Shaper *of* Seattle

Builder of ports, wrangler of rivers, mover of mountains and men—no one shaped the Northwest's largest city as much as R.H. Thomson. William H. Wilson's exhaustive biography is a sympathetic yet reasoned portrait of the man who made and remade Seattle.
—*Matthew Klingle, author of* Emerald City: An Environmental History of Seattle.

For half a century, William H. Wilson has explored the history of city planning while publishing, among other works, two books on the City Beautiful movement.

Now he adds a fascinating account of a "Shaper of Seattle," Reginald Heber Thomson. A Scot, Hoosier, Presbyterian, Republican, and college-educated engineer, the young man moved in 1881 to the then-small, primitive city on Puget Sound, and there, mostly as city engineer, he shaped the place in basic ways, building sewer and water systems, leveling hills, filling hollows, and contributing to the development of electric power, railroads, and the ship canal.

Wilson, writing about a man of controversy and historical significance, gives us an impressively researched, forcefully argued, and richly documented biography that places Thomson in his late 19th, early 20th century context.
—*Richard S. Kirkendall, The Scott and Dorothy Bullitt Professor Emeritus, University of Washington, Seattle.*

Shaper *of* Seattle

Reginald Heber Thomson's
Pacific Northwest

William H. Wilson

Washington State University Press
Pullman, Washington

Washington State University Press
PO Box 645910
Pullman, Washington 99164-5910
Phone: 800-354-7360
Fax: 509-335-8568
E-mail: wsupress@wsu.edu
Web site: wsupress.wsu.edu

Library of Congress Cataloging-in-Publication Data

Wilson, William H. (William Henry), 1935-
    Shaper of Seattle : Reginald Heber Thomson's Pacific Northwest / William H. Wilson.
        p. cm.
    Includes bibliographical references and index.
    ISBN 978-0-87422-301-9 (alk. paper)
    1. Thomson, Reginald Heber, 1856-1949. 2. Municipal engineers--United States--Biography. 3. Public works--Washington (State)--Seattle--History. 4. Municipal engineering--Washington (State)--Seattle--History. 5. Seattle (Wash.)--Buildings, structures, etc.--History. I. Title.
    TD140.T5W55 2009
    628.092--dc22
    [B]
                                                                                    2009016161

Fine Quality Books from the Pacific Northwest

Contents

For Kitty, again

Acknowledgments

ONE NAME APPEARS as the author of *Shaper of Seattle* but, like most books, it is a collective enterprise. It is my pleasure to thank those who helped make it a reality.

When I used the large collection of Thomson papers at the University of Washington Libraries, they were housed in the Manuscripts and University Archives (MUA) section, now folded into the Special Collections Division. Karyl Winn, the head of the MUA, and her staff, including Nan Cohen, Gary Lundell, and Janet Ness, were extraordinarily sympathetic and helpful. I benefited especially from Gary's knowledge of collateral collections. Nicolette Bromberg of the Special Collections Division, and Carolyn Marr of the Museum of History and Industry in Seattle, helped with valuable photographs. Greg Lange, Michael Saunders, and Philippa Stairs of the Puget Sound Regional Branch of the Washington State Archives discovered Thomson material despite my sometimes inexact requests. Special thanks for similar invaluable services are due to Jeff Ware, Scott Cline, and Anne Frantilla of the Seattle Municipal Archives and its excellent photo collection.

My look at Thomson's college records would have been impossible without the firm knowledge of Doug Denne at the Joseph Wood Evans Memorial Special Collections and Archives Center of the Agnes Brown Duggan Library at Hanover College, Indiana. The Samuel Hill papers at the Maryhill Museum of Art, where Colleen Schafroth and Betty Long-Schleif guided me, enlarged my understanding of Thomson. At the James J. Hill Reference Library, W. Thomas White and Eileen McCormack found relevant letters and documents in the various Hill collections, now housed in the Manuscript Collection of the Minnesota Historical Society. Other useful archives are listed in "A Note on Sources," and I thank the staffs of all of them.

Sally Hepler, a granddaughter of Thomson's, generously granted me an interview about her grandfather, extending over parts of two days, June 15, 1999, and January 5, 2000, at her home on Bainbridge Island, Washington. The late Mrs. Hepler also allowed me to copy an invaluable autobiographical statement of Thomson's—his recollections of his early childhood to his 1877 graduation from Hanover College. Pat Soden, the director of the University of Washington Press, graciously opened the press files concerning the publication history of Thomson's memoirs, *That Man Thomson*. John Powell of the Special Collections and Archives, Utah State University Libraries, sent manuscripts related to *That Man Thomson* from the Grant

Hubbard Redford Papers. Redford edited Thomson's memoirs, which were published in 1950.

Over the years I presented papers on Thomson at meetings of the Pacific Northwest History Conference and a meeting of the Pacific Northwest Historians Guild, where commenters and auditors made helpful observations on my subject. The board of directors of the James J. Hill Reference Library awarded a much-appreciated grant, while the University of North Texas allowed a year's leave to advance the research on Thomson.

The *Pacific Northwest Quarterly* (*PNQ*) published two articles featuring Thomson. I thank Kim McKay, the editor of the *PNQ*, for permission to use conclusions first published in "The Rising and the Setting of Seattle's *Sun*," in volume 92 (spring 2001), and "'Names Joined Together as Our Hearts Are,' The Friendship of Samuel Hill and Reginald H. Thomson," in volume 94 (fall 2003). Much longer extracts from "Reginald H. Thomson and Planning for Strathcona Park, 1912–15," in *Planning Perspectives*, volume 17 (2002), are used by permission of Taylor and Francis Ltd. (copyright Taylor and Francis Ltd.). Christine Orange Dubois, the managing editor of *Columbia: The Magazine of Northwest History* granted permission for reuse of some sections of "The Mythic and (Virtually) Unknown Reginald H. Thomson," appearing in volume 15 (winter 2001–2002). I thank the editorial staffs and the reviewers of those journals for helping me focus my views of Thomson and his era. Tim Cannon, permission coordinator of Harvard Business School Publishing, granted permission to reproduce maps appearing in Von V. Tarbill, "Mountain Moving in Seattle," *Harvard Business Review*, volume 8 (July 1930), pages 483–84.

At the Washington State University Press, Glen Lindeman, editor-in-chief, responded positively to the original manuscript and constantly encouraged me. Mary Read, Nancy Grunewald, Kerry Darnall, Caryn Lawton, and Jenni Lynn also played important roles in seeing the book through to completion.

Special thanks go to a Shuttle Express driver in Seattle, whose name I do not know, who suggested the writings of engineering historian Henry Petroski. It is impossible to list all of the friends, relatives, and colleagues who have influenced me directly and indirectly, so this blanket thank you is issued to all of you. One friend, relative, and colleague of five decades standing is my wife Kitty, without whose love and patient support neither this book or any other positive achievement of mine would have happened.

Introduction

REGINALD HEBER THOMSON was one of the great triumvirs of West Coast city engineers—Michael M. O'Shaughnessy in San Francisco, William Mulholland in Los Angeles, and Thomson in Seattle. The three men brought to their cities potable water, absolutely essential to urban public health. All three eased their cities' phenomenal growth. All three engendered passionate loyalties and bitter hatreds.[1]

Thomson set himself four major tasks and succeeded in all. Sewers, the first and most technically formidable, provided the outlet for the city's coming abundant water supply. The second, the Cedar River gravity system, brought water 26 miles to Seattle to replace water pumped from turbid Lake Washington, increasingly an area sink. The third and most debated, then and later, was the leveling of some of the city's steep hills and filling the worst of its hollows. During his first and longest tenure as city engineer, Seattle embarked on 17 major regrading projects.[2] They remade the face of the 19th and early 20th century city. His fourth task was establishing a city light plant, originally at the site of the Cedar River dam.

Thomson succeeded partly because of remarkable personal qualities. He combined extraordinary intelligence, energy, diligence, and perseverance with an ability to select capable subordinates. As city engineer, he enjoyed far-reaching authority over the quotidian development of Seattle, but used it judiciously. He was well aware of the political nature of his job. Other city engineers whose abilities he respected were fired or were vigorously attacked, as he was.[3] He did not need their experiences to warn him of his tenuous situation, for he lost his city surveyorship in 1886, and later, if only temporarily, his engineership in 1894. Politics inspired both removals. After returning to his city engineer job in 1894, he kept it until 1911, then resigned to accept other work. Many years afterward, when in his 70s, he returned to the city engineer's post in 1930–31. It was an exceptional expression of confidence, although he was forced out after a little

less than a year, again for political reasons. He survived in office as long and as well as he did because of his leadership abilities, his knowledge of Seattle's urban systems, and, when he chose to use them, his considerable charm and well-developed sense of humor.

Thomson's involvement with complex urban development raises the issue of his relationship to the progressive era and the progressive movement. The late 19th and early 20th centuries witnessed the rise and refinement of systems of transportation, communication, food processing, lighting, heating, and public health, which the progressive movement sought to harness for public benefit. Thomson was a progressive in the general sense in that he believed government should intervene in economic and social life to meliorate and improve the lives of ordinary people. He practiced nonpartisanship on the local level and supported city planning, municipal ownership of public utilities, and prohibition—all progressive enthusiasms. He believed that government should enable private enterprise to function efficiently and effectively, and that the resulting prosperity would solve most social and economic imbalances. He did not believe in elaborate regulatory schemes, radical democratization, or uplifting the masses through purposeful intervention in individual lives.

For his own personal guidance and support, Thomson adhered less to the progressive movement and more to other institutions. He was a deeply religious Presbyterian, staunch Republican, and devoted family man, but wore none of these convictions on his sleeve. Seattle was, for much of his life, an "open town," where flourished the three pillars of public licentiousness—gambling, prostitution, and the liquor trade. He deplored them but segmented them from his job, which was to encourage population growth, public health, civic patriotism, and legitimate commerce by making Seattle as well paved, topographically level, and fully supplied with water and sewers as he could make it.

Although he is best known for his city engineership from 1892 to 1911, there are other aspects of his life to consider. He spent his formative years mostly in two villages—Hanover, Indiana, near the once-thriving city of Madison, and Healdsburg, California, north of the San Francisco Bay area. Though family relationships kept him tied to both places for a time, Thomson was an urban man in aspiration and outlook from his early maturity forward. He spent his free time after college graduation (1877) searching for a proto-metropolis where he could develop his talents, finding it at last in Seattle. After his first long term as city engineer, he became, briefly, the engineer of the newly-formed Port of Seattle, then the first superintendent of British Columbia's Strathcona Park, and, finally, an active consulting engineer during and after his stints as city engineer.

None of this means that he could have decided to become an engineer and move to Seattle from California without family support. He owed his existence in Indiana and California to his family. Family members encouraged him to leave California for Seattle, and relatives there provided him with a place to live and gave him a job when he arrived. More than that, his success as an engineer depended partly on the spectacular growth of western cities in the late 19th and early 20th centuries. It also rested on amazing developments in construction materials, a revolution in the structure of city government, and the organization of engineering management that blossomed concurrently with the long western boom. It was Thomson's gift, however, to seize the opportunity provided to reform Seattle physically and to influence other developments in the Pacific Northwest.

The chapters that follow concern all these aspects of Thomson and his career. The first two narrate and analyze his years in Indiana and California from his birth in 1856 to his move to Seattle in 1881. His varied activities in Seattle and elsewhere for his first eight years there are the subject of chapter 3. Chapter 4 establishes the practical and theoretical basis for engineering in Thomson's time. The next three chapters focus on his role in developing the sewer system, gravity water system, and regrades. Chapter 8 discusses his role in Seattle's railroad planning, principally with the Great Northern and its imperious president James J. Hill, with the city's first light plant, and with the ship canal linking Lake Washington to Puget Sound. Chapter 9 involves a miscellany of engineering developments, including his controversial plans for trash incineration and his equally controversial first trip to Europe. It also brings his private life up to date from his marriage to about the time he resigned the first time from the city engineership.

> ## Chronology of R.H. Thomson's Municipal Career in Seattle
>
> City Surveyor—
>   Appointed August 1884
>   Removed August 1886
>
> City Engineer—
>   Appointed June 1892
>   Removed January 1894
>   Reappointed February 1894
>   Reappointment under successive city charters
>   Resigned November 1911
>
> Port Commission—
>   Four months 1911–12
>
> City Council—
>   Elected first term 1916–19
>   Re-elected 1919–22
>
> City Engineer—
>   Appointed August 1930
>   Resigned July 1931

Chapter 10 looks at his brief time as engineer of the Port of Seattle, his park superintendency in British Columbia, as well as two matters of great importance to him—his civil suit against the *Seattle Times* and its editor-publisher, Alden J. Blethen, and his disastrous investment in an evening newspaper, the *Seattle Sun*.

Chapter 11 considers his activities during two terms as city councilman, and as a World War I patriot, consulting engineer, loyal friend, husband, and father of his four children. Chapter 12 involves his return to the city engineer's job at age 74 in 1930, his break with James D. Ross, the powerful head of the municipal lighting system, and his resignation under threat of dismissal. Chapter 13 deals with his other involvements during the second term as city engineer, and his later consulting, especially regarding efforts to control the White and Puyallup rivers, the issues surrounding the collapse of a railroad tunnel, and the building of the first Lake Washington floating bridge. The fourteenth and final chapter reaches some conclusions based on Thomson's record as delineated in the previous chapters. It demonstrates how all of his varied activities and responsibilities may be seen as the expression of a life unified around his religious faith, his political party convictions, his family, and his belief in a glorious urban future.

Notes

1. For O'Shaughnessy, see William Issel and Robert W. Cherney, *San Francisco, 1865–1932: Politics, Power, and Urban Development* (Berkeley: University of California Press, 1986), 175–76, 181–84, 196–97; Robert W. Righter, *The Battle over Hetch Hetchy: America's Most Controversial Dam and the Birth of Modern Environmentalism* (New York: Oxford University Press, 2005), 7, 108–11, 134–64, 170–206; and John Warfield Simpson, *Dam! Water, Power, Politics, and Preservation in Hetch Hetchy and Yosemite National Park* (New York: Pantheon, 2005), 179, 224–25, 233–35, 240, 246–47, 256–57. For Mulholland, see Margaret Leslie Davis, *Rivers in the Desert: William Mulholland and the Inventing of Los Angeles* (New York: HarperCollins, 1993); and Catherine Mulholland, *William Mullholland and the Rise of Los Angeles* (Berkeley: University of California Press, 2000).

2. Reginald H. Thomson (hereafter RHT) to John P. Hartman, 25 February 1909, accession number 89, section 1 (hereafter 89/1, and all other accessions listed by number only), box 2, letterpress book (hereafter book) 1, RHT Papers, Special Collections Division, University of Washington Libraries (hereafter UW). The letter to Hartman gives a detailed account of fourteen major regrades, omitting three also undertaken during his tenure to 1911.

3. RHT to J. C. Ralston, 14 February 1908, 89/1, box 2, book 5; and to William Mahlon Davis, 5 December 1911, 89/1, box 4, book 11, RHT Papers, UW.

Formal portrait taken about the time Thomson left a long tenure as city engineer (1892–1911) to become the engineer at the Port of Seattle. *University of Washington Libraries, Special Collections, UW 18678.*

1
Boyhood and Adolescence in Indiana

REGINALD HEBER THOMSON entered the world on March 20, 1856, the fifth living child of Samuel Harrison Thomson and Magdelene Sophronia Clifton Thomson. The world he entered had little knowledge of sanitation and often stank. In the towns, horses deposited manure and urine on poorly graveled streets. Human bodies, normally fully bathed just once a week, frequently emitted foul odors. Outdoor privies and acrid smoke from home fireplaces and small industries added to the olfactory assault. On the farms, animals and humans were as noisome, but with fewer numbers, and wind, rain, and spring blossoms meliorated the reek.[1]

Early death was commonplace. The etiology of disease was unknown; sepsis and uncertain anesthetics made childbirth dangerous and surgery a nightmare. In the towns, hogs scavenged garbage thrown into the unsewered streets, and they bit people, too. So did feral dogs. Travel exacted its toll on roads of gluey mud. Steamboats wrecked. Railroads, the wonder of the age, were just as lethal, with their link-and-pin couplings dangerous to crewmen, and ineffective brakes and poorly engineered roadbeds.

In a time of high infant mortality, the Thomson family was among the advantaged and only one infant died. However, of the eight surviving children, Alma, or Almira, the youngest, died at 18. Meeda, the next youngest, died at 20. May, the next child after Reginald, lived long enough to marry and bear a daughter, but tuberculosis killed her at 24. James Harrison, eight years older than Reginald, died before he was 30. Henrietta, or "Retta," three years older and already a widow, lived to be 40. Only Reginald and his older brothers Henry Clifton and Williell survived to savor middle age.[2]

The Thomsons were steadfast Presbyterians and several family members, Reginald's father among them, were teachers or preachers in a time when those callings were not so different or separate.[3] Newspaper notices of Alma's death capture the flavor of family piety. One praised the "dear girl" who possessed "an intelligent faith in the gospel of Christ," and was, on her deathbed, "gentle, considerate of all about her, and full of tender affection." Alma, an "attractive person," fought against her "invincible malady," undefined in the notice but probably tuberculosis, "until the will of the Father was manifest," whereupon "with lovely resignation she surrendered the struggle, and passed without a fear to the heavenly rest." Another notice recounted previous deaths in the family, but assured its readers that the surviving members "bear these deep griefs with faith in God, knowing the holy joys of their departed ones and waiting with confidence the time of their reunion in that better country where they will part no more forever." Readers much later removed in time might consider these lines strange in a newspaper account, but to the Thomson family they were comforting assurances of the close connection between the temporal and spiritual worlds, a bond reserved for the righteous.[4]

Samuel Harrison Thomson's people were Scotch-Irish. James, his grandfather and Reginald's great-grandfather, immigrated to the colony of Pennsylvania in 1771, when he was 30 or 31. He and his wife Mary produced a brood of nine, one of whom, James Henry, was the father of Samuel Harrison. James, born in Pennsylvania, moved to Kentucky where he continued the family's strong commitment to Presbyterianism, becoming in the meanwhile a judge and a sheriff. He and his wife Sarah had eight children, large families being a hobby with the Thomsons until Reginald's generation. Samuel Harrison, the sixth child, arrived on August 26, 1813, in Nicholas County, Kentucky, from where the family moved to southeastern Indiana in 1828. Six years later Samuel, or Harrison as he was better known, entered the then-fledgling Hanover College, in the hamlet of the same name located some 40 miles south of his home.

Hanover College in 1834 was tiny—113 college students, a number that would soon substantially decline, and two faculty members, although the faculty increased to four during Harrison's student years.[5] Instead of size, Hanover offered discipline and doctrinally sound Presbyterianism. Young Harrison graduated with the class of 1837, and was granted a master of arts in 1840.

During those years he was the principal of the Female Academy at Crawfordsville, northwest of Indianapolis. Female academies were then secondary or finishing schools for polite young ladies. It was pioneer country in comparison with the more settled southern section and there were few ladies or, for that matter, few people of any sort, in northern Indiana in the 1830s and 1840s. Harrison stayed only until 1841. Over the next few years he turned his hand to newspaper editing, teaching in a grammar school, and college and seminary teaching. He married while teaching at the seminary in the village of New Castle, Kentucky, not far from Hanover.

In 1844 he found his long time vocation when he was appointed professor of mathematics and natural science in his alma mater, Hanover College. The same year he and Magdelene Sophronia celebrated the birth of their firstborn. By the time of Reginald's birth, Harrison held the chairs of mathematics and mechanical philosophy, and of astronomy. Although for a time a teacher in a seminary, he never attended one, but he "studied privately for a number of years,"[6] and two years before Reginald's birth the Presbytery of Madison, Indiana, licensed him to preach. He was ordained the year after Reginald was born. Harrison never became a pastor but his pursuit of the ministry through ordination was a testimony to his deep religiosity.

Harrison was in academic life an example of what Donald F. Carmony termed the rural and semi-rural pioneers of the era: "they were *generalists* who could do a variety of different things." He taught a heavy load of varied courses, as many as 30 class hours per week, and attended the compulsory Sunday afternoon service. He gave added assistance to students in need. Harvey W. Wiley, later the famed father of the Pure Food and Drug Act, was "an invalid at home" during "a good part" of his sophomore year at Hanover, the result of a Civil War wound. Many years after, he recalled the help he received from "S. Harrison Thompson [sic], my professor in mathematics," and other professors, that enabled him to return to regular work by the end of the year and to graduate with his class in 1867. Wiley's misspelling of Harrison's last name was an error, not a slight (many other people also misspelled his name). Wiley ruminated on "the debt which I shall never be able to repay to Hanover College," for professors "who insisted upon thoroughness rather than multiplicity of studies, and the fundamental groundwork that I received in mathematics" and other disciplines.[7]

Another student recalled Harrison's "illuminating" discussions of outer space, and his "very searching" examinations. Mathematics was a "solemn" class, with Harrison an "extremely quiet, solemn, impressive character." Still another recalled that "Professor Thomson was one of the most learned, and certainly the most widely read, of the faculty." The same student recalled how Harrison "rode a cream-colored horse" from his home "on the beautiful bluff" across a ravine "from College Point." An "irreverent undergraduate at one time converted" his horse "into a zebra by a judicious application of green stripes," but the incident did not appear to disturb the equanimity of horse or rider. "It is to be regretted that as yet the College authorities have not given this really great man the recognition his eminent service to the institution merits."[8]

While Harrison's career advanced, Magdelene managed the household. Born in New Castle, Kentucky, she was the daughter of Henry Clifton, a farmer whose holdings embraced land in Carroll and Henry counties. New Castle, the county seat of Henry County, was hardly more than an outpost hamlet, but Magdelene's father was a man of substance, as demonstrated by his raising a regiment during the War of 1812. He saw no combat but attained the rank of major.[9]

The Cliftons traced their English ancestry to Charles Clifton, a migrant from Bristol to Virginia, where he farmed. Most of his six children moved to Kentucky, where Henry continued the farming tradition. He and his wife Mary had four children who survived to maturity, of whom Magdelene was the third.

Although Harrison and Magdelene named their fifth child Reginald Heber, neither family nor school chums called him Reginald. He was instead known by Heber. He may have been named for a Thomson ancestor or for Reginald Heber, a famous Anglican bishop of Calcutta and author of the thunderous Protestant hymn, "Holy, Holy, Holy."

Young Heber grew up in an environment scarcely typical of the time. He was a professor's son, and while that legacy imposed expectations of academic excellence, it also entailed a respect for knowledge and learning not invariably present in southern Indiana households during the 1850s and 1860s. Heber lived up to the expectations—he was intelligent and industrious—and he enjoyed the benefits. Moreover, the house in which he was born and its grounds were unusually lavish. His parents chose land on the crest of an Ohio River bluff west of Madison and a mile or so east of Hanover. The large house, a story and a half, was built of bricks "moulded and burned on the site." The views would have moved a real estate agent to inspirational writing. From its lofty perch the house looked east, down on Madison, which at Heber's birth was the largest or second-largest town in the state. To the south, at a bend in the river, vistas unfolded "along the beautiful Ohio for several miles."[10]

Heber enjoyed the added advantage of living in the most matured, settled part of his home state. Madison's beginnings trace to 1808, when three pioneers bought almost 700 acres of public land on high ground over-looking the Ohio River, at the junction of the Ohio and an Indian trail later renamed the Michigan Road. The Michigan Road, despite its often dreadful condition, was a major highway for settlement in the interior of the ter-ritory. Madison stood at the crossing of the two transpor-tation routes, growing rapidly following the first lot sales in 1811. By 1830 its population reached 1,752, making it the largest town in the new state. It was the seat of Jefferson County, which in 1835 held one-eighth of all of Indiana's taxable property. By then the town boasted the outpost industries of a booming distribution center: flour mill, sawmill, pork packing houses, and manufacturers producing wagons, furniture, hats, and pottery. Its first bank—the first in the territory—opened in 1814, two years before Indiana statehood. In 1834 Madison became the site of a branch of the State Bank of Indiana. The Madison & Indianapolis Railroad, the first constructed within Indiana, began building in 1836. The same year a boatyard opened at the east edge of town, stimulated by steamboating on the Ohio. A drumbeat of the usual boosterism and antipathy toward competing towns accompanied this growth.[11]

Madison survived the depression of the late 1830s in relatively sound economic shape. The slackened boom resumed, and by the year of Heber's birth the town was a major manufacturing center. Even before completion of the 86 mile long Madison & Indianapolis Railroad in 1847, the line hauled hundreds of hogs to pork pack-ers, the town's industrial mainstay. In the early 1850s there were 14 or more packing houses or warehouses devoted to handling hogs, as well as linked industries that processed hog bristles, skins, and lard, or built saddle trees or barrels. Expanded flour milling, brewing, horse marketing, a railroad car and wheel foundry, and a new shipyard, together with regular steamboat service on the Ohio, a ferry to the Kentucky shore, new wharves, and improved if still primitive roads, made Madison one of the major manufacturing and distribution centers of what was still called "the West."[12]

But the boom peaked while Heber was still in his cradle, if indeed it had not already crested. Migration, geography, and railroad expansion and consolidation all militated against Madison's preeminence. Indiana enjoyed a huge population increase in the second half of the 19th century, one moving it to rank sixth among all states in the censuses of 1860, 1870, and 1880. But it was the population distribution within the state that mattered to Madison. In 1850, the southern third of Indiana held 418,373 people, while in 1880, shortly after the Thomsons decamped for California, it regis-tered 737,215. That was significant growth, but pales in comparison to the rest of the state. The central section contained 404,734 in 1850, fewer than the southern, but it had surpassed the southern tier by 1870, climbing to 778,465 in 1880. The comparative growth of the indus-trializing northern third was the most spectacular, from a mere 165,300 in 1850 to 462,621 in 1880.[13]

Had Madison maintained its relative position within the southmost third of Indiana, growth elsewhere might not have mattered so much. But it failed to do so. The shift in migration patterns within Indiana exacerbated Madison's geographic limitations. A ring of high, "rugged and precipitous hills" combined with the Ohio River to limit accessible building sites to "a valley three fourths of a Mile wide and three Miles long." The Michigan Road and the Madison & Indianapolis Railway pierced the hills but much of Madison's near hinterland lay in the Muscatatuck Regional Slope. The area supported market gardens but was otherwise one of the least invit-ing agricultural areas of the state. Indiana contained coal and other minerals in mineable quantities, but not near Madison. The Ohio River proved to be less than an unimpeded artery of commerce. Madison lay upriver from the falls of the Ohio at Louisville, therefore the drought of 1854 and its resulting low water stymied its navigation without harming the Indiana towns across from Louisville. Those two, Jeffersonville and especially New Albany, Madison's commercial and industrial archrival, continued to prosper.[14]

Railroad expansion harmed Madison more than altered patterns of population growth or its geographi-cal relationships. The Madison & Indianapolis (M&I) line—to be considered in a moment—was Indiana's first railroad but hardly its last. By 1850, 212 miles of track, including the M&I's 86, had been laid, with a thousand additional miles under construction. By the early 1850s, anyone with an atlas of Indiana and its neighboring states could see that railroads, once they became reliable enough to surmount the tyranny of waterborne transportation, should build toward three objectives. The first was to link a major Indiana town with Cincinnati and that city's rail connection to the east coast. The second was to connect with southern Lake Michigan, either at a major town or over the northern part of the state, perhaps to the feverishly growing lake port of Chicago. The third was to tie a major town with Jeffersonville and New Albany at the falls of the Ohio, thus reaping the benefits of a sure connection with both upriver and downriver traffic, periods of river icing aside. Those roads were the nemesis of the M&I. By 1854 the Jeffersonville line reached Columbus, Indiana, effectively cutting off the M&I from much of its hinterland, while the New Albany road stretched all the way to Chicago. The "major town" was of course Indianapolis, centrally located in the state and more the beneficiary of the M&I than Madison. A series of disastrous industrial fires in Madison, the panic of 1857, and the rise of pork packing within Indiana and elsewhere, aided by favorable freight rates, combined to doom the town's aspirations. [15]

The M&I management was not free of responsibility for Madison's predicament. In the early 1850s it spent time and effort, and perhaps money, lobbying against the successful general railroad incorporation law that weakened it. Beyond building a spur through better agricultural country than that around Madison, it showed no interest in expansion. It spent money nevertheless. Sixty miles of track laid with iron strip rail on top of wood had to be torn out and replaced with heavier "T" rail. The road added buildings and rolling stock, all at considerable expense. A new right of way, to replace the original almost prohibitively steep grade through the hills, failed after $3,000,000 had been wasted. The expenditure was mind-bogglingly huge at the time. Control of the road passed to distant investors loath to consider either more attempts at innovation or consolidation with competing lines. The M&I went broke, bought in a sheriff's sale in 1862 by the rival Jeffersonville road. [16]

Had Madison done a better job of putting its own urbanizing house in order, its limitations might have been overcome or at least meliorated. There were some efforts at urban sophistication. A water system, a gasworks, a major hotel, numerous dry goods and grocery stores, and a new jail and courthouse raised the municipal tone somewhat. Problems remained: roaming hogs and dogs, building supplies piled in the dirty, graveled streets, and carelessly parked wagons detracted from the scene. So did the lack of street signs and numbered business blocks. So did reeling drunks. The aptly named Crooked Creek became a depository of refuse and industrial waste where it meandered through town.

The Civil War, however, brought renewed prosperity despite the demise of the M&I and Madison's faltering

urbanity. Continued good times down to the depression of 1873 produced a sewer system, an improved water works, better streets and sidewalks, and a municipal pound for roaming hogs. A trotting park, a streetcar line, and ambitious building programs fostered the illusion of permanent prosperity. But the boomlet was over for good by the mid-1870s. Population figures told the story. In 1850 Madison's population was 8,012, scarcely growing during the troubled 1850s to 8,130 in 1860. The Civil War and postwar boom raised the total to 10,709 in 1870, but only 8,945 people lived in Madison in 1880. Despite its incorporation with outlying villages, the town's population continued a slow decline into the early 20th century. [17]

Madison's gradual eclipse meant little or nothing to young Heber, who grew up next to what was one of the state's prime, if flagging, commercial and industrial areas, and, with Hanover College, one of its educational centers. Heber's first brush with formal education was the Hanover "village school." Civil War loyalties and experiences conditioned his schoolyard behavior. Most Indiana opinion swung to the Union after the firing on Fort Sumter and the Thomsons were no exception. But the war brought privation even to loyal Republicans: "we were short of food, clothing, money, and in addition were kept in a constant state of apprehension" about "rebel" military raids. The war sundered friendships. One of Thomson's early memories was of a Kentuckian, "a bitter rebel" who had been close to Thomson's parents. He "came over" from his house opposite theirs across the Ohio "and was very ugly in his talk with Father." Heber "stood by, not knowing what it all meant" but was dismayed by the man's anger. "We never saw him nor heard from him again." The large military hospital complex at Madison required a battalion composed of soldiers who "were kindly men, but terrible foragers." The "great droves" of mules driven "right past our house" on their way to army service were in the charge of muleteers who "were not always as careful as we desired." Heber's older brother Henry Clifton enlisted, and although he was "a topographer" rather than a combat soldier, his service "of course added to our excitement." [18]

The youngster "did not understand the war as it proceeded, but was under the excitement of it," as well as the sadness. "When news came of the assassination of President Lincoln, I saw a sorrow and anguish overspread my Father, such as [I] hope never to witness again." Heber and other children carried these events and emotions to school, where conflicting loyalties set boy against boy. "There was of course some learning, but with it much fighting. There were some Democrats whom we called copperheads, whom we felt should be disciplined. The scars on my legs and breast testify to some of the results of my efforts."[19] Heber more than likely gave as good as he got, for he probably was big for his age, growing toward his eventual six feet two to four inches tall.

Fortunately for young Heber's intellectual development, he depended not on "some learning" in grammar school, but on his parents and their friends, other adults, his siblings, and on political rallies. "As I grew up life was serious," he recalled. "There were no children in the vicinity," except for his proximate siblings. The nearest neighbors were half a mile distant, and anyway, "were of advanced age." His childhood, his combative schoolmates aside, "was thus spent with my own brothers and sisters." Adults played key roles in Heber's upbringing, no little thanks to southern Indiana's prominence and the importance of Harrison Thomson and his colleagues at Hanover. Madison and Hanover had lost their primacy but remained obligatory stops for distinguished travelers. Some of them called on the Thomson household. "Visitors at the home were College professors, ministers, and politicians," all of them literate and most of them well educated.[20]

The visitors were "all persons of age," to young Heber, but their maturity and wisdom were stimulating. One of Harrison Thomson's colleagues, John W. Scott, a professor of natural science from 1860 to 1868, was Benjamin Harrison's father-in-law. Although 20 years younger than the senior Thomson, Benjamin Harrison, the rising Indianapolis attorney and later 23rd president, visited the Thomsons when in Hanover. "Ben Harrison and wife were often at our house[,] Mr Harrison and Father discussing National affairs[,] Mrs. Harrison visiting Mother and helping to teach me my A.B.C.s" The Liberal Republican campaign of 1872 brought another eminent visitor, the successful Democratic politician, Thomas A. Hendricks. The Liberal Republican program of opposition to the corruption of the regular Republican Grant administration, promotion of civil service reform, and affirmation of a free labor market interested Democrats only marginally. But they did respond to the Liberal Republican conviction that the federal government's intrusive experiment—post-Civil War Reconstruction— had done enough to assist the ex-slave and should be ended. Therefore the Democrats endorsed the Liberal Republican presidential candidacy of New York editor-publisher Horace Greeley. "Abe" Hendricks, as Thomson remembered him, "came several times to our house to see if my Father could not be persuaded to vote for Greely

[sic]. That could not be," for the elder Thomson was an undeviating regular Republican.[21]

Political rallies were educational as well as entertaining. They helped to shape Thomson's lifelong commitment to the Republican Party and his fascination with politics. "The great days were [those of] political processions when we could go to Hanover and see the loyal people"—that is, the Republican-Union people—"go by on their way to Madison" to hear partisan oratory. The Thomsons "watched intently" for the representatives of one district, because "[t]hey always had banners and made a great show." The Liberal Republican movement that prompted Hendrickson's visits to the Thomson home galvanized the Madison area. Ulysses S. Grant's easy reelection and Greeley's crushing defeat as the Liberal Republican-Democrat candidate make the outcome appear forgone, but hindsight was unavailable to partisans in 1872. Thomson remembered that "the very air was alive." "With my brothers I was taken to Madison," probably by their father, "to hear Governor Oliver P. Morton," a dedicated Radical, pro-Reconstruction, and regular Republican, "tell why every one should vote against Greely [sic]."

The Thomson women, in the days before woman suffrage, enjoyed no formal involvement in politics, but on this day the large, excited crowd was reason enough for them to stay away. Morton spoke "nearly all afternoon" to "twelve thousand people in the rink," a huge building some 300 feet long by 150 feet wide containing a roller skating and velocipede rink with a gallery, an "ice cream saloon," and other rooms. "The intensity of the audience was at high pitch. I doubt if any hour in the midst of the war was more tense than the hours while Morton spoke." James A. Garfield, then an Ohio Congressman, sat on the platform with Morton, and addressed the crowd in the evening.[22]

Heber left the "village school" when he was 13, and entered Hanover's preparatory program. The preparatory department was by no means a high school; it was Hanover's "college prep" division at a time when public high schools were scarce in Indiana. The preparatory curriculum probably was as rigid and demanding as the regular college courses. In 1871 Heber enrolled "with the class that graduated in 1875."[23] By then Hanover, though still struggling with severe underfunding, had rebounded from the slump in student population during and after the Civil War. At the war's beginning, the enrollment in the preparatory and colleges courses stood at 110, but trended downward until its nadir in 1868, with a mere 56 students evenly split between the preparatory department and the college. Still, the college expected much and exacted much from its faculty.[24]

The college was scarcely innovative. It was proud of its conservatism and proud of preparing graduates for the ministry. As late as 1926 more than 26 percent of its active alumni served as ministers or missionaries, and more than 54 percent were either religious workers or educators. Some of the educators were ordained even if not active pastors or missionaries. The faculty adhered to a high standard of Christian rectitude. During and shortly after the Civil War, the teaching load doubled. Harrison, as a senior faculty member, probably enjoyed a salary of $800. His pay would have the purchasing power of a gross salary of perhaps $30,000 in the currency of a century and a half after—it was scarcely generous. Worse, by 1858 Harrison's salary was $2,353.29 in arrears! Nevertheless he was expected to soldier on, and he did.[25]

The college demanded as much from its students. They lived by a strict schedule of compulsory class attendance, readings, recitations, and daily chapel at 7:30 a.m. on weekdays and a relaxed 8 a.m. for Sundays. Heber enrolled in the "full classical course," a required rigorous program of Greek, Latin, Bible study, and ancient and modern history, leavened by, among others, advanced mathematics, surveying, philosophy, astronomy, geology, rhetoric, and civics. The elective curriculum promoted by Harvard's Charles Eliot had not reached Hanover. The only electives allowed were granted to students in the "Scientific Department," limited to substituting French and German for Greek and advanced Latin. This liberalization coincided with Heber's matriculation, with the award of a bachelor of science to those opting for the modern languages. The B.S. degree, however, was not an option available to Heber, who may have taken some comfort in the exclusion of Hebrew from the curriculum in 1871, the year he entered the college.[26]

Heber's grades were strong to exceptionally high, fulfilling the family and his expectations. He first appears in the "Recitation Register" of Hanover in 1869 as a "Jr. Prep," with an overall average of 97 against a class average of 94.67. Surpassing the class average by that much, or more, proved routine. As a "Sr. Prep," he bested the average by five and a half points. His college grades were generally better still, dropping below the class average only twice in eight of the first nine terms for which class averages were recorded. Then, having completed his junior year, he started over again in the fall of 1874 as a sophomore! He repeated the sophomore and junior years, completed his senior year, and graduated in June 1877. Once again he did well in his studies, topping the class average for eight of nine terms. Heber's college career certainly seems unusual, but no direct explanation for it survives.[27]

Thomson's own memory of his college chronology is not supported by the record, but offers some clues about his life then and after. According to him, he contracted an illness, possibly pneumonia, leaving him debilitated, and perhaps explaining his lifelong susceptibility to severe colds and flu-like illnesses. About the end of "my sophomore year," he remembered, "my strength was so small that it was deemed necessary that I quit study and work to build up my strength. This I did." No doubt he was ill, experiencing 33 absences during the fall term of 1873, though he kept up his grades and creditably completed his junior year. The next fall, he dropped back to the sophomore year. However, his memory of a two-year regime of "carpentering, blacksmithing, stone quarrying, etc., together with working in our garden," while keeping "persistently at my greek" [sic], is clearly mistaken.[28] Doubtless he worked at those tasks during term breaks, while at the same time maintaining and improving his Greek. Any one of those intervals could have seemed like two years. The best explanation for his unusual attendance may be due to his youth. He entered Hanover at 15, not unheard of then or afterward, but nevertheless an early age for a future matriculant. Perhaps his parents decided that repeating two years of college would allow Heber more time to mature and yet graduate at the respectable age of 21.

A universal undergraduate dictum is that significant learning occurs outside the classroom and assigned studies, and Heber's experience was no exception. While he was still in the preparatory department Frank H. Bradley joined the faculty. Bradley replaced John W. Scott, Benjamin Harrison's father-in-law, as professor of natural science. Bradley remained for only one year, 1869–70, but he influenced the young scholar mightily. Thomson remembered him as a "Geologist and Mineralist. He came much to our house, and many were the points in Geology and Minerology that were given me by him. I drunk his words in a[s] sacred words of wisdom."[29]

There were other extra-academic developments. About midway through Heber's college studies, "at Mothers [sic] suggestion Father sold our house overlooking the river and moved into Hanover. Mother wished closer companionship for her self [sic] and for the children." Probably it required more than a "suggestion" to persuade Harrison to surrender the large brick house, but it was done. Besides, the village of Hanover, "closer companionship" aside, lacked street lighting and paved streets until the 20th century. Whether the move resulted in more companionship for Heber is doubtful. If any close female companionship developed outside his family circle, no record of it survives. There is no hint of a crush, courtship, or romance until Heber moved to California and met his beloved Addie. The college was exclusively male except for those few young women admitted to courses not offered in the nearby village schools. Open or surreptitious consorting with young women beyond the borders of the college could happen, of course. There would have been relatively few suitable women in Hanover, however, and they would be known to Heber whether or not they attended the college. The staples of later undergraduate life—dances and informal socializing, sports events and other entertainment, and easy, widely ranging travel—did not exist to the same extent as later, if they existed at all. Besides, Heber's devotion appears to have focused on his family until his graduation and the move to California.[30]

There were no barriers to male bonding. Heber became an initiate of Beta Theta Pi, a strong national collegiate fraternity. He cherished his Beta associates, "high class Christian men. They gave me fine Christian fellowship." Beta satisfied his craving for organized companionship outside his family, for he did not mention an interest in the two literary societies then flourishing on the campus. Travel beyond the Madison-Hanover axis also figured in Heber's life for the first time. "I was allowed to have two trips away from home." One, no great distance downriver, was to Louisville, to take in the sights of the 1872 Exposition. He did not note who accompanied him but it probably was a family excursion. The other venture was far afield—"a trip with the class on a Geological expedition with Prof. John M. Coulter," to Charleston, possibly the Indiana town, but probably the West Virginia city, the longest trip Heber took until the move to California. Two other trips were within Indiana. On one, Heber accompanied his brother Williell to Versailles, some 50 miles north by rail and road. The journey was, apparently, his brother's idea, for Thomson left no record of the trip's purpose. The only trip he took alone was by steamboat upriver to Vevay, Indiana, to visit Minard Sturgis, a fellow Beta. Sturgis, who became a life-long friend, was then teaching school at Vevay. The town itself was unremarkable except as the birthplace and sometime residence of Edward Eggleston, the author of many books, of which the most enduring is *The Hoosier Schoolmaster.*[31]

In 1877 Heber claimed his degree and left with his parents and four sisters for California. His geographically circumscribed life was over. Although he spent almost one fourth of a long life in the Madison-Hanover area, he wrote little about it, save for one autobiographical fragment that he cut from a notebook and separated from the bulk of his papers. Almost all of his biographical statements record only his birth and graduation from Hanover, leaving a 21 year void between. Even the fragment is depreciatory of the significance and attainments of those 21 years. From the perspective of 50 years, Thomson declared, "I came to my Commencement day in June 1877 a fairly well educated man so far as preliminary College work goes," but he was once more "frail of body," perhaps from academic overwork, and "ignorant of the world," a possible reference to his relatively cloistered life. He had, however, "made my peace with God."[32]

Heber's memoirs, published as *That Man Thomson* in 1950, are much less revealing of those Indiana years. "While a youth, living on the Ohio River in Indiana," he wrote in the opening sentence, "I used to hear discussions on the causes of city growth." Four brief sentences follow, their import being that the cities under discussion were Louisville and Cincinnati, and that their growth was said to be due to an undefined "competition." In the next paragraph he noted that some three years before he graduated, "friends in California advised me to continue in civil engineering and to take special courses in geology and chemistry" to prepare for a career in mining engineering. "I equipped myself fully and, following their plan, rushed to California in 1877."[33]

This published summary works well as a "creation story" for Thomson's purpose in furnishing a teleology to reveal his inexorable intellectual and geographical hegira from Indiana to California to Seattle, where he discovered a city young, vibrant, and awaiting the application of his talents. In other respects these extracts from the first two paragraphs of his memoirs are misleading. Thomson heard mostly political discussions according to his unpublished recollections. If he did hear talk of Louisville and Cincinnati, the chances are it focused on the growth of those two cities as background to the decline of Madison, a decline at first relative, then absolute. "About three years before my graduation"[34] would locate him in the midst of his adherence to Hanover's prescribed curriculum.

The required courses included geology—including a field trip—and chemistry. Frank Bradley's informal geological and mineralogical tutoring had already occurred. A freshman course, already taken, did include surveying but that hardly qualified as a program in civil engineering. His unpublished fragment about his early years suggests that his father, in addition to other achievements, was also a civil engineer. Civil engineering, sometimes crudely performed in Harrison Thomson's day, was a profession then easy enough to enter. Heber may have learned some additional surveying and construction techniques from his father, but such off-hours instruction, if it occurred, was not the type Thomson's "friends in California advised me to continue" would infer. Nor had he "rushed to California in 1877," language suggesting a headlong charge westward, a dynamic expression of rugged, individualistic get-up-and-go. In fact, he moved there with his parents and four sisters, and on his father's initiative. The most that could be said for his technical education was that, as he himself once wrote, he graduated "with full classical course, and special courses in surveying, chemistry, and geology."[35]

In any case, Thomson's purpose was not to equivocate or to deceive, but to draw a firm line of personal development from the banks of the Ohio to the shores of Puget Sound. As in all other autobiographical accounts save his brief remembrance of his early years, his life focus really begins in 1877. In his mind, commencement at Hanover marked the advent of his adult career. Readers could be presumed to care only about Thomson's later activities, not about his childhood and youth. Then, too, 1877 was the year in which he became an independent person. Young Heber was no longer an extension of his parents and family despite continuing to live with them from time to time during his four years in California.

Whatever Thomson's judgment about his earlier years, there is no question they were formative. His Presbyterianism was by far the most important influence. Recall that he concluded his roster of educational and physical shortcomings with the affirmation "having made my peace with God." He did not brag about or often mention his faith, but his belief in his salvation nevertheless explains his supreme self-confidence, as well as his conviction concerning the obligation of a member of the elect to serve humanity while advancing his own interests in a morally upright manner. His innumerable kindnesses to people, who might not have been considered on a worldly basis to be among the saved, attest to a willingness to take people as he found them. Nor was he overly involved with sorting out the schisms, hierarchical arrangements, or other disagreements among Presbyterians. His religious attitudes were conservative, forming a system of belief allowing him to be in the world and to work in the world, but not be of it.

His religious attitude was a gift from his father whose profound faith allowed space for human sympathy. Harrison Thomson did believe that God created the earth in six 24-hour days, "a work performed on materials already in existence," a brief, busy time that should be "interpreted literally" from the Bible. Biblical literalism did not, however, justify a belief in human depravity. People, he held, were not "all good" or "wholly inclined to do evil"; therefore their actions and tendencies did not always result in bad works. Similarly, he believed suffering to be simply a part of life on earth and not in itself a punishment for sin.[36]

Certainly the younger Thomson subscribed to the "essential" doctrines promulgated by the Presbyterian Church of the U.S.A. General Assembly of 1910: "belief in the inerrancy of the Bible; the virgin birth of Christ; his substitutionary atonement; Christ's bodily resurrection; and the authenticity of miracles." He was especially focused on Christ's sacrifice, for as he believed, it was reason to accept "the propitiation made for us through the blood of our Savior." This acceptance he related to the work of the world, as "it is necessary for us to be crushed for service so that we may rise again into a new life and to a new beauty, as it was for the rock to be crushed that it might display itself in the flower." The natural world provided proof, for "everything relating to the next life is simply a following out of the laws of nature as we see them executed every day." Beyond the essentials of 1910, he agreed with the 1913 General Assembly's endorsement of federal prohibition. Not that he waited until 1913 to oppose the consumption of liquor—religious tradition and the less than edifying spectacle of Madison's inebriates were sufficient to set him against strong drink. In 1889, eight years after he arrived in Seattle, he signed a petition asking that a saloon be barred from locating next to the post office.[37]

Next to religion, Thomson's devotion to his family, immediate and extended, stood at the core of his belief system. He revered his father. "You will know and appreciate the fact that my father's life was given to building up Christian manhood among the students at Hanover," he wrote to a Madison newspaper editor. "His was a higher work than mine and it will doubtless be more far reaching." A lengthy paragraph in his memoirs affirms his father's command to serve the public in the face of those who shrank from carrying out their social responsibilities. As he remembered his father's phrasing, there would be "persons present fully able to understand the necessary work, but, lacking any sense of 'must' they just do nothing." Harrison Thomson enjoined his son to investigate "the matter," and if he believed it "indeed demanded for public good, let the 'must' put you to work" and "persevere to the end." The son concluded: "during my many years in Seattle I have tried to be guided by what I considered the 'must' of any situation."[38]

Thomson's regard for his mother was considerably more emotional. He loved his "own dear mother" deeply. She "possessed a remarkably keen analytic mind," and was, after brief acquaintance, able to determine "almost" anyone's "probable value in the moral scale," a gift of insight greater than his own. She was, he wrote, a woman who "regardless of all consequences... stood only for that which she believed to be right before Almighty God. The void in our family, left by her departure, will never be filled." He generalized his profound affection, making mother love itself a test of character. When writing to a man whom he had helped in the past, praising the man's "high regard" for his mother, Thomson noted: "when I find a young man in love with his mother, I am sure there is the opportunity of doing something with him."[39]

Thomson behaved affectionately toward his surviving brothers and sister, remaining close to them throughout their lives. His affection, of course, embraced his wife, the former Adeline "Addie" Laughlin. In 1929, on their 46th wedding anniversary, he summarized their married life as "46 years sweet companionship with sweet, patient Addie." He took pride, tempered with realism, in the maturation of their four children, and he doted on his grandchild, Sarah "Sally" Porep. He remained keenly interested in family genealogy.[40]

He extended his regard for his mother and wife to all womanhood, or at least to those women—obviously a large number of them—deserving of solicitude. Writing about a rape case, he declared, "if the death sentence were imposed for every assault upon woman's virtue, that the difficulty would be gotten over. Of course, this may seem like harsh language to you" (he was writing to a New York divine), "but having been born in south eastern Indiana in the neighborhood of some of the most violent men in the country, and having spent my life upon the frontier, I perhaps view these things differently from those who have been in the more refined regions of the world, where maudlin sympathy is common and where weak women are in the habit of carrying flowers to male murderers." He acknowledged "that nothing but the love of our Lord and Savior, Jesus Christ, will ever make men right, but it is barely possible that the fear of death might prevent a certain line of crimes from being committed, next to the fear of God."[41]

In Thomson's mental firmament, devotion to the Republican Party shared space with faith and family. Childhood experiences during the Civil War annealed his Republicanism. From the perspective of 35 years, the struggle remained "the war of the Rebellion" to him. His father was a steadfast regular Republican voter. As did other partisan progressives, however, he supported urban reformers irrespective of party affiliation. His national and state commitments nevertheless were unwavering. In 1932, with unemployment approaching 25 percent, the economy sinking, President Herbert C. Hoover descending into gloom, and Prohibition enforcement collapsing, the country abandoned the Republican Party and voted Democratic. Thomson commented: "Election day. U.S. goes crazy and votes in Democrats and whiskey." Nor did two years of Franklin D. Roosevelt's administration and some economic improvement reconcile him. In 1934 he confided unhappily to his diary: "State election. The Demo-Communistic party wins."[42]

Finally, there is his college education, a rarity in his time. In 1877 he joined only 10,914 others in receiving bachelor's or first professional degrees out of a population of more than 47 million. He was a "college man," and fraternity member besides, and conscious of his status among a formally educated elite. He was proud of the honorary degrees that Hanover bestowed upon him: a master's of art in 1887, and a doctorate in 1901. He worked hard to boost Hanover's endowment.[43]

All this he did with an acute awareness of the limitations of his bachelor's degree. As he later admitted to an acquaintance, "what we learn in college is very largely that which fits us to...appraise those things with which we come in contact" later. "The power of appraisal is a gift which has been denied a great many people and it seems impossible to bestow it upon them simply by a college education," however an "inborn" analytical ability could be "developed during student life." He valued college, too, for the opportunity it gave for learning how to concentrate on the task at hand. "Power of concentration must also be developed during student life, else a man will always be frittering away his time upon useless things. The best that we can get out of college, however, is the direction and right development of our temperament, so...that we may...possess some spirituality. Without the spiritual, we are wholly animal."[44] Thus did he blend faith and education.

Equipped with his lifelong tenets—the Presbyterian faith, commitment to family, and Republicanism, all buttressed by education—he decamped for California. He would not see Hanover again for many years.

NOTES

1. Discussions of public health and related issues in the 19th century include Michael P. McCarthy, *Typhoid and the Politics of Public Health in Nineteenth Century Philadelphia* (Philadelphia: American Philosophical Society, 1987); Charles E. Rosenberg, *Explaining Epidemics and other Studies in the History of Medicine* (New York: Cambridge University Press, 1992); and Susan Sessions Rugh, *Our Common Country: Family Farming, Culture, and Community in the Nineteenth-Century Midwest* (Bloomington: Indiana University Press, 2001). For a look at rampant illnesses in Indiana, with references to the southern part of the state, see Thurman B. Rise, M.D., *The Hoosier Health Office: A Biography of Dr. J.N. Hurty and the History of the Indiana State Board of Health to 1925* (Indianapolis: Indiana State Board of Health, 1946), 45–56. For transportation conditions, see Edwin L. Dunbaugh, *The Era of the Joy Line: A Saga of Steamboating on Long Island Sound* (Westport, CT: Greenwood, 1982), 10, 12, 22; and Mark Aldrich, *Death Rode the Rails: American Railroad Accidents and Safety, 1828–1965* (Baltimore: Johns Hopkins University Press, 2006), 1–180.

2. For "Retta," the sister to whom Thomson was closest, see RHT, "Sketches from 1877 to 1932," (hereafter "Sketches") 1893 entry, 1602-2, box 2, folder 10, RHT Papers, UW. For the deaths of other siblings, see 1602-2, box 1, folder 2, RHT Papers, UW.

3. RHT, "History of the Thomson Family," 1602-2, box 1, folder 2, RHT Papers, UW.

4. Both unattributed notices are in 1602-2, box 1, folder 2, RHT Papers, UW. The second notice cited is signed J.C. Eastman.

5. William Alfred Millis, *The History of Hanover College from 1827 to 1927* (Hanover: Hanover College, 1927), 203 for faculty, 223–24 for students. The online version of the Millis text by the Hanover Historical Texts Project notes the original pagination.

6. The quotation is from RHT's biographical sketch of his father, from which other biographical information is taken, 1602-2, box 1, folder 2, RHT Papers, UW.

7. Carmony, *Indiana, 1816–1850: The Pioneer Era* (Indianapolis: Indiana Historical Bureau and Indiana Historical Society, 1998), 47. Harrison Thomson's class load is surmised from Millis, *History of Hanover College*, 199, 200–1. Wiley, "The Education of a Backwoods Hoosier," *Indiana Magazine of History* 24 (June 1928): 89.

8. Millis, *History of Hanover College*, 210–11. The third student is quoted in Ibid., 275–76.

9. Here and elsewhere, material on the Clifton family is taken from James Harrison Thomson, "A Brief Statement of the Ancestors of My Mother, Mrs. Magdelene Sophronia Clifton Thomson," arranged by RHT, 1602-2, box 1, folder 2, RHT Papers, UW.

10. RHT notebook fragment, copy in author's possession.

11. Except as noted, information on Madison is from John T. Windle and Robert M. Taylor Jr., *The Early Architecture of Madison, Indiana* (Madison and Indianapolis: Historic Madison, Inc., and Indiana Historical Society, 1986), xv–xvi, 3. For an example of a local newspaper booster, see Frank S. Baker, "Michael C. Garber, Sr., and the Early Years of the Madison, Indiana, *Daily Courier,*" *Indiana Magazine of History* 48 (December 1952): 397–408.

12. Emma Lou Thornbrough, *Indiana in the Civil War Era, 1850–1880* (Indianapolis: Indiana Historical Bureau and Indiana Historical Society, 1965), 1, 323.

13. Ibid., 537, 539.

14. "Madison, Indiana, October 16, 1851," *Indiana Magazine of History* 43 (June 1947): 140. John D. Barnhart and Dorothy L. Riker, *Indiana to 1816: The Colonial Period* (Indianapolis: Indiana Historical Bureau and Indiana Historical Society, 1971), 2, 4, 6.

15. Thornbrough, *Indiana in the Civil War Era*, 331–33.

16. George S. Cottman, "Internal Improvements in Indiana," *Indiana Magazine of History* 3 (December 1907): 150, 154–57, 178–80.

17. Thornbrough, *Indiana in the Civil War Era*, 556. *Seventeenth Census of the United States, 1950* vol. 2 (Washington, D.C.: GPO, 1952), pt. 14, p. 15.

18. Thornbrough, *Indiana in the Civil War Era*, 85–123. Quotations from RHT notebook fragment, copy in author's possession.

19. RHT notebook fragment, copy in author's possession.

20. Ibid.

21. Ibid.

22. Ibid.

23. Ibid. For public high schools, see Thornbrough, *Indiana in the Civil War Era*, 490–91.

24. Millis, *History of Hanover College*, 224.

25. Ibid. Information on students and faculty during and after RHT is scattered through Millis. In order of pagination, see 67–69, 114, 142–44, 167–72, 180–82, 200, 263, 271–72.

26. For information on the curriculum see Millis, *History of Hanover College*, 166–71. See also the *Fortieth Annual Catalogue and Circular of Hanover College, Hanover, Indiana, 1871–1872* (Madison, IN: Courier House, 1872). This and other Hanover materials are in the Joseph Wood Evans Memorial Special Collections and Archives Center, Agnes Brown Duggan Library, Hanover College, hereafter HC.

27. *Recitation Register 1862–1888 Grades*, 63, 67, 71, 75, 88, 94, 99, 102, 106, 110, 112, 116, 119, 122, 123, 127, 131, 134, 138, 142, 145, 149, 152. HC.

28. RHT notebook fragment, copy in author's possession. For the absences, see *Recitation Register, 1862–1888 Grades*, 112, HC.

29. Quotations, RHT notebook fragment, copy in author's possession. For Bradley, see Millis, *History of Hanover College*, 204.

30. Millis, *History of Hanover College*, 71, 77, 183–84, 279–80. Quotations, RHT notebook fragment, copy in author's possession.

31. RHT notebook fragment, copy in author's possession.

32. Ibid. For an example of an autobiographical statement, see 89/1, box 5, book 12, no date but late May 1913, RHT Papers, UW.

33. RHT, *That Man Thomson*, ed. Grant Redford (Seattle: University of Washington Press, 1950), 9.

34. Ibid.

35. RHT, autobiographical account, 1602-2, box 1, folder 1, RHT Papers, UW. Engineering education during Thomson's collegiate years was limited both in number of institutions and in the graduation rate, see Charles Riborg Mann, *A Study of Engineering Education: Prepared for the Joint Committee on Engineering Education of the National Engineering Societies*, bn. 11 (New York: Carnegie Foundation for the Advancement of Teaching, 1918), 6.

36. The first two quotations are from S. Harrison Thomson, "The Mosaic Account of Creation," *Methodist Quarterly Review* 4th ser, 4 (October 1852), 516, 519. The last two are from *Discussion of the Doctrine of Human Depravity, in New Albany Presbytery, Sept. 2, '73; April 2, '74* (Madison, IN: Courier Steam Printing, 1874), pamphlet. For sin as inheritance from Adam, but not punished by life events, see S.H. Thomson, *Our Fall in Adam: Discussion, Exegentical and Doctrinal, of*

Romans V. 12-21 (Cincinnati: Elm Street Printing, 1878). The publications and others are in MSS12, S. Harrison Thomson Collection, HC.

37. For questions about doctrines, see Randall Balmer and John R. Fitzmer, *The Presbyterians* (Westport, CT: Greenwood, 1993), 87. For other Presbyterian issues, see David F. Wells, ed., *Reformed Theology in America: A History of Its Modern Development* (Grand Rapids, MI: William B. Erdmans, 1985), especially 1–12, 15–35, 89–101, 135–52, 247–62; and Howard Miller, *The Revolutionary College: American Presbyterian Higher Education, 1707–1837* (New York: New York University Press, 1976). Thomson's words are in RHT to W.L. Hoffenditz, 10 April 1911, 89/1, box 4, book 10, RHT Papers, UW. For the petition, see Norman H. Clark, *The Dry Years: Prohibition and Social Change in Washington*, rev. ed. (Seattle: University of Washington Press, 1988), 60–61, 111.

38. RHT to M.C. Gardner, 26 September 1910, 89/1, box 3, book 9, RHT Papers, UW; and RHT, *That Man Thomson*, 13–14.

39. RHT to F.G. Stranger, 27 November 1906, 89/1, box 2, book 4, RHT Papers, UW. The "my own dear mother" quotation is in RHT to Emma Walker, 14 March 1908, 89/1, box 2, book 5, RHT Papers, UW. For the "high regard" and concluding quotation, RHT to W.L. Hoffenditz, 10 April 1911, 89/1, box 4, book 10, RHT Papers, UW.

40. RHT diary, August 29, 1929, 1602-2, box 2, folder 1, RHT Papers, UW. For RHT's family, see chapters 9, 11, 13, and 14. For genealogy see note 3.

41. RHT to H.C. Weber, 26 April 1909, 89/1, box 2, book 6, RHT Papers, UW.

42. For "war of the Rebellion" quotation, RHT notebook fragment, copy in author's possession. RHT diary, November 8, 1932, 1602-2, box 2, folder 2; and RHT diary, November 6, 1934, 1602-2, box 2, folder 3, both in UW.

43. *Historical Statistics of the United States* (Washington, D.C.: GPO, 1975) pt. 1, 8, 386. For honorary degrees, see RHT, "Personal Record, Reginald Heber Thomson," RHT Papers, 1602-2, box 1, folder 1. The record of the M.A. is missing from HC, but see *Hanover College Board of Trustees, Minutes June 9, 1896–Sept. 25, 1927*, meeting of June 11, 1901, p. 73, awarding RHT the Ph.D., the only Ph.D. awarded that year, HC. For the endorsement, see RHT to Harry Mansfield Waggoner, 5 May 1914, 89/1, box 5, book 13, among many similar letters in RHT Papers, UW.

44. RHT to A.G. Long Jr., 9 September 1911, 89/1, box 4, book 10, RHT Papers, UW.

Thomson, then known by his middle name "Heber," stands in the center of the back row, just left of a corner window of the Healdsburg Institute, California. Thomson taught here under his father's direction. His favorite sister, Henrietta, "Retta," stands in front of him, slightly to the viewer's right. Thomson was 23 years old when this 1879 photograph was taken. *Healdsburg Museum and Historical Society*.

2
Young Manhood in California

A fair inference from Heber Thomson's various accounts of his life is that he went to California in search of a suitable city and a career in engineering, preferably mining engineering. All else when he got there, teaching and tending a lending library, was fill-in work. His search was frustrated, so he presented his four years in California as a brief hiatus in his personal teleology, disposed of in little more than a page. His narrative says he arrived in 1877 to find mining almost entirely suspended because of opposition to hydraulic mining's detritus—the tailings, the muddy, gravelly, sandy, sometimes gluey "slickens." Tailings raised the beds of creeks and rivers, causing flooding. In Thomson's words, they "polluted the streams and killed the land," and "the resulting near-shutdown cut off the use of quicksilver [mercury]—in the mining of which I was particularly interested." No wonder that the faces of the friends who urged him to come to California "were dark." Worse, Dennis Kearney of the radical Workingmen's Party of California, based in San Francisco, threatened to seize "all the railroads and ferries" and "operate them *for the people.*" To cap off an already miserable situation, the price of wheat "had dropped so low that operators of small farms gave up." [1]

In this appalling environment, Heber "found various kinds of work," but only one operating mercury mine, though apparently there was no mutual interest in an association with it. Finally, "late in 1881, after a disappointing trip up the coast as far as Arcata," he decided to take the advice of T.B. Morris, a railroad and mining engineer, and move to Seattle. Thomson identified Morris as "a warm friend of my brother" who had located mines in the Puget Sound area, among them one "with Mr. F.H. Whitworth…on a creek out from Tacoma." On board ship, Thomson joined Morris and other prominent Northwesterners in a discussion of the attributes of urban location, a discussion occupying almost as much space in his memoirs as that of his life from birth through 1881. He arrived to be greeted by the prominent pioneer Henry L. Yesler. It seemed that "my relatives, the Whitworths," had advised Yesler of his pending arrival. Then he went in a hack to the "Rev. George F. Whitworth's home where I enjoyed a good breakfast, after which we all attended church." [2]

Those comments, plus Thomson's discussion of later engineering projects with cousin F.H. "Harry" Whitworth, leads to the conclusion that the Whitworths were on good terms with the local elite and were functioning as a beachhead family for Thomson, preparing the way for his arrival. His brother's "warm friend," T.B. Morris, also played a vital role in connecting Thomson to Seattle. Those conclusions are correct so far as they go, but Thomson's narrative clouds the real impetus for his moves to and from California, and employs more fiction than fact in recounting his time there. [3]

Not that Thomson intended to dissemble or deceive. Indeed, he wrote illuminating narratives of his California sojourn, at least one of them written for his memoirs. The autobiographical *That Man Thomson* limited recollections of California because of Thomson's determination to present his life as an unbroken chain of personal growth culminating in his role in Seattle's development. His stay in California was, it is true, unproductive from the vocational point of view. He could find no emerging city to engage his talents, nor any attractive engineering jobs. Yet his sojourn was important in other ways. He maintained close family ties while suffering the grief of watching a sister die young. He taught in his father's academy and refined his skills in presentation, which would stand him in excellent stead later in life. And he met the young woman who became his wife.

Heber depended on family connections from the beginning to the end of his California experience. The first family member in this case was his older brother Williell, who arrived in San Francisco "two or three years" before Heber's graduation in 1877. There is no direct record of why "Willie" decided to study theology at the Presbyterian Seminary, but possibly the decision was influenced by the Thomsons' formidable uncle, George Frederick Whitworth. The fiercely determined Whitworth had married their aunt, Mary Elizabeth Thomson, in 1838, and took their family by wagon train to the Oregon country in 1853. Whitworth's missionary zeal led to his founding of a dozen or more Presbyterian churches in Oregon and Washington territories. His obsessive quest for Presbyterian higher education would result in, ultimately, Whitworth University in Spokane, Washington. It is plausible to assume that his relatives' trek westward and their tales of the great missionary work to be done in the burgeoning west influenced Williell to go to San Francisco. The family tradition of preaching and teaching was also a probable cause for one of Harrison Thomson's children to decide to study for the ministry.[4]

Williell promptly pressured the rest of the family to follow. "He had been urging my father to move to California, and recommended him to take over the Healdsburg Academy," actually the Alexander Academy, a school located at Healdsburg in Sonoma County, north of San Francisco. "Father finally consented. We started for California July 1 1877." Harrison had put off Williell until after Heber's graduation, but the delay, while reasonable enough, does not explain why Harrison decided to relocate the entire family. This was, after all, a major move involving two parents, a son, and four daughters. The issue is further confused by the general agreement that poor health forced Harrison's retirement the same year, following 33 years of teaching at Hanover. If his health really was poor, it is unlikely that he would plan, organize, and carry through an exhausting trek more than halfway across the continent to assume the demanding task of operating a grade and high school.[5]

It is logical, however, that Harrison's decision was influenced by the economic buffeting in southeastern Indiana. The depression of 1873 hit the area hard, dropping Madison's population from 10,709 in 1870 to 8,945 ten years later, not a good sign in a growing country. The loss prophesied more decline to follow, as the Madison-Hanover area became the sleepy backwater beloved of romanticists and preservationists, but despaired of by people trying to make a living. Nevertheless the area's retreat into a quasi-bucolic state could have been ideal for a retired 64-year-old professor, but it was not. The depression and a series of fiscal expedients had driven Hanover College to the edge of collapse. The student population, which recovered in the post-Civil War days to 176 in 1872, fell to 111 in Heber's graduation year. It would fall for two more years. In 1878, the year after the Thomsons left, a motion to suspend the college until its financial affairs could be righted failed by one vote at a meeting of the board of trustees. It was no time for Harrison to relive the crushing teaching loads and the pecuniary travails of the past decade. He might well have given poor health—perhaps poor mental health—as a reason for resigning.[6]

So the Thomson family headed west. Nothing is known of the trip except for Heber's statement that it began July 1 and ended at Healdsburg early in July.[7] The family had to have traveled by train. It was possible but unlikely that the Thomsons took a less well integrated route using the Kansas Pacific from St. Louis. Travel through Indiana, on the other hand, would have been more familiar and convenient, if slightly less direct. Assuming they rode the old Madison & Indianapolis railway, they traversed country familiar enough to Heber. Indianapolis was growing and almost flat as a pancake, unlike shrinking Madison with rumpled hills. There was more insipid country from Indianapolis to dirty, frenetic, flat Chicago. A change of trains there brought the family through the Illinois prairies and over the Mississippi at Burlington, then across the lush, green, rolling hills of Iowa. By the time the Chicago, Burlington & Quincy engine chuffed into Council Bluffs on the Missouri, Heber had traveled farther from home than ever before. When it rattled over the bridge into Omaha, he was about to experience his first visual taste of the Great West.[8]

A few miles out of Omaha the landscape changed, becoming drier with hints of rough hills in the distance. The train followed the great bend of the Platte and rose mile by mile toward the hills, which became more rugged and barren. At the fork of the Platte, the Union Pacific struck due west into the Nebraska panhandle, then into Wyoming Territory. Here there were real mountains, the Laramies, but also the lovely valleys around Cheyenne and Laramie. At Laramie the road swung again, this time northwest to Medicine Bow, the northernmost point of the trip save Chicago. The train climbed through the Rockies, then the tracks bent southerly into the Great Divide basin, some of the most desolate, treeless, windswept terrain in the northern temperate zone. At otherwise insignificant Dale Creek, the train crept over a new, soaring iron bridge, the "spider web," 707 feet long between bluffs and 127 feet above the lowest point of the creek bed. After stopping at oases-like Green River, the train plunged into Utah, changing to Central Pacific cars, through the rough Wasatch Range, skirted the Great Salt Lake, crossed into Nevada, and followed the wild canyon of the Humboldt River as it curved southwestward, to near the fetid Carson Sink. It struggled up the eastern slope of the Sierra Nevada, then careened down the western, chugging through eerie tunnels and snow sheds along the way. Heber saw railroad engineering at its most triumphant.

The Central Pacific rolled into California's vast, fecund Central Valley, so rich and green after the wastes of sand, snow, and spiky peaks. At Vallejo, on the northeast bight of San Pablo Bay, the transcontinental trip ended. There the family debarked and proceeded by local train to Healdsburg, in the valley of the Russian River, some 70 miles north of San Francisco.

It was for good reason that Thomson wrote little about the trip. In 1877 rail travel from Indiana to Healdsburg was no jaunt. It required at least a week's time. Stops were frequent and the trains slow. The food at trackside lunchrooms was usually edible but scarcely ever above that level. Wooden coaches swayed and bumped over track not yet brought to high-speed standards. Windows raised to allow air circulation in the summer heat also admitted insects, along with smoke and soot from the locomotive. Dangerous kerosene heaters fended off the cold in the high country and mountains. The total cost of a bare-bones trip would have been in the neighborhood of $325, quite a sum for Harrison, whose annual salary was only about four times that. If the family rode in a Pullman sleeper and ate in dining cars, it would most likely have been on the Omaha-California run. In any event, much of the trip was tedious except for the sometimes breathtaking scenery during daylight hours.

What Heber found in California was not at all as he described in his autobiography—a desolate scene, compounded of closed mines, wild socialist agitation, and failing farms. The trouble with Heber's account was that he faced none of those situations at first. True, hydraulic mining had caused problems for a decade before his arrival, but the tailings had not "killed the land" and certainly had not forced a suspension of mining. Indeed, the *Keyes* decision, the first of a series of findings against the mines, was not handed down until almost two years after the Thomsons' arrival. Investment in hydraulic mining did decline after the decision, possibly affecting Heber's opportunities, though the mines continued to operate for years. Nor had Dennis Kearney's rabble rousing yet begun. Kearney came into view about two months after the Thomsons arrived. Given Heber's opposition to the 1886 anti-Chinese riot in Seattle, he should have condemned Kearney's vaporings against San Francisco's Chinese. He did not. A possible explanation is that his later disgust with the Democratic New Deal electoral and legislative triumphs in the 1930s condi-

tioned his view of Kearney's labor radicalism while he was writing his memoirs. He may have seen Kearney's unbridled wooing of workingmen as a precursor of the New Deal's position on national issues, a stance he considered radical. Perhaps it was enough for him to denounce all of Kearney's works without distinction. In any case, Kearney's Workingmen's Party was practically a spent force when Heber left California. So far as farming went, the depression of 1873 resulted in lower farm prices, but the serious decline began the year after the Thomsons came to California. It had in part lifted by the time Heber left for Seattle. The long-term trough in farm commodity prices that lasted from the late 1880s to World War I was in the future. [9]

In short, Heber's explanations concerning unsettled economic times explain little or nothing about his inability to find a job in mining engineering. Family commitments do, however, clarify why he "found various kinds of work," a statement only partly true. The people who found the most work for Heber were his father and Williell, who is identified only as "my brother" in Heber's autobiography. Heber had already obligated himself to teach in his father's academy. "School was not to open until in September," however, so Williell "got me to take charge of a mission school on the Oakland waterfront until school opened." When the academy did open, Harrison Thomson "was, as it were, President—all the rest of us, helpers." Heber, his mother, and four sisters "all did something, and the fees paid supported us fairly well." [10]

In mid-July 1877, Harrison Thomson officially took charge of the Alexander Academy, a two-story frame building near the southeast side of Healdsburg. The academy had a checkered past, opening in 1857 on the strength of hopes for Healdsburg's future and a yearning for education among its 300 residents. It operated with different names and headships for ten years, then failed. Cyrus Alexander, a leading pioneer and the school's mortgagee, donated it to the Presbyterian Church, whereupon resuscitation came under the name Alexander Academy. The academy struggled along with fewer than 60 students, even though Healdsburg boomed, soaring from a population of 300 to 1,600 twelve years later. The building, apparently not well constructed, drained funds from staff salaries and supplies to pay for maintenance. Meeting tuition costs was a struggle for Healdsburg families, especially during the hard times of the 1870s. Overcrowding in the public schools was little incentive to enroll offspring in the Alexander Academy when money was tight. [11]

Possibly, the elder Thomson did not know of a recent competing development making his new circumstances potentially just as desperate as those escaped in Hanover. The fresh challenge for the Thomson family appeared in the shape of Gilbert Butler, who arrived perhaps as early as January 1877 and set about drumming up support for a new "Healdsburg Academy." Butler was a promoter. He wangled enough in donations and pledges to have his plans well formed by the time the tired, dusty Thomsons arrived. His conception of a bigger, better, more centrally located school was fulfilled at the dedication on January 1, 1878, of "an edifice that stands as a monument to the liberality of the citizens of this city and vicinity," a handsome frame building of two stories set on a three-foot brick foundation. The 56 by 75 foot "edifice" was "supplied throughout" with blackboards, water, and gas lighting. Butler or his board may have selected the exterior paint, of "a drab color," to suggest the serious activities to be conducted within. The doors, however, were grained in imitation oak and the interior wood in imitation walnut. "The painting and graining," a local newspaper proudly announced, were "equal to any in Sonoma County."[12]

The only concession to the competing Alexander Academy was a change in name, to Healdsburg "Institute." Despite the gala event featuring a free day and night concert by the Healdsburg Brass Band, and despite the subscription of some 65 seats in the new building, things went poorly for Healdsburg's latest center of learning. Butler quickly decamped. Whether someone questioned his credentials as a former teacher's college professor or whether it was always his intention to milk the community financially and then move on is unknown. In any event, by July the institute's stockholders were too discouraged by the school's prospects and more than $2,300 debt to raise a quorum at a meeting. In November the institute consolidated with the Alexander Academy under Harrison Thomson's leadership. Heber, Retta, and May were his assistants, and the school was to be "conducted on the nonsectarian order" in the much newer and better institute building.[13]

The combined school retained the name "Healdsburg Institute." For a time things went well enough. Fifty-eight students enrolled and performed creditably during Christmas-time closing exercises in December. By May 1879 the *Healdsburg Enterprise* reported that Harrison Thomson and his children "have spared neither labor nor money to make the Institute a crowning honor and acquisition to the city." Heber made his contribution to the institute's reputation. In the spring of 1879, a group

of students—who had failed their teaching certification test after enrolling in a "private school under a gentleman who made a very fine appearance," possibly the departed Butler—approached Thomson to ask if they could enroll in his classes. Test-based teaching was not, in the late 1870s, something new. Heber noted "that I had had no experience with California methods, but that I would ground them in such principles as I believed the examination questions might touch upon." The class was successful, despite one student's complaint that Thomson "did not make the lessons [as] entertaining" as those of the previous teacher. His instruction continued until November 1879, when the class traveled south to Santa Rosa and sat for a three-day exam. All but one of about 20 students passed. Thomson took the exam with them and passed, too, receiving a "first grade County and State" certificate.[14]

Despite the Thomson family's best efforts, and the addition of "a splendid electrical apparatus" to "the valuable surveying, engineering, astronomical and philosophical apparatus," enrollment declined. A report noted that "the stringency of the times has caused the pecuniary returns to fall far below just remuneration." The attendance in all departments including the primary grades averaged about 40. The only way to support the family "fairly well" was for Heber to use his newly-minted certificate and find another teaching post. Thus he began teaching, perhaps as a fill-in schoolmaster, and possibly as early as the last month of 1879. His first job was at the nearby hamlet of Green Valley, where he boarded with the mayor, almost certainly the prosperous farmer Isaac W. Sullivan. In any event, the job saw him through the spring term of 1880. That autumn he "took the school near the Groves and Hotchkiss place, about four miles South of Healdsburg. On Saturdays I took charge of a Lending Library in the Healdsburg Institute."[15]

Heber's memory was probably correct, but he did neglect to mention most of his extensive efforts to find a viable alternative to teaching. He also failed to note that the "Lending Library" mentioned in his "Sketches" probably fell to his care because of his well-cultivated love of books and learning. This dimension of his life was not one that he mentioned in his memoirs. Nor, probably, did he dwell on it except to family and a few close friends. In any event, the "Lending Library" was in young Heber's mind a great deal more than that. A letterhead, probably printed late in 1878, noted that "R.H. Thomson" was the "Librarian" of the "Healdsburg Public Library," located in the "Healdsburg Institute Building." Established in 1876 by a private association, its first home had been the second floor of the Masonic Lodge. The library was "Open Fridays from 3 to 5 P.M." After accepting his public school position south of town, however, Heber could not return for a Friday afternoon opening, so moved the operating time to Saturday. The severely limited hours are incomprehensible to library patrons of a later time, especially for a "public" library. What is remarkable about this library, however, is that it existed at all in a small farming community only a few years removed from geographic isolation.[16]

The teaching stint four miles south of Healdsburg lasted until the spring of 1881, a pivotal year for Heber. By then one of his sisters was dead and two others were not in good health, "so it was determined to close all teaching." Health aside, Heber did not mention the main reason for suspending the school—dwindling student numbers. Continuing hard times, Healdsburg's stagnant population growth, and the (at last) "firmly established" public school all contributed to the decision. The family moved to Pasadena, where Harrison Thomson died the next year.[17] Heber struck out on his own, though still within the protective envelope of his extended family. In September of that year, he sailed for Seattle, the one event of his pre-Pacific Northwest career celebrated at length in his memoirs.

Understanding Heber's move to Seattle requires consideration of his four years in California from the perspective of his search for a promising city with good job prospects. Despite a distinguished family tradition of teaching, his experience, and abundant local opportunities, he decided not to continue pursuing a teaching career. Nor was he interested in moving to San Francisco, then the largest city on the Pacific Coast. San Francisco's maturity likely alienated Heber. In 1880 the city held almost 240,000 people—not large by national standards but its elites were well established. Those elites did not include any Thomson relatives. Heber could have looked south to Los Angeles, then on the verge of a delirious boom, but either the absence of relatives or its alien if salubrious climate, or both, deterred any serious consideration.[18]

Oddly, given his supposed "special courses in geology and chemistry in preparation for good offers that would be awaiting me in California," Heber evinced no interest in gold mining. The mines needed engineers, or at least people who called themselves engineers, for damming projects, hydraulic operations, and quartz mining. By the time Thomson arrived, the industry had matured, taking its direction from capitalists in San Francisco and elsewhere. Fresh opportunities in mining were available only

to those with capital or extraordinary luck. And most gold mining was on the eastern side of the state, where there was no family.[19]

The summers that Heber spent in California, save the first and possibly third, he eschewed teaching in favor of seeking an engineering opportunity or an incipient city. After the spring term of 1878, the first year of teaching at the Healdsburg Institute, he and Williell drove a horse and buggy around Lake County north and east of Sonoma, looking for operating mercury mines. They found "many tunnels" dug out in unsuccessful searches for quicksilver. They returned to the Healdsburg area and, together with their father, visited an operating mine on Sonoma County's Mount Jackson. It was hardly the lone effort Heber depicted in his memoirs, a search undertaken in the context of a supposedly failed gold mining industry. In fact the gold mining industry would plunge ahead unabated for many more years. The reality of a large and steady gold production propelled the Thomson brothers' investigation of quicksilver mining possibilities, even if nothing came of it.[20] Again, with father and brother joining him, Heber subdivided the Rancho Tzabaco, "up Dry Creek" near Healdsburg, using their surveying skills. Their survey suggests that California's famed residential land boom of the 1880s actually began earlier and was not confined to the southern part of the state.[21]

Heber left no record of his activities during the summer of 1879. Possibly, he did not record them because he spent most of the time courting his future wife, "Addie" Laughlin, the daughter of a prosperous farmer. The Laughlins, like the Thomsons, were pillars of the local Presbyterian church, and it is probable that Heber and Addie met there. In any event, Heber returned to his mining investigations during the summer of 1880. He and a young man named Sullivan, probably Charles C., the oldest son of Isaac W. Sullivan of Green Valley, went to Mendocino County to "examine a great water wheel in the Garcia River a mile or two before reaching Point Arena." There the two watched a "monster" overshot waterwheel turn gears, lifting lumber up to a tram at the top of a ridge. The tram then hauled the wood to a small harbor for loading on ships. When Thomson asked why the proven, turbine-driven Pelton wheel was not used, "they challenged me to equal the service given by the overshot wheel and equipment by any other method."[22]

Thomson and Sullivan returned to Cloverdale, where they found a sort of miners' folly nearby. Years before, Heber wrote, "there was a rather continuous slide down the mountain side," near "a geyser, or steamboat spring,

as the local people called it, and out of the geyser the
steam carried a large amount of sulphur." The sulfur con-
densed and "settled on the face of the slide," leaving sul-
furic traces. "Anxious miners insisted there must be tons
of sulphur just a little back from the front of the slide, so
they erected a large mill" to extract the mineral. "After
long tests they found that the percentage of sulphur compared with the gravel and earth in the slide was almost
infinitely small, so the plant remained idle." [23]

Next the young men renewed Heber's search for
quicksilver, in a more extensive trip, examining "great
numbers of abandoned quicksilver mines in Sonoma,
Mendocino, and Lake Counties." Despite those failures,
they "met men who proclaimed themselves superior
miners," and eager to share "their secret methods."
Unimpressed, the duo returned to the Healdsburg area,
where they "found," but really revisited the "actually
operating quicksilver mine" on Mount Jackson, "where
we remained long enough to take in the entire system
used in sinking mines, hoisting, and refining the ore." [24]
Nothing developed from the second trip to Mount
Jackson, just as there were no results from the first, except
to affirm Heber's continued interest in mining engineering. As he was discovering, there was little or nothing
in Sonoma or its adjacent counties to hold him. What
placer gold mining existed in the Russian River Valley
"never paid much more than ordinary wages," scarcely
the setting for an active mining engineer. Coal mining
at Taylor Mountain, southwest of Santa Rosa, may have
piqued Heber's unrecorded interest but was fading as
he left California. Within a decade after his departure,
"the old tunnels, slopes, and shafts" were "so thoroughly
dilapidated and caved in, that…no coal can be seen in
place anywhere underground." Coal found there and
elsewhere nearby was of dubious quality and in severely
faulted seams. The state mineralogist found that alleged
surface coal was actually volcanic rock. [25]

Meanwhile, the valleys and rounded hills supported
grain farming, stock raising, and dairying. Abundant
orchards produced apples, pears, plums, cherries,
peaches, and table and raisin grapes. Ever since his
gardening days in Indiana, however, Heber showed no
interest in farming. Ironically, given the abstemious
Thomsons' choice of residence, hops and wine grapes
grew in abundance in the area. Hop raising and vinicul-
ture, of course, were not occupations that Heber could
consider. His one surveying job aside, there was next to
no employment for civil engineers. Healdsburg was a
pretty little town set in the midst of lovely agricultural
country, but it was just that and no more. [26]

A modern-day view of the restored Laughlin farmstead in the Mark West
community south of Healdsburg, California, suggests the prosperity of
the family into which Thomson married. *Katharine L. Wilson.*

For good personal reasons, 1881 was Heber's last
year in California. That summer he took the longest
trip of his California sojourn, about three quarters of
the distance from Healdsburg to the Oregon border.
In his autobiography, he describes this journey as, in
effect, forcing a decision to leave the state. He recalled
how, "late in 1881, after a disappointing trip up the
coast as far as Arcata, I took my baggage and started to
San Francisco to take steamer to Seattle." Thomson did
not explain his disappointment, except to note it came
after a "constant strain of kindly advice wore on me,"
advice offered by that "warm friend of my brother," T.B.
Morris, the Seattle booster. Heber further described
Morris as the "first chief engineer of the Northern
Pacific railway," who, with a partner, had founded "a
coal mine at Renton, a town about twelve miles from
Seattle," and who, with F.H. Whitworth, had begun to
develop another. [27]

Thomson's cousin, Frederick H. Whitworth, already
was firmly established in Seattle. Heber would later
admit, as we have seen, the family connection, which was
a powerful one in the small world of Seattle in 1881. But
what was the advice, supposedly from T.B. Morris? It was
to "not be satisfied" with the San Francisco area, but to
"go to Seattle," where "you can find a coal vein to reward
your search." Moreover, Heber recorded Morris as saying,
"if you make a good search, you can very cheaply acquire
a timber claim." Both a coal vein and timber claim
would increase in value because San Francisco "brings the
greater part of its coal from Seattle," and "secures much
of its most choice building lumber from Seattle." In sum,
Heber would have his reader believe that, after the long
and "disappointing" trip in north California, he took

the persistent advice of a booster and moved to Seattle, which, Morris claimed, would be important principally as a distant industrial suburb of San Francisco.[28]

Really understanding Thomson's last summer in California begins with that lengthy trip. Heber left two versions of the journey, and they may be reconciled, except for his statement that he made the trip alone. Discounting his usual for-publication description of individualistic travel and investigation, and his much later claim that it was a railroad location "reconnaissance," a context for the trip may be developed. To begin with the personal aspect: By 1881 he and Addie were almost certainly engaged, if not yet formally so. It was high time for 25-year-old Heber to demonstrate his ability to support a family and establish himself in some occupation other than teaching in tiny communities combined with itinerant fortune hunting. Worse, from the personal viewpoint, he was, during the winter of 1881 "troubled with either colonitis [colitis] or enteritis"— inflammations of the large and small intestines respectively. The most evident symptom of either is diarrhea. Two doctors, one of them a brother-in-law, treated him "with no good effect." The medical stalemate encouraged him, not for the last time, "to pick some out of doors employment," as anodyne to an ailment.[29]

Fortunately for Heber's health, the "Rev. F.G. Culver of Green Valley seeing my condition asked me to ride with him on a Good Templar trip." The "Good Templar" of Thomson's recollection was the Independent Order of Good Templars, a reformist "total abstinence" group responsible for founding the national Prohibition Party in 1872. The Rev. Culver "began Hom[e]opathic treatment." As they progressed northward in the name of temperance, Heber also "made careful examination of the profits that were made in lumbering" while seeking out any settlement with future urban prospects. Thus the trip had four purposes: recruiting adherents to alcohol prohibition, seeking out a profitable enterprise, finding a community destined to grow into a city, and restoring health.[30]

Thomson's at least partial return to health was the only positive result that he recorded. Culver's homeopathic treatment probably involved small doses of herbal laxatives. "Under his treatment I improved," Heber wrote, although horseback riding, walking, and a return to a summer diet of fresh foods probably helped as much or more than Culver's medicine. In any event, the two moved up the coast to Eureka, on Humbolt Bay, then on to nearby Arcata. While scanning the possibilities of the Humbolt Bay region, for doing good and doing well,

they "gave some help to building a bridge across Mad River, a short distance above Arcata. There was some physical exertion necessary in building that bridge, as we had to whipsaw all the lumber." Neither place offered more than a site for strenuous exercise. "Not seeing any hope of either Eureka or Arcata becoming more than a sawmill town for a long time to come, I made up my mind to make a trip to Seattle and determine what the outlook was there and…whether or not there was really a chance of Seattle becoming a great city, as some of its advocates insisted."[31]

One of Seattle's "advocates" to whom Heber responded was undoubtedly his brother Williell, who had originally lured the family to California. Williell had visited the Whitworth family up north at least once before. A handwritten "History of the Thomson Family" notes it was "Transcribed & revised by me Williell this 3rd Oct. 1877 at Seattle W.T. from Aunt Eliza's copy." Some time thereafter, Williell returned to Seattle to work in cousin "Harry" Whitworth's engineering firm. Although Williell eventually returned to California, he was in Seattle when Heber arrived. Thus T.B. Morris' supposed exhortations and the Whitworths' successes were not the only influence on Heber. He was also pushed, and not only due to the limited possibilities of Eureka and Arcata. By the time Heber returned home in August, the Harrison Thomson family had decided to leave Healdsburg.[32]

Heber's decision to go to Seattle and associate with a family business should not be interpreted as weakness or laziness. For him, family was a cradle of mutual help and culture, not a crutch. During the four years in California he had worked hard, searched for significant openings in civil or mining engineering, and tried to find a small settlement that would become the next San Francisco. At any time, he could have settled for a humdrum job adequate to support Addie and himself. Or he could have put down roots in any one of a dozen towns, hoping against hope for a population boom. Or he could have tried to succeed his father, nurturing the Healdsburg Institute in an era of struggling private colleges and rising support for public education. The negative example ever before him was the near-collapse of his alma mater, Hanover College. Healdsburg itself was among the several California towns apparently headed nowhere, if "becoming a great city" was Thomson's measure of community success, as indeed it was.

Declining family fortunes in California, and a pressing need to find a broad avenue to success in the expanding West, form the context for Thomson's auto-

Seattle's central area in 1886, viewed from the south slope of Denny Hill. The photographer's stance on the prominence indicates Denny Hill's massive height and its hindrance to northward expansion of the city. *Seattle Municipal Archives #2868.*

biographical statement that "after a disappointing trip up the coast as far as Arcata," he moved to Seattle. His steamer landed at Yesler's wharf 30 years to the day from the putative founding of Seattle, though the first settlement was abandoned for the better location where the *Dakota* docked. After a decade and a half, the city remained ragged, unkempt, and small. Its population was perhaps 4,000, mostly clustered on the hills around Elliott Bay, a concave stretch of Puget Sound. Almost all of the residents needed better lighting, water, and sewage services than they had. The place was primitive, but Heber was used to that. Thus, Heber Thomson, a 25-year-old college and fraternity man, devout Presbyterian, and well-connected in Seattle from the moment he arrived, stepped from the steamer *Dakota*. Henry L. Yesler, 70 years old, lacking formal education, irreligious, and probably the leading reprobate among Seattle's founders, "welcomed" the young man "very cheerily."[33] Thomson was used to men such as Yesler, too. By age 25, he had learned how to live in the world, yet not be of it.

NOTES

1. RHT, *That Man Thomson*, 9–10.
2. Ibid., 10–12.
3. Ibid., 12–13, 15–16.
4. For Whitworth and former Whitworth College, see Alfred O. Gray, *Not By Might: The Story of Whitworth College, 1890–1965* (Spokane: Whitworth College, 1965); and Dale E. Soden, *A Venture of Mind and Spirit: An Illustrated History of Whitworth College* (Spokane: Whitworth College, 1990). For RHT's quotations, RHT, "Sketches," 1877 entry, 1602-2, box 2, folder 10, RHT Papers, UW.
5. RHT's quotations, RHT, "Sketches," 1877 entry, 1602-2, box 2, folder 10, RHT Papers, UW. Millis, *History of Hanover College* 198, states that Harrison Thomson "retired on account of health."
6. Millis, *History of Hanover College*, records the student population on page 224 and the near-suspension on page 116.
7. RHT, "Sketches," 1877 entry, 1602-2, box 2, folder 10, RHT Papers, UW.
8. There are voluminous sources for the reconstruction of RHT's presumed trip. They rest on the author's observation of much of the route; D.W. Meinig, *Transcontinental America, 1850–1915*, vol. 3 of *The Shaping of America* (New Haven: Yale University Press, 1998), 3–55, 89–113, 133–67; Albro Martin, *Railroads Triumphant: The Growth, Rejection, and Rebirth of a Vital*

American Force (New York: Oxford University Press, 1992), 52–55, 76–77; and Stephen E. Ambrose, *Nothing Like It in the World: The Men Who Built the Transcontinental Railroad, 1863–1869* (New York: Simon and Schuster, 2000), 261.

9. For environmental problems, see Robert L. Kelley, *Gold v. Grain: The Hydraulic Mining Controversy in California's Sacramento Valley* (Glendale, CA: Arthur H. Clark, 1959), 116–18. For Dennis Kearney and the Workingmen's Party, see Issel and Cherney, *San Francisco, 1865–1932*, 126–30, 206, 208. For farm commodity prices, see *Historical Statistics of the United States* pt. 1 (Washington, D.C.: GPO, 1975), 208.

10. RHT, "Sketches," 1877 entry, 1602-2, box 2, folder 10, RHT Papers, UW. See also note 3.

11. *Russian River Flag*, February 4, 1869, and May 12, 1870. For public school overcrowding, see *Russian River Flag*, January 18, 1877.

12. Butler's card appeared in the *Russian River Flag*, January 18, 1877, together with a supporting editorial. The description of the new building appears in the *Healdsburg Enterprise*, January 3, 1878.

13. For the stockholder's meeting, see *Healdsburg Enterprise*, July 4, 1878; for the combining of the schools, *Healdsburg Enterprise*, October 31, 1878, and for quotation, November 7, 1878.

14. For the number of students, see *Healdsburg Enterprise*, November 7, 1878. For the closing exercises, see *Healdsburg Enterprise*, December 26, 1878. For quotation, see *Healdsburg Enterprise*, May 22, 1879. Thomson's account is in RHT, autobiographical statement in 89/1, box 6, folder 3, RHT Papers, UW.

15. Quotations are from the *Healdsburg Enterprise*, May 22, 1879. For the number of students, see the *Healdsburg Enterprise*, February 18, 1926. RHT's quotations are from "Sketches," 1880 entry. See also 1881 entry, box 2 folder 10, RHT Papers, UW. For Sullivan, see *An Illustrated History of Sonoma County, California* (Chicago: Lewis, 1889; Salem, MA: Higginson, 1997), 349–50.

16. The letterhead is in 1602-2, box 1, folder 2, RHT Papers, UW. For the origins of the library, see "Not by Bread Alone: A Social History of the Healdsburg Public Library," *Russian River Recorder* 34 (Fall 1988): 3–5.

17. RHT quotation, "Sketches," 1881 entry, 1602-2, box 2, folder 10, RHT Papers, UW. For the public school, see "Healdsburg Schools, 1853–1880," *Russian River Recorder*, issue 23 (April 1982): 2. For population, see the chart in the Healdsburg Museum listing the 1869 population at 1,600; 1880s at 2,000; and 1910s at only 2,011.

18. Sources on San Francisco and Los Angeles abound. Standard are Issel and Cherney, *San Francisco, 1865–1932*; and Robert M. Fogelson, *The Fragmented Metropolis: Los Angeles, 1850–1930* (1967; reprinted with a foreword by Robert Fishman, Berkeley: University of California Press, 1993).

19. Malcom J. Rohrbough, *Days of Gold: The California Gold Rush and the American Nation* (Berkeley: University of California Press, 1997), 197–204, 267–70.

20. For quotation, RHT autobiographical statement in 89/1, box 6, folder 3, RHT Papers, UW. See also "Sketches," 1878 entry, 1602-2, box 2, folder 10, RHT Papers, UW.

21. RHT remembered the name as "Rancho Izsbaco" in "Sketches," 1872 entry, 1602-2, box 2, folder 10, RHT Papers, UW. The ranch had passed out of the hands of its original Mexican grantees and into those of a D.D. Phillips. See Hannah M. Clayborn, "Teenage Rancheros on the Tzabaco: The Piñas of Dry Creek," *Russian River Recorder* 30 (Summer 1985): 8–15; and Louise Davis, *History of Sonoma County and Geyserville* (Geyserville, CA: 1985), 22–23.

22. RHT's quotations here and in the following paragraphs are from his autobiographical statement in 89/1, box 6, folder 3, RHT Papers, UW. The Sullivans are listed in U.S. Bureau of the Census, Manuscript 1880 Census, Mendocino Township, Sonoma County, California, 272A.

23. RHT autobiographical statement in 89/1, box 6, folder 3 RHT Papers, UW.

24. Ibid.

25. California Division of Mines and Geology, *Report of the State Mineralogist*, vol. 10 (San Francisco, 1890), 676–77, quotation on 677.

26. For agricultural developments, see J.P. Munro-Fraser, *History of Sonoma County, California* (Oakland: Pacific Press, 1879; Petaluma, CA: Charmaine Burdell Veronda, 1978), 20; C.A. Menefee, *Historical and Descriptive Sketch Book of Napa, Sonoma, Lake, and Mendocino* (Napa City, CA: Reporter, 1873), 2, 262–63; and Gaye LeBaron, Dee Blackman, and Harry Hanson, *Santa Rosa: A Nineteenth Century Town* (Santa Rosa: Clarity, 1985), 60–61.

27. RHT, *That Man Thomson*, 10.

28. Ibid.

29. The "Reconnaissance" claim is in RHT, "Personal Record: Reginald Heber Thomson," 1602-2, box 1, folder 1; RHT Papers, UW. The three following quotations are from autobiographical accounts, in order, , and 1602-2, box 1, folder 1; 89/1, box 6, folder 3; and 1602-2, box 1, folder 1, RHT Papers.

30. For the Good Templars, see Norman H. Clark, *Deliver Us from Evil: An Interpretation of American Prohibition* (New York: Norton, 1976), 69–70. For Thomson's first two quotations, see the autobiographical account in 1602-2, box 1, folder 1; and for the last one, the account in 89/1, box 6, folder 3, RHT Papers, UW.

31. For the first quotation, see the autobiographical account in 1606-2, box 1, folder 1, and for all others, see the account in 89/1, box 6, folder 3, RHT Papers, UW.

32. For Williell's history, see 1602-2, box 1, folder 2; and for Thomson's move, see RHT, "Sketches," 1881 entry, 1602-2, box 2, folder 10, RHT Papers, UW.

33. RHT, *That Man Thomson*, 12. For one example of Yesler's extramarital activity, see "Henry Yesler's Native American daughter Julia is born on June 12, 1855," www.historylink.org/essays/output.cfm?file-id=3396.

Pioneer Square waterfront in 1896, with a view up Mill Street (now Yesler Way). These bustling blocks encompassed Seattle's commercial core. *Seattle Municipal Archives #29984.*

3

Early Years in Seattle

BEFORE HEBER THOMSON stepped from the aging *Dakota*, he had set two tasks for himself. One was to investigate the possibilities of the town of Seattle, still rough and raw 30 years after its founding. The second and equally important charge was to assess the future of the coal mines spreading out in a fan east of the town, beyond Lake Washington. His companions aboard ship spoke of the great future of coal mining in the Puget Sound area, although they hotly debated whether Victoria, British Columbia, or Seattle would become the dominant port for coal development.[1]

Euroamerican culture had invaded nature in and around the scraggly settlement of Seattle by September 1881. Glaciers, volcanoes, and earthquakes had left a land of great beauty on the horizons. The Cascade Range to the east, including the glistening slopes of Mount Rainier to the southeast, complemented the peaks of the Olympic Mountains to the west. Closer at hand, however, the view was less promising. An eastern ridge of five hills, littered with stumps left from cuttings for rough lumber and firewood, surrounded the town in a semicircle—locking it into a shallow rectangular ledge of perhaps 120 built up blocks, tilting steeply up from south to north and west to east. Within the double incline the hillocks and hollows frustrated pedestrians, builders, and city crews attempting to make streets and sidewalks over mud or dust. "Nature," in Welford Beaton's apt phrase, "left the townsite itself like a tousled, unmade bed."[2]

The waterfront then lay some two blocks farther east than in the 21st century after projects filled it in. A polluted Elliott Bay lapped close to the backs of frame buildings along the west side of Front Street (now First Avenue). Front Street ran downhill from Pike Street south to Yesler's Wharf, then the most prominent man-made structure on the bay. The wharf was a widened, 200-foot-long extension of Mill Street (now Yesler Way). It formed a miniature commercial district in itself, with a shifting array of warehouses, stores, and saloons, plus a blacksmith shop, ice house, and water tank. South of Mill Street, dry land ran another four blocks until it surrendered to the bay, an area now filled in.[3]

A tidal flat of the bay extended from about the present location of King Street to the foot of Beacon Hill, or roughly to the route of today's Interstate 5. As much as 15 feet of water covered the tidelands at high tide; during the brief tidal ebb, it was a mass of mud. The tidal flat extended south along Beacon Hill to the mouth of the Duwamish River, a looping, turbulent stream, larger than its tamed descendent of today, the Duwamish Waterway. The northeast bend of this huge tidal sheet was fill, mostly sawdust dumps from the Yesler mills that succeeded one another after consuming fires. In 1881 the area was still being filled in, and extended east until meeting the old high tide mark at about present-day Fourth Avenue South. The sliver of land and older fill to the west contained the town's leading commercial, entertainment, and hotel district, strung north-to-south along the aptly-named Commercial Street (now First Avenue South). When Thomson joined his cousin's surveying business, the firm was located on Main Street, just east of Commercial.

Lively and flourishing, the peninsula district was nevertheless doomed. Just east, the newer fill supported a growing vice district, "down on the sawdust," or the "lava beds," so called because some of the wood slab, trash, and sawdust fill smoldered, now and then flaring into flame. The peninsula's southwest corner sported the King Street coal wharf of the Columbia & Puget Sound Railroad, thrusting west into the bay. Directly south, wood products factories and the shops of the Columbia & Puget Sound Railroad edged out over the bay on pilings, pointing toward the present sports stadia district. To the north, Mill Street crossed Commercial's connection with Front, a blockade not removed until after the great fire of 1889. There was nowhere for the peninsula commercial district to go; one portent of its decline was the 1880 regrading of Front Street from Pike south to Mill. The regrading smoothed Front's humps and hollows, making it more palatable to business.

The completed regrading of Front during the year before Thomson's arrival shifted the commercial focus back to the main section of town. But here, a view of

The tideflats south of Seattle's downtown eventually were filled in with spoil from nearby city regrades and other projects. Vertical posts, or "squatters pilings," indicate property claims out in the tideflats. *Seattle Municipal Archives #130374.*

the area was less than impressive. A mix of low frame buildings straggled up and down muddy streets. Most dated from the 1860s and 1870s, with false front second stories, and lettered signs overhanging wood plank sidewalks. The houses, with some exceptions, were simple boxes with unadorned hip or gable roofs.

There were only a few brick buildings in town, with Henry Yesler's new three-story edifice among the most prominent. Most structures, whatever their materials, were low and undistinguished. Among the most prepossessing of the early buildings was the Opera House on the east side of Commercial Street, a three-story, vernacular-styled, yet graceful building.

Utilities were crude to nonexistent. A few small, private water companies, notably Henry Yesler's, served customers scattered here and there. The other residents made do with wells or cisterns. The Spring Hill Company, formed the year of Thomson's arrival, had not yet become the dominant supplier. Gas lighting existed,

but was confined mostly to commercial establishments. Candles and kerosene lamps illuminated ordinary houses. Noisome trench sewers were being replaced with underground or (in a few instances) above ground pipes. The pipes dumped the contents of chamber pots, tin bathtubs, and a few flush toilets into Elliott Bay, without benefit of intercepting sewers. High tides sometimes forced sewage up the pipes, with unpleasant results, while low tides left sewage exposed on the soggy mud flats. Hundreds of rats scurried around under Yesler's wharf and the plank sidewalks. In some seasons, people approaching Seattle smelled the town before they could see it.

A scattering of houses stood north, near the southern shore of Lake Union, also a sewage dump. Residences rambled up the hills as far east as Eighth Street (now Eighth Avenue), dispersed over the rough ground. The commercial peninsula south of Mill Street aside, the compactly settled area comprised some 40 blocks

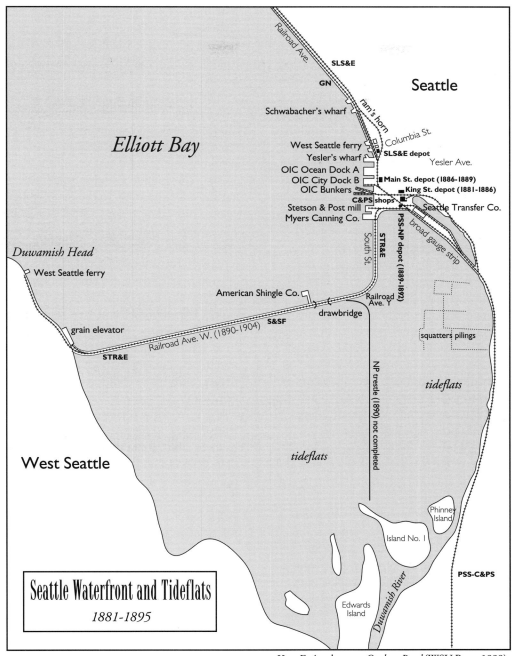

Seattle Waterfront and Tideflats
1881-1895

Kurt E. Armbruster, *Orphan Road* (WSU Press, 1999).

bounded by Front east to Fourth, and Pike south to Mill. Most of the year, the drizzly, showery, and rainy weather amplified the mud, filth, and stench. Many mottled days of rainy and sunny periods, and generally dry summers, brought forth flower gardens and vegetable plots in house yards, somewhat relieving the drabness. Thomson summarized the town's condition succinctly. A few days after he arrived, September 27, the town fathers conducted memorial services for the assassinated President James A. Garfield. "Photographs taken that day show quite a crowd of people but show very little city development," he wrote.[4]

Seattle was a tough place. Respectable people such as the Whitworths and the attorneys Thomas Burke and Orange Jacobs, out of necessity, lived and worked near "disreputable" people, whom they could no more escape than the olfactory nuisances. The disreputable crowd could be dangerous. Jacobs' description, even allowing for some frontier gasconade, was sobering: "Hold-ups on the streets, with pistol accompaniments, were frequent in the City of Seattle." Burglaries, too, "were the regular order of business; no man was safe in the streets after nightfall," and an evening time visitor to another's house "after proper precautions, was received with pistol in hand." All this leads up to Jacobs' account of the January 1882 murder of a "popular business man," the lynching of two suspects in the case, and, for good measure, the lynching of a third man in jail awaiting trial for another murder. According to Jacobs, the hangings were a deterrent to the criminal element; they left town for more hospitable places. Thomson noted the lynchings in his diary, without comment.[5] Violence and the threat of it had hardly disappeared from the Seattle scene, as Thomson himself discovered soon enough. Experiences in southern Indiana and northern California, however, had inured Heber to an environment like Seattle's.

He was concerned about development of the town's economic possibilities, the first solid evidence of potential growth being the harbor itself. Ten years before, a *Portland Oregonian* editor found "more steamboats, sailing vessels, steam tugs, and small crafts of one sort or another than we saw in all the other harbors."[6] The busy harbor was one of Seattle's several "natural advantages," to use a promotional phrase repeated by numberless 19th-century urban boosters. The town's central location on the eastern sound made it a sensible stop-off and outfitting point for the entire Puget Sound basin, though direct steamship service from San Francisco was in the future. Thomson's vessel had stopped first at Victoria, British Columbia's capitol and a thriving city of some 10,000 people compared with Seattle's 4,000 or so.

Modest though it was, Seattle showed more promise than the proven backwaters of Madison, Indiana, or Healdsburg, California, and not just because of its maritime advantages. Good farm land, marketable timber, and, especially, mineable coal lay within arm's reach. Coal and timber were the resources Thomson had been told to investigate. He lost no time in doing just that. Long before 1881, however, the major timber harvesting and lumber milling had shifted away from Seattle to other Puget Sound locations. Nevertheless, the city's milling days were not by any means past, due in part because securing a timber tract and setting up a shingle mill required little capital. Shingle prices were volatile, though. Heber had seen plenty of shirt-tail operations in California and was not looking for any chancy enterprises in the boondocks. There was Addie and their future to think about. Even if his fiancée was as smitten

with him as he with her, and willing to live with him anywhere, the well-settled Laughlin family would hardly approve of a son-in-law drifting from timber claim to timber claim in the back woods east of scruffy little Seattle.

The coal situation was more difficult from the individual investor's viewpoint. Shingle milling required little capital whereas coal mining did. Local men with more resources than a schoolteacher had tried to make a go at mining and transporting coal from Newcastle, near Seattle. They sold to a reconstituted local group, including Heber's famous uncle, the Rev. George F. Whitworth, who combined deep piety with a shrewd business sense. This group, in turn, sold out to a San Francisco company featuring Samuel Dinsmore, one of Heber's shipboard savants on the subject of successful urban location. The Dinsmore investors had sold to another combine, which in its turn disposed of the property in 1880 to railroad builder Henry Villard and the Oregon Improvement Company. Heber's erstwhile advisor's dictum, "if you go to Seattle, you can find a coal vein to reward your search," was true for others but valueless for him.[7] Much bigger capital than Heber could invest controlled Puget Sound mining and would continue to do so.

Another element essential to any consideration of timber and coal development was getting these extractive resources to market. Heber had to consider the state of Seattle's railroads, both in relation to coal hauling and the promise of a future transcontinental connection. The hills and valleys around Puget Sound, where level space was at a premium, were potential impediments to economic and urban development despite Seattle's undeniably brisk water trade. One day, "the boys," with whom Heber was investigating rail and coal properties, affirmed that the existence of "some of the largest cities in the world" had been "built up and around mountains," yet nobody could identify such a city. Also, to those who linked the inevitable growth of Seattle to the providential future appearance of a railroad, Heber "retorted that I could name a number of cities which had had a full measure of railroads and showed no sign of enlargement after years of railroad service." Potentially rich hinterland resources were valueless without an effective transportation web. Worthwhile transportation required easy grades and as few breaks between transport modes or systems as possible. Preferably, coal loaded at a mine's mouth on railcars should be hauled by rail in those same cars and over relatively flat terrain until reaching the bunkers of a specialized coal wharf, into which it would be dumped to await loading onto coal ships for a long water haul.[8]

Hauling coal or any other extractive resource in this manner was far from simple. In Thomson's time there were many obstacles to a smoothly flowing transportation system. Fall lines in rivers, plus lakes, unbridged streams, ridges, and hills were barriers, often forcing "breaks" during which a commodity was unloaded and reloaded, and its container shifted from, say, tracks to a barge and back again. Long expensive detours often were required. Obstacles could be reduced or overcome, of course, with the proper application of technology, capital, and labor—all with the catalyst of human will and understanding. That was the meaning of Thomson's often-quoted observation: "Looking at local surroundings, I felt that Seattle was in a pit, that to get anywhere we would be compelled to climb out of it if we could."[9]

When the second local group had sufficiently developed the mines along Coal Creek to warrant regular shipments, they built a complex transportation system from their field headquarters at Newcastle. Newcastle stood east of Lake Washington, about ten miles from the Seattle waterfront as the crow flies.[10]

What the local investors could afford to build was a cobbled-together arrangement consisting first of a three-mile wooden tramway over which horses and mules pulled loaded cars from Newcastle to Lake Washington's southeastern shore. Then the cars were winched down an incline to barges, boated on the lake past Mercer Island, then north and west to a narrow portage with Lake Union. Here, another tram took over, hauling the cars up from Union Bay, then down a steeper ramp to Portage Bay on Lake Union, some nine or ten feet below the level of Lake Washington. Then another team of barges floated the cars to the south end of Lake Union. Once more the cars were moved on a tram, south to Pike Street, and then southeast to another incline, a chain

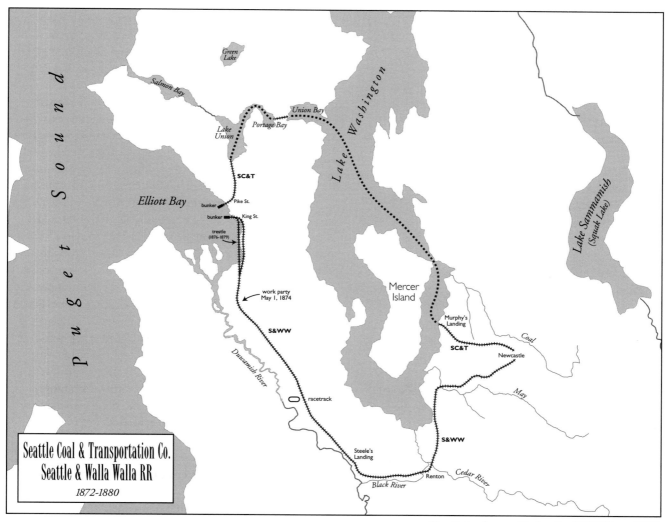

Kurt E. Armbruster, *Orphan Road* (WSU Press, 1999).

apparatus that let the cars down to the foot of Pike Street, where they were dumped at the company's bunkers.

The operation was crude. The cars were small, carrying only two tons, and the tramways were wooden with strap iron rails. The barges and tugs were all that the company could afford. The operation also was unsafe. Emily Inez Denny, of a local pioneer family, recalled traveling up the 900-foot incline from Lake Washington's eastern shore in an otherwise empty coal car, "duly warned by the operatives that the day before a car load of furniture had 'let go' over the incline and smashed to kindling wood long before it reached the bottom." At least one barge capsized, with a string of coal cars sinking to the bottom of Lake Washington.[11]

Neither the length of the coal route—about 17 miles versus an air line distance of 10 miles from Newcastle to Seattle—nor an occasional accident bothered the coal men as much as the transfers. Depending on how the coal men counted, there were up to 11 transfers in moving coal from the mine to securing it in a ship's hold. This elaborate transportation scheme drove up operating costs, depriving local capitalists of the margin they needed to retain control of the Newcastle properties. In 1872 the Dinsmore group imported the town's first locomotive, accompanied by inordinate hoopla, and set it to work on the run from Lake Union to the Pike Street incline. Two years later it put a second engine on the leg from Newcastle to near the eastern margin of Lake Washington. Replacing mules and horses with locomotives, and wood and metal straps with ties and rails, did not alter the basics—the system proved too unwieldy and expensive. What was needed was a railroad running south-southeast from Seattle following Elliott Bay and the Duwamish River until reaching the Black River, and then turning eastward, striking the Cedar River south of Lake Washington, swinging north, and finally, northeast to Newcastle.

This is what eventually developed as an offshoot from a pivotal event in the railroad history of the Puget Sound country—the Northern Pacific Railway's (NP) selection of Tacoma as its western terminus. The NP chose Tacoma, 40 miles south of Seattle, because it could develop its own townsite on Puget Sound and also meet its contractual construction deadline with the federal government. The NP's actions earned the undying enmity of a generation of Seattleites, compounded by

The Bavarian born financier Henry Villard gained control of the Northern Pacific in 1881 and oversaw completion of its transcontinental route to Washington in 1883. *Washington State University Libraries.*

the transcontinental railroad's later reluctance to extend full service and rate equalization to Elliott Bay. The NP made its decision in 1873, the year between the arrival of Seattle's first coal road locomotive and the coming of its second engine. This proved to be the catalyst for the first eruption of the "Seattle Spirit"—the decision to create the Seattle & Walla Walla Railroad (S&WW). In town meetings during July 1873, the citizenry pledged support for the line. They intended to build over the Cascade Range, pass through fertile valleys in eastern Washington, connect with Spokane, and terminate at Walla Walla in the territory's southeastern corner. They would wrench the growing wheat trade from steamboats traveling down the Columbia River to Portland.

In reality the little road had as much hope of arriving in Walla Walla as it did of reaching Jupiter. It lacked sufficient local capital, the same scarcity that condemned the coal entrepreneurs to their ramshackle delivery system from Newcastle. Nevertheless, locals subscribed for shares of stock or offered their services. On May 1, 1874, the male citizenry gathered three miles south of town, near the mouth of the Duwamish, to begin clearing and grading the S&WW right of way. The women served a hearty lunch. Though this effort has risen to fabulous historical proportions, its principal results were bruises, blisters, sore muscles, and a mile of rough roadbed, soon to begin crumbling and reverting to the wild. The depression of 1873 compounded the difficulties of raising capital until early in 1876, when James M. Colman took a hand.

Colman, a "canny Scot," was a native of Dunfermline, also Andrew Carnegie's hometown. From his early 1860s arrival in the Puget Sound country, Colman proved to be a first-rate businessman and mechanical engineer. He proposed refinancing the S&WW and put up the lion's share of the money himself. With financial help from Henry Yesler and others, Colman worked tirelessly—supervising grading, tracklaying, and building wharves, shops, and trestles. He orchestrated the purchase of locomotives and rolling stock. By 1877 his crews had pushed the line to Renton. In March, Colman himself stood at the throttle of a locomotive making the inaugural run out of Seattle. A year later, the S&WW reached Newcastle. Meanwhile, the original coal bunker at the foot of Pike Street collapsed—the pilings bored through by ravenous shipworms. The coal company rerouted its deliveries from its makeshift transportation system to the S&WW.

Two years later, Henry Villard's Oregon Improvement Company (OIC) bought both the coal company at Newcastle and the S&WW, renaming it the Columbia & Puget Sound. Villard, a German émigré with an excellent command of English and dazzling financial ability, closed the deal late in 1880. Almost immediately he began improvements to the little narrow-gauge line. By the time Thomson arrived in September 1881, the Columbia & Puget Sound's coal bunkers and dock stood on pilings far into Elliott Bay, well beyond Henry Yesler's more massive, multi-use wharf. Villard and others were planning new mines and new rail lines in the coal-rich semi-circle east of Seattle. Villard's actions concluded the recent development of mining and railroading in Seattle's hinterland as Thomson would initially come to understand it. Primitive and parochial as the mining and railroading were, their continued expansion offered opportunities for an enterprising engineer. So did Seattle's infrastructure, crudely built, poorly organized, and in desperate need of engineering to overcome its "very little city development."

ഇറ

Thomson's plunge into the transformation of Seattle must be understood in several contexts. First and most obviously, he was a reformer affiliated with those who worked to transcend nature's limitations on Seattle by filling in tideflats, reducing ridges and hills, leveling hollows, and connecting Lake Washington and Lake Union with the sea. Restructuring nature would be conducted in tandem with the radical reorganization of the city's sewage, water, and lighting. These revampings would provide for a healthy growing population, able and willing to advance Seattle economically. Conceptions held by young Heber at the time may rather poorly fit some precise definitions of "reform," but he was indeed and literally a "reformer" who sought to reshape Seattle for its greater well-being, happiness, and prosperity. These strivings united him in spirit with generations of Americans seeking to transcend or supplant nature, whether through agriculture, urban development, great

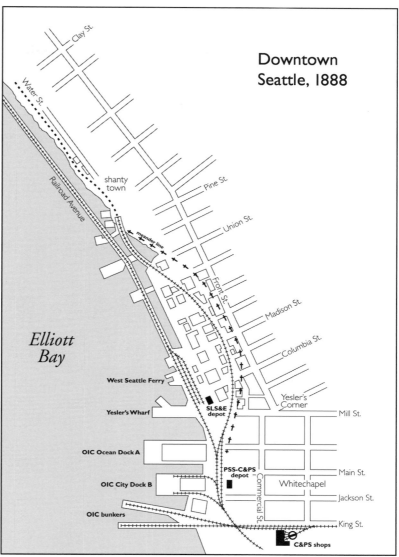

Kurt E. Armbruster, *Orphan Road* (WSU Press, 1999).

works such as the transcontinental railroads, or land surveys that reduced the rumpled earth to neat metes and bounds. His drive for making these changes meshed well with his Presbyterian conviction about obligations of the advantaged to provide a better earthly life for the deprived.

None of this, however, should be pushed too far. In 1881, Heber, at age 25, was hardly yet the active reformer that he later became. Even if he had been, the self-conscious use of the phrase "progressive reform" was far in the future. The realization of restricted opportunities for small investors in activities dominated by big-business oligarchs also lay ahead. His big, not to say grandiose, engineering feats and plans were not yet developed. Nevertheless, by entering a surveying firm in a booming

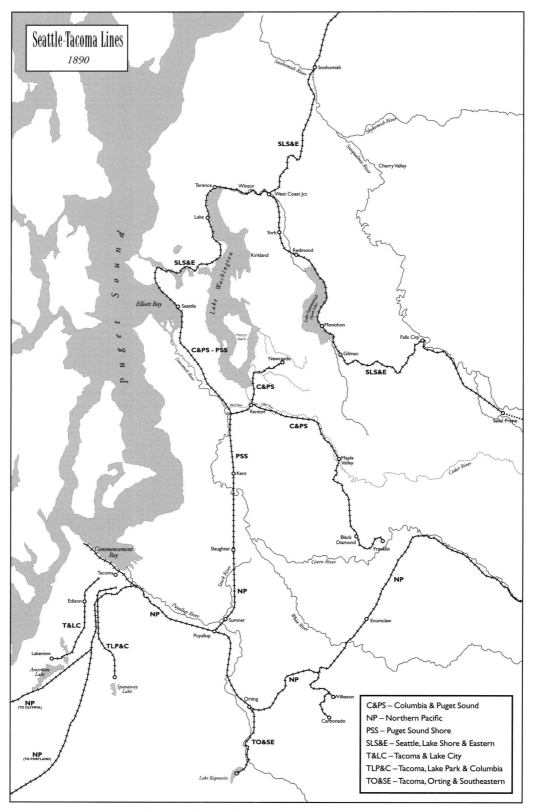

Seattle-Tacoma Lines
1890

SLS&E

Snohomish River
Snohomish

Skykomish River

Snoqualmie River
Cherry Valley

SLS&E

Terence
Winsor
West Coast Jct.

Lake

York

Redmond

Kirkland

SLS&E

Lake Washington

Puget Sound

Elliott Bay
Seattle

Lake Sammamish
Sammamish Lake

Monohon

Falls City

Mercer Island

C&PS - PSS

Newcastle

Gilman

SLS&E

Duwamish River

C&PS

Black River
Cedar River
Renton

Saltal Prairie

C&PS

PSS

Maple Valley

Cedar River

Kent

Black Diamond

Franklin

Commencement Bay

Green River

Slaughter

NP

Tacoma

Soos River

White River

NP

Edison

Puyallup River

Enumclaw

NP

Sumner

T&LC

TLP&C

Puyallup

Lakeview

American Lake

NP

Orting

Spanaway Lake

Wilkeson

NP
(TO OLYMPIA)

Carbonado

NP
(TO PORTLAND)

TO&SE

Lake Kapowsin

C&PS – Columbia & Puget Sound
NP – Northern Pacific
PSS – Puget Sound Shore
SLS&E – Seattle, Lake Shore & Eastern
T&LC – Tacoma & Lake City
TLP&C – Tacoma, Lake Park & Columbia
TO&SE – Tacoma, Orting & Southeastern

Robert E. Ficken, *Washington State: The Inaugural Decade, 1889–1899* (WSU Press, 2007).

town he was turning away from the traditionalism of villages like Hanover and Healdsburg and toward a future of dynamic urban change.

The second context involves Thomson's commitment to Seattle, a commitment ultimately practical. From the time he arrived, he was busy with survey work for cousin Harry Whitworth, who also served as city surveyor, an office approximately analogous to the later designation of city engineer. The firm of Whitworth & Thomson would have plenty of work to do, whether for public or private clients.

Indeed, Thomson would have his hands full in the many years ahead as he became, successively, the city surveyor, a railroad locating engineer, a Seattle-based consulting engineer, city engineer, park superintendent, and freelance engineer, broken by a brief return to the city engineer's post. During his freelance career he also would serve two terms on the Seattle city council. Twice he would leave Seattle for extended periods—a year in Spokane for railroad work, and three years on Vancouver Island superintending the newly-established Strathcona Park. He seemed willing to consider appealing jobs elsewhere, if they had implied time limits. Perhaps it is possible he would have left Seattle for permanent employment elsewhere, but the fact is, he did not. Doing so would have separated him from a rich web of associations and from the bulk of his interests. Years after his arrival he told Clarence B. Bagley, the Thucydides of Seattle, of early on spending "considerable periods at Tacoma, Bellingham, Everett, Seattle, and other places," including Renton. Other towns failed to measure up to his expectations as being the entrepot of Puget Sound, so he "once more devoted his attention to Seattle."[12]

Renton, despite proximity to the coal fields, was never in the running for his permanent attention. Renton coal operations would continue to be reliant on Seattle. Tacoma, although the designated terminus of the Northern Pacific, boasted about three-quarters of Seattle's population. It would share in the Puget Sound boom of the 1880s but could not overcome Seattle's dominance, however vital the struggle seemed to contemporaries. Everett scarcely existed and Bellingham was nothing more than three town sites. No other location on or near Puget Sound posed a serious challenge to Seattle.[13]

The third context of Thomson's means of entry in Seattle life was surveying, the most widely practiced branch of civil engineering at the time. Young Heber remained a surveyor, mainly, until after he became city engineer in 1892. Surveying was an ancient art and science, as old as humanity's first attempt at earthly mensu-

ration. It was a special necessity in the early and middle years of the United States, when almost all the vast, expanding territory needed to be surveyed. After land was claimed, it had to be resurveyed, and then resurveyed again as ownership disputes arose and property repeatedly changed hands. Surveying was fundamental to a society that commodified land and had so very much of it. Schools and colleges taught surveying, as would be expected. Heber learned it at Hanover, with extra coaching from his father. Almost all the men in his family, immediate and extended, knew surveying. Surveying was so much a part of basic education that it was taught at New York City's St. James School, where Alfred E. Smith, future governor of the state and the 1928 Democratic presidential candidate, took instruction. Even this Roman Catholic institution in an intensely urban environment required the subject in 1872.[14]

By the time Heber entered Hanover, there were five major accoutrements for surveying land—an instrument for measuring horizontal angles, a rod for gauging height, a chain for reckoning horizontal distances between the instrument and the rod, an axe for clearing away brush and small trees from the line of sight between the angle-reckoning instrument and the rod, and a field book in which the angles and distances were recorded. A variety of nails, tacks, pins, hammers, strips of cloth, pencils, and other small items made up the complete survey kit.[15]

An elaborate surveying team might include an instrument man (in those days, surveying was men's work), two rodmen, two chainmen, two axemen, and a recorder keeping the field book. Back in the office, a computer checked the data in the field book and, using trigonometric functions, he or she prepared a diagram of the land surveyed. Surveyors, however, rarely enjoyed the luxury of such a large crew. A survey team often only included an instrument man who also kept the field book, a rodman doubling as head chainman, and a rear chainman. An axe man might be along, but absent an axeman, one of the team of three would chop away brush and limbs.

In any case, most surveying was crude, which was recognized at the time. Today's surveyors have access to the satellite-driven global positioning system (GPS) and easily achieve accuracies within one unit of error in 50,000 units of measurement[16]; in the late 19th century, however, the time and expense involved in achieving that level of certitude in any place but "the heart of a great city"[17] was not worth it. Seattle was no great city, so the permissible error was larger and varied from survey to survey, depending on the skill and instruments of the surveyors. In Seattle the competent surveyor's task was complicated by poorly located and maintained "datum points"—points of known elevation on which all other heights were based. The town council temporarily resolved the problem in 1883 by setting a new datum point at a supposedly permanent stone structure, a downtown bank, in the heart of the old commercial district. This datum point remained until the great fire of 1889. It was positioned too low, making the accurate reading of other verticals on the steeply rising terrain to the north and east more difficult, and it was too far south and west of the main thrust of commercial and residential development. Worse, the best early horizontal measurements were done with a Gunter's chain, just the thing for the careful surveyor when invented around 1620, but hardly up to the task of accurate measurement in the later 1800s. Worse still, some surveyors used rope, a flexible material utterly unsuited to surveying. This gave wildly varying readings, depending on the tension applied when stretched, and the affects of wind, temperature, and humidity. [18]

When Heber, Williell, and their father subdivided Rancho Tzabaco in California, they probably relied on a compass, adjusting for the deviation between magnetic north and true north, and likely the Gunter's chain. The Gunter's chain was effective enough when used with care. Sixty-six feet long, the chain had handles for pulling it taut, and included 100 links, each link with its attaching ring being 7.92 inches. The chain was good for land surveying using traditional English measure, because 80 chains equaled a mile, while 10 chains on four sides of a square enclosed an acre. The compass and Gunter's chain were adequate in California's Dry Creek and other rural areas in the 1870s, but had shortcomings when used in cities and towns. Iron in urban settings—horseshoes, wagon wheels, decorative building fronts, utilities pipes, streetcar tracks, and other metallic objects—distorted compass readings. The Gunter's chain also could give different readings over the same ground when pulled taut because the tension varied a little during each time of use. Variations in marking a break in elevation with pins (the job of the chainman), extreme temperature swings, windy conditions, and links straightened after being damaged could all affect accuracy. The chain also wore a little on each of its linking surfaces with every use, lengthening the chain and therefore lengthening distances measured. Careful and experienced use in rural areas could bring accuracies within one unit of 5,000, or one-tenth of what is readily achievable today with GPS. But the rural 1/5,000, as it was often expressed, was not good enough for urban lots and streets, where closer quarters and commercial buildings built to lot lines demanded great precision.

In cities during the later 19th century, the compass and Gunter's chain gave way to the transit and steel tape. The transit included a mounted telescope designed to read heights on increasingly sophisticated rods. A familiar sight wherever civil engineers worked, it included a scale for measuring horizontal angles and three or four horizontal vials, each with a bubble. Using adjusting screws, the transitman would place each bubble exactly in the center of its vial, accurately leveling the instrument. The apparatus rested on a tripod of adjustable legs, each leg having a sharp steel foot securing it in the ground. A transit's location over the center of a datum point or other marker could be secured by suspending a plumb bob from the center underside of the instrument, and moving the instrument until the weighted cord hung directly above the center of the marker. The steel tape was much more accurate than the chain. Properly cared for, it did not wear, and could be read more precisely. Nevertheless, use of the transit, a better rod, or the tape were not foolproof. Wind could move the plumb bob, as well as a rod, however carefully it was held. A transit could be carelessly leveled by the operator or knocked out of level. The tape, usually 50-foot or 100-foot models, could sag over gullies. Better instruments were no substitute for meticulousness and experience.

In our era of precision mensuration, it is easy to scoff at engineers who worked with relatively crude instruments over rough terrain. It was, however, an essential task, which if performed conscientiously brought accuracies within acceptable limits of 1/10,000 or 1/20,000.

෧◌ඏ

Heber's uncle, Frederick Whitworth, did as well at surveying as he did with his other secular tasks. Cousin "Harry" Whitworth did better still at surveying and other engineering work, taking Heber into his firm in the year of Heber's arrival, 1881. Heber would quickly rise to a partnership. His brother "Willie" could have continued with Harry and been a competitor, but Williell's calling was the ministry, not engineering; he returned to California at the end of November. That left James Edwin, cousin Harry's brother. James Edwin, known by his middle name in the family, could see the handwriting on the wall regarding his future when Heber became a partner less than four months after arriving in Seattle. Nevertheless, Edwin continued to do competent work for the firm until 1884. (Finally, in the summer of that year, about the time Heber would be selected city surveyor, Edwin began farming full time at his "ranch" southeast of Seattle.)[19]

On January 2, 1882, Heber "agreed with Cousin Harry to attend to the office work," while Harry did engineering duties for Villard's Columbia & Puget Sound Railroad, which strove to open new mines and lay track to them. Heber was "to receive 2/3 of net income."[20] Meanwhile, Harry also served as county surveyor and city surveyor—there was no concept of conflict of interest at the time, so these public tasks were considered compatible with his private railroad engineering work. In any case, not all that much public work was required by the city and county. Heber undertook whatever city work there was until Harry resigned from the surveyor's post in 1883. The partnership continued when Heber himself became city surveyor, lasting until near the end of 1886. At that time, Harry entered the real estate business and Heber became an engineer for the locally fabled Seattle, Lake Shore & Eastern Railroad.[21]

Heber's duties at Whitworth & Thomson included railroad engineering, government and private surveying, and mining engineering, in no neat sequence. Immediately after he arrived in Seattle, Heber worked in what was then south Seattle, relocating part of the Columbia & Puget Sound route, probably with Harry keeping a close eye on progress. Next, Harry sent Heber to a then-promising coal field southeast of Seattle to post claims.

Heber's acceptance into partnership with Harry coincided with one of Seattle's delirious growth spurts, when the population of perhaps 4,000 (allowing for the usual census undercounting) rose to at least 81,000 by 1890—an astonishing 4,000 percent increase. The fact that other western cities registered similar gains at one time or another was small consolation to Seattle's harried officials, struggling to cope with an average yearly increase of nearly double the 1880 population.[22]

In such an environment, what was needed was a competent engineering firm capable of performing diversified tasks. Whitworth & Thomson was that firm. One day, Heber, Edwin, and a crew could be surveying an original 1850s "donation claim," or an "addition" to the town (later commonly called a subdivision). Singly or together, they also might remain at the office working on a map. Or they could be leveling; i.e., establishing heights from a point of known elevation. Because Harry served as city surveyor, there was public street surveying to do, or more probably, the resurveying of inadequately measured streets. Edwin's more detailed diary indicates that Heber was in charge. On August 9, 1882: "Hawthorn & I & Fred helped Heber on the street today," or, from June 12, 1883, "afternoon on Jackson St[.]—Hawthorn & I helping Heber." Heber did not always appreciate the help. "Assisted by Edwin and Hawthorne," he wrote in January 1882: "They did not keep tally well." The next day Heber was "assisted by Hawthorne & Wilson. Retarded by Palmer."[23]

There were additional tasks. With Harry and perhaps others, Heber surveyed "a town plat," better described as "a swamp," which fortunately had frozen solid during a bitterly cold day in February 1882. More city work continued until August 1883, when Harry finally resigned as city surveyor, and the position went to another man. Nevertheless, Heber kept busy surveying for other projects in mining engineering and railroad location. He conducted a preliminary survey of the curving extension of the Villard line, the Columbia & Puget Sound, from Black Diamond east to the Villard-controlled town of Franklin, perched on a ledge above the Green River gorge. Villard soon lost control of his regional development empire, but his Oregon Improvement Company and other concerns left a legacy of more mines and railroad spurs east and south of Seattle. Years later, in 1889, Thomson returned to Franklin where the OIC wanted to build a spur track but had suffered a falling out with the contractor. The upshot, as Heber remembered, was that "the task was turned entirely over to me; so I located a line, employed the laborers, bought the material, and supervised the entire work."[24]

Mill Street streetcar line to the Rainier Boat House on Lake Washington, 1886. *Seattle Municipal Archives #2865.*

Mining engineering included surveying of the sort similar to work in towns, though it involved "tracing the tortuous course of gangways under ground," then plotting that "tortuous course" on the surface. Thomson did not exaggerate, for some of the coal veins out from Seattle were severely twisted and folded, and were affected by faults, ancient shears in the earth, usually far enough below ground as to give no surface clue to their whereabouts. The faults, the product of strong prehistoric geologic forces, meant that miners working a coal seam might suddenly confront a rock wall. In these instances, it was up to the mine engineer to locate the displaced seam, and quickly. A mining engineer also was supposed to estimate the volume of mineable coal based on surface indications, as well as from readings in prospecting shafts or tunnels. It was the kind of work that Heber had hoped for in California. Despite the problems, the mines near Seattle usually produced good bituminous or mid-grade coal, making the struggles worthwhile. It was essential fuel in a region where locomotives, ships, industries, and households used coal. [25]

A year after cousin Harry had left the city surveyor's job, the mayor and city council appointed Heber to the same position on August 6, 1884. It was a testimony to Thomson's competence and influence in the booming town. On the other hand, it was no sinecure. In fact, heavy political pressure would force him out of office two years later. As city surveyor, he faced the problem of Seattle's poor sewage, about which he could do little. The city's sewers could hardly be called a system in 1884. Typhoid, cholera, diphtheria, and the dreaded bubonic plague were constant threats to public health. Bacteriology, or the "germ theory," was still on the cusp of public acceptance, though the eventual obviating of the threat of disease had more to do with a clean water supply than with effective sewers. Combating the bad smell or "miasma" of sewage was at the time at least as important as establishing a potable water supply acceptable to ordinary sight and taste. The only sewer built during Thomson's term stretched along Union Street near the north end of town, from what is now Eighth Avenue west to existing sewers emptying into Elliott Bay. Thomson, to his credit, recommended an oval-shaped cement sewer line rather than a repetition of the existing and less-than-satisfactory wooden-box sewers. Property owners along Union Street settled for a box sewer by petition, asking for the improvement and sharing its cost. Construction began in 1885, and was continuing at the time of the pivotal anti-Chinese riots in February 1886. The only other far-reaching action regarding sewers came

with an 1885 ordinance requiring "inhabited" land to be connected to sewers where they existed. It would be gratifying to note that Thomson came out foursquare for an inclusive sewer system at this time, but there is no evidence that he did. [26]

Thomson could do nothing regarding the lighting system or the water supply, then in private hands. Besides, Washington would remain in territorial status for five more years, with towns such as Seattle suffering from restricted taxation and borrowing powers. If these restrictions were not enough, Heber's calls for street improvements met serious resistance as landowners sometimes blocked his suggestions. Also frustrating was his inability to remove the old coal train track from south Lake Union to Pike Street, and replace it with a street designed to open up the southwest and west sides of Lake Union— the improvement would ease communication with areas north of town. Thomson insisted that a councilman, who wanted to retain a view of the passing traffic in front of his house, three blocks east of the proposed street, killed the measure. Years later, the street was put through as the present Westlake Avenue North. A plan for traffic relief on the south end of town, extending Second Avenue to the then Grant Street, also was defeated. This time, grocers who had built stores on east-west streets successfully objected. The diagonal would have cut off their traffic from the south. Part of Thomson's proposed diagonal was later put through at much greater expense. Together with other street improvements, it shortened a southern trip by a few blocks. [27]

There were, of course, more satisfying aspects to the work. He approved private subdivision plats into which the soaring population spilled. Heber's acceptance of these subdivisions was not automatic; he insisted a plat had to be properly surveyed, mapped, and named. Any deviations sent the plan back, so to speak, to the drafting board. He also supervised the construction of a sidewalk beginning along "upper 1st Ave" skirting massive Denny Hill, then north and west to Harrison Street at the base of Queen Anne Hill, then to the north-south Queen Anne Avenue "and North for some distance." This sidewalk construction was consistent with his view that the citizenry needed easy passage between Seattle's commercial core and the north parts of town. In other work in the town's expanding areas in 1885, Heber ordered some 30 stone monuments to be surveyed and correctly placed, providing better access to accurate reference points than the distant older "city datums." A year and a half earlier, the lack of accurate monuments proved so severe that cousin Edwin had placed some monuments for Henry Yesler.[28]

Heber's greatest triumph proved to be the construction of the Grant Street bridge, a wooden trestle thrusting southerly over the tideflats below town. It ran on pilings hammered into the soggy soil for more than 1½ miles from present South Dearborn Street to present South Hinds Street. The council ordered an 800-foot extension on dry ground from South Hinds to about the present West Seattle Freeway. Airport Way now traverses some of the path of the Grant Street bridge. At the time, it was "a gigantic undertaking" and "an innovation upon the traditional Sleepy Hollow methods and scales of public improvements in vogue in King County and Seattle." Thomson designed it to replace the "old beach road," a gooey mess in wintertime despite its location above high tide. The council had no authority to borrow money for the project and no power to amend the city charter in those territorial times. Therefore, the city attorney went to the legislature, asked for, and obtained an amendment empowering the council to issue bonds. The bonds sold at a premium of a little more than one percent. The successful bidder began work in August 1886, and finished up just before Christmas, having strained the capacity of four local sawmills so severely that they "could only keep the contractor's force of workmen busy in a sort of intermittent manner." Despite Thomson's frustrated hopes for building a direct diagonal from the trestle to Second Avenue, the trestle eased travel between south Seattle and downtown for many years. It comprised driving lanes, each ten feet wide plus a five-foot wide sidewalk, generous dimensions for the time. Unfortunately, the trestle was poorly maintained, leaving Thomson as early as 1894 "in daily, if not hourly dread" of a fatal accident on part of it. [29]

Thomson's work on the Grant Street bridge roughly paralleled the anti-Chinese agitation in Seattle, which would impact his livelihood. Resentment against the Chinese was a social staple in the West during the late 19th century, exacerbated in the Pacific Northwest by the national depression of the mid-1880s and the temporary suspension of railroad construction. Many working people deplored the Chinese due to their willingness to work long and hard for low wages, their odd clothing and customs, their crossing the Canadian border in defiance of the Chinese Exclusion Act of 1884, and their unassimilability into American culture. Their critics, of course, did not want them to assimilate. The sentiment turned violent often enough, usually resulting in the loss of property or even lives among the Chinese. In Seattle,

the anti-Chinese movement featured mass meetings, a parade, threats of forced removal, and antagonism toward their white defenders. Threats persisted even though the Chinese, when pressed, overwhelmingly agreed to leave. Their defenders grudgingly concurred, insisting only that the removal of the vast majority be conducted lawfully and humanely. Violence occurred in Seattle on February 8, 1886, when a crowd blocked the path of armed home guardsmen returning about 150 Chinese from the waterfront to their homes, since no steamer was immediately available to take them to San Francisco. In the confrontation, some members of the home guard fired their weapons, wounding five in the crowd, and inflicting a mortal wound on another, a street tough named Charles Stewart. The governor, in town at the time, quickly declared martial law. Federal troops arrived three days later to enforce the order. The city returned to civil control on February 22, but the troops remained for half a year. [30]

Thomson was not a leader of the counter movement to defend the Chinese, nor did he enroll in any of the local units aiming to keep order in Seattle, although cousin Harry Whitworth was a member of the home guard unit that fired into the crowd. Yet, Heber played a part. Thomson had, probably, observed the industry and dedication of Chinese workmen the year before when Harry won the contract for engineering the first canal between Lake Washington and Lake Union. This was not a ship canal but a relatively shallow trough designed to move logs between the lakes by the current from Lake Washington, then some ten feet higher than its smaller neighbor, Lake Union. The laborers on the western section from Lake Union to Salmon Bay were Chinese and it is probable that Chinese worked on the eastern portage between the lakes as well. In any case, Thomson's language leaves the strong impression that he was responsible for hiring Chinese without his stating the fact explicitly. "During the height of that trouble," he wrote, "I was working on a sewer from Sixth Avenue to the Sound, on Union Street, with Mr. John T. Jordan, an old settler, and he was busy with our workmen keeping them there and supporting me in protest against this shameful riot. Several persons gathered around us while our discussions were going on, the result of which was that the advocates of the riot became very bitter and insisted that when they could get a change in city government they would have me removed." [31]

The change was not long in coming—a short-lived Peoples Party rode the anti-Chinese sentiment to victory in August 1886. In anticipation of that possibility,

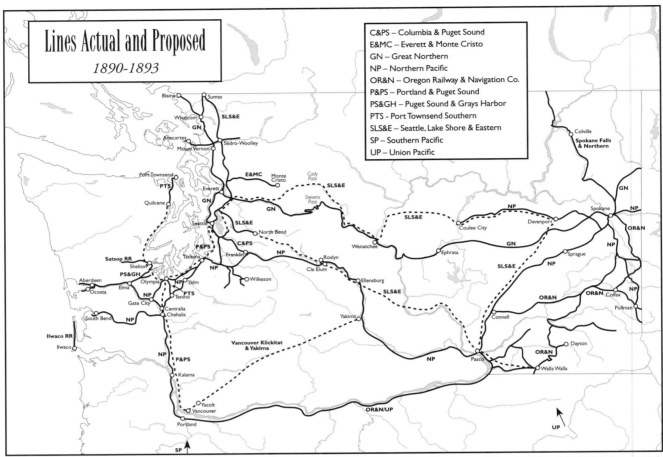

Lines Actual and Proposed
1890-1893

C&PS – Columbia & Puget Sound
E&MC – Everett & Monte Cristo
GN – Great Northern
NP – Northern Pacific
OR&N – Oregon Railway & Navigation Co.
P&PS – Portland & Puget Sound
PS&GH – Puget Sound & Grays Harbor
PTS - Port Townsend Southern
SLS&E – Seattle, Lake Shore & Eastern
SP – Southern Pacific
UP – Union Pacific

Robert E. Ficken, *Washington State: The Inaugural Decade, 1889–1899* (WSU Press, 2007).

the council approved a contract dated July 14, signed by Thomson, Mayor Yesler, the city clerk, and the city attorney, listing Thomson variously as the engineer, superintendent of construction, and contractor of the Grant Street bridge. The contract carried no time limit, so Thomson was within his rights when he faced down the policeman sent to arrest him, refusing to leave the project until its completion. The new mayor, William H. Shoudy, though frustrated in his effort to remove Thomson from the Grant Street bridge project, could and did replace him with another city surveyor. By then, Thomson was ready to return to the private sphere, this time as a locating and all-around engineer for a fresh local railroad venture, the Seattle, Lake Shore & Eastern (SLS&E).[32]

Indeed, Thomson had already signed on with the SLS&E, incorporated in 1885 as the most recent effort to build a line eastward and break the NP's grip on the Pacific Northwest. The redoubtable Thomas Burke served as the mainstay of the SLS&E in Seattle. A pioneer attorney, promoter, politician, and investor, Burke

compensated for his unprepossessing appearance with a penetrating, ingenious legal mind, boldness, and steadfast determination. Burke skillfully kept creditors, naysayers, and an anti-railroad territorial legislature at bay while pressing track, surveys, and mineral development forward. He persuaded the city council and adjacent landowners to endorse the construction of Railroad Avenue on pilings in Elliott Bay, giving the SLS&E a right of way. The trestle was patently illegal—neither the city council nor anyone else had authority to usurp any part of coastal waters belonging, until statehood, to the federal government. With the same insouciance, Burke deftly dodged a territorial law requiring a majority of the board members of any railroad to be territorial residents, thus ensuring effective control of the line by the SLS&E's eastern investors.[33]

Daniel Hunt Gilman acted as the conduit for those eastern investors. Physically, Gilman was everything that the stubby, paunchy, pug-nosed Burke was not. Tall, slender, and handsome, with a slight jut to his jaw and piercing eyes, Gilman overlaid his fine physique with fashionable suits. He exuded confidence, although he depended on others for money and seemed always to run through whatever funds he obtained in the course of his financial plunges. A relative newcomer to Seattle (in 1882), he claimed important connections from his days as a lawyer in New York City. Combining persistence with persuasive charm, Gilman in 1886 landed an investor group centered on the banking house of Jameson, Smith & Cotting. The biggest fish of the lot was James D. "Commodore" Smith, past president of the New York Stock Exchange and commodore of the New York Yacht Club. One of the early consequences of the Gilman presence for Thomson was their life long association, which flourished despite Thomson's conservatism and Gilman's flamboyance. Thomson, no dreamer of small dreams himself, was not for the last time drawn to a man with a similarly expansive vision.

There were, however, more practical reasons for Thomson's joining the SLS&E. The line's first chief engineer was none other than cousin Harry Whitworth, who surveyed a preliminary line before leaving to pursue more promising interests in coal mining and real estate. Also, there was no future for Thomson in city work after the anti-Chinese riot of February 1886. The new chief engineer, John G. Scurry (who later became city surveyor), knew about Thomson's meticulous surveying. Late in December 1886, Scurry and Thomson returned together on horseback to the locality where Thomson's survey crews were working—an area running from Gilman (now Issaquah) near the foot of Lake Sammamish, about 20 miles east and south of Seattle, and on toward Snoqualmie Falls, some 60 miles from Elliott Bay. A tip from a member of Thomson's crew alerted the engineers of a planned move by OIC surveyors to mark a line through a critical area near the falls, which would deny passage to the SLS&E and frustrate its announced purpose of building from there through Snoqualmie Pass in the Cascade Range. The Oregon Improvement Company crew intended to arrive "about two days after Christmas." Despite deep snow and it being Christmas Eve, Thomson and his crew quickly secured the preliminary line. They continued working along the Snoqualmie River on Christmas Day and for a few days afterward, until they met an advance man from the OIC. They cheerfully informed the OIC man that "Scurry and his dudes" had beaten him to the mark. [34]

Following this episode, Thomson and his crew continued surveying up the Snoqualmie valley. They struggled against snowfall and bitter cold that sometimes sent thermometers plunging to -14° Fahrenheit. Finally,

Thomson gave it up and turned his crew to more manageable sections of the projected line for that time of year. But then it rained. And rained. In the midst of this inclement weather, he proposed running a survey along Issaquah Creek from Issaquah to Raging River, some five miles south of Fall City. By clambering high above the creek to get a birds-eye view, he discovered a feasible right of way. He took great satisfaction from having bested an engineer sent from Pennsylvania, who while working from creek-side could not find a route that "wouldn't bankrupt the company." Not all of Thomson's time was spent in camp or on the survey line. He returned to Seattle regularly to visit his wife Addie, catch up on office work, consult with Scurry and cousin Harry who was busy with the mining work of the SLS&E consortium, and to involve himself in the Presbyterian church. [35]

After more Snoqualmie area surveying, the SLS&E sent Thomson to Spokane on the so-called Eastern Division, a line running from Spokane 40 miles west to Davenport. For the cash-strapped road, the shift in emphasis meant easier terrain for construction. But it alienated eastern investors, who were not apprised of the re-direction, and lent plausibility to claims that the SLS&E never would build the really tough miles through the Cascades. Thomson's concerns would be more immediate. On March 27, he arrived in Spokane and began a series of meetings and reconnaissances with Paul Mohr, the latest chief engineer. He studied Mohr's proposed crossing of the Spokane River. "I had to admit," he wrote many years afterward, "that for beauty of line and economy of railroad transportation the site selected was good, but I called attention to the fact that the expense of construction would be extreme," and probably more than the SLS&E could bear. Thomson selected a cheaper crossing, but balked when informed that he would superintend bridge construction at that point. He objected to the prevailing belief that the bridge's center pier would rest on sound rock; he believed instead that the bedrock actually was "thirty or forty" feet below. A freshet in the river, undermining the pier, proved him correct. Not for nothing had Thomson learned to read surface indications for deeper geologic meanings from Frank H. Bradley at Hanover College. He devised a crib bracing for the tilting pier, and it worked. The bridge held, but eventually the Great Northern Railway, the subsequent owner of that part of the SLS&E line, built an expensive replacement "at practically the same site" as Mohr's initial projected crossing. [36]

With the bridge work done, Thomson located branch lines and later supervised construction of the

SLS&E's station, roundhouse, and other buildings. By then, the SLS&E was in financial deep water. Early in 1889, its management offered Heber the job of supervising track construction northward to Sumas on the Canadian border. Wisely he declined, and returned to Seattle in March. Cousin Harry and he had closed the office the year before, so Thomson established his own business. He engaged in a variety of tasks—railroad surveys (one of them producing a charming "roughing it" story for his autobiography), mining engineering, in-town surveying, and, as a deputy United States mineral surveyor, proving up a variety of claims for people hoping for a connection to the SLS&E. His business survived Seattle's great fire of June 6, 1889, although many of his maps did not. Meanwhile, the SLS&E staggered to its demise and ultimate absorption by larger lines, chiefly the Northern Pacific and the Great Northern. In 1890 the NP bought control of the little road. During its brief independent existence, the SLS&E had built tracks looping north and east around lakes Washington and Sammamish, then south to Issaquah, as well as lines north to Snohomish and west from Spokane. "By no means was our work lost or a failure," was Thomson's apt summation.[37]

Engineering absorbed much of Thomson's time and talent but not all of it. The Presbyterian church and his new family engaged him, too. He spent part of his first day in Seattle in church, and attended regularly thereafter. His diary entries are sprinkled with references to churchgoing and theological discussion. After one doctrinal debate at cousin Harry's he noted: "No satisfactory conclusion" to the questions raised. News of others' wandering from the Christian path provoked sadness, as when in January 1882 he noted that he was "sorry to learn that Mr. Atherton's sons dance &c." A longer exposure to people who danced "&c" increased

his toleration but did not diminish his commitment to Presbyterianism. Five years after the discussion at Harry's house, he was at Harry's coal mining camp in the midst of what citified folks would have considered a howling wilderness. Here the two, and perhaps others, held forth on the matter of Christian truth and error. Practical church concerns were also his meat. In January 1888, although he was not feeling well, he and another believer went to "Bell Town," then a residential area eight or ten blocks north of the commercial district, to "visit Presbyterian families there in regard to organizing a 2d Church."[38]

If the Presbyterian church served as one pole of his emotional and spiritual life, his wife Adeline "Addie" Laughlin was the other. Born in 1856, she was two months older than her husband. Though not pretty, having large features set in an oval face, she was intelligent, and a Presbyterian. Moreover, she was willing to leave the comfort of her home in California and go with Heber to rough and tumble, foggy, rainy Seattle. Although the two were informally affianced when Heber left for Seattle in 1881, a July 1882 visit to Mark West in California clinched things. Thomson's diary for July set the stage. On the seventh he "came to Mark West, and was enraptured." The next day was "a day of rapturous joy," while the following day "does not need much written record." Evidently during those days of rapture Addie agreed to marry him, and Heber obtained the consent of her parents. Then, the happy couple left to visit his parents in Pasadena, where "on July 15 I pressed the engagement ring on Addie's finger." The next year, "looking forward to marriage I built a house at 701 Yesler Way" (a site now part of the Interstate 5 right-of-way). They married on August 29, 1883. The first two of four children followed. James Harrison, "Harry," was born in 1886 to a doting father. "Baby tries to blow the moon out," Thomson's

---

The Thomson Family

Reginald Heber Thomson (1856–1949) — Adeline "Addie" Laughlin Thomson (1856–1945)
Married, August 29, 1883

ഇരുതു

Children
James Harrison "Harry" Thomson (b. 1886)
Marion Wing Thomson (b. 1889)
Reginald "Rex" Thomson Jr. (b. 1894)
Frances Clifton Thomson (b. 1897)

diary entry recorded on February 17, 1886.[39] Marion Wing, their first daughter, arrived on May 20, 1889.

Thomson titled the second chapter of his autobiography "The Years of Preparation." He declared that during the first "ten and one-half years" he spent in Seattle, "almost everything I did was unplanned but most valuable preparation for my many years as city engineer."[40] The statement leaves the impression of someone under the control of Divine Providence whose personal teleology, disconnected in California, resumed its relentless advance in Seattle. It is unnecessary to discount the workings of Divine Providence to find plenty of intelligent calculation behind Thomson's actions—becoming a partner of Harry's, accepting the city surveyor job, taking the correct if temporarily unpopular position regarding the Chinese workforce, moving to the SLS&E at a critical moment, refusing the failing concern's offer of continued employment, and opening a successful consulting engineering firm. In the course of all this activity, he more than incidentally became well-known to everyone who was anybody in Seattle, and became that late Victorian apotheosis, the devoted family man. Those were years of preparation, to be sure, but the preparation was deeper and wider than successfully completing a variety of engineering tasks.

NOTES

1. RHT, *That Man Thomson*, 11–12. RHT delivered a somewhat different version in a 1939 Pioneer Days speech, 1602-2, box 2, folder 10, RHT Papers, UW.
2. *The City That Made Itself: A Literary and Pictorial Record of the Building of Seattle* (Seattle: Terminal, 1914), 64.
3. For descriptions of 1881 Seattle, see Paul Benoit, "The Man-Induced Topographic Change of Seattle's Elliott Bay Shoreline from 1852 to 1930 as an Early Form of Coastal Resource Use and Management," (Master's thesis, University of Washington, 1979) fig. 2, p. 7; Paul Dorpat, *Seattle Now & Then*, vol. 1, 2nd ed. (Tartu, 1984, secs. 8, 9, 10, 14; and David M. Buerge, *Seattle in the 1880s*, ed. Stuart R. Grover (Seattle: Historical Society of Seattle and King County, 1986), 1–14, 49–55, 89–108. A more extensive survey is in Matthew Klingle, *Emerald City: An Environmental History of Seattle* (New Haven: Yale University Press, 2007), 14–23.
4. RHT, *That Man Thomson*, 12.
5. Jacobs, *Memoirs of Orange Jacobs* (Seattle: Lowman and Hanford, 1908), 129 for quotation, and for the remainder of the incident, 129–37. For RHT's entry, see diary, January 18, 1882, 1602-2, box 1, folder 1, UW.
6. Quoted in Kurt E. Armbruster, *Orphan Road: The Railroad Comes to Seattle, 1853–1911* (Pullman: Washington State University Press, 1999), 29.
7. RHT, *That Man Thomson*, 10.
8. Ibid., 13, 14.
9. Ibid., 14.
10. Clarence B. Bagley, *History of Seattle from the Earliest Settlement to the Present Time* (Chicago: S.J. Clarke, 1916), 1:125–27. Klingle, *Emerald City*, 46–60, is the most recent discussion of rail, coal, and related issues.
11. Emily Inez Denny, *Blazing the Way: True Stories, Songs, and Sketches of the Puget Sound and other Pioneers* (Seattle: Rainier, 1909), 448. J. Willis Sayre, *This City of Ours*, (Seattle: Seattle School District No. 1, 1936), 22–23. RHT's contribution to coal mining history is "Some Notes on Early Coal Mining in Washington Territory," 89/1, box 6, folder 9, RHT Papers, UW.
12. Bagley, *History of Seattle*, 1:359.
13. See the tour de horizon in Robert C. Nesbit, *"He Built Seattle": A Biography of Judge Thomas Burke* (Seattle: University of Washington Press, 1961), 9–18.
14. Robert A. Slayton, *Empire Statesman: The Rise and Redemption of Al Smith* (New York: Free Press, 2001), 29. See also Edmond R. Kiely, *Surveying Instruments: Their History and Classroom Use* (New York: Bureau of Publications, Teachers College, Columbia University, 1947), 243–47.
15. Basic studies of surveying, other than Kiely, above, include J.B. Johnson, *The Theory and Practice of Surveying*, 16th ed. (New York: John Wiley and Sons, 1908); William G. Raymond, *Plane Surveying for Use in the Classroom and Field*, 2nd ed. (New York: American, 1914); Harry Rubey, George Edward Commel, and Marion Wesley Todd, *Engineering Surveys: Elementary*, 3rd ed. (New York: Macmillan, 1950), and Lowell O. Stewart, *Public Land Surveys: History, Instructions, Methods* (1935: Minneapolis: Meyers, 1977). A good study containing references to Seattle problems and practices is Herbert Judson Flagg, "A Study of the Methods of City and Town Surveying," (B.S. thesis, University of Washington, 1912).
16. For systems, see 1–8; for techniques, 22–102, and for accuracies of 1/50,000, 31, in *NAVSTAR: Global Positioning System Surveying: Technical Engineering and Design Guides as Adapted from the U.S. Army Corps of Engineers*, No. 28 (Reston, VA: ASCE Press, 2000).
17. Raymond, *Plane Surveying*, 368.
18. Myra L. Phelps, *Public Works in Seattle: A Narrative History of the Engineering Department, 1875–1975*, ed. Leslie Blanchard (Seattle: Seattle Engineering Department and Kingsport Press, 1978), 237–38. A discussion of the early datum points and the difficulties associated with them is in F.H. Whitworth to Herbert Strandberg, 26 April 1927, copy in 89/5, box 1, folder 1, RHT Papers, UW. Whitworth's recollection gives different dates than Phelps does, but its account of the difficulties is almost certainly accurate.
19. For Willie in the firm, see RHT, "Sketches," 1881 entry, 1602-2, box 2, folder 10, RHT Papers, UW. For Willie's leaving, see James Edward Whitworth diary, November 29, 1881, 4967/1, box 1, James Edwin Whitworth diaries (hereinafter JW diaries), UW.
20. RHT, 1882 diary, 1602-2, box 1, folder 5, RHT Papers, UW.
21. Phelps, *Public Works in Seattle*, 277; and RHT's biography in Bagley, *History of Seattle* 2: 821.
22. RHT, notebook "1881–1889," 1881 entry, 1592/3, box 1, RHT Papers, UW.
23. For various tasks, see RHT diary, 12 and 13 January; 3 February; 3 August; and 9 August 1882, 1602-2, box 1, folder 5, RHT Papers, UW. JW Diaries, UW. RHT, 1882 diary, 9 January, 10 January, 1602-2, box 2, folder 5, RHT Papers, UW.
24. RHT, "Sketches," 1882 and 1883 entries, 1602-2, box 1, folder 10, RHT Papers, UW; RHT, notebook, "1881–1889," 1885 entry, 1592/3, box 1, RHT Papers, UW. For the Villard

holdings, see C. William Thorndale, "Washington's Green River Coal Company: 1880–1930," (Master's thesis, University of Washington, 1965), map, vii. For RHT quotation, RHT, *That Man Thomson*, 25–26.

25. For quotation, RHT notebook, "1881–1889," 1885 entry, 1592/3, box 1, RHT Papers, UW; Johnson, *Theory and Practice of Surveying*, 356–69; and Thorndale, "Green River Coal Company," 25.

26. Nancy Moore Rockafeller, "Public Health in Progressive Seattle, 1876–1919" (Master's thesis, University of Washington, 1986), 1–45; RHT to City Council, September 18, 1884, 993245, Seattle Municipal Archives (hereafter SMA), and Phelps, *Public Works in Seattle*, 199. Phelps misdates the sewer 1883. See also RHT, *That Man Thomson*, 16, 19; and RHT, "Sketches," 1884 and 1885 entries, 1602-2, box 2, folder 10, RHT Papers, UW.

27. Limits on territorial government are noted in Robert E. Ficken, *Washington Territory* (Pullman: Washington State University Press, 2002), 26–30; and Bagley, *History of Seattle* 2:546–47. For street problems, see RHT, *That Man Thomson*, 17–19. Here and elsewhere Keith D. Revell's conception of progressive era expertise and its concerns for the interdependence of the sections of a city is useful; see *Building Gotham: Civic Culture and Public Policy in New York City, 1898–1938* (Baltimore: Johns Hopkins University Press, 2003), ix, although Thomson's understanding of traffic movement as an urban unifier antedated the progressive era.

28. An example of plat correspondence is RHT to Mayor and Council, 2 October 1885, 992339, SMA. For the sidewalk, see RHT, "Sketches," 1884 entry, 1602-2, box 2, folder 10, RHT Papers, UW. For monuments, see RHT to W.R. Forest, 7 October 1885, 993155, SMA; and JW diary March 14, 1884, JW Diaries, UW.

29. The *Seattle Daily Press* described the Grant Street bridge in detail in its editions of December 22 and December 31, 1886. See also RHT, *That Man Thomson*, 18–19. For RHT's "dread" see RHT to Board of Public Works, 6 August 1894, 991251, SMA.

30. The most careful study of the riot and its foreshadowing, in the context of other western anti-Chinese activity, is Robert Edward Wynne, *Reaction to the Chinese in the Pacific Northwest and British Columbia, 1850 to 1910* (New York: Arno Press, 1978), 207–83. See also Nesbit, *"He Built Seattle,"* 166–212; and Bagley, *History of Seattle*, 2:455–77.

31. For Harry Whitworth, see Bagley, *History of Seattle*, 2:474. For the construction, see RHT, *That Man Thomson*, 16–17; and Phelps, *Public Works in Seattle, 98*. The quotation is from RHT, *That Man Thomson*, 19.

32. For the contract, see 993839, SMA. RHT's account is in RHT, *That Man Thomson*, 19.

33. Nesbit, *"He Built Seattle"*, 90–165; Armbruster, *Orphan Road*, 121–41; and Bagley, *History of Seattle* 1:248–52.

34. For first quotation, see RHT, *That Man Thomson*, 20. The second quotation is from the *Post-Intelligencer*, quoted in Armbruster, *Orphan Road*, 124. See also RHT, "Sketches," 1886 and 1887 entries, 1602-2, box 2, folder 10, RHT Papers, UW.

35. RHT, *That Man Thomson*, 21–23, quotation on 22. For return to Seattle, see RHT, 1887 diary, entries for April 30 and September 20, 1602-2, box 1, folder 5. For the temperature, see RHT's note on F.H. Essig to RHT, 8 March 1946, folder BIOGRAPHY, Thomson, Reginald Heber, pamphlet files Washington (State) Biography, UW.

36. For quotations, in order, see RHT, *That Man Thomson*, 23 and 25.

37. RHT had no apparent connection with the labor troubles in mines associated with the railroads; see Robert A. Campbell, "Blacks and the Coal Mines of Western Washington, 1888–1896," *Pacific Northwest Quarterly* (hereafter *PNQ*) 73 (October 1982): 146–55. The quotation is from RHT, *That Man Thomson*, 25, but see also 25–33 and RHT, "Sketches," 1889–1891 entries, 1602-2, box 2, folder 10, RHT Papers, UW.

38. The quotations, in order, are from RHT, 1882 diary, 1 January, 8 January, 22 January; 1887 Diary, 27 March; and 1888 Diary, 20 January, all in 1602-2, box 1, folder 5, RHT Papers, UW.

39. For Addie, see *Illustrated History of Sonoma County*, 469; Munro-Fraser, *History of Sonoma County*, 2; and two photographs, one in the possession of the present owners of the Laughlin farmstead, the other in the possession, in 2000, of Sally Hepler. RHT, diary 1882, 1602-2, box 1, folder 5, RHT Papers, UW. For "on July 15" quotation, see RHT "Sketches," 1882 entry, 1602-2, box 1, folder 10; and for "I built" quotation, RHT "Sketches," 1883 entry, 1602-2, box 1, folder 10, RHT Papers, UW. For "Baby" quotation, see RHT, diary 1886, 1602-2, box 1, folder 5, RHT Papers, UW; and for Marion's birth, RHT, "Sketches," 1889 entry, 1602-2, box 1, folder 10, RHT Papers, UW.

40. RHT, *That Man Thomson*, 15.

Thomson entitled the third chapter of his memoirs "My Work as City Engineer Begins." It is a brief chapter, scarcely more than three pages long. On first reading it is a loosely-organized collection of his activities and an analysis related to the major issues confronting him on June 1, 1892, when he became Seattle's city engineer—street paving and grading, sewer construction, and water supply. Curiously, it omits railroad matters, problems as vexing as the others. Adding the relevant parts of his memoir's previous chapter's last two pages, which belong to the third chapter organizationally, this brings the length of the discussion to four full pages. Abbreviated though it is, the entire statement could have been pressed into a page or so of tightly organized prose, even including the railroads. [1]

A second, reflective reading suggests why the end of the second chapter and the whole of the third chapter are brief, yet discursive and a bit disorderly. They are that way because Thomson was using two incidents to affirm his courage and knowledge, attributes essential to success in his new job.

The first, and dangerous, incident involved his survey on the Sucia Islands, a small group in the southern Strait of Georgia, west of Bellingham. Thomson went to the islands in October 1892 to survey a quarry claim, later a source of stone for street paving in Seattle. His companions included two of the Seattle claimants, Simon P. Randolph and John A. McGee, who already had mining claims on the main island. P. Brooks Randolph, the son of Simon and a "naturalist" as biologists were then called, also was in the party. It is probable that Simon, a well-known boat owner, piloted the vessel bringing the group to the Sucias. Brooks was there, probably, to collect specimens to advance his work in conchology; the junior Randolph was a founding member of the Young Naturalists Society who conducted a country-wide correspondence and exchange of aquatic shells. [2]

Thomson's party walked south to north on the main island without incident until they reached a trail, an oddity on an island supposed to be uninhabited. As Thomson was casting about for a place to set up his transit, three armed "smugglers"[3] appeared. They ordered the Thomson party off the island. This inflamed Brooks Randolph, who threw a stone, barely missing one of the interlopers. Randolph was ready to throw again when the man whom he had targeted raised a rifle and pulled the trigger, but it misfired. Misfire or no, the situation appeared desperate and nearly lethal, so Thomson took charge. Thomson, commandingly tall, hefted his tripod with the sharp steel points toward the man who had fired and told the trio to drop their weapons. He ordered Randolph back to the boat.

With the situation somewhat defused, he told "those men that I was a United States officer; that I was there in the name of the United States; and regardless of what they thought, my business was to survey the islands and that is what I would do." It was a bluff. A U.S. deputy mineral surveyor was an independent contractor appointed to survey mining claims. He was not a "United States officer" with enforcement powers. Nor was he there to survey the Sucias, only to survey one claim. On the other hand, the smugglers had an illegal livelihood to protect, so "with some grumbling" they decided against a showdown and stayed out of the way of Thomson's party. [4]

Whether or not the confrontation happened exactly as Thomson described, it is less important in itself than the broader understanding of his purpose in writing the account as he did. What he was stating, in so many words, was that he possessed the courage to surmount the difficult situations he would face during his "work as city engineer." Many future circumstances, though personally not potentially deadly, would nevertheless require quick thinking, decisive action, and determination. His account of the Sucia Island incident demonstrated his mastery of those qualities in full measure.

The second autobiographical story involves Seattle's first park and boulevard plan, the work of Bavarian-born Edward O. Schwagerl, an experienced landscape architect serving as superintendent of the city's original park board. Thomson relates how he worked with "a Mr. Schwagerel," to "show him what ought to be done." He

Thomson sits at left in an armchair while presiding over a luncheon with members of the Seattle City Council and others at Volunteer Park, May 1, 1900. The gathering probably involved an inspection tour of the abuilding water system that tapped the Cedar River. *University of Washington Libraries, Special Collections, UW23488z.*

reports a conversation with Schwagerl in which the landscape architect said that if Thomson's vision for Seattle proved correct, the city would be "very large" but at least "for some time" an "attenuated" one. Thomson concludes with the assertion that the city council dropped Schwagerl's 1891–92 plans because of "much criticism" of them.[5]

The four paragraphs required for this story do not lead anywhere unless it is understood how keenly Thomson believed himself to be the father of Seattle's boulevard system. He made the claim, however tenuous it was, in a 1916 autobiographical sketch. He also claimed that he began with a bicycle path, thus avoiding the "criticism" that he was planning a boulevard. His piecemeal and cumulative approach was, therefore, much cleverer and ultimately more effective than the elaborate plans of Schwagerl or his successors, the contracted Olmsted Brothers of Brookline, Massachusetts.[6] There is still more to the purpose of this story. However obvious the four anchor points of a quadrilateral park and boulevard system were to anyone familiar with urban planning in the 1890s, it was Thomson who "was supposed, among other things, to take him [Schwagerl] all over the city and the neighboring country and show him what

ought to be done."[7] With that assertion Thomson also could claim great foresight. Although other parks were developed after his time, the quadrilateral parks eventually became the city's Magnuson Park and Seward Park on Lake Washington, Discovery Park on Puget Sound, and, though reduced in size and concentration, the parks and playgrounds around Alki Point. Not only that, but Thomson's claims salved his stinging defeat in 1904, when Seattle voters adopted a charter amendment stripping his public works board of effective control over the city's parks and placing them in the hands of an independent board of park and boulevard commissioners.[8]

Finally, Thomson adverted to the three immediate problems confronting him—completing the North Tunnel trunk sewer and developing a sewer plan for the whole city, securing an adequate water supply "at first from Lake Washington and later from Cedar River," and organizing a rational street system that kept property damages to a minimum. The three problems were a tall enough order, but as he concluded, "others were added in the course of time."[9]

Had Thomson been writing in the 21st century, he might have added three topics to broaden and deepen the perspectives of his third chapter. They are technology,

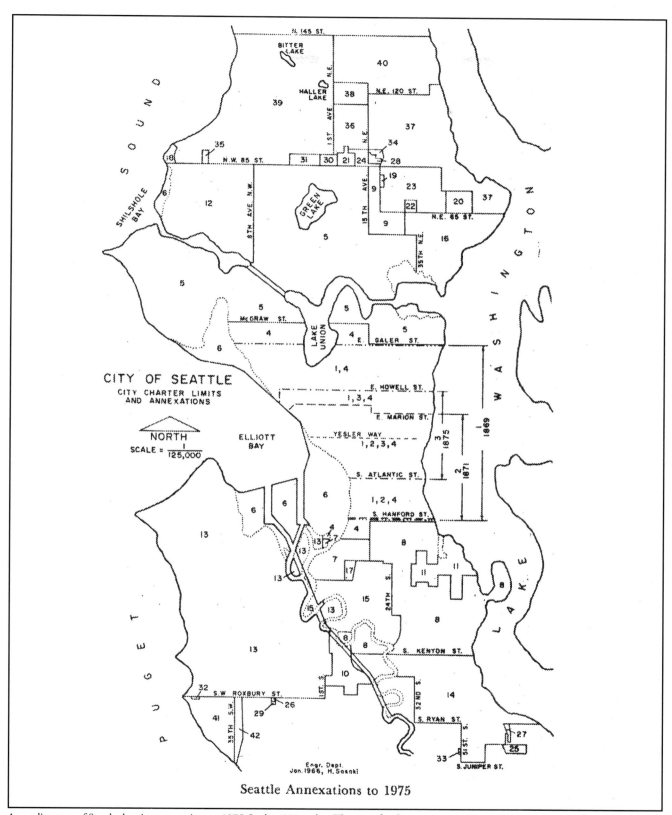

Seattle Annexations to 1975

An outline map of Seattle showing annexations to 1975. In the 1880s, when Thomson first became active in Seattle, the city's "built-up" area only extended from the south shore of Lake Union to the Elliott Bay tideflats (the oval area labeled "6"). *Office of the City Clerk of Seattle & Seattle Municipal Archives.*

nature, and the professional obligations summarized in the phrase "conflict of interest." Thomson could contemplate sewer construction, a huge water project, and street development and redevelopment because technology in the early 1890s was quite adequate to the task. Water-carriage sewage systems employed vitrified clay pipe for small sewers, vitrified brick for lining trunk sewers, street manholes for access to the larger sewers, flush tanks for cleaning the main sewers, and catch basins to limit storm water debris from entering sewers. Overflows designed to dump water out of the sewers and into bays, lakes, or streams not normally used to receive sewage were designed to prevent sewers from backing up into streets and basements. In regard to water systems, by the early 1890s they included a complex of dams, steam-driven pumps, reservoirs, cast-iron, copper, lead, or stone piping, pressure tanks, gates, valves, and, for power production, water wheels, turbines, and penstocks. Turning to heavy street work, regrading was accomplished with steam shovels, small steam engines and dump cars on temporary narrow-gauge tracks, refined surveying equipment, and dynamite. Engineers confronted with complex trigonometric and logarithmic problems could consult such aids as John C. Trautwine's *The Civil Engineer's Pocket-Book*, a compendium of procedures and calculations. Stationery steam engines—"donkeys"—simplified the tasks of clearing, cutting, and construction when harnessed to power equipment. [10]

Exciting advances in applied technology lay just beyond the horizon in 1892. Electric motors, control panels, and the concomitant cascade of electric lamps, switches, sockets, relays, transformers, insulators, and the like already existed, but steady improvements would facilitate the work of engineers while enormously expanding their activities. High-pressure water cannons that blasted hillsides away, a technique first developed in California gold mining, would speed street regrading. Better concrete sewer pipes, treated steel trunk water pipes, concrete and asphalt street surfaces, reinforced concrete in its many applications—all these and more—would extend the reach of engineers. [11]

The mind-numbing complexity and stupendous scale of late 19th century undertakings, combined with almost

In 1896, the Green Lake locality remained mostly forested with only scattered settlement. This view is of the eastern shore taken from Prospect Point. *Seattle Municipal Archives #29248.*

constant innovation in equipment and techniques, could not have happened without a revolution in the way engineers approached their work. Engineers learned that the new technologies required new techniques for saving lives and time, for splitting work between off-site and on-site construction, for managing the order of on-site operations, and for the effective control of operations over considerable distances. [12]

Advancing technology and systems development would enhance, not replace, the human element. Engineering would continue to be guided as much by common sense as by calculations, as much by insight as by ingenuity. Nor would technology quiet disagreement among engineers over the best construction technique and procedure in any given situation. It would enhance the scope and success of engineering projects, but it would also tempt engineers to overreach, to engage in imprudent ventures that failed. In Seattle and elsewhere, dams or their abutments collapsed, water pipes burst, sewer pipes leaked or backed up, pavements crumbled, and earthmoving induced landslides. The results of failure were, too often, catastrophic—a loss of life, significant property damage, large repair bills for works with already high capital costs, and expensive lawsuits. At the least, failure involved inconvenience—muddy or impassible streets, barricades around repairs, and interrupted water, sewer, or electrical service. At the same time, engineering advances made city life healthier and more comfortable for the mass of urban humanity. [13]

An imaginary 21st century Thomson, having considered the technological context of his work, would next turn to nature. He would take up the topic for two reasons—first, because of heightened environmental awareness after his time, and second, because virtually every engineering work modified nature. In the later 20th century, growing concerns over these modifications and the environmental damage they sometimes caused has stimulated the study of environmental history. Urban environmental historians have placed engineers and other city builders in a historical witness box, forcing confessions about the expense and inadequacy of their attempts to overcome nature.[14] Placed on the defensive, engineers are now required to explain themselves in their relation to the natural world. In his own time, however, Thomson was not at all defensive about his view of nature. For the purpose of establishing him within his milieu, and of relieving him of some of the burden of guilt, his multidimensional view of nature should be considered.

At the macrolevel, he saw nature as a unity, God's provision for humankind to use in trust and stewardship.[15] Wantonly destroying or befouling nature was anathema, a violation of trust and stewardship. Nevertheless, some considerable destruction or modification of nature was necessary if human health and happiness were to flourish in bustling, productive cities. This was necessary, too, because cities required tributary regions for extractive industry, usually a destructive enterprise. He praised the efforts of local investors who developed early coal operations and projected the ramshackle hauling system west to Seattle. They had "exhausted their entire credit in an attempt to build a city," and had to sell to outside capital after they "had spent their very vitals." They had, however, "received that profit which usually befalls the Pioneer, the satisfaction of knowing they had conquered Nature."[16] Agriculture, not as destructive, likewise resulted in some environmental modification. These necessary tributary activities legitimized keeping some people away from cities in mining, lumbering, or in linked businesses such as sawmilling, transportation, or trade. Thomson never extolled these exurban occupations for themselves, only insofar as they contributed to the urban economy. He was not, in other words, an advocate of rural or small town life as pleasant or virtuous. From his birth in 1856 until he arrived in Seattle in 1881, he had lived mostly in semi-rural areas or small towns. He wrote little about that life and demonstrated even less desire to return to it. Thomson knew, as only a city man could, the imperfections of urban living. He was determined to overcome them within his sphere of activity, as it related to the city's natural setting. When and where it was possible to work with nature he did; for example, in the basic designs and patterns of the sewer and water systems. When it was not, in the case of street regrading, he planned to destroy hills and fill hollows, creating streets of unnaturally gentle grades for greater ease of travel.

None of this conflicted with Thomson's belief in the 19th century doctrine of "natural advantage,"[17] although he did not use the phrase himself. As he told the 1911 Washington State Good Roads Association, the "great cities of the world…are those which have the most easy and the most direct means of access to the ocean, or are located upon some great inland lake or sea, or at the confluence of freight bearing streams."[18] Seattle's location on Puget Sound qualified it for greatness, but the same might be said for a least a dozen other waterfront communities. What distinguished Seattle was its central situation and its harbor, the deep and remarkably well protected Elliott Bay. No other aspirant to regional dominance could claim those advantages. Just as firmly, however, Thomson believed in the concept of human agency. God had marked out the main features of Seattle's site but had left plenty for humans to improve or rectify. Thomson's determination to make "Seattle accessible to the hinterland"[19] as well as to smooth the serrated city itself, testified to his conviction that God intended people to get busy with schemes to improve His handiwork. God also left a troublesome inheritance of seismic activity in the Seattle region, a reality defiant of human agency. The 1906 San Francisco earthquake aside, Thomson shared none of the contemporary concern about earthquakes. Severe tremblors were rare. Seattle's buildings, even the tallest, were relatively low in stature and its at-risk population relatively small. Seismology, with its worrisome discoveries of tectonic shifts, complex faults, and the liquefaction of fill earth, was either for the future or little heeded during Thomson's time.

Once natural advantage was conceded, Thomson laid down four requisites for urban growth, all of them requiring human thought and action against nature's backdrop. They were "Cheap Bread," his phrase for a low cost of living achieved through an effective network of "highways" combining the use of oceans, rivers, canals, roads, and railroads. Next came "Good Sanitation," with its first requisite being "good water," followed by a sewer system, and "perfect streets and perfect drainage." To these he added "stable Government," a precondition of "security to the investments [in] manufacture and commerce," and "Honest Tradesmen," defined as "confidence on the part of the producer that goods committed to…the tradesmen will be honestly accounted for, and confidence on the part of the consumer that the goods transmitted to them…will be the identical goods designated in the bill." Thomson's last requisite strongly suggested not simply a "stable government" but a regulatory one as well.[20]

None of this means that Thomson did not love nature for itself. He was in his element "in the field," working and tramping through country that, if not strictly wilderness, was too remote or rugged for intensive exploitation. His elaborate, unrealized plans for British Columbia's Strathcona Park included substantial modifications of relatively small areas to enhance the tourist experience. The major features, the beautiful Lady Falls, rivers and larger creeks, Buttle Lake mirroring the mountains, to say nothing of the mountains themselves, were left "as nature intended" them to be.[21]

Finally, after technology and nature, a 21st century Thomson would consider the problem of conflict of interest. Broadly considered, conflict of interest is any situation in which an officeholder uses a public position to advance any personal interest, or give the appearance of doing so. It is an area less sharply defined than older, grosser forms of abuse involving officeholders and those trying to influence them—giving and accepting bribes, bid rigging, contract kickbacks, and vote or office buying.[22]

Thomson scrupulously avoided these ethical lapses during his term as city surveyor and city engineer, and during his later two terms on the city council. Indeed, when Seattle's leading newspaper accused him of accepting a bribe, he sued the paper and its editor and won a judgment. But those were simpler times, as later generations are fond of telling themselves. Today the bounds of ethics are drawn much more closely around officeholders. By later standards, Thomson was involved in conflicts of interest. For example, while city engineer, he accepted a houselot from a leading citizen, given in recognition of his municipal work. It was an obvious *quid pro quo* under later conflict-of-interest codes. Both men would have been horrified at the suggestion that Thomson was expected to deliver a favor in return. Today, their professions of ethical purity notwithstanding, the probable outcry would have forced Thomson to return the property, to resign, or to do both in hopes of avoiding a fine or incarceration. No prohibitions on conflict of interest, as later conceived, existed in his day, and to criticize him for violating non-existent standards is to indulge in that bane of historians, "presentism." None of this means that Thomson was perfect. He made mistakes. But as he set about his work as city engineer, he was more often right than wrong.

NOTES

1. RHT, *That Man Thomson*, 33–38.
2. Ibid., 35–36. For Simon P. Randolph and Brooks Randolph's later career as a steamboat captain, see Gordon Newell, ed. *The H. W. McCurdy Marine History of the Pacific Northwest* (Seattle: Superior, 1966), 477; and Gordon R. Newell, *Ships of the Inland Sea: The Story of the Puget Sound Steamboats* (Portland: Binfords and Mort, 1960), 69–70, 79–80, 97. Brooks Randolph's work in the Young Naturalists' Society is described in Melville H. Hatch, "The Young Naturalists' Society (1879–1905)," in Melville H. Hatch, *Studies Honoring Trevor Kincaid* (Seattle: University of Washington Press, 1950), 29–34, especially 30–32. Keith R. Benson, "The Young Naturalists' Society: From Chess to Natural History Collections," *PNQ* 77 (July 1986): 82–93, concentrates on others than Randolph. The Young Naturalists' Society Records, 70–68, UW; and R.B. Randolph Collection, 495, Washington State Museum and Burke Memorial Museum, shed relatively little light on Randolph's career, except that the latter contains letters to Randolph.
3. The "smugglers" were identified as such in RHT, "Sketches," 1892 entry, 1602-2, box 1, folder 10, RHT Papers, UW.
4. RHT, *That Man Thomson*, 36. RHT's work as a United States deputy mineral surveyor is in Washington series 14, box 82, Oregon State Office (Portland); series 94, box 694-1, vols. 1–6; box 694-3, vol. 7–10, box 694-3 vol. 11–14, Record Group 49, Bureau of Land Management, National Archives and Records Administration, Pacific Alaska Region, Seattle, WA. Thomson surveyed a placer mining claim for Simon P. Randolph and others in October 1892 and March 1893, series 94, box 694, RG 49. The Guye claims mentioned in RHT, *That Man Thomson*, 31–33, are in Mineral Survey Files series 14, box 81, RG 49, above.
5. For Schwagerl, see his obituary, *Seattle Daily Times*, January 28, 1910. *Seattle Daily Times* and the *Seattle Sunday Times* hereafter cited as *Times*. RHT, *That Man Thomson*, 37.
6. RHT's claim is in Bagley, *History of Seattle*, 2: 822–23.
7. RHT, *That Man Thomson*, 37.
8. Bagley, *History of Seattle*, 2: 522, and 1: 273–75; and William H. Wilson, *The City Beautiful Movement* (Baltimore: Johns Hopkins University Press, 1990), 156–57, 159.
9. RHT, *That Man Thomson*, 37–38, quotation on 38.
10. Jon A. Peterson, *The Birth of City Planning in the United States, 1840–1917* (Baltimore: Johns Hopkins University Press, 2003), 30–39; Joel A. Tarr, *The Search for the Ultimate Sink: Urban Pollution in Historical Perspective* (Akron, OH: University of Akron Press, 1996), 131–97; John W. Oliver, *History of American Technology* (New York: Ronald Press Company, 1956), 411–12; and Terry S. Reynolds, *Stronger Than a Hundred Men: A History of the Vertical Water Wheel* (Baltimore: Johns Hopkins University Press, 1983). RHT probably consulted different Trautwine editions over the years; it was published at least until the 1930s; see John C. Trautwine and John C. Trautwine Jr., *The Civil Engineer's Reference Book (Formerly "Pocketbook")*, John C. Trautwine, 3rd. ed. (London: Chapman and Hall, 1937). For advances in equipment, see chapter 7.
11. A clear explanation of electrical developments, although related to Edison's work, is Martin V. Melosi, *Thomas A. Edison and the Modernization of America* (Glenview, IL: Scott, Foresman/

Little Brown Higher Education, 1990), 58–76. See also Neil Baldwin, *Edison: Inventing the Century* (New York: Hyperion, 1999), 102–14, 135–38. For street surfaces and the like, see chapter 9. For advances in materials and in energy production and transmission, see Tom F. Peters, *Building the Nineteenth Century* (Cambridge, MA: MIT Press, 1966), 35–78, 101–57.

12. Peters, *Building the Nineteenth Century*, 81–93; 159–207, 281–345.

13. For engineering problems and failures, see Henry Petroski, *To Engineer Is Human: The Role of Failure in Successful Design* (New York: St. Martin's Press, 1985; New York: Barnes and Noble Books, 1999). Dams and their related works are especially vulnerable, see Norman Smith, *A History of Dams* (London: Peter Davies, 1971); Elizabeth M. Sharpe, *In the Shadow of the Dam: The Aftermath of the Mill River Flood of 1874* (New York: Free Press, 2004); and David G. McCullough, *The Johnstown Flood* (London: Hutchinson, 1968). For public health improvements, see Rockafeller, "Public Health in Progressive Seattle."

14. For two examples of strident historical environmentalism, see Eric Sandweiss, "Paving St. Louis's Streets: The Environmental Origins of Social Fragmentation," 90–106; and Katharine T. Corbett, "Draining the Metropolis: The Politics of Sewers in Nineteenth Century St. Louis," 107–25, in Andrew Hurley, ed., *Common Fields: An Environmental History of St. Louis* (St. Louis: Missouri Historical Society Press, 1997).

15. For RHT's view of nature in an urban setting, see Wilson, *The City Beautiful Movement*, 217–18.

16. RHT, "Some Notes on Early Coal Mining in Washington Territory," 89/1, box 6, folder 9, RHT Papers, UW.

17. Beaton, *City That Made Itself*, 5–6; and 14–16; Bagley, *History of Seattle*, 1: 101.

18. RHT, "How and Why Cities Grow," a version of a speech RHT gave regularly, n.d., but internal evidence suggests the date and audience, 89/1, box 6, folder 9, RHT Papers, UW.

19. RHT, *That Man Thomson*, 13. See also Beaton, *City That Made Itself*, 7–11.

20. RHT, "How and Why Cities Grow," see note 18.

21. RHT to C.E. Remsberg, 10 July 1912, 89/1, box 4, book 11, RHT Papers, UW; to A.E. Flagg, 2 December 1912, 89/1, box 5, book 12, RHT Papers, UW.

22. Andrew Stark, *Conflict of Interest in American Public Life* (Cambridge, MA: Harvard University Press, 2000), 36–42, 74–77, 235–36, 264–65.

Portrait of city officials in 1895, with Thomson sitting next to his long-time secretarial assistant, Katharine Stream—highly competent, fully trusted, and practically a part of the Thomson family. Sitting at the far right is George Cotterill, an engineering collaborator, future Democratic mayor, and good friend. *Seattle Municipal Archives #130344.*

5
The Sewers

Sewers preoccupied Thomson. In his autobiography, the subject fills the first substantive chapter about his city engineering career, chapter four. Not until chapter seven does he turn to the most visible and controversial reforms—the regrades. Historians of Seattle's physical shaping have instead given the regrades, along with the city's water supply, primary space. They have devoted much less attention to, or even ignored, the sewers.[1]

One reason for this inversion of interest is that the regrades—knocking down hills, flattening streets, and causing disruption and expense—were vastly more dramatic, both contemporaneously and historically. The other is Thomson's overwhelming concern for clean water as the basis for urban civilization. Focusing on this concern is all very well, but it ignores the fact that when clean water was used and became dirty it had to go somewhere. Surface receptacles, street gutters, streams, ditches or underground catchments, and cesspool pits or privy vaults were insufficient. The surface outlets quickly became unsightly and smelly at best, clogged at worst. Cesspools and privy vaults collecting bodily and other wastes from each house or business required frequent cleaning. If cesspools and privy vaults (the terms were at least partly interchangeable) were not completely tight, and most were not, they leached contents into the surrounding soil and nearby ground water. Exposing the public to putrescence and filth through open sewers and inadequate pits negated the positive influence of potable water.[2]

Neither Seattle nor any other city was as keen on building a sewer system as it was a water system. A problem with building a water system without attention to a sewer system was that the availability of clean water dramatically increased its use. Increased wastewater could overwhelm cesspools and privy vaults. The cesspool-privy vault system depended on well-functioning pits on each lot, but the cesspools and vaults could not handle the torrent. They overflowed, with their contents saturating lots, seeping into basements, and collecting in low places.

The fact that convenient new water systems encouraged greater use was well known at the time Thomson became city engineer. In the words of historian Joel A.

Tarr, Chicago "went from 33 gallons per capita per day in 1856 to 144 in 1882; Cleveland increased from 8 gallons per capita per day in 1857 to 55 in 1872; and Detroit from 55 gallons per capita per day in 1856 to 149 in 1882." As Tarr points out, the increase was not all in households, for industrial and other uses claimed larger portions, too. The increases per person per day are astounding, especially when the late 19th century's rampant urban growth is considered. Water systems encouraged the use of flush toilets. Tarr estimates that about a fourth of urban homes had them by 1880. To the extent that flush toilets dumped their contents into underground pits, they exacerbated the problem.[3]

Sewers also supposedly were built to prevent the polluting of nearby bodies of water. This motive, however, was not really accomplished during the 19th century.[4] Seattle did not have a large river within its boundaries, therefore its sewage went into Elliott Bay, which was saltwater and not a source of drinking water, or into freshwater lakes Union or Washington. It would be many years before both became reasonably clean again. Before that happy day, the city shifted its water source to the Cedar River.

Three preliminary actions influenced Thomson's sewer work of 1892 and after. They were the sewage construction activities of the 1880s and the George Waring and Benezette Williams' sewer reports. Unsatisfactory as Seattle's sewage arrangements were, qualitative improvements had been made in the early 1880s. In 1883, to cite one declaration of olfactory inadequacy, Mayor Henry G. Struve denounced "cesspools filled with decaying animal and vegetable matter, distilling poisonous gasses." These affronts were located on the waterfront and "on both sides on the lower end of Washington Street and intersecting streets," near the offices of Whitworth & Thomson. Struve complained about "filth and garbage" and "defective house drains without proper ventilation creating noxious and sickening odors." Struve's denunciation of Seattle's sanitary deficiencies included the Chinese, whose "filthy habits and customs" encouraged "contagion" among a people "coming in daily contact with our citizens as servants, laundry men and laborers." In a way, his condemnation presaged the anti-Chinese riots of less than three years later.[5]

The Chinese aside, Struve was correct in criticizing the lack of proper sewers and, separately, the low streets near the waterfront in the retail-commercial district. Low streets lacked the elevation to keep bay water from backing up the sewers. Raising the streets "several feet" was also advisable to lessen the steep grades eastward toward the then more residential streets of town.[6] The 1889 fire would provide the opportunity for wholesale street raising. Meanwhile, Struve and Joseph M. Snow, Thomson's predecessor, were busy building sewers. "Large, durable, and capacious sewers have been constructed on Washington, Mill [now Yesler Way] and James streets," Mayor Struve reported in 1884. Thanks to the new sewers, "that district, which for the last twenty years has been the place of deposit for all garbage and offal, has at last been penetrated by a proper drain."[7] Snow, the engineer, was not so sure. He acknowledged that there were six sewers from Mill north to Pine Street but these only "in some cases" discharged their contents above high water on the waterfront. In any event, some sewage was "flowing westerly across Front street" (now First Avenue), hardly an endorsement of Front's commercial prospects. To solve the problem, he suggested a collector sewer along Front from Pike Street south to Mill.

Thomson's 1886 sewer along Union Street (see chapter 3) was a wooden box, even then a less-than-durable solution, but for only about two blocks. From Front to near Sixth Street (now Sixth Avenue) it was of "the best vitrified ironstone"[8] for a distance of some six blocks. Thomson's report of that year did not, as already noted, propose a system or even an interceptor to carry away the sewage from his and the other east-west sewers dumping into the bay. His brief, dry, statistical report may be excused on the grounds that he had his hands full opposing the anti-Chinese riot and finishing the Grant Street bridge.

In any event, neither Thomson nor his predecessor, nor his successors, were able to create anything resembling a proper sewer system. Poor sewers sometimes resulted from "privatism," that is, property owners financing their own sewer without any consideration or concern for other citizens, nor were adverse conditions limited to private sewers along the waterfront. Geology and hydrology contributed to making Lake Union a convenient cesspool. Seattle's sanitary officer noted that in the area of the "alley" between Fourth and Eighth "and extending to Lake Union,…all excavations immediately

fill with water." This situation helped drainage into the lake but rendered privy vaults impossible unless they were made of stone, brick, or cement. He recommended the opening of a street "from the vicinity of Pike street northerly to Lake Union with public sewer therein."[9] In 1889, City Surveyor John G. Scurry was even more critical. "Pipes now being laid are not in conformity with any general plan," he wrote. Detailed topographical surveys would have helped future planning, but as things stood, there was no good map of existing sewers, or even good records. Scurry criticized Thomson and his other predecessors when he wrote that "no systematic attempt has been made heretofore to preserve a proper record of the operations of this office," or if preserved "they have been considered as the personal property of the surveyor" and removed at the end of his term. Worse, "the records on file in this office of surveys constructed, are very imperfect; in fact, they are practically worthless."[10]

Little wonder, then, that half a year before Scurry's scathing remarks, George E. Waring Jr. came to Seattle to make a sewer plan. Scurry rejected Waring's program. Before assuming that Scurry maliciously condemned Waring's work in order to pose as a voice crying in Seattle's planless wilderness, we must consider Waring, his beliefs, and his works. Waring's personality was later termed "charismatic,"[11] while a contemporary declared that "there was so much personal magnetism in Colonel Waring."[12]

Waring, although wrong on some public health and sewage issues of the day, should not be lightly dismissed. In an age when colonels, honorary and self-described, sprinkled the economic upper crust of American cities, Waring was the real thing, having been a Union cavalry officer during the Civil War. He absorbed, as did others, the ideas of Edwin Chadwick of England. In the 1840s, Chadwick developed the vision of an endlessly circulating urban water system where fresh water, piped into houses and businesses, ran into the sewers after use. The sewer water itself, though foul with excreta and other pollution, as well as rainwater carrying its own offal, performed an essential function; it cleaned sewers as it charged through them. The trick was to design a complete system of gravity-powered sewers of ever-increasing size from the house drain to huge collector or intercepting sewers, all performing the ultimate task of whisking the contents out of the city.[13]

This is where Waring's personal beliefs came in. Waring was an advocate of the "filth" or "sewer gas" theory, believing that decaying organic matter such as human feces produced disease. That is, he was an "anti-

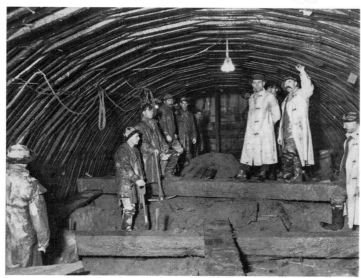

An extension of the North Trunk Sewer under construction, January 27, 1913. Completing the first section of the North Trunk project after another engineer declared it hopeless was perhaps Thomson's greatest engineering triumph. *Seattle Municipal Archives #6229.*

contagionist" who rejected the idea that contact with a diseased person or a carrier caused "contagion" or transmitted illness. In this he was more wrong than right, as "sewer gas" and "filth," however unpleasant, could not produce infection in and of themselves. Respectable doctors, sanitarians, and engineers, including Chadwick himself, nevertheless accepted the proposition until advancing 19th century medical knowledge produced the "germ theory," the concept of a specific pathogen for each disease.[14] Waring's second belief was in the so-called "separate" system of waste removal. He rejected the "combined" system in which stormwater joined household and commercial waste for three reasons, again ultimately derived from Chadwick. First, he argued for the rapid removal of human wastes from households through tightly fitted pipes of small diameter before the wastes decomposed and produced unhealthy gases. Second, he maintained that the small pipes were relatively inexpensive, when compared to the high costs of the huge combined sewers designed to carry off both stormwater and sewage. Third, he asserted the value of human waste as fertilizer for crops. The fertilizer proposition soon proved to have limited utility.[15]

It is easy to misunderstand Waring's "separate" system as calling for a parallel network of underground pipes, one for sewage, the other designed to handle stormwater and all other surface drainage (some dual separate systems, indeed, were built). Most systems, however, relied on streets to dispose of the surface liquid. A double system of pipes would have negated Waring's argument

for lower cost. His design for Memphis, following yellow fever epidemics there in 1873, and again in 1878 and 1879, involved underground sewers for household waste, and streets and their gutters for everything else. A special commission created for settling on a sewer system accepted Waring's plan, despite considerable dissent. It was five times cheaper than a competing combined system and it responded to the prevailing miasmatic or "sewer gas" theory. It was built during 1880.[16]

The controversy surrounding acceptance of Waring's plan was nothing compared to the wrangling that arose after his system went into operation. To put the matter gently, it did not work. Pipes clogged, and flush toilets designed to move sewage could not function well until the water system was extended to them, at a cost not included in the original plans. Plumbers called to free clogs sometimes broke pipes. To save money, Waring had omitted manholes, forcing crews to dig up the streets to make repairs. Manholes were installed later at additional expense. Not all the problems were Waring's fault. Householders surreptitiously diverted their gutters into sewers, overloading them, and the city did not provide an outlet to the Mississippi River until 1886, although that outlet was part of Waring's original plan.[17]

The hubbub over the Waring system was confined, largely, to Memphis and to engineering circles. Waring unhesitatingly declared his system successful in numerous speeches and articles. He developed a wide, loyal following despite behaving in a way that some other engineers found unprofessional. For example, he formed a company to build sewers and promoted the company as relentlessly as he did himself. His fame as a sanitarian probably accounts for his arrival in Seattle late in 1888. At the end of November, he "communicated informally" with the city council about his preliminary findings. He advised dividing the city into four sewer districts, each with its own outfall. He emphasized building sewers along the north-south streets rather than running sewers from the ridgetops down every east-west street to the bay, endorsed the idea of a collector sewer beneath Front Street, and called for a major sewer from Lake Union to the bay.[18]

In his meeting with the council, Waring did not make a point of his proposing a separate system, but it was obvious enough. His trunk sewer from Lake Union would be "about three feet in diameter," versus the six-foot sewer eventually built. Waring's final plan was presented in February or March 1889. It made the case for a separate system on the Memphis plan. The council turned it over to City Surveyor Scurry for a report. Scurry found the plan "well gotten up and complete" as would be expected "from so distinguished a source," but "defective in the arrangement of the pipes, in the location of the outlet sewers, in the method of flushing and other particulars." He saw fatal limitations in Waring's scheme, and did not recommend it. The council adopted Scurry's report, effectively killing the Waring plan.[19]

It was left to the next expert, Benezette Williams, to attack Waring's separate system. Williams, less well known to history than Waring, was nevertheless a major urban engineering figure in the late 19th and early 20th centuries. Among other achievements, he designed a double-pipe, separate sewer system for Pullman, Illinois. But Pullman was a company town of limited size and massive funding, not a proto-metropolis chronically under financed.[20]

Williams completed his report in August 1891. He criticized Waring's solution on three grounds. First, he ridiculed Waring's contention that Seattle was, to quote Waring, "well situated for the removal of surface water" without the need for storm sewers. This was a mistaken position. Steep grades east to west in what was then the main part of town would send rainwater rolling across the north-south streets at a furious rate, flooding them at intersections. The elaborate system of gutters and culverts necessary to move surface water, "will not only cause inconvenience and annoyance, but will in the long run be more expensive than to provide for it in underground sewers." Aesthetics were important too. Surface water systems made it practically impossible to build "handsome" streets. Williams cited "the accumulated experience of all populous cities and towns" as favoring "a combined system." Also, a separate system with two pipes, one for sewage, the other for stormwater and surface runoff, would "materially" increase costs over combined sewers.[21]

Next Williams turned to the public health aspect and Waring's belief in the serious consequences of "sewer gas." Williams wisely refrained from taking either a contagionist, anti-contagionist, or "germ theory" stance. Instead he used Waring's statement that 95 percent of all sewer gas was generated between the plumbing fixtures in the home and the street sewer. Even allowing for Waring's flamboyant exaggeration, Williams wrote, if a high percentage of sewer gas is indeed generated so close to home, the solution was to move it promptly to the street sewer. This could be accomplished just as readily through a properly constructed house drain connected to an efficient combined sewer, as it could in a separate system.[22] Third, Williams warned that a separate system consisting only of small pipes would be "overcharged in a few years," as happened in Memphis. This was because of surreptitious house downspout connections, and because, as in some parts of Memphis, there was no way to drain stormwater except through the sewers. Williams admitted that his combined sewers for Seattle would overflow during heavy downpours, when the overflows would go into the lakes instead of the Sound. But this situation would occur "seldom" if the city built adequate sewers. Of course, it was financially impossible to build sewers to handle every conceivable heavy rainfall. Williams and his readers knew that. In some areas, unfortunately, overflows would occur more frequently than "seldom."[23]

Williams, although handicapped by inadequate rainfall reports, an insufficient number of established street grade plans, unfamiliarity with tidal behavior in the sound, and uncertainty as to when and where the city would grow, nevertheless produced a plan that guided sewer developments for years. The Williams scheme retained the trunk sewer from Lake Union to the sound and projected future developments on Queen Anne Hill and around Green Lake. Williams was especially concerned about the future diversion of sewage away from Green Lake and Lake Washington's Union Bay. For the rest, he carved the city into five districts; four of these— Lake Union, the built up section around downtown, Lake Washington, and a district between Lake Washington and the ridge east of the built up section— demanded immediate attention. The trunk sewer to the sound would serve much of Lake Union. In the "Central District," or "nearly all the business part of the town," sewers already laid would, with some modifications, carry effluent to an interceptor sewer beneath Front Street, to a main sewer on John Street, and thence to Elliott Bay. The Lake Washington strip would discharge into the lake. Sewage from the district between the lake and the area in and adjacent to the business area would collect in a sewer south of the area. Then it would be discharged to the tideflats.[24]

Williams was pleased that his plan reduced the area of natural drainage into Lake Washington, Lake Union, and Green Lake from 18 square miles to "about two." Still, his arrangements could be criticized for dumping too much sewage into the lakes, even in 1891. Some engineers were beginning to doubt the idea of "dilution," that sewage in running water or a large body of water purified itself. Williams' only expressed concerns were that efflu-

Building the Lander Street sewer across the tideflats, 1910. Later this tidal area was filled and raised. *Seattle Municipal Archives #52074.*

ent be conducted far enough into Elliott Bay or the sound so as not to return on the tide, and that the lakes be replaced with other sources of drinking water.[25]

In any event, Thomson and his predecessors and successors carried out and extended the Williams plan for many years. They made modifications as circumstances and experience dictated, but all things considered, Williams' efforts were remarkably prescient. Even before he finished his report, work had begun on the Lake Union tunnel, the first leg of what became the North Trunk Sewer. The North Trunk would be Thomson's triumph. A look at its genesis will show why.

Williams planned the tunnel to run from what was then the south end of Lake Union near Rollins (now Westlake Avenue North) and Republican streets, southwest to Fifth Street, then to Depot Street (now Denny Way), then west to Elliott Bay. His plan avoided tunneling through much of Denny Hill, a dome of almost 150 feet at its summit, athwart the street leading from the city's center to the lake. Through laterals—secondary street sewers—the tunnel would drain the soggy ground south of Lake Union, keeping its sewage from further fouling the lake's waters.[26]

Planning the sewer was one thing; designing and building it was something else. For the designing and construction stage, Williams passed the ball to Albro Gardner, the city engineer. Gardner passed it back. Gardner's work exhibited the tentative, uncertain quality

of a man who had convinced himself from the beginning that the project was beyond his grasp. As he noted to the Board of Public Works in February 1891, he had done the location engineering and performed other "preliminary" work. Williams, Gardner noted, would "definitely" establish the grade, although fixing the grade would seem to be the province of the man on the ground. The next month, Gardner asked Williams to "fix the thickness of the lining of the tunnel," another task supposedly belonging to the city engineer. At the end of March, Gardner concluded a discussion of the tunnel by telling Williams, "I presume you can suggest a better plan." In two weeks, he wrote again informing Williams of a tussle between the chamber of commerce, which wanted a brick-lined tunnel, and a majority of the Board of Public Works, which favored concrete lining, as did Williams. Gardner wanted a letter from the Chicago consultant "stating your reasons and authority for recommending" concrete. "It will require some backbone to resist" the advocates of brick, Gardner wrote, "and I want to fortify myself." The stiffening of Gardner's spine would have to wait for a letter from Chicago.[27]

Meanwhile, backed by a bond issue, work on the tunnel went forward. Unfortunately Gardner's oversight of the tunnel's construction confirmed his tentative approach to the problem. In mid-March, his crews began excavating from under the foot of Depot Street, the west end of the tunnel. By July 8, they had picked and shoveled their way 450 feet from the Elliott Bay outlet. Gardner reported only light timbering was needed for the last third of the bore, but the honeymoon conditions with the earth along the 5,400 foot route soon ended. What began well enough through "good ground" quickly turned into a nightmare of shifting types of clay, water rivulets, and quicksand. Caving soil at the face, or front, of the work cost one life and frustrated efforts to advance the tunnel. Then the struggling crews encountered "an underground lake," forcing Gardner to abandon the project. Faced with a fatality, cost overruns, a flooding tunnel, and no apparent solution to the dilemma, the hapless Gardner resigned in May 1892.[28]

Unfortunately, sanitary conditions in Lake Union and the area south of it deteriorated as the efforts to rectify the situation stumbled. By the end of 1891, when Gardner was groping his way to failure, three "immense" open trenches dumped "the sewage of 10,000 people into Lake Union." The city health officer, not surprisingly, found the lake smelling of sewage, its color "yellow," and the water "turbid." In an exemplary piece of bureaucratic understatement, he wrote: "I would recommend that no more [drinking] water be taken from Lake Union."[29] This is when Thomson stepped in, for the 1892 election brought the conscientious reformer James T. Ronald into the mayorship. Ronald realized that something had to be done. According to Thomson, the first man offered the city engineer's post (Edwin Hall Warner) looked over Gardner's work and declined the job on the grounds that the tunnel was hopeless. Thomson disagreed. The tunnel, he knew, passed through glacial till containing water lenses; it had bored through a lens, i.e., the "underground lake." His solution was to drain the lens while work continued. Not for nothing had Thomson continued his informal studies of Seattle-area geology. With the understanding that he could carry the tunnel through to a finish, Thomson was offered the job of city engineer beginning June 1, 1892.[30]

Thomson continued tunnel construction from both ends, as had Gardner, but he made two important changes. First, he delegated the immediate supervision of the work to Edward T. Morgan, an experienced miner. Morgan admitted his ignorance of the local geology but he had plenty of practice with tunneling. Selecting Morgan was an early example of Thomson's ability to choose effective subordinates. His second departure was to abandon concrete for the tunnel lining, specifying brick instead. Before his resignation, Gardner backed away from concrete as the preferred lining material, perhaps because of political pressure or doubts about

concrete, or some combination of the two. Williams had recommended concrete at least in part because he believed local suppliers were incapable of making durable brick. Thomson's endorsement of local brick, however, asserted that its new standard "relieves us from the odium cast upon our city and our County by the statement of Mr. Benezette Williams that there was no brick in this country…suitable for sewer linings." Williams' "statement when made was doubtless true," but the combination of excellent brick clay and conscientious work from brick makers had "put us on a par with the best average of Eastern made sewer brick."[31]

Heber's intervention did not end the troubles, for Seattle's sewer bonds sold slowly in the severe 1890s economic depression. Work was suspended during 1893 but resumed when more bond funds became available. Careful timbering and adequate drainage moved the project forward to its completion in the fall of 1894. By then work on the collector-interceptor South Tunnel under Bayview Street, a six-foot high sewer, was also complete, but because of delays in constructing other sewers, it was not put into use until 1901.[32]

Thomson's reputation received a second boost while the two major sewer projects were under way. This time he added fiscal probity and responsibility to his engineering repute. As Thomson explained in his published account, he and his assistants were determined to build desperately needed sewers with the greatest possible economy consistent with good construction. However, there were two sets of circumstances affecting their stand. The existing sewers were not just inadequate, some of them were failing. The "large, durable, and capacious sewers" of 1884 on the east-west streets James, Yesler, and Washington were "now decayed, and may any day collapse," Thomson reported at the end of 1892. So much work was needed that not everything could be done. Two years after Thomson warned of collapse, part of the Washington Street sewer gave way. Second, the searing depression struck with full force in 1893, converting the sewers and any other city construction into unemployment-relieving public works.[33]

Other members of the Board of Public Works were equally aware of the need for sewers and unemployment relief, but their emphasis was different. They were less anxious about the quality of the sewers than they were with hiring the "great many idle men" who needed jobs. When they told Thomson to remove some of his assistants and replace them with men less concerned with good construction and "more reasonable with the workmen," he refused. The board then went to Mayor

Ronald, who assured them that he and Thomson would expand a Thomson policy already in place. The new policy would limit hires to men who were Seattle residents and who were supporting families. They would be hired on a non-partisan basis for two weeks, then replaced with an equally qualified crew for the next two weeks.[34]

Ronald and Thomson's arrangement, however humane, did not address the board's intent. Board members wanted a shift away from demonstrated competence to crowding the payroll with the unemployed. Thomson suggests that their motives were partisan, as well. Once again the board approached the city engineer, and again he rejected their entreaties. Thereupon, the board ended Thomson's supervision of sewer work, turning it over temporarily to one of their number, the superintendent of streets, then it dismissed Thomson. His autobiographical notes record only that the board removed him from the sewer project on January 16, 1894, replacing him with Edwin Hall Warner as the new city engineer. (Warner had earlier been offered the job following Gardner's resignation in 1892, but declined the position after inspecting the difficult, uncompleted North Tunnel sewer.)[35]

Warner proved to be complaisant toward the board and the politically-oriented superintendent of streets, as well as indifferent to rigorous inspection. The bond issue funds flowed into the pockets of workmen, and perhaps into other pockets as well. To that extent, the board achieved its purpose of providing work relief. There were two hitches, however. The board was not rotating workmen as the mayor expected, and it was not making much progress toward finishing the sewers. Ronald's attempts to have the employment issue resolved were stonewalled, even when he discovered that some workmen labored for extraordinarily long hours, according to the time sheets. At least one worker realized the superhuman and supernatural achievement of toiling for 26 hours in a single day.[36]

Such obvious padding could have been overlooked had the work been well managed but it was not. Thomson's favorite illustration of incompetence—the long-advertised and long-awaited Front Street interceptor sewer—was at last under construction from Union Street on the north to King Street on the south. Its 12-block length would collect sewage from the several east-to-west sewers then dumping their contents all along Elliott Bay. The

North Trunk Sewer overflow tunnel, April 1, 1912. *Seattle Municipal Archives #6037.*

task should have been relatively simple—to follow the downgrade of Front Street as it ran from Union to King. For some reason the sewer was, instead, rising toward the surface of the street. When Ronald found out about the blunder, he ordered Warner to investigate. Warner, perhaps visiting the construction site for the first time, informed Ronald that an unknown person had cut off part of a pole used to maintain a uniform depth between the street and the sewer line. Warner's explanation was absurd, for a single cut of the pole would have caused the sewer to rise only until the next measurement, when it again would have followed the descending grade of the street, although at a level closer to the surface. The shallower depth could have caused problems with lateral connections. Depending on circumstances, however, a relatively short hump in the sewer could have been cleared by the siphoning action of the sewage flowing through it. Only repeated cuts of the pole would explain a persistent rise in the grade of the sewer. Farce piled on absurdity when the investigation focused on an attempt to discover "who cut the stick"; i.e., identifying the supposed miscreant who shortened the pole. "Who cut the stick?" quickly became the derisive byword for all the ills of Warner's brief tenure. [37]

Mayor Ronald had had enough. He removed two members of the Board of Public Works and appointed his personal choices in their stead. The reconstituted board dismissed Warner and reappointed Thomson, effective February 16. Thus, he returned to the work after a one month hiatus. Thomson restored the lapsed system of prudent, economical construction, thereby confirming his reputation for fiscal responsibility. As he explained the situation in his memoirs, from the time that the superintendent of streets took over on December 20, 1893, to the date of Thomson's reappointment, sewer work estimated at $30,000 had cost $101,000. Even assuming low preliminary estimates, the Board of Public Works should not have spent above $35,000. To put it another way, sewers costing no more than $3.00 per running foot under Heber's management were priced at $9.00. The same type of sewer, after his return, was built for the former price. [38]

In an important way, however, Thomson's autobiographical account minimizes the problems he encountered. The "Who cut the stick?" episode aside, much of the sewer work had been prosecuted in a careless, discontinuous way, with cost overruns plaguing almost every aspect. Thomson conducted a triage, deciding which sewers to abandon, which to finish only in the portions then under construction, and which to rush to comple-

tion. The city council reinforced the necessity with an order to stop work on all bond issue sewers, and to deliver a report on the financial and physical condition of each. It was easy enough to conclude that sewers unbuilt would remain so until they could be financed in some other way, for example by assessment against benefited property. But other sewers had to be finished. The Front-Commercial streets sewer was long overdue and those streets were choked with construction materials. An east-west sewer on Main Street could be finished if halted short of its planned upper portion; the street at last could be restored to traffic. Thomson worried about what could happen here should a conflagration erupt and fire apparatus could not reach a burning structure. Memories of the great fire of 1889 remained. One sewer, intended to connect the south part of the commercial district with the mostly unused South Sewer Tunnel, could be finished only at its exposed junctions, then closed for lack of funds. [39] A combination of rigorous cost control, and money saved from closed, partially completed, or uninitiated projects, plus additional council appropriations, allowed Thomson to finish some of the most critically needed sewers. What was also important in the short run, he restored a sense of fiscal responsibility, integrity, and discipline to the office of city engineer.

Over the next 17 years, Thomson directed an enormous expansion of Seattle's sewer system, which health officials credited with reducing the rate of infectious disease. The extension of the North Trunk Sewer north to and around Green Lake was an engineering and personal political triumph. From Green Lake, the sewer system ran south and east almost to Lake Washington, looped around the University of Washington grounds, then ran west to Puget Sound, emerging on the northwest shore of Fort Lawton (today, Discovery Park). One of Thomson's most trying but ultimately rewarding experiences was obtaining federal permission to tunnel the sewer under the northern edge of Fort Lawton. [40]

As early as 1903, Thomson had asked for permission to locate a sewer outfall on the rocky beach about midway between the Fort Lawton area's West Point and the southern shore of Shilshole Bay, in the Magnolia district. As usual, the circumstances surrounding his efforts arose from a near-emergency situation; 1903 was years before the completion of the North Trunk Sewer into the Green Lake area north of Lake Union, but permanent sewer or no permanent sewer, something had to be done. The Board of Health found that all of the wells and springs in the area were polluted and condemned them. Seattle had to extend water mains to the rapidly growing number

An attractive new bridge built to carry the North Trunk Sewer line over Montlake Boulevard, April 1, 1912. *Seattle Municipal Archives #6042.*

of residents, leading, as Thomson put it, to "those facilities, which in a city, accompany the introduction of city water in the house." There had to be some outlet for the resulting surge of sewage, so the Board of Public Works requested a temporary discharge into Salmon Bay through the site of the future federal ship canal between Lake Union and the sound. The officer in charge of the U.S. Army engineering district at first denied a permit, increasing the urgency of a permanent solution.[41]

From the fall of 1904 through most of 1905, the situation prompted Thomson to begin an elaborate study of wind, tides, and currents along the Seattle waterfront. A trusted employee, Ferdinand "Fred" Dehley, used a boat to set out floats wherever a current "touched any place on the Seattle waterfront from two miles south of Alki Point to three miles north of Shilshole Bay." Dehley could not check on every float over so great a distance on the same day, which is why the labor required so much time. During the year or so that he and at times an assistant worked at the task, they numbered, dated, and charted the course of the individual floats. They tracked each float until it either washed up somewhere on the shore, suggesting that sewage released at that point would return to plague the coast, or it moved north toward the sea.[42]

These studies convinced Thomson that his earlier, pragmatic conclusion based on the observed behavior of log booms was correct. The best place for a sewer outfall was in deep water beyond the rocky beach at Fort Lawton. Even from there, however, insufficiently diluted sewage could wash up on a far shore of Puget Sound before reaching the Strait of Juan de Fuca and heading out to the Pacific Ocean. Nevertheless, this was the best place. Thomson's next task was to convince the United States government, including the War Department and Congress. The task would not be easy.[43]

Thomson managed his campaign boldly and carefully, enlisting the aid of two members of the Washington delegation, Congressman William E. Humphrey and Senator Samuel H. Piles. He also brought in Major Hiram M. Chittenden, the U.S. Army district engineer, as well as a close friend, Samuel Hill, the persuasive, well-known Washington and Oregon entrepreneur and bon vivant. Matters drifted until 1907, during which time the War Department consistently refused to issue a permit allowing the city to tunnel under Fort Lawton. "It is going to be necessary to introduce a bill, and pass it too," Thomson wrote to Humphrey in October, in order to grant Seattle the authority to "tunnel under a portion of the extreme northwest corner" of Fort Lawton.

Both Humphrey and Piles worked for passage of the bill but the War Department withheld its assent to the legislation.[44]

Thomson suspected that Fort Lawton's commandant, Colonel T.C. Woodbury, was blocking any action on the sewer tunnel despite his courteous manner. During the struggle over the tunnel, Woodbury transferred to Vancouver Barracks, Washington, but he retained command of Fort Lawton and control over decisions regarding it. During and after a conference with Woodbury at Vancouver Barracks, Thomson wrote, "it had become very clear to me that he had definitely planned to compel the City of Seattle" to buy "Fort Lawton for Park purposes" because Woodbury believed the grounds were "unsuited" to U.S. Army use. Further, Woodbury wanted the city to purchase "another tract of ground, which just suited him," for a new post. Until the city met his wishes, Thomson believed, Woodbury would continue his opposition to the sewer tunnel. Thomson's assessment probably was correct. Colonel Woodbury was most likely holding the city hostage to his desire for another post. In any case, he continued to oppose the sewer.[45]

At the conference, Woodbury "talked very pleasantly," agreed with Thomson that the proposed outfall location "was for the best interests of all," and insisted that the army officer in charge of the area lighthouse district objected to the tunnel. Thomson informed Senator Piles, and Piles requested Secretary of War William Howard Taft to have the head of the lighthouse district investigate the situation. The lighthouse officer and Thomson went over the ground, taking "a very careful observation of all the surroundings." The officer assured Thomson of his support for the outfall, and informed him of his "impression that Col. Woodbury would also, now make a favorable report." But Woodbury's report was hardly favorable. Not only did Woodbury not reveal his belief in the inadequacy of Fort Lawton for military purposes, he reiterated a statement condemning the proposed outfall for its destructive effect on the post's swimming and bathing beach. He made the statement despite the fact that the garrison did not use that stretch of the shore for swimming. He criticized the outfall despite the city's careful study of currents—a study demonstrating that Thomson's proposed location would have the least impact on any and every bathing beach in Seattle.[46]

When Thomson received a copy of Colonel Woodbury's report, his reply to Woodbury stayed within the bounds of civility. Otherwise, his reaction was volcanic: "I am unable to determine whether the gentleman has lost his mind, or whether he is attempting to deliberately job me," he wrote to Piles. To Samuel Hill, then in Washington, D.C., lobbying for the outfall, he seethed about the report, "the most idiotic and contemptible statement and distortion of facts that I have ever seen." Thomson refused to have anything further to do Woodbury, for "I don't know what to do with a man, holding a place of public trust, who is a hypocrite." Instead, he had already determined, as he told Hill, "to keep this thing going until they give us the outfall to get rid of us." He appealed to Major Chittenden, who acquiesced in an independent study of the tides, if Thomson provided the funding directly to him. Chittenden would pay his independent expert from those funds without revealing their source, and the expert would report only to Chittenden. After receiving a report from his expert confirming Dehley's findings, Chittenden toured the beach at various times with his expert and with Thomson's skilled photographer, Asahel Curtis, who made a panoramic photograph of the beach. By doing these things, Chittenden made a great concession to Thomson, an indication of his growing friendship with the city engineer and of his increasing enchantment with Seattle and its surroundings. The sewer was a major matter for Thomson, but a minor concern for Chittenden, who was wrestling with what was almost certainly relapsing and remitting multiple sclerosis, and who himself was battling for numerous significant projects, most importantly the Lake Washington–Lake Union Ship Canal.[47]

Meanwhile, Piles, Humphrey, and Hill were busy discrediting Woodbury and pressuring the War Department for another review of the sewer situation. Humphrey prevailed on Secretary Taft to submit the question to Chittenden, whose favorable report at last broke the legislative logjam. A bill granting Seattle the right to build the tunnel passed Congress in April. The city council accepted the congressional conditions in May. Thomson acclaimed the work of Senator Piles and of Will H. Parry, a local politician and businessman who had warned him about Woodbury, but he reserved his highest praise for Representative Humphrey and Chittenden. "Mr. Humphrey is the one who stood by the guns and fought the bill through." Chittenden, he declared, "is a prince among men and one of the most loyal friends that the City of Seattle ever had." At last the city's outfall needed only its construction.[48]

Any review of Thomson's work must deal with his strident criticism of Benezette Williams, whose 1891 sewer plan became the basis for Seattle's drainage development. Heber's criticism of Williams by name in his autobiography is unusual. Typically, Thomson provided the names of those people with whom he disagreed only if they later came around to his point of view, for which conversion both they and he received full credit. Others were granted anonymity, while still others were ignored. Why Williams should be the target of such treatment is not self-evident. Perhaps Thomson may have believed that he or his cousin F.H. "Harry" Whitworth should have been called to consult the city on sewage or water supply. His attacks on Williams' plans for tapping Cedar River water are even more scathing (see chapter 6). But the fact that the city did not select local men, who had little direct experience in sewage and water matters except in Seattle, and little enough there, could be expected. Unquestionably, Thomson believed in his own ability, but it is doubtful whether he believed himself qualified at the time to consult the city on so significant a matter. It is more likely that Thomson's disapproval of Williams resulted from a perceived affront to his cousin Harry. Williams had challenged cousin Harry's position regarding Seattle's water supply, a serious transgression in Thomson's eyes that he could not forgive, even after the passage of more than half a century.

Thomson's bill of particulars against Williams consisted of two points. First, the Chicago engineer advocated emptying sewage into Lake Washington, then the major source of the city's drinking water. Williams made a bad idea worse when he underestimated the natural drainage into Lake Washington by at least 5,200 acres. Second, Williams arranged for sewage to run into Elliott Bay, instead of Thomson's selected spot of "perpetual outflow," the Magnolia Bluff area—later the object of his successful struggle for a sewer outfall. The places Williams selected would return some sewage to shore. When the Board of Public Works invited public comment on Williams' plans and Thomson objected to his locations, Williams supposedly retorted, "that young man has a lot to learn yet. You just forget his theories, and go ahead." [49]

The best that may be said for Thomson's criticism is that it is unfair. If Thomson challenged the Williams plan before the board of Public Works, he could not have done so in 1889, as he claimed, because the board did not exist until the following year. Dating errors are fairly common in his memoirs and in any event are a minor matter. What is more to the point is his statement that Williams did not refer to a map while making up his sewer districts. In fact, Williams did so, and while it is true that he limited what he termed the Lake Washington District to 800 acres, he recommended intercepting sewers to carry sewage away from the lake in almost all other areas naturally draining

into it. Thomson, in fact, followed the Williams program in those sections of the city. The only other exception was a relatively small part in the southwestern area of the lake shore, a location undeveloped at the time. It is true that Williams recommended discharging some sewage into Lake Washington, and into Lake Union and Green Lake for that matter. But if, as Thomson claimed, it was already necessary to boil Lake Washington water, then the additional sewage could have made little difference to water customers. Indeed, Thomson recommended sending sewer overflows into the lake just as soon as its level was lowered, following the construction of the ship canal. [50]

Concerning sewage into Elliott Bay and other parts of Puget Sound, the problem could not wait upon an ideal solution. Something had to be done to save the city from the surface sewage flowing into Lake Union and over Front Street. Williams' call for a tunnel from Lake Union to the bay and an interceptor along Front Street echoed Waring's earlier suggestions. It was better to have an imperfect solution than none; better to act than to wait for the protracted confirmation of an untested theory. Besides, Williams foresaw a time when washed-up sewage could become "objectionable." If the time came, Seattle would "carry out disposal works" to "deliver the sewage well out into the main channel of the Sound," where it would be dispersed without "serious effect upon the main body of water." Williams may or may not have told the Board of Public Works that Thomson was ignorant—"You just forget his theories, and go ahead"—it actually was excellent advice under the circumstances. [51]

Finally, Thomson's autobiographical condemnation of the Williams plan hardly comports with his contemporaneous view of its value. In only one instance did he criticize a type of sewer outlet favored by Williams as not "in accord with economy and common sense." At other times, he recommended sewers because they agreed with the Williams plan. "The sewers asked for in the accompanying petition are in conformity with the Benezette Williams plans," he informed the Board of Public Works in November 1892. On another occasion, he wrote the board about a sewer laid down contrary to the Williams plan, a sewer that "should be taken up and replaced according to the system." In 1894 he told the *Engineering Record* that the Lake Union tunnel conformed to the "Williams plan." The same year, in a letter to James J. Hill, he described Williams as "the eminent engineer of Chicago." In 1895 he discussed the difficulties with the Pike Street sewer, which backed up "during heavy storms." "Mr. Benezette Williams foresaw this state of affairs and his plan provides relief," Thomson informed the Board of Public Works. Yet more than half a century later, Thomson leveled what came close to an ad hominem attack on Williams, an attack against a man whose work he once praised and few readers would have recalled. His scorn is incomprehensible, except as a defense of a relative whom he much admired, Harry Whitworth.[52]

Thomson's difficulties and quarrels aside, the sewer system was enormously important for him and for Seattle. The North Trunk Sewer secured his reputation while his rescue of sewer projects following the "Who cut the stick" fiasco confirmed his financial probity. Critics then and later disputed both his expertise and his financial acumen but none were able to overturn his position in Seattle. The enormous expansion of the sewer system helped to secure Seattle's standing as a healthy city, while it matched the city's stupendous growth in the late 19th and early 20th centuries. At the end of 1892, the sewers totaled 18.5 miles and were utterly inadequate to the city's needs. By 1902 sewer length passed 75 miles, and by the end of Thomson's administration had become a system of 358 miles. There was much to be done, and in the nature of things, all that could be done with the funding and technology of 1911 would not be enough. Nevertheless, Seattle's 1911 population of some 240,000 received much better sewer service than did its 45,000 citizens of 1892. Sewers were expensive, especially as their costs were piled on top of those for street regrading and paving, and for retiring city bonds. To a correspondent who complained of the high cost and location of a branch of the North Trunk Sewer, Thomson defended the route as the most economical and practical, while admitting that it was expensive. "High prices are a natural concomitant of the rapid growth of the city," he explained, "and prevail in other commercial lines as well as in constructing." Expensive but essential, the sewers enabled the city's continued expansion.[53]

Notes

1. For example, Richard C. Berner, *Seattle 1900–1920: From Boomtown, Urban Turbulence, to Restoration* (Seattle: Charles Press, 1991) includes nothing about sewers, and has no entry for them in an otherwise elaborate index. The title is vol. 1 in the series, *Seattle in the Twentieth Century*, but it frequently discusses 19th-century issues in the early chapters. Klingle, *Emerald City*, pays some attention to sewers, see, for example, 89–90, 93.

2. For sewage problems in general, see Joel A. Tarr, "Sewerage and the Development of the Networked City in the United States, 1850–1930," in Tarr and Gabriel Dupuy, eds., *Technology and the Rise of the Networked City in Europe and America* (Philadelphia: Temple University Press, 1988), 159–85; and Jon A. Peterson, "The Impact of Sanitary Reform upon American Urban Planning: 1840–1890," in Donald A. Kruecheberg, ed., *Introduction to Planning History in the United States* (New Brunswick, NJ: Center for Urban Policy Research, 1983), 13–39.

3. Tarr, "Sewerage and the Networked City," 162 for quotation, but see also 162–63.

4. Ibid., 169–71.

5. Struve, *Annual Message of the Mayor of the City of Seattle…30 June 1883* (Seattle: C. Hanford, 1883), 13–14.

6. Ibid., 16–17, quotation on 17.

7. *Annual Message of the Mayor of the City of Seattle for the Fiscal Year Ending 30 June 1884* (Seattle: C. Hanford, 1884), 16. Snow's quotations are from the report of the city surveyor contained in the mayor's annual message, 51. Snow's recommendation is on 50.

8. For quotation, see RHT's report in *Annual Message of the Mayor of the City of Seattle, Washington Territory…1886* (Seattle: Lowman and Hanford, 1886), 37–38.

9. For quotations, see the report of Laurence Cummings, in *Annual Message of the Mayor of the City of Seattle for the Fiscal Year Ending 31 May 1889* (Seattle: Koch and Oakley, 1889) 43–44.

10. For quotations, see Scurry, "Report of the city Surveyor," in *Annual Message of the Mayor, 1889* 49, and also 47–50.

11. Tarr, "Sewerage and the Networked City," 135.

12. Quoted in Martin V. Melosi, *The Sanitary City: Urban Infrastructure in America from Colonial Times to the Present* (Baltimore: Johns Hopkins University Press, 2000), 157.

13. Peterson, "Impact of Sanitary Reform," 18; and Tarr, "Sewerage and the Networked City," 137–38.

14. For the "sewer gas" theory, see Tarr, "Sewerage and the Networked City," 137–38.

15. For aspects of Waring's program, see Melosi, *Sanitary City*, 53, 93–94; and Peterson, "Impact of Sanitary Reform," 17.

16. Melosi, *Sanitary City*, 153–56.

17. Ibid., 153–60.

18. Ibid., and Tarr, "Sewerage and the Networked City," 140–48. For Waring in Seattle, see the *Seattle Post-Intelligencer*, December 1, 1888, hereafter cited as *P-I*.

19. For Waring quotation, see *P-I*, December 1, 1888. Scurry is quoted in the *Seattle Daily Press*, March 23, 1889. For the council's action, see *Journal of the Proceedings of the Common Council of the City of Seattle*, March 22, 1889, p. 764, SMA.

20. Tarr, "Sewerage and the Networked City," 146.

21. Williams, "Appendix to Annual Report of Reginald H. Thomson, City Engineer, for the Year 1894, Including the Report on Proposed Sewerage System for the City of Seattle, Submitted by Benezette Williams, C.E., August, 1891," 2–4. City of Seattle, Engineering Department, file 248, North Trunk Sewer, 1891–1914, in Damage Cases, 1891–1914, box 1, Puget Sound Regional Archives of the Washington State Archives, hereafter PSRA. "City of Seattle" hereafter omitted, 2–4.

22. Ibid., 4–5.

23. Ibid., 5–6, for quotations, see 6 and 16.

24. Ibid., 10, 11–12, 17.

25. Ibid., for quotation, see 8, and also 12. For dilution, see Melosi, *Sanitary City*, 162–65.

26. RHT, "Sketches," 1892 entry, 1602-2, box 2, folder 10, RHT Papers, UW.

27. Gardner to Board of Public Works, 5 February 1891 (first quotation); Gardner to Williams, 9 March 1891 (second quotation); Gardner to Williams, 27 March 1891 (third quotation); and Gardner to Williams, 10 April 1891 (fourth quotation), all in City Engineer's Correspondence, 1890–1898, book 1, PSRA.

28. Ibid., Gardner to Williams 16 March 1891; and Gardner to Williams, 8 July 1891. See, for quotations, Phelps, *Public Works in Seattle*, 188.

29. "Report of the Board of Health," in *Seattle Municipal Reports for the Fiscal Year Ending December 31, 1891* (Seattle: Koch and Oakley, 1892) 282–83.

30. RHT, *That Man Thomson*, 33–34.

31. Gardner to Board of Public Works, 13 May 1892, City Engineer's Correspondence, book 1, PSRA. RHT report to the Board of Public Works, n.d. but mid-October 1892, 992843, SMA.

32. Aspects of the North Tunnel sewer are in Phelps, *Public Works in Seattle*, 188–89; *Seattle Telegraph*, July 3, 1892; "Report of the City Engineer," in "Report of the Board of Public Works," in *Seattle Municipal Reports for the Fiscal Year Ending December 31, 1892* (Seattle: Koch and Oakley, 1893) 209–12; the address of the mayor, in *Seattle Municipal Reports for the Fiscal Year Ending December 31, 1893* (Seattle: Sunset, 1894); and *P-I*, September 16, 1901.

33. RHT to City Council, 5 December 1892, 990598, SMA; and RHT to Board of Public Works, 14 January 1895 City Engineer's Correspondence, book 4, PSRA.

34. For quotation, see RHT, *That Man Thomson*, 40. For RHT's policy, see RHT to Mrs. Pierce, 18 August [1893], City Engineer's Correspondence, book 3, PSRA.

35. RHT, "Sketches," 1894 entry, 1602-2, box 2, folder 10, RHT Papers, UW.

36. RHT, *That Man Thomson*, 41.

37. Ibid. For a discussion of sewage problems in Washington, D.C., which places the Seattle problems in context, see Alan Lessoff, *The Nation and Its City: Politics, "Corruption," and Progress in Washington, D.C., 1861–1902* (Baltimore: Johns Hopkins University Press, 1994), 44–129. Warner's only report to the council provided the cost of the North and South sewer tunnels but included no information on their progress, *Seattle Telegraph*, January 26, 1894.

38. RHT, *That Man Thomson*, 41–42.

39. Sewer problems generated a heavy correspondence. For examples, see RHT to J.G. [*sic*] Ronald, 14 March 1894, City Engineer's Correspondence, book 3; and RHT to Board of Public Works, 14 January 1895, book 4, PSRA. For a comprehensive explanation, see RHT to J.T. Roland [*sic*], 20 January 1908, 89/1, box 2, book 5, RHT Papers, UW.

40. Rockafeller, "Public Health in Progressive Seattle," 40–43. For the North Trunk Sewer, see RHT to Fred Johnson, 14 November 1910, 89/1, box 3, book 9, RHT Papers, UW. A narrative and chronology of the sewers is in Phelps, *Public Works in Seattle*, 186–92.

41. RHT to John Millis, 10 August 1904, 89/1, box 1, book 3, RHT Papers, UW.

42. For quotation, see RHT, *That Man Thomson*, 43; and for RHT's account of the work, 43–47.

43. Ibid., and "Outline of Address Given by Mr. Blackwell Before the Board of Public Works, City Council and others, in the Mayor's office, July 16, 1925," in City of Seattle, Engineering Administrative Services, subject files, box 23, folder 2, PSRA.

44. Those developments may be traced in many letters in 89/1, box 2, book 5, RHT Papers, UW, including the letter to Humphrey, 7 October 1907.

45. For "unsuited" quotation, see RHT to Woodbury, 24 March 1908, 89/1, box 2, book 5, RHT Papers, UW. Other quotations are in RHT to Humphrey, 17 April 1908, 89/1, box 2, book 5, RHT Papers, UW.

46. For quotation, see RHT to Piles, 3 March 1908. Other pertinent letters are to Woodbury, 24 March 1908; and to Chittenden, 31 March 1908, all in 89/1, box 2, book 5, RHT Papers, UW.

47. RHT to Woodbury, 24 March 1908; to Piles, 25 March 1910; and to Hill, 26 March 1908; 89/1, box 2, book 5, RHT Papers, UW. For Hill's lobbying, see *P-I*, March 22, 1908. For Chittenden, see Gordon B. Dodds, *Hiram Martin Chittenden: His Public Career* (Lexington: University Press of Kentucky, 1973), 128–43, 204.

48. On Humphrey, see RHT to Parry, 30 April 1908; and on Chittenden, RHT to Humphrey, 30 April 1908, 89/1, box 2, book 5, RHT Papers, UW.

49. RHT, *That Man Thomson* 42–43, 47. For quotation, see 43.

50. Williams, "Report on Proposed Sewerage System," 10–12. RHT's recommendation is in his letter to C. Malmo, 6 October 1910, 89/1, box 3, book 9, RHT Papers, UW.

51. Williams, "Report on Proposed Sewerage System," 12–13.

52. For first quotation, see RHT to Board of Public Works, 12 October 1892, City Engineer's Correspondence, 2602-2, book 2, PSRA. For second quotation, see RHT to Board of Public Works, 18 November 1892, City Engineer's Correspondence, 2602-2, book 2. For third quotation, see RHT to Board of Public Works, 9 November 1892, City Engineer's Correspondence, 2602-2, book 2, PSRA. RHT to *Engineering Record*, 27 April 1894, City Engineer's Correspondence, book 3; RHT to Hill, 27 July 1894, book 3; and RHT to Board of Public Works, 4 January 1895, Office of the City Engineer, *Reports*, book 1, PSRA.

53. Rockafeller, "Public Health in Seattle," 91, and see 40–43 for an appraisal of the yearly work of RHT from a public health standpoint. Report of the City Engineer, in report of the Board of Public Works, in *Seattle Municipal Reports for the Fiscal Year Ending December 31, 1892* (Seattle: Koch and Oakley, 1893), 217. For 1911 mileage, see the chart "Sewers" in A.H. Dimock, "Annual Report of the City Engineer to Mayor George W. Dilling, December 26, 1911," Engineering Department Administration, Annual Reports 1900–1954, box 1, PSRA.

Cedar Lake on the upper Cedar River, located southeast of Seattle in the Cascade Range. *Seattle Municipal Archives #5914.*

6
Cedar River Water System

IN THOMSON'S MIND the Cedar River water system was his greatest triumph, and his most essential victory. Sewers were necessary, to be sure, but only to carry away urban detritus. Thomson's greatest goal was to "attract population and encourage business and trade." How should the goal be achieved? There were surely many means to the end, but one overrode the rest. "It seemed obvious to me, as well as to many others, that a plentiful supply of pure water was a prime requisite for the growth of the city." It had to be universally available, so that "every citizen would be able to have water and have it at a cost he could afford."[1]

The chapter in *That Man Thomson* from which the quote is taken validates his critical concern in other ways. The chapter on Cedar River water is the longest by far, and the locus of some of his most vigorous writing. For the second and last time, he invoked his father, who had "drilled" into him the fact that clean, abundant water was "the life blood of a city." "Father," he wrote, "was once healed of some sickness by" clean water and ever after preached the gospel of pure water and air. The "sickness" could have been one of a number of food or water borne illnesses and his father's recovery probably was incidental to clean water. What is reasonably certain is that the disease occurred during Harrison Thomson's early life and was not one of those readily identified by its symptoms, such as typhoid fever.[2] Whatever the reality of his father's illness, Thomson demonstrated his filial piety, as well as his commitment to private enterprise, urban expansion, and national and international trade.

Otherwise, the chapter is reliable in its broad outlines. Private water sources, even after purchase and supervision by the city, supplied inadequate amounts for firefighting, the city's projected consumption, and purity. Sewer planner Benezette Williams had drawn up an 1889 scheme for tapping Rock Creek, a tributary of the Cedar River, for Seattle's water supply. Subsequently, in an 1891 report he shifted to the Cedar River itself, a Cascades tributary that flowed into the Black River near the south end of Lake Washington. After Thomson became city engineer, there were no funds to develop the Cedar

River works, but he hired a former associate, George F. Cotterill, to work on plans for a financially self-sustaining system. Meanwhile he and others surveyed Benezette Williams' proposed route and construction, concluding that both were inadequate. Thomson wrote about encountering "disputed and lost corners" in the Williams survey and other problems, making it a "paper theory" requiring "practical demonstration upon the ground." In any case, the severe post-1893 economic depression (which Thomson does not mention) and a city treasurer's defalcation limited what could be done. None of that prevented Seattleites from debating the issue of public versus private water development, Thomson from developing far-seeing plans for an intra-city distribution system, or George Cotterill from working out a plan for repaying the cost of the system from its revenues.[3]

A breakthrough began in August 1895 when the partisans for municipal ownership received word of a state supreme court case allowing the City of Spokane to finance a water system with revenue bonds. Thomson, Cotterill, and their council allies put through an ordinance in October allowing for a public vote on a municipal water system. After a hard fight, the voters endorsed the ordinance in December. Location surveys, descriptions of the land to be acquired through condemnation, and detailed specifications followed. At last, in 1898, all was ready for bidding, but only one bid was received and opened in November. Thomson regarded it with suspicion; the bidder and the city council rewrote some provisions of the contract. The Board of Public Works was directed to accept it. Meanwhile, Robert Moran, who as mayor had hired Benezette Williams, secured an injunction against the contract. The case was carried to the state supreme court, which invalidated the bid.[4]

The Board of Public Works let new contracts in April 1899. However, an attorney for the president of a Snoqualmie Falls power company, at a point about 25 miles east of the city limits, sued to prevent construction of the Cedar River system. The power company also wanted to sell water to the city. Thomson, as he often does, omits the background and salient points of this matter in his recollections, but he is correct in declaring that the suit failed. Next, Thomson had to force the suppliers to bring their work up to specifications. Two capable assistants, M.W. Glenn and Henry W. Scott, oversaw construction. They finished their work at the end of 1900, and in January 1901 the city received the first Cedar River water. This pipeline served as the foundation for a water supply that by 1945 provided as much as 161,000,000 gallons per day to Seattle and its suburbs. It was a far cry from Benezette Williams' guess that Seattle could get along with 10,000,000 gallons for "a great many years." Finally, Thomson saw the need to secure the watershed from pollution. Working with others, he laid the groundwork for city and federal cooperation to that end. [5] So runs Thomson's account.

What the reader of Thomson's memoirs would lack, even if he or she diligently supplemented Thomson's account with other published sources, is a deep understanding of the 1895 vote, or the bases for the lawsuits against the city. The reader would assume, incorrectly, that Benezette Williams was a poor hydrological engineer who failed to comprehend Seattle's future. He or she would credit Thomson with understanding the dangers of watershed pollution from the outset, a credit he does not deserve. None of this suggests that Thomson often deliberately misled his reader—note, for example, his careful discussion of stave and steel pipes. He treats Williams unfairly, however, for a reason already suggested—that "Cousin Harry" Whitworth should have had the contract for the proposed sewer and water systems. There is no direct evidence for this assertion, save Thomson's high regard for his cousin's comprehension of engineering problems, and of his grasp of the topography of Seattle and its environs. An analysis even less kind to Thomson would suggest that Thomson himself coveted the job given to Williams or, at least, expected to be Whitworth's assistant in the enterprise, but there is no clear evidence for such a conclusion. [6]

ഇരു

The beginning point for any discussion of the new system is the Cedar River itself. The stream's north fork rises in Yakima Pass near Tinkham Peak in the Cascade Range at an elevation of about 2,500 feet. Some six riverine miles later, it joins with the south fork to flow another 40 miles or so to the south end of Lake Washington (after modification, the final 1¾ miles flowed rather ignominiously between the banks of the Cedar River Waterway). When Thomson undertook the task of bringing its water to Seattle, the Cedar flowed to the Black River, then Lake Washington's natural outlet. (That arrangement would end in 1916, when the lake level was lowered ten feet with the opening to the northwest of the Lake Washington Waterway and the Montlake cut, designed to give the lake access to and from Puget Sound.) Meanwhile, the Cedar tumbled and fell through rough, broken, heavily forested areas almost impenetrable to humans. Twelve miles from its source, it entered Cedar Lake, then 1,530 feet above sea level, next roiling along for many more miles until it reached the broad valley south of Lake Washington. Its basin comprised 240 square miles, with the watershed being some 140 square miles, mostly in the upper three-fifths of its basin. [7]

The Cedar was considered a source for gravity-supplied water long before much else was known about it. The ultimate success of the Cedar system generated the usual paternity claims. Clarence B. Bagley, the much-cited chronicler of Seattle's past, awarded the palm to the weekly *Fin-Back* for a Christmas Day prediction in 1880. The next year, Harry Whitworth, in his role as city surveyor, endorsed the project. A prior claim comes from the biographer of the pioneer leader John J. McGilvra. Because McGilvra will be heard from again, it is important to understand his enthusiasm for Cedar River water, an avidity dating from 1878 at the latest. In that year, a campaign biography supporting his run for the territorial senate referred to him as "an ardent supporter" of moving Cedar River water to Seattle. Whatever the claims for Cedar River paternity, the basics of gravity water systems—those that began at a higher point and end at a lower—were in place before Seattle's founding. Such systems included aqueducts, conduits, reservoirs, and distribution mains, and, where necessary, pumps. Pumps and pressure piping improved during the years that Seattle's residents struggled with water supply issues. By the time of Benezette Williams' arrival in 1889, a panoply of apparatus, including standpipes, and in the home, distribution pipes, bathtubs, water closet toilets, and sinks, was available if not widely diffused. Antibacterial treatment of water was yet in its infancy, and filtration little used except by households wealthy and wise enough to install and maintain individual systems. [8]

The problem for Seattle's government was that it had no means of ordering up the technology. Municipal debt was too great, and there were other problems and issues beginning with Mayor Robert Moran's call for a possible municipal system. On September 28, 1888, Moran asked the city council to investigate the possibility, and the council turned to its fire and water committee. The committee dispatched John G. Scurry, the city

Cedar Lake Dam, December 12, 1911. *Seattle Municipal Archives #5915.*

surveyor, to report on the cost of a gravity system from Rock Creek, a tributary located about 12 miles from the Cedar River's junction with the Black River. On October 19, Scurry recommended a system he estimated to cost just under $765,000. The day before, the fire and water committee, evidently having access to Scurry's as yet undated report, urged the mayor and council to hold a $1,000,000 bond election in November to fund construction of the system. The higher figure from the council committee may be explained in part because Scurry included no land acquisition costs in his budget. A lapse of less than three weeks from the mayor's initial request to the council and the council's response, to say nothing of Scurry's oddly post-dated report, suggests that the groundwork for all of this was carefully laid in advance. The council's probable pre-selection of Rock Creek as the source of supply suggests it was the farthest accessible point up the Cedar basin where a swiftly flowing stream could be diverted into a pipeline in quick time and at minimum expense.[9]

Legal reasons postponed the bond vote until July 1889. Meanwhile, the great fire struck in June 1889, engulfing the ramshackle wharves, incinerating the business district, and indicting the city's hapless fire department and its woefully inadequate water supply.

Not surprisingly, the voters overwhelmingly approved the bonds. But the bonds voted in July would never be issued because, in the next month, the state constitutional convention limited city debt to, in effect, 5 percent of assessed property valuations. With Seattle's valuations reduced to rubble with the destruction of most of its expensive property, the $1,000,000 worth of bonds would have been over the debt limit.[10]

The alternative was to purchase and improve private water works, especially the largest, the Spring Hill system. By then, Benezette Williams was in town. Among other tasks, he evaluated the Spring Hill works, then helped the city buy it. The city completed the purchase early in 1890, selling bonds for the purpose. The voters also approved bonds to expand the Spring Hill system's pumping capacity on the western shore of Lake Washington. The city established a water fund to absorb revenues from water rates, pay the expenses of operation, and retire the bonds issued for purchasing and expanding the system.[11]

From the end of 1890 and for more than ten years, Lake Washington served as Seattle's main municipal water source. Yet the attraction of the Cedar River never diminished. Understanding the goal of moving away from pumping Lake Washington water to using a Cedar

River gravity system involves a comprehensive examination of the transcendent circumstances involved. Of first importance, no responsible person argued that pumping water from Lake Washington was a permanent solution for the city. All agreed, implicitly at least, that further urbanization of the lakeshore would render Washington's water unfit to drink. Besides, pumping was expensive. The question was not whether the city would shift to the Cedar River, but when.

The national economic cycle affected the timing of the shift. Hard times began in 1893 with a "tide of failures and disasters which swept down upon the city during the latter part of the year."[12] The hard times lifted decisively with the arrival of the steamer *Portland* from Alaska with a "ton of gold" and confirmation of the big Klondike strike in the Yukon. Seattle became the Alaska-Klondike entrepôt. Through a combination of shrewd advertising, favorable geography, developed rail and maritime transportation, and luck, it surpassed Tacoma, Portland, San Francisco, and other contenders for that trade.[13] Reviving national and regional commerce erased the depression but spiked the demand for everything in Seattle, water included.

Other crosscurrents in play included debate about who would collect and distribute water, and whether, or how, power production could be linked to the water supply. Advocates of municipal control and of private ownership contested these issues, until they were finally settled in favor of the city—first, for water, and later, for electric power. Finally, the law—whether constitutional, legislative, or judicial—determined what could be done to advance Seattle's municipal water works.

All of which returns us to the first effort to create a gravity supply and to John G. Scurry's efforts of October 1888. His report presented the fundamentals of a gravity system in a brief, readable form. The first fundamental for any gravity system was a sufficient "head" or height above the city to carry water to its distribution point, allowing a gravity flow to most or all water customers. Scurry planned a headworks (a diversion dam, settling basin, the mouth of a water carriage pipe, and other apparatus) at a point on Rock Creek about 500 feet above high tide at Seattle. Water from the creek would flow parallel to the Cedar River near its south bank, cross the Cedar River-Black River valley, and ascend the ridge bisecting the city, "which it follows to a point on high ground near Seattle, to be selected as a site for a distributing reservoir." The site probably was at or near the present reservoirs on Beacon Hill, then south of the city

limits. Scurry estimated the "total fall from headworks to reservoir" at about 300 feet.[14]

Next, he addressed the issue of purity. Scurry conducted no tests of the water. The testing available in 1888 would not have revealed much, although the connection between polluted water and diseases such as typhoid was empirically known. He advocated Rock Creek because its course was "unfitted for agriculture or lumbering and not likely to be contaminated by manufacturing or settlement to any injurious extent. I know of no stream more eligibly situated for supplying the city with pure water." Time proved Scurry wrong about "injurious" intrusions but his judgment was reasonable then. Moreover, Scurry recommended a 30-inch steel pipe to carry water from the headworks to the reservoir, making it safe from pollution. The pipeline, if not the Rock Creek headworks, would be an important precedent for Thomson.[15]

Third, Scurry estimated that the gravity system could supply far more water than the Lake Washington plant. At a time when the Spring Hill works pumped at best 2,500,000 gallons daily, Scurry figured the capacity of a 30-inch pipe at 10,000,000 gallons, enough to supply a population of 100,000 with 100 gallons per person per day, though his per capita estimate proved conservative even for 1888. On the other hand, in the late 1880s Seattle probably stood shy of its 1890 population, 43,000, not to mention its swollen Klondike and post depression 1900 enumeration of 81,000. Even allowing for the typical census undercount, these numbers were considerably less than a population of 100,000 when Scurry wrote, and would remain so for a number of years thereafter. He was on safe ground when asserting that his program would "amply meet all requirements for two or three years at least."[16]

Finally, Scurry looked forward to the expansion of the system. He estimated the flow of Rock Creek at between 550,000 and 650,000 gallons per hour, and probably more. A flow near his tentative upper limit would increase the city's supply by a third or greater. If the 30-inch pipe alone could not meet the city's needs, adding a second pipe would. He did not mention the lakes near the Cedar River but one or more of them could be used to impound and deliver water. Additional reservoirs also could be built in the city. Mayor Moran's call for the July 1889 vote left open the possibility of expanding Scurry's program as well as making other changes. Moran's proposal mentioned a "distributing reservoir or reservoirs," and a water supply from "such lake, stream, creek, or other watercourse" as the council should decide.[17]

To his credit, John Scurry had defined the basics of any gravity system—adequate fall, purity protection, sufficient supply, and the possibility of expansion. Not that he had all the answers. As Thomson's chapter on water indicated, Rock Creek was eventually abandoned, and, in any event, the council never endorsed Rock Creek. Scurry underestimated the practical distance between Rock Creek and a serviceable reservoir, either because of an inadequate survey, or because he wished to conceal the true cost of the pipeline, or both. His assumption that there would never be a threat to the purity of the water supply was naïve. Also, a Rock Creek plan would limit any expansion plans to that source. But whatever the limitations, Scurry had made a beginning.

Benezette Williams built on Scurry's work. Arriving in October 1889, and with Scurry's assistance, he submitted a "preliminary report" to Moran and the council, dated November 12. Williams endorsed Scurry's choice of Rock Creek but made several significant additions to the plan. For one thing, he published earlier tests of Lake Washington and Rock Creek water, revealing that Lake Washington water contained "2.68 grains of organic matter per gallon, while that for Rock Creek shows but a trace." The disparity between the two would grow. In an oblique reference to a future ship canal, Williams mentioned the lake's potential as "the fresh water harbor for Puget Sound shipping." Whether or not that development occurred, the population and pollution around the lake were bound to increase, rendering what Scurry called the "tepid and unwholesome waters of Lake Washington" becoming increasingly unfit. [18]

Williams abandoned Scurry's plan to run water directly from Rock Creek to a reservoir near the city. Instead, he proposed turning the water into Swan Lake (now Lake Youngs), some six miles west and a little north of the mouth of Rock Creek. The lake would become the "impounding reservoir" for the system. At 475 feet above Puget Sound's high tide mark, the lake would provide enough elevation for a headworks. To meet what he regarded as a needed volume of 25,000,000 gallons per day, he proposed including three small lakes near Swan Lake into the system. Those three—Wilderness, Pipe, and Spoon (now Shadow) lakes—would supplement Swan Lake's 600 acres. Williams did not cite Scurry's figures on the flow from Rock Creek. Assuming a volume of 50,000 gallons an hour above Scurry's high estimate—an

estimate that Scurry himself considered conservative—Rock Creek would supply 16,800,000 gallons per day if all of it were diverted to Swan Lake. While this was far short of the "nearly enough" [19] for Williams' 25,000,000 gallons, he was probably correct that the lakes, if drawn down, would supply the needed additional 8,200,000 or so gallons per day. Of course, the lakes could not be emptied at such a rate for more than a few months, especially not the relatively small Wilderness, Pipe, and Spoon lakes. Williams' latter reports called for a dam at Swan Lake to raise its acreage to 800, the better to supply the city. [20] In any case, the 25,000,000 gallons would not be needed right away.

What is important to remember is that Williams rejected Scurry's reliance on a figure of 10,000,000 gallons for use each day and upped it to a minimum of 25,000,000 gallons. This set the stage for Thomson's attacks on Williams' water reports. According to Thomson's memory, Whitworth read a copy of Williams' preliminary report, dropped his work at the mines east of Seattle, and came to town to inform Williams that Rock Creek could not produce even 10,000,000 gallons per day. When Williams disputed Whitworth's assertion, Whitworth checked Williams' figures and discovered a misplaced decimal point. With the decimal in the right place, Rock Creek's flow was shown to be 1,000,000 gallons a day. Even so, Whitworth said, Seattle's needs would be closer to 100,000,000 gallons per day. Thus chastised, Williams put his engineering forces back in the field, "withdrew" his first report, and in a second statement confirmed the wisdom of Whitworth's choice of the Cedar River. [21]

Swan Lake (now Lake Youngs), located several miles southeast of Renton, was included in early plans for the Cedar River gravity system. Thomson bypassed it because of concerns about costs. *Seattle Municipal Archives #50822.*

It takes nothing away from Thomson's considerable achievements to regard his "decimal point" story as utterly unbelievable. Williams' report did not rate Rock Creek at 10,000,000 gallons per day or any other gallonage. What he argued was that Rock Creek, together with four lakes, could supply 25,000,000 gallons. It was Whitworth's and Thomson's local colleague, John G. Scurry, who declared that 10,000,000 gallons were available from Rock Creek and would do in the short run. Williams' report was not withdrawn, but was instead replaced by two later, more detailed reports. There is little doubt that Rock Creek and the four lakes would have been hard pressed to supply Seattle with 25,000,000 gallons per day year around, but they probably could have done so with a dam at Swan Lake. If that were insufficient, Williams identified another tributary of the Cedar River that could have been added to the volume of water. It is likely that Whitworth staged a confrontation with Williams, but the quotation that Thomson put in cousin Harry's mouth about the decimal point is pure fancy. Finally, Williams did not turn to surveying the Cedar River or recommend the Cedar River because of Whitworth's objections. He intended to supplement his preliminary report with more thorough studies. His subsequent report named the Cedar River because tapping the Cedar was obviously simpler and cheaper than running lines from two creeks and three lakes into Swan Lake.[22]

Twice more Thomson returned to attack Williams—on the related issues of population growth and water consumption. Eight paragraphs after his fanciful account of the Williams-Whitworth encounter, he repeated his contemporaneous judgment "that Mr. Williams had no concept of the size to which Seattle would certainly grow." Near the end of his Cedar River chapter, Thomson enlarged on his earlier story of Whitworth's con-

Digging a trench in the bottom of the Black River for laying the Cedar River pipeline, October 13, 1899. *Seattle Municipal Archives #7258.*

frontation with Williams and the limitations of Williams' vision of Seattle's water use. He stated that Williams' ultimate projection for Seattle was 15,000,000 gallons. In fact, as already noted, Williams had urged the mayor and council to prepare its initial gravity system to handle 25,000,000 gallons. His second report analyzed a system designed to provide 50,000,000 gallons. Then Thomson quoted Williams' third report, in which the Chicago engineer had stated "that to provide for a new easy capacity [without straining the Lake Washington pumps] of nine or ten million gallons per day would be…the maximum limit…in the way of enlargement." While Thomson's quotation is accurate, the implication is wrong. Williams was writing only about the Lake Washington-based system, a fact that Thomson elides. Indeed, Williams predicted that by the time 8,000,000–10,000,000 gallons per day was used, the city should have the money to build its gravity system.[23]

Williams' population projections do not sustain Thomson's criticism either. Future population estimates, even at a time of soaring urban growth in the West and Far West, were largely guesswork, as Williams recognized. By late 1889, when he issued his preliminary report, Seattle's growth had surpassed Tacoma's. The city was thriving, without any premonition of the scarifying depression that lay almost four years in the future. At a time when its population was about 43,000, Williams declared that it was neither "safe nor advisable" for Seattle "to proceed with the construction of [water] works…on a basis of less than 250,000 population," a number not actually reached until after 1910. In Williams' second (February 1890) report, he noted that water use expanded with its availability, thus if "our large cities" supplied "a sufficient quantity of water, under an adequate head, the amount of water consumed by them could be vastly greater." If Seattle furnished an abundant supply, "I would prefer to predict that before the population reaches 150,000 a shortage of water will be felt." In his third (February 1891) report, Williams once more took up the population question. Projecting Seattle's growth from cities reaching a similar size "during the last two decades," he forecast a population "of at least 150,000" in ten years but also cautioned, "in six years it may reach 200,000. For my part I believe these are not extravagant expectations." They were in fact extravagant, for in 1900, the population, although it almost doubled, reached about 81,000.[24]

Whatever the value of Williams' population forecasts, they are scarcely the predictions of a man who had "no concept" of Seattle's future growth. Yet Thomson fought a running battle with Williams for almost 60 years, criticizing his fellow engineer in terms that he had to know were misleading, to say the least. However misguided his sentiments, Thomson was writing not to deliver an impartial account, but to defend "Cousin Harry" who bravely confronted Williams with the inadequacies of his estimates. "Mr. Whitworth to the end of his life kept affirming that, as no man could determine what the population might be in a reasonably near future, we should secure an almost unlimited supply of water." Thomson added, "I held the same views."[25] That Williams planned for "an almost unlimited supply" by shifting to the Cedar River cut no figure. That Williams' population estimates were overly optimistic was irrelevant. A man intensely devoted to his family, Thomson could do nothing less than support his cousin, whose great vision of Seattle's future the city fathers snubbed in favor of the outlook of an imported expert.

Thomson stood on firmer ground when criticizing Williams' means for conducting the water to its distribution points. In his first report, and the second more detailed report, Williams called for an "open channel" or "V-shaped flume" to carry water for most of the distance between the intake and Swan Lake. The flume would be a coated wooden conduit "in earth" for much of its length, but would be elevated "for about 1,700 feet of the way…from 40 to 60 feet" in order to maintain the grade. A 48-inch pipe would carry the water a relatively brief distance. Then the flume would resume, discharging into Swan Lake, dammed to raise its water level. When Thomson examined the plans he concluded that Williams "exhibited no sensible idea as to either sanitary or physical danger which would result from miles of open flume."[26]

Thomson's criticism was apt, but it took no account of the compromises inherent in any waterworks plan,

including his own later proposals. As did any other engineer, Benezette Williams had to contain costs. When he rejected Rock Creek as a source of Seattle's water, he believed that he should find a spot with a similar height on the Cedar River. Scurry, who was doing the bulk of Williams' surveys, found a location for a dam and headworks about 2½ miles above Rock Creek. The new proposed headworks location, along with the flume running westward to Swan Lake instead of a direct northwesterly route to Seattle, and piping to Williams' more realistic distribution system, significantly increased the length of the supply conduit. Scurry planned for 22 miles of line from the source to the points of distribution; Williams for 29. Assuming the grading costs for an "in earth" flume and a 48-inch pipe to be the same, the cost of the flume with its coating was less than $2.27 per foot, while the pipe cost $4.50. The 36,100 lineal feet of "in earth" flume from the Cedar to Swan Lake, running through what was then practically uninhabited country, represented a significant financial saving.[27]

Williams strove to cut costs because there were less expensive ways to bring abundant water to town. Scurry's scheme, although it delivered a lower volume initially, cost an estimated $764,380, versus the Williams plan's estimate of $1,200,793. Scurry's and Williams' systems were in no way comparable but the fact remained that Williams' plan, even with the inexpensive flume, cost over two-fifths more. As Williams surely knew, and as later Seattle events confirmed, stingy citizens were inclined to compare costs while ignoring or discounting the distinctions between different water delivery proposals. Williams needed to watch expenses for a second reason—he had to make a case for his gravity system supplanting the Lake Washington pump as soon as it was financially feasible. In his second report, Williams admitted that expanding the present Lake Washington pumping system would be cheaper than building the gravity system. He argued, however, that as water use grew, the cost of a gravity system would become more and more practical, "even if the water to be had in the two cases would always be equally pure."[28]

Thomson's attack on the Williams flume for sanitary reasons was valid, even if it resulted less from a contemporaneous assessment than it did from hindsight. Indeed, Williams does not appear to have spent much time outside of Seattle, preferring to rely on Scurry's judgments about insignificant human settlement in the near-wilderness of the upper Cedar River and around Swan Lake. Neither was Williams much concerned about potential pollution problems. Thomson, although his early responses to sanitary dangers were themselves inadequate, had a greater appreciation of the possibilities of even small settlements in remote and difficult country. His work in railroad and mining engineering, as well as his observations of timber cutting, taught him that human activity and settlement would open up virtually any country that promised an economic return. The flume in the Williams reports would have been subject to unintentional damage as well as vandalism, in addition to the risk of pollution. Williams made a mistake that Thomson rectified.[29]

The Cedar River gravity system brought water through rugged country to Seattle. Here, a section of the original pipeline undergoes testing, March 9, 1900. *Seattle Municipal Archives #7305.*

In at least three ways, though, Thomson benefited from Williams' plans. The Chicago engineer recommended wooden stave pipe for almost all the distance from Swan Lake to the distribution system, on the grounds of economy and durability. Thomson chose a different route but he adopted wood stave pipe. In the strongest language, Benezette Williams insisted on bringing the pipe beneath the Black River. "Under no circumstances should any plan of crossing above the stream be considered," he wrote. Thomson followed Williams' trenchant advice. Thirdly, Thomson accepted the Williams report's careful analysis of the reservoirs and standpipes necessary to the distribution system. Williams understood Seattle's topography as well as anyone because of his obligation to develop a functional sewer system. He planned what he called a "low gravity service district," a "high gravity service district," and a "high pumping service district" to distribute the water throughout a city rumpled with ridges and hills.[30]

The Spring Hill water company had a Beacon Hill reservoir, which the city acquired in 1890 along with the rest of the Spring Hill system. While the reservoir would do for the time being, it was too low and too small for a permanent impound, so Williams suggested a low service reservoir on higher ground. Later Thomson located the present Beacon Hill reservoir on the same ridge, on land bought from the federal government, 13 blocks

south and three east of the Spring Hill tank. Williams suggested a second reservoir on present-day First Hill at the intersection of Broadway and Madison. Thomson put a bid on land nearby at an estate auction—land four blocks north of Williams' location. Williams plotted his highest reservoir on Capitol Hill in modern-day Volunteer Park. Thomson did the same, adding a standpipe to increase pressure. Under his direction, a pump was installed from the First Hill reservoir to Volunteer Park, also as Williams planned. Later, the water department added standpipes on Queen Anne Hill, where Williams planned a reservoir. No reader of Thomson's autobiography would know that Williams' reports placed the reservoirs about where Thomson located them. In Thomson's defense it should be said that he placed them at what were, most likely, the best combination of inexpensive land and maximum height for each. Further, Thomson's standpipes on Capitol and Queen Anne hills were better locations than the low service reservoir on Beacon Hill. Yet the reader of Thomson's "I came to the conclusion that we would need three good-sized retaining reservoirs from the beginning" would not suspect that Williams had favored facilities in the same general locations. It was part of the price Williams paid for his conflict with cousin Harry.[31]

Whatever the value of the Williams plan, it could not be implemented because of the constitutional limit on city debt. Then there were the double blows of the 1893 depression and the defalcation of the city treasurer, not to mention the additional funds diverted to upgrade the existing plant purchased from the Spring Hill company. Nevertheless, the economic bad news did not prevent Thomson from focusing on the ultimate goal of a gravity system based on the Cedar River. Without an appropriation for a supplementary survey and with other work crowding his office, he could do little about righting the perceived wrongs of the Williams plan. But he did what he could to familiarize himself with the territory, "tramping" over portions of the proposed line. With his assistant Charles J. Moore, he conducted preliminary surveys during the summers of 1893 and 1894. Their visits to the Cedar River convinced them of the need to replace Williams' "very bad engineering" in two critical respects.[32]

First, and most important for the future, they decided to bypass Swan Lake. This was a profound change. It wiped out the use of Swan Lake as a reservoir, and as an alternate supply in case of a failure of the headworks or the line leading to the lake. Instead, the first line as constructed would run from the intake on the Cedar River to near the eastern shore of Swan Lake, thence to the city. Second, and wisely, they decided to replace Williams' flume from the intake to near the lake with a buried pipe, except at two crossings of the Cedar River, where the pipe would be elevated but remain enclosed. Thomson thereby shielded the water supply—from its intake to reservoirs—against pollution or tampering. Financing bound the two changes together, because to get his buried pipe Thomson had to give up Swan Lake.[33]

Consider Williams' estimated cost of $1,735,847.40 for both the delivery and distribution system. The Williams estimate dated from early 1891. No prudent engineer would advocate more, especially during the depression years, 1893–97. Indeed, when in 1895 the city council passed and the voters ratified a proposal to build the Cedar gravity system its maximum cost was listed at $1,250,000. To return to Williams' figures one more time, he estimated the Swan Lake overflow tunnel at $63,600, and other lake apparatus at $2,200. Some portion of his proposed item, "excavation in reservoirs, dams and in grading pipe and flume lines," should also be charged to Swan Lake, but leaving all of that almost $135,000 aside, it comes to at least $65,800 off the top of the Williams estimate. Subtracting $65,800 from the total Williams estimated leaves $1,670,047.40, still above the 1895 maximum but closer. Assuming that 25 percent of the excavation and grading budget would have been spent at Swan Lake allows another reduction to $1,636,347.40, as yet higher than the 1895 figure but within $386,347.40 of it. Ultimately the successful bids on the entire project were at the post-depression price of $939,019.07. Assuming an extraordinarily high engineering and supervision charge of 10 percent, the system built out at more than $217,000 under the ordinance amount. Even so, Thomson recommended against bringing in Swan Lake at an estimated cost of $116,000, and instead urged applying the funds "to the acquisition of Cedar Lake and the proper lands in the Cedar River watershed, thus securing to all posterity the absolute

ownership, purity and sufficiency of our water supply." But that was in late 1899, 5½ years after Thomson and Moore reached their decision. By then a lot of water had gone over the metaphorical dam.[34]

This long exercise in figures means, obviously, that Thomson had to live by the numbers as well as any other engineer. But it also means that he and Moore chose, prudently, to keep their mouths shut about their proposed changes in the Williams plan. In their view, it was better to play along with the Williams proposal for the time being. Williams, whatever Thomson thought of him, was a respected, successful engineer. A challenge to his reasoned reports based on nothing more than a reconnaissance by two men who lacked his stature could have thrown the entire gravity system scheme into disarray. It was better to be less than honest about their future intentions than risk being subjected to an absolute mandate to build on the Williams scheme. It was better to live with the ordinance figure of $1,250,000 than to risk having it lowered.

In sum, Thomson and Moore opted for some dissembling and an abundance of caution in hopes of avoiding an emotional debate over the water supply. They failed, and instead lived through a series of stormy clashes. There were more than enough twists and turns along the way to a successful gravity system to satisfy the most ardent thirst for adventure.

Thomson's fellow engineer, Theron A. Noble, raised the curtain on the adventure in 1893. Noble knew more about the Cedar River than anyone else, having surveyed the area for the federal government for possible homesteading under federal law. On Noble's advice, or independently, a promoter named Edward H. Ammidown purchased land along the Cedar River at the site of Williams' intake, while Noble built a bridge and a small dam on the river and began taking measurements of the stream's flow. As George Cotterill, Thomson's erstwhile partner and sometime assistant, wrote of Noble: "Nobody knew he was there. Communication did not reach over such distances, and it was quite a while later that we knew these things." They already knew about Ammidown who was cut from a cloth similar to that of Daniel H. Gilman, Thomson's friend and associate, except that Gilman appeared to be more often self-deceived than deceiving. Ammidown arrived in 1891 after a failed speculation in New York. He and Noble took advantage of the city's inability to fund its gravity system by forming the Seattle Power Company to exploit the Cedar River for water and hydroelectric power. Although Ammidown's credentials were not the best, he worked hard to ingratiate himself with the Seattle business community. Besides, he and

Noble were doing something about using the Cedar River, while Thomson, however legitimate his reasons, was not.[35]

Thomson certainly learned about the Noble-Ammidown scheme late in 1893, although he may have had intimations or heard rumors before then. His certain dose of reality came in November or December when Noble walked into his office and asked to review Williams' maps, reports, and other data. Though Thomson would have liked to refuse, he could hardly do so because the material was public record. He did insist that Noble examine the Williams information in his office, a condition Noble accepted. By April 1894, Noble was drafting his own scheme. His proposal was similar to the Williams design, except that the overflow pipe in the Williams program, instead of merely returning excess water from Swan Lake to the Cedar River, would be used to generate electricity. Noble's power plant would supply current to Seattle and Tacoma. Two other aspects of the Noble-Ammidown scheme made it all the more intriguing. Noble proposed consolidating the steam-generating plants in Seattle and operating them in conjunction with the Cedar River powerhouse. Secondly, he planned to divert water to a company created to cut a canal from the south end of Lake Washington to Puget Sound through the formidable bulk of Beacon Hill. Water, fired through huge hoses at tremendous pressure, would sluice down the hill, a technique perfected in California gold mining. The dislodged earth would be spread over the tideflats to bring them up to grade level, converting new acreage into industrial lots. [36]

Their project was exciting but Noble and Ammidown's Seattle Power Company faced serious obstacles among the citizenry. The greatest of these was the mistrust of outsiders, a suspicion trumping all other considerations. Although the city's commercial-financial elite generally opposed a municipal water supply on the Cedar River, partly because it could or would lead to municipal power production, such a sentiment did not necessarily endear the elite to Ammidown. Diverting water to the south canal project raised the specter of one outside private undertaking helping another, with neither controlled by the city. In addition, the south canal project—though the brainchild of a visionary, the former Washington territorial governor Eugene Semple—had plenty of local foes who wanted a canal, but wanted it elsewhere. Another important issue was the fear that a company financed and controlled by outside capital would dictate the terms of water use to the city. The matter of outside private control came to the fore in 1895, when the national Populist movement was nearing its crest in 1896. One tenant of populism was its opposition to ever-increasing financial centralization, while one tenant of the emerging progressive movement advocated municipal ownership of basic utilities. The two meshed in opposition to the Seattle Power Company or any other private organization dictating terms of the city's water use.

Thomson and his assistant Cotterill were not populists. They were progressives committed to private enterprise, who saw municipal ownership as the handmaiden of private commerce and manufacturing. Their allies in the city council and city administration were scarcely

Placing iron hoops around staves, January 26, 1900. *Seattle Municipal Archives #7297.*

enthusiastic about municipal ownership but as politicians they recognized a groundswell when they felt it. Meanwhile, Cotterill was casting about for a way to evade the debt limit. The problem, however, remained—a municipal water plant was tied to city bonds and therefore to the state constitutional debt limit.[37]

A disaster in Spokane led to a way out, and to what are now called revenue bonds. In 1895, Spokane bonded itself above the limit to finance a new intake on the Spokane River, replacing a pumping station. Then, as Cotterill expressed it, "in early June a freshet occurred in the Spokane River, with a terrific rush of water that took out their whole intake system, ruining their water system completely." The resulting revenue bond concept has several fathers but the actual paternity goes to the Chicago banks that financed the now-destroyed improvement. They proposed that Spokane issue new bonds, "warrants," which the banks would buy to finance rebuilding the intake. The bonds would be repaid from water system revenues over and above the cost of operation. The city would direct those revenues into a fund exclusively for the purpose of repaying the bonds. No taxes or other obligations of the city would be involved, thus avoiding the constitutional limit and creating a new type of debt to be repaid strictly from the revenues of an income-producing public work.[38]

A test case of the Spokane ordinance creating these arrangements double-timed through the courts. In late August, the state supreme court validated the ordinance in a 3-2 decision, *Winston v. Spokane*. It held that the arrangement was legal old hat. The majority opinion cited, for example, a case affirming the legality of Seattle warrants issued to a street improvement contractor to be paid from property assessments, not city revenues. Whatever the validity of the comparison, the court determined that the city's liability was too indirect to be considered a constitutional debt. The court had opened the way for a new class of obligations based solely on revenues from utilities.[39]

In Seattle, the drafting of an ordinance reflecting the court's decision fell to George Cotterill. The council passed the ordinance in October, only to have it vetoed by the mayor on technical grounds, principally that the city's project should be ratified by Seattle voters. The council redrafted the ordinance to meet the mayor's objections. Ordinance 3990 became law, subject to popular ratification, at the end of the month. As it happened, the measure's passage was timely for the advocates of a municipal system. Ammidown, who had been wooing Seattle politicians and business leaders with promises of inexpensive Cedar River water and abundant power, returned to Seattle following a trip to acquire the necessary capital. He had, he announced, secured the backing of mostly English financiers and was ready to proceed, as soon as all the details could be worked out and an agreement reached with city government.[40]

Ordinance 3990, which Ammidown and its other opponents had to contend with, "specified and adopted" basically the Williams plan with slight modifications. It provided for a headworks or intake on the Cedar River, using Swan Lake as a reservoir, and three service areas in the city. The Cedar River-Swan Lake conduit would have a capacity "not less than" 50,000,000 gallons per day, with the whole, including all land and other acquisitions, to cost an estimated $1,250,000. The vote was scheduled for December 10. If ratified, the Board of Public Works would advertise for bids on the work, with the successful bidder to be paid from warrants on the "Cedar River Water Supply Fund of Seattle," composed of 75 percent of receipts from the waterworks, less water for municipal use. The warrants were to bear interest at 5 percent. Other provisions were designed to bind the city "irrevocably" to its contract.[41]

The campaign for and against voter ratification of Ordinance 3990 did not wait upon Ammidown's plans. It began the day before he announced his return to Seattle, when the evening *Times* published a letter from John J. McGilvra opposing the ratification of Ordinance 3990. McGilvra's letter, if not the first, was an early broadside. Because of the importance McGilvra's position assumes in accounts of the battle over the Cedar River system, it is critical to establish just who McGilvra was, what he proposed, and why Thomson worked, successfully, to convert him into a supporter of his idea of a gravity supply. McGilvra, born in New York state in 1827, moved with his parents to Illinois when he was 17. He read law in two different law offices, then a common way of entering the legal profession. Later he claimed to have been "excellent friends" with Abraham Lincoln, a claim disputed by his biographer who contends that the two may have known each other only casually. In any event, McGilvra's Republican credentials were sufficient to land him the job of U.S. district attorney for Washington Territory. It was hardly a political plum. He held the office from 1861 to 1865, meanwhile moving to Seattle where he began buying land. After resigning his government position, he practiced law, expanded his real estate operations, and became a mildly progressive civic booster. He was, his biographer wrote, a man who "operated effectively in the second level of the city's

Testing Cedar River Pipeline No. 1 at Molasses Creek, January 26, 1900. The gauge at station #647 recorded 140 pounds of pressure. *Seattle Municipal Archives #7326.*

leadership." He was, in other words, a contributing member of Seattle's commercial-financial elite but far from a controlling one. His frontier society bestowed on him the honorific "Judge" as uncritically as it accepted his claim of closeness to Lincoln.[42]

McGilvra's letter opposed the ordinance, but not the concept of a gravity system. What he did propose was, in its way, more far-reaching than the ordinance. He argued for the immediate acquisition of "Swan Lake as a supply reservoir, Cedar Lake as a source of supply," the works themselves to be constructed at a future time on a pay-as-you-go basis. McGilvra insisted that there was no need to rush the matter or incur a large debt, for the "supply from Lake Washington is sufficient for years to come." He pointed out that if the Seattle Power Company located a facility at Cedar Lake or anywhere along the 12 riverine miles above the city's proposed intake, it could "adulterate or divert" any amount of water from the river. He did not object to a private firm's using surplus water, but he did insist that "the city must own the land around" the lakes as well as the lakes themselves, "for sanitary and other purposes, and it must have the prior right of appropriation for its own use even to the extent of the entire supply." McGilvra recommended paying for the purchase or condemnation of the necessary property

by setting aside 25 percent of receipts from the existing waterworks, together with any other "available" funds. McGilvra's letter was notable for its acceptance of the need for a gravity system, its early warning against source pollution, its revelation that the Seattle Power Company was moving its proposed power operation miles upriver to Cedar Lake, and its offer of a funding alternative to Ordinance 3990. At the same time, McGilvra refused to concede the opening provided by *Winston v. Spokane.* Noting that the city was "in debt up to the constitutional limit at least," he counseled against assuming "an additional indebtedness directly or indirectly for speculative purposes" unrelated to immediate needs. [43]

Thomson quickly if indirectly responded to McGilvra's letter in an ultimately successful effort to persuade him to accept Ordinance 3990. As he remembered it in his 1950 memoirs, he and McGilvra discussed the problem in a series of conferences, after which McGilvra asked for "us to provide a brief showing the city's side of the case." McGilvra would prepare a brief in opposition. Thomson's memory is supported in a passage from Bagley's 1916 history, but neither is accurate. This is what happened: Cotterill and McGilvra discussed the letter about the time that McGilvra filed it with the city clerk and before few, if any, *Times* readers saw it. After their talk, Cotterill rushed to his typewriter and produced a response. Thomson endorsed it, and Cotterill mailed it to McGilvra on November 9, the day after the letter appeared in the *Times*.[44]

Cotterill was conciliatory. He agreed that Swan Lake was "an ideal impounding reservoir," a statement placing him at odds with Thomson's conclusion to bypass the lake, though Cotterill probably was unaware of his boss's decision. He assured McGilvra of the city's determination to provide an ample supply of water and to prevent "any subsequent pollution or contamination." He demonstrated that an upriver power project, whether private or public, would return water to the Cedar, where it would be available to the city. He assured McGilvra that the language of Ordinance 3990 permitted the maximum flexibility in choosing sites and purchasing property. Then he turned to the question of finances. He reiterated that no money would be spent until the gravity system was in operation, whereupon 75 percent of the receipts would be sequestered to retire the warrants issued for its construction. He admitted that, with the pumping system superseded, no income from that source could be used to repay the bondholders who financed its expansion. A tax increase would be necessary to fund the bond repayment. However—and here he played upon McGilvra's fear of taxes to fund "speculation"—the pumping works would require substantial expansion if the gravity system were not built. Cotterill estimated the costs at about $125,000 to expand the pumping plant to meet future needs, a great "burden for something to be eventually discarded." He reminded McGilvra that approval of the gravity system would allow the city to "secure the most favorable condemnations possible." Finally, he reminded McGilvra that approval of the system was not a mandate to build it. If the construction bids were too high or other circumstances made "it advisable not to proceed," the council could "suspend" the installation of the Cedar River works.[45]

Cotterill's letter had its intended effect. On November 18, McGilvra accepted Cotterill's "clear" and "cogent" arguments, as supplemented by his reading of other documents. These included an uncirculated proposal for bids on an entire water system to be leased to a corporation, an arrangement that Ammidown repudiated on his return from his financing trip. McGilvra did not like Ammidown, the Johnny-come-lately promoter. He now saw Ammidown's Seattle Power Company as moving toward control of the entire output of the Cedar River—"a cold and bloodless, as well as soulless creature of the law, called a corporation,...seeking to levy tribute

on the City of Seattle." Admitting that his position was "considerably modified," McGilvra swung to support of Ordinance 3990, however reluctantly.[46]

McGilvra's switch to support the ordinance was but one incident in the fight over Ordinance 3990. Bagley and Thomson would have it that McGilvra financed public meetings with band music and speeches, and, as Thomson wrote, "his strong advocacy of the plan had much to do with it being very strongly approved." Thomson's judgment was wide of the mark. This is not to suggest that Thomson and McGilvra did not meet as he and Bagley suggested, or that McGilvra's help was unwelcome. The Thomson-McGilvra meetings probably did occur, and they probably related to a second, more technical response that Cotterill prepared, of which more later. Thomson and Bagley simply confused causes and effects. McGilvra and Thomson probably had something akin to a father-son relationship, for 29 years separated them. What had united them was a devotion to Seattle, the Republican Party, and McGilvra's presumed friendship with Lincoln, already an iconic figure among Republicans. It was a close relationship confirmed years later with McGilvra's gift to Thomson of a view lot overlooking Lake Washington.[47]

The reality was, despite McGilvra, that the fight was just getting under way. On the morning of McGilvra's rather hesitant endorsement, the *Post-Intelligencer* came out against Ordinance 3990 on the grounds of high risk and potentially heavy expense. Three days later, Ammidown made four proposals, or one proposal and three variations. The gist of them was that the Seattle Power Company would deliver a copious supply of water to the city more cheaply than the city could do the job at its pumping plant. Rates would vary depending on the obligations of the Seattle Power Company; e.g., they would be higher if the company were required to build a new reservoir to supplement the old Spring Hill tank. When or if the city decided to purchase the water system, it could do so through a process of appraisal and binding arbitration. Meanwhile, the company would retain the right to all surplus water. Ammidown did not mention the intended use of the surplus water—it was to sluice for a south canal and use the earth to fill the tideflats.[48]

Ammidown addressed his letter to the mayor and city council but also supplied a copy to the chamber of commerce. A chamber committee asked Thomson for an analysis. Cotterill again produced the response, but this time it was more analytical, bristling with figures on eight pages of legal-size paper. To summarize Cotterill's contentions, he admitted that under three of Ammidown's plans, water could be provided more inexpensively from the Seattle Power Company than by pumping, but in all cases a city gravity system could provide the water at less cost. Looking at the situation over a period of 12 years, Cotterill found that under all of Ammidown's proposals, the city would own only those distribution facilities it paid for, would have to buy out the company's installations at future prices (1895 was the depth of the depression), would purchase deteriorated equipment, would not own either Swan or Cedar lakes, would not control the surplus water, and would not, as a practical matter, be able to generate municipal power from the Cedar River. Cotterill's assumptions could be challenged but they were a reasonable statement of the city's case.[49]

On November 29, the chamber of commerce met to review two reports from the committee. The majority report opposed Ordinance 3990, while the minority report endorsed it. "After a vigorous debate," the chamber accepted the majority report, 52 to 8. The arguments in favor of the majority opinion were essentially those made in the majority report; i.e., city debt was already high and over the constitutional limit, the concept of revenue warrants had been tested for Spokane only, the pumping system bonds would have to be retired, new debt of whatever character was inadvisable, revenue warrants placed the entire burden on users while undeveloped property held for speculation paid nothing, the city could condemn any private water works at any time if needed, and the present pumping system was, in any case, adequate for the time being. If Thomson cherished any illusions about McGilvra's influence over the chamber, the meeting shattered them. McGilvra objected to a time limit on speeches but was overruled. When he spoke, derisive laughter and cheers greeted him. The audience listened to speeches favoring Ordinance 3990 with ill-concealed impatience. The vote against it was decisive, though it was no endorsement of Ammidown and his scheme. Whether or not his water and power plans would be realized was left to the future.[50]

The intense public debate continued. In an interview with the

Queen Anne Hill standpipe under construction, February 22, 1900. *Seattle Municipal Archives #7310.*

Times, James M. Colman reiterated some points made at the chamber meeting, but with his own emphasis. Colman, it will be remembered, was the savior of the early Seattle & Walla Walla Railroad. A mechanical genius, hardworking, spare, and frugal, he used city figures to demonstrate that Seattle would be paying more for a new gravity system than the existing pumping system. His contention would have been correct had the city been required to pay all charges from both systems, as Colman insisted it would. Examining Cotterill's estimated expenses for maintaining the gravity system, he concluded that "the estimation must have been made by some one not at all familiar with such works," and declared it to be too low by at least two thirds. Such a "debt would not help our credit, nor encourage favorable immigration to our city." A contract for such a huge job, with the contractor paid in warrants—warrants the contractor would have to sell to finance the construction—would force bids up by 50 percent. All city work, he declared, should be handled on a pay-as-you-go basis.[51]

Two points need to be made about Colman's claims. The first is that they actually gave no comfort to the Seattle Power Company. If the city accepted any of Ammidown's propositions there would be no cost savings, because it would be paying for water from his company while also paying an additional amount to retire the debt on the pumping system. Under Colman's holistic view of the issue, it made no difference who—taxpayers or ratepayers—was paying what. All the money came out of the same pot, as it were. The second point is that Colman's clash with Cotterill demonstrated how readily two students of the same problem could disagree. That point would be made again more than three years later when suit would be brought to suspend the city's work on the pipelines.[52]

Two days after Colman's remarks appeared, McGilvra delivered his riposte at a crowded pro-Ordinance 3990 gathering at the armory. He declared that Colman "was no authority on engineering, although he might be a good machinist." McGilvra's thrust could be expected, but other aspects of the meeting foreshadowed the favorable vote on the ordinance. The meeting passed a strong resolution recalling the water famine of the great fire, warning of the reach of the Seattle Power Company, and minimizing the costs of the gravity system. A prominent Populist also responded with a fiery address against the water company and its newspaper supporter, the *Post-Intelligencer*—an address that was "continuously broken by uproarious applause." The "inclement weather" proved no barrier to attendance. On the main floor, "standing room was at a premium," and "the gallery was crowded with men." Even though the *Times* opposed a city gravity system for the present, it did print these comments and more. The *Times* reporter found the meeting to be "peculiar" in that "many of the 'blue bloods' of the city were conspicuous by their absence," yet "a good many of the best people of the town" were there as well as "many" attendees "who never before took part in the political affairs of the city." Workingmen turned out "in great numbers," and so did populists.[53]

On December 10, the voters decisively supported the city gravity system—2,656 in favor, 1,665 opposed. Ordinance 3990 faced its heaviest opposition in the most prosperous wards, but it won everywhere, with solid middle-class support and more tentative working-class endorsement. In the end, the chamber of commerce and newspaper opposition counted for little. The value of McGilvra's support, on the other had, was "hard to ascertain" according to his biographer. It helped, certainly, but it is doubtful that it determined such a lopsided vote.[54]

From the perspective of the holiday season of 1895, it would seem that the city's gravity system would be ready in short order, perhaps even within the two years predicted in Cotterill's letter to McGilvra. Instead, more than five years elapsed before Cedar water flowed into Seattle's distribution mains. Surveys and condemnation proceedings occupied Thomson, his office, and the corporation counsel (city attorney) from April 1896 through August 1898. Several problems hampered the surveys—a small crew, inadequate appropriations despite Thomson's efforts at wooing the mayor and important councilmen, the need to discover the best possible route through meticulous surveying while taking copious notes on exactly what lands needed to be purchased or condemned, great and growing demands on the engineering department in connection with street and sewer work, especially after the gold rush boom began in 1897, and heavy rains during the fall and winter of 1896–97. Meanwhile, Thomson maintained a private practice as well as conducting his public

work (see chapter 4). This was not illegal, but it kept him busy to the point of distraction and, occasionally, past it. The corporation counsel, also overwhelmed, moved slowly on land purchases and condemnations. These stumbling blocks negated Thomson's advantages—his access to both Williams' and Noble's reports, his preliminary surveys of 1893 and 1894, and his visit to Portland's famous Bull Run waterworks, first opened in 1895. Bull Run, a gravity system built through almost impassable country in the Oregon Cascades, involved problems similar to the Cedar River project. Thomson's visit confirmed, not surprisingly, his earlier decision to alter the Williams plan in basic ways.[55]

Voter approval of Ordinance 3990 appeared to open the way for construction, but in fact it did not. Seattle's financial experts assured Thomson that no bank would accept warrants drawn on the Seattle water fund merely on the strength of a 3-2 state supreme court decision and a city ordinance. A supporting state law would be necessary. Thomson once more turned to Cotterill, who drafted a bill based on the court decision. The two engineers and at least two other representatives journeyed to Olympia, where they secured easy passage of the measure during the 1897 session. Like the court decision and the ordinances in Seattle and Spokane, the law limited its effect to existing systems undergoing expansion.[56]

At last the way seemed clear, but there was new trouble over the contract. Here again the reader of Thomson's memoirs would come away with the correct view of the outcome but not of the specifics. These are contained in the state supreme court case *Moran v. Thompson* [sic]. In brief, the Board of Public Works called for bids on September 22, 1898, based on specifications gotten up by Thomson and Cotterill, and on the relevant provisions of the city charter. One bid came in, on November 15, from the Chicago firm of Gahan & Byrne. The bid departed from the charter requirements but the board reported it to the city council without a recommendation for or against. In subsequent negotiations the council and the contractors agreed that the warrants would draw interest from the date they were issued and not, as the ordinance stipulated, on completion and acceptance of the work. On completion and acceptance, Gahan & Byrne would refund the interest received in the interim. In effect, this meant that Gahan & Byrne would purchase warrants from the city as portions of the work progressed and were provisionally approved, collect and spend the interest on each block of warrants, then return the interest when they purchased their final warrants.[57]

The council and the contractors also agreed that the city would withhold 30 percent of the contract price for 30 days to satisfy the legitimate claims of laborers and suppliers against the contractor, as provided by the city charter. (The charter subordinated all other claims to those of workers and suppliers.) The agreement between Gahan & Byrne and the council added—and here was a second issue—a clause giving equal standing to "any valid claims for fees or royalties on any patented invention, article or arrangement connected with the work, and as security for the replacement or completion of any defective or uncompleted work which may be found, and to secure the repayment of any interest moneys advanced." This change, whatever its intention, potentially diluted the protection of working people and materials suppliers provided for in the charter.[58]

The council passed an ordinance confirming these changes on November 22. Three days later, Mayor Thomas J. Humes, elected on a promise to push the Cedar River project, approved the ordinance. The council directed the Board of Public Works to proceed on the basis of the new ordinance. Thomson opposed the new ordinance, referring at the time to his "scrap with the Council as to the right thing to do in the premises," contending "that the bid and the proposed contract" were illegal. Former mayor Moran agreed; he began the proceedings leading to the supreme court decision of February 7, 1899.[59]

The court found, as Moran contended, that the revised contract was a new agreement with significantly different terms than the original. If the council wanted such substantial changes, it would have to put the revised contract out for bids. But it could not in fact do so. The court found the arrangement whereby Gahan & Byrne collected interest on the warrants, then refunded the interest at the end of the contract, to be a violation of the state constitution prohibiting cities from loaning money. The court held that the provision retaining 30 percent of the contract price to pay claimants other than workers or suppliers to be a violation of the city charter. So was the council's directing the Board of Public Works to accept the revised bid. Noting that the revisions were negotiated publicly, the court declared them to be above board, and "characterized by the utmost good faith on the part of all parties concerned."[60] Nevertheless, they were illegal.

With the Gahan & Byrne contract dead beyond revival, Thomson and his subordinates revised their specifications to make the job more appealing to bidders. Among other changes, they broke the contract into four divisions, the first for the supply system from the

Laying 12-inch main pump line along East Harrison Street from the original Volunteer Park reservoir to the Queen Anne standpipe, September 8, 1899. *Seattle Municipal Archives #7292.*

intake to the distribution system, and the other three for parts of the distribution system within the city. The Pacific Bridge Company took the contract for the supply system, while Smythe, Wakefield & David successfully bid on all three segments of the distribution system. The Board of Public Works awarded all the contracts on April 19, 1899. Smooth sailing for the Cedar River works was still some distance away, however. The events of this fresh disputation are convoluted but this is their essence. Ammidown realized that his private plans for water and power on the Cedar River were doomed after the 1895 vote approving Ordinance 3990 and an 1896 amendment to the city charter requiring voter ratification for any private water or power franchise (see chapter 7). He sold his land and other property around and near Cedar Lake to an influential group organized as the Washington Power Transmission Company (WPTC). The WPTC had the resources to build an up-to-date dam and powerhouse at the lake.[61]

Into this scene entered Charles H. Baker, a civil engineer and operating head of the Snoqualmie Falls Power Company, located at the river's spectacular falls east of

Seattle. Baker saw the WPTC as a threat to his Seattle franchise, in which assumption he was probably correct as he and the WPTC group were rivals of long standing. Using a friend as a cat's-paw, he sued the city on the grounds that its new Cedar River contract departed materially from the terms of Ordinance 3990, and could not deliver the daily gallonage under the ordinance. Simultaneously, he began a publicity campaign against the city's gravity water supply, claiming that upriver sources polluted the Cedar River. The city's only solution, he claimed, was to garner the WPTC property and still more lands in the watershed, to protect the water supply from pollution.[62]

Taking the legal matter first, on April 17, 1899, Baker's friend Tracy H. Robertson filed suit against the Board of Public Works claiming three significant departures from Ordinance 3990. First, Thomson's design would not deliver the 25,000,000 gallons daily suggested by the ordinance. At best it would provide 18,000,000 gallons. Second, because Thomson's pipeline, in effect, bypassed Swan Lake, the lake could not serve as an impounding reservoir. Therefore the impoundment at Swan Lake and the pipeline of 50,000,000 gallons daily capacity from the Cedar to Swan Lake, both specified in the ordinance, were wrongfully omitted from the new provisions. Thirdly, according to a later, amended complaint, the new language improperly nullified the ordinance declaration that 75 percent of gross receipts from the waterworks, not counting water for strictly city uses, would be committed to the "Cedar River Water Supply Fund." The fund would be used to redeem warrants, interest on the warrants, and other expenses associated with the system's construction. The new language provided for at least $100,000 per year for those purposes, not the 75 percent of receipts designated in the ordinance.[63]

Judge William Hickman Moore heard the suit in superior court. He granted a temporary restraining order against awarding the contract, but other preliminary actions did not bode well for Baker and his friend Robertson. The day after Robertson filed his suit, Moore dismissed an unrelated action brought by disappointed bidders against the award of gravity system contracts to Pacific Bridge and Smythe, Wakefield & David. He also dissolved his temporary restraining order in the Robertson case, allowing the contracts to be signed. But Robertson persisted. On April 27, Moore heard arguments on the matter of issuing a permanent injunction. After hearing Robertson's attorney, Moore ruled that "no ground whatever for the granting of an injunction

had been shown" and dismissed the case. There was, he declared, insufficient evidence to justify an injunction, especially given Thomson's assurances that he had carefully made his calculations on water volume. The rest of Robertson's complaints were immaterial.[64]

The suit was settled, but Thomson's recollection of the trial was radically at variance with the contemporary accounts. According to Thomson's memoirs, Robertson's complaint made "no statement" about the "incompetence" of the amended plans, yet Robertson's attorney "was accompanied by several very fine-looking engineers who had been brought from the East to prove the incompetence of the plans." Thomson's testimony cleverly deceived the easterners into believing that he was a hick. Then Robertson's attorney asked him to work out nine calculations related to the gravity system. In a little more than two hours he worked out all nine. One of his solutions confounded the learned engineers, who had arrived at the wrong answer.[65]

Despite the elaborate detail accompanying Thomson's recollection, his account is almost certainly false. Robertson's complaint stated the basis for his suit in no uncertain terms. Instead of "several" engineers, only one represented the plaintiff, Baker's engineer, Thomas J. Johnston. Both Johnston and the Chicago engineer, John Ericson, who served as Williams' assistant years before, submitted affidavits against the plan. But Thomson and other four engineers with ties to him or to the city affirmed its adequacy, thus the preponderance of expertise was on Thomson's side, not Robertson's. The transcript of testimony, if it was taken, does not survive, but according to a newspaper account, Robertson's attorney asked Thomson to make one computation, not nine. That one was unfinished after two and one-half hours. While the attorney's request could be considered a red herring to divert attention from legal issues, Thomson's testimony had, in fact, made much of the soundness of his calculations. He was not a trained hydraulic engineer, and it is possible that Cotterill or someone else made the calculations for which he took credit. In any event, the matter did not seriously influence Judge Moore. Nor does Thomson's poor memory make him a liar. It is probable that his elaborate misrepresentation was a false memory designed to replace the unpleasant truth that two engineers who knew their business opposed his plan, and the humiliation he suffered when he was unable to complete a relatively simple calculation in a reasonable time.[66]

Baker had more luck with his second thrust, a publicity campaign against the WPTC's control of Cedar

Lake and the company's potential pollution of the upstream sources. A spokesman for the WPTC was quick to reply that running Cedar Lake water through the company's turbines would not harm it for domestic use. Furthermore, if it wished, the city would "have supervision of the dwellings of our men at the lake the same as if they were located in the city." Yet Baker's attack eventually forced the city to buy out the WPTC. He succeeded in part because the pollution issue was of long standing. Over the years, the partisans of the gravity supply discussed pollution from human and animal waste, decaying organic matter, and industrial activity, principally mining. Meanwhile, Thomson had taken no steps to secure the Cedar River watershed against pollution, despite the concerns of others and despite his keen awareness of the dangers of Williams' flume design. In his autobiography, Thomson leaves the impression that he fought an uphill battle to secure the watershed from contamination, against the indifference of councilmen and others. While there may be some truth to his assertions regarding individual council members, it was the council as a group that pressured Thomson to respond. He at first did nothing. His inaction created the perfect opening for Baker, who went to the *Times* with his tale of official unconcern. [67]

Baker's description of the public outrage his revelation provoked is almost lurid in its pretentiousness, but the reality was arresting enough. On April 14, the *Times* burst forth with a five-column headline with quotation marks around the words: Pure Cedar River Water! The last of three deck headlines read: "If Engineer Thomson's Scheme Goes Through Seattle's Investment of $1,200,000 Will Be Worse Than Wasted." The story, written in publisher Alden Blethen's direct, unadorned prose, condemned the "scheme" in columns sprinkled with capitalized words. The article warned against pollution from several sources, called for the acquisition of Cedar Lake and turning it into a reservoir, and the purchase or condemnation of all land necessary to the protection of the water supply. The accompanying map enclosed a large area around the city's intake in dotted lines, labeling it a "polluted area." The *Times'* attack on Thomson for his "folly" and "foolish expenditure" may have been its first assault on the city engineer. It would not be the last. [68]

After the Robertson suit was settled, the council requested Thomson to survey the watershed for potential contamination. That was in May. In June he wrote the Northern Pacific's Western Land Agent: "From examinations on the ground, I am satisfied that the City of Seattle will wish to purchase a large amount of land from you" in the Cedar River and Cedar Lake areas, "your company receiving the right to remove timber" and all minerals "which can be extracted without tending to pollute the watershed." In August he reported that pollution was not then a major problem. To prevent future private development, however, he recommended buying extensive tracts around Cedar Lake, along the river, and in adjacent areas. At last Thomson, already suffering under a censure from the council for failing to purchase all the land required for the gravity system, responded to the problem. In his 1899 report, he recommended spending the money saved from bypassing Swan Lake, some $116,000, for acquiring "Cedar Lake and proper lands in the Cedar River Watershed." The "absolute ownership, purity and sufficiency" of the gravity supply had become "the most urgent question before our City to-day." [69]

Once Thomson tumbled to the need to secure Cedar Lake, its surroundings, and other watershed lands, he proceeded to do so with vigor and skill. Clarence B. Bagley's encomium, that Thomson's concern antedated his city post, that he continued his course "when it was charged that his activities were the outgrowth of an impracticable dream," or that the water supply protection was "due solely to the foresight, determination and perseverance of Mr. Thomson," may be dismissed as a pleasant if inaccurate panegyric. But nothing changes the fact that he worked closely with the NP, the U.S. government, and various private landowners to purchase the necessary lands or secure them through condemnation. The acquisitions began in 1901, well before voter approval in 1905. At first, the city allowed landowners to harvest timber from their property. Next, the engineering department would supervise the necessary reforestation. After 1904 some timber harvesting rights were also obtained, the better to control timber use in the watershed. Later the city secured the right to condemn land for watershed protection. Up to the late winter of 1908, Seattle owned 10,000 acres. By the spring of 1910 it held 25,700 acres of "surveyed and patented lands" by purchase, and was condemning another "28,750 acres of patented lands." Yet another 11,030 acres were scheduled for purchase from the NP as soon as surveys were completed. [70]

The fight for the government lands was so furious that the struggle left Thomson embittered against the U.S. Forest Service. The bureau argued that it was more qualified to control timber cutting and reforestation on its lands than the city. Thomson and other partisans of the city answered that much of the government-owned land was in scattered sections, was commercially worthless, and in any case would have to be patrolled by the city to guard against pollution. The battle against the Forest Service ran in part coincidentally with Chief Forester Gifford Pinchot's attacks on Interior Secretary Richard A. Ballinger, whom Thomson greatly admired. To Thomson, Pinchot was "guilty of criminal conspiracy" and was hurting Seattle commerce by limiting Alaskan resource development.[71]

Unfortunately for Thomson, Pinchot's resignation in March 1911 did not alter federal policy. The spare, wealthy Pennsylvanian's successor, Henry S. Graves, was just as adamant about keeping federal lands away from the city's grasp. A local forester's valuation of the 16,350 acres of federal land—more than $600,000—fueled the government's reluctance to part with the property. In a denunciatory letter, Cotterill claimed that, among other outrages, the report valued the land at "over $30,000 a section for mountain tops." He accused the forester of drinking an "elixir" before making his report, "an insult to the intelligence of mankind and an affront to the city" and "not based on truth." Although a bill granting the land to Seattle was introduced in the Senate during January 1910, it languished because of opposition from the Department of Agriculture, U.S. forestry's administrative home.[72]

Early in February 1911, Thomson and Ralph H. Ober, a member of the Board of Public Works, arrived in Washington, D.C., in an attempt to break the deadlock. They met with Chief Forester Graves and James Wilson, the Secretary of Agriculture. Their effort availed them nothing, even though Washington's senator, Samuel H. Piles, and the ubiquitous Thomas Burke, strongly supported their case. The scene then shifted back to Congress, where Piles and Congressman William E. Humphrey saw the bill through to passage by an adroit combination of brashness and clever procedural footwork. Thomson left office that year, and the Department of Engineering eventually canceled the purchase plan in favor of a cooperative agreement with the federal government.[73]

Meanwhile, work on the supply and distribution systems advanced. After some initial problems with a supplier and a contractor, the work went smoothly given the complexity of the large undertaking. Though he delegated authority over construction contractors to others, Thomson was no armchair administrator. He wrote detailed suggestions and admonitions to his assistants concerning construction and financing details as the work progressed. On January 10, 1901, Cedar

River water flowed to the taps of Seattle. By early 1901, the original reservoir system was almost finished. Eight years later, water mains stretched almost 443 miles underneath the city. In 1910 the original supply pipe delivered 23 million gallons per day, while a larger, parallel conduit (completed 1909) brought in about 40 million gallons every 24 hours. The combination was vastly more than the city could use, so the surplus went to contractors sluicing down hills in the city's massive street regrading, or was simply wasted down a tube from the Volunteer Park reservoir into Lake Union. Still, the people and industries of Seattle consumed about 30,000,000 gallons every 24 hours, or roughly 125 gallons per person per day. A new system of standpipes, reservoirs, and mains was under construction or planned to meet the rising demand.[74]

Meanwhile, the gravity system made money. Taking the years from 1903 to 1907 as examples, Thomson figured the net income for the system at $1,632,402.64, after deducting maintenance, operation, and debt retirement. He set aside nothing for depreciation, but allowing the generous sum of $1,000,000 for that category, the net income would have been more than $632,000, then an enormous figure. The gain occurred despite a reduction in the rates charged by the old pumping system.[75]

One major failure marred Thomson's water supply system; it happened shortly after he left office. On November 19, 1911, "a flood of unprecedented magnitude" struck the Cedar River. Among other damage, the roiling waters smashed the trestle carrying the city's pipelines. For six days Seattleites struggled to secure drinking and cooking water. Water was available for other purposes, because the engineering department reactivated its old pumping station on Lake Washington and operated three pumps at Swan Lake, turning lake water into the undamaged portion of the supply pipes south and west of the break. The University of Washington activated a pump for its use, while the Seattle Electric Company operated a pump at its amusement park on Lake Washington. Sprinkling carts carried additional water to people who gathered at intersections to take it home "in pitchers and pails."[76]

Charges that Seattle suffered a water famine for a week while a temporary trestle was rebuilt are not true. The city government urged residents to boil drinking and cooking water despite its treating some of the emergency supply with chloride of lime. Nonessential activities, such as sluicing for the regrades, were temporarily suspended. Aside from these inconveniences, life went on.[77]

Cedar Lake Dam during the severe flooding of November 1911. *Seattle Municipal Archives #5897.*

The *Times*, whose editor, the pugnacious Alden J. Blethen, loathed Thomson, laid the entire incident at his door. The burden of the *Times'* complaint was that the city engineer, in bypassing Swan Lake and refusing to connect newly-completed reservoirs, had allowed the disaster to happen. In his fury, Blethen overlooked significant issues. Thomson bypassed Swan Lake to save money on construction costs and to divert funds to what he came to understand was a more important matter, securing the Cedar Lake and Cedar River watershed from pollution. The reservoirs remained unfilled because simply keeping up with current demand strained the water department's resources to the limit. While it was possible in theory to hook up and divert hundreds of thousands of gallons of wasted water into the reservoirs, that activity would have diverted money, time, and manpower from expanding the infrastructure necessary to accommodate a population that mushroomed from some 80,000 in 1890 to almost 240,000 in 1910.[78]

Thomson blamed the Milwaukee Road, then under construction, for creating the break by changing the Cedar River's channel above the pipelines, thereby wiping out two of the railroad's own bridges and some of its

nearly completed right of way as well as the city's trestle. The weekly *Town Crier* replied that it was Thomson's job to protect the pipeline trestle against all eventualities. What such armchair engineering overlooks is that few man-made works of any sort are able to withstand "unprecedented" natural rampages. Thomson and especially Luther B. Youngs, the head of the water system, were in fact worried about a channel change that the Milwaukee Road introduced. Their concern was, however, to deal with the problem in the context of normal high water. The railroad denied responsibility, arguing that the flood carried away the breast boards raised above the original city dam at Cedar Lake. The resulting torrent tore away a tree. The tree then smashed the railroad's works and the city's pipeline trestle. So, if the flood damage was anyone's fault, the fault was with the city. Whatever the source of the damage, to build against all possible destructive freaks of nature would raise building costs to prohibitive levels.[79]

If Thomson could be faulted for any design lapse, it was his extraordinary faith in the value of untreated wood stave pipe for long-distance supply, except where excessive pressures required the use of steel. "I am a great friend of

Cofferdam destroyed by the November 1911 flood. *Seattle Municipal Archives #5899.*

wooden pipe," he once wrote. Wood stave pipe, properly strengthened with steel bands, performed well enough. It did not, however, live up to Thomson's claim that it was as good or better than steel when the price difference was considered. Thomson claimed that wood staves permeated with water both inside and out would last 50 or 60 years, when engineering department records showed that 20 years was the best that could be hoped for.[80]

When all was said and done, the striking fact about the Cedar River system was that it worked. Thomson masterminded the program, but of course he had vital assistance. Here as elsewhere he picked his subordinates well. Cotterill did most of what would now be called the cost-benefit calculations. He shouldered much of the legal work as well. The able Henry W. Scott supervised construction. Thomson sensibly followed the third and best survey of the Cedar River, even though it was the brainchild of his erstwhile rival, Theron A. Noble. Others, including attorneys, state representatives, and federal senators and congressmen, helped along the way. Thomson's memoirs are correct on the major points and do give others their due, although they are woefully inaccurate in places. Nevertheless, in the final analysis only one pair of hands held all the strands in the effort to bring "a plentiful supply of pure water"[81] to Seattle. Those hands were Thomson's. To him belongs the credit.

NOTES

1. RHT, *That Man Thomson*, first quotation, 57; second quotation, 60.
2. Ibid., 60.
3. Ibid., 57–60. Thomson to William Chapman, 25 September 1897, "Water System Miscellaneous #1," PSRA. For a different perspective than that presented here, Klingle, *Emerald City*, discusses the Cedar River system on 92–94, 98–99, 106–8.
4. Ibid., 68–74.
5. Ibid., 78–84; quotation, p. 82.
6. Ibid., 78–81, for RHT's discussion of pipes.
7. John Lamb, *The Seattle Municipal Water Supply Plant.* (Seattle: Seattle Water Department, 1914), 75–78; and map of the Cedar River watershed following 152.
8. Bagley, *History of Seattle*, 1: 266; Ivan Clark Doig, "John J. McGilvra: The Life and Times of an Urban Frontiersman, 1827–1903," (PhD diss., University of Washington, 1969), 172–73; Letty Anderson, "Fire and Disease," in Tarr and Dupuy, *Technology and the Networked City*; 137–56; and Melosi, *Sanitary City*, 134–44.
9. Lamb, *Seattle Municipal Water Supply*, 19–24.
10. Ficken, *Washington Territory*, 210; Gregory Grey Fitzsimons, "The Perils of Public Works Engineering: The Early Development of Utilities in Seattle, Washington, 1890–1912," (Master's thesis, University of Washington, 1992), 44–45; and Lamb, *Seattle Municipal Water Supply*, 33.
11. Lamb, *Seattle Municipal Water Supply*, 26–30. See also Mary McWilliams, *Seattle Water Department History, 1854–1954: Operational Data and Memoranda* (Seattle: City of Seattle Water Department and Dogwood Press, 1955), 54–56.
12. Bagley, *History of Seattle*, 2:481.
13. Lisa Mighetto and Marcia Montgomery, *Hard Drive to the Klondike* (Seattle: University of Washington Press, 2002),

18–67. The Klondike and subsequent strikes did not, however, lift Seattle to primacy over Portland, which occurred after 1960; see Carl Abbott, "Regional City and Network City: Portland and Seattle in the Twentieth Century," *Western Historical Quarterly* 23 (1992): 293–322.

14. Lamb, *Seattle Municipal Water Supply*, 22, 24.

15. Ibid., 149. For purity tests, see Melosi, *Sanitary City*, 136–39.

16. Lamb, *Seattle Municipal Water Supply*, 26 for gallonage, 24 for quotation. Population figures are from Mighetto and Montgomery, *Hard Drive to the Klondike*, 57.

17. Lamb, *Seattle Municipal Water Supply*, 24, 25.

18. Williams' preliminary report is in Ibid., 33–40. For quotation, see 34. See also *Journal of the Proceedings of the Common Council of the City of Seattle* October 31, 1889, p. 288; and November 15, 1889, p. 319, SMA. Scurry's comment is in "Report of the City Surveyor," July 18, 1890, in *Annual Report of the Mayor of the City of Seattle* (Seattle: Koch and Oakley, 1890), 102.

19. Lamb, *Seattle Municipal Water Supply*, 36, 37.

20. Williams' guess of 475 feet was off by 7, see Ibid., 44, 46.

21. RHT, *That Man Thomson*, 57–58, quotation on 58.

22. RHT told a different story to O.A. Piper, 18 May 1939; and 21 May 1939, 993412, SMA. See also the council's order for November 15, 1889, note 18; and the council's committee of the whole on March 18, 1890, leaving the source or sources of the water system to be settled "at a future time," *Journal of the Proceedings of the Common Council of the City of Seattle*, 319, SMA.

23. RHT, *That Man Thomson*, 60, 82. For Williams' estimates, see Lamb, *Seattle Municipal Water Supply*, 51, 72.

24. For population figures in context, see Mighetto and Montgomery, *Hard Drive to the Klondike*, 56. Williams' statements are in Lamb, *Seattle Municipal Water System*, 37, 72.

25. For an early RHT criticism of Williams, see Fitzsimons, "Perils of Public Works Engineering," 122. RHT, *That Man Thomson*, 82.

26. For quotations, in order, see Lamb, *Seattle Municipal Water System*, 38, 44. Here as elsewhere Williams probably accepted some advice from Scurry, who did most of the surveying, Lamb, *Seattle Municipal Water System*, 43. For quotation, see 60–61.

27. Ibid., 43, 45, 64.

28. In order of my reliance on them, the pages in Ibid. are 24, 64, 52–53, 60–63, 72. For quotation, see 53.

29. For Williams' indifference, see Ibid., 35, 54–55, 67–68.

30. For the Black River crossing, Ibid., 69–70, quotation on 69. For the service districts, see 36–37, 57–59, and 70–71. For the Spring Hill reservoir, see Bagley, *History of Seattle*, 1: 266.

31. RHT, *That Man Thomson*, 61–63, 81. For quotation, 61.

32. Ibid., 61. See also RHT, "Sketches," 1893 and 1894 entries, 1602-2, box 2, folder 10, UW.

33. RHT, *That Man Thomson*, 61.

34. Lamb, *Seattle Municipal Water Supply*, 64–65; and, for some figures and quotation, see City Engineer to H.J. Humes, 9 December 1899, 38, box 9, folder 19, George Cotterill Papers, hereafter cited as Cotterill Papers, UW.

35. For quotation, see Cotterill's unpublished 1949 memoir, 38, box 27, folder 6, Cotterill Papers, UW. For Nobel and Ammidown, see Fitzsimons, "Perils of Public Works Engineering," 91–103.

36. Cotterill memoir, 38, box 27, folder 6, Cotterill Papers, UW; Fitzsimons, "Perils of Public Works Engineering," 95–97; and Alan Hynding, *The Public Life of Eugene Semple* (Seattle: University of Washington Press, 1973), 142–63.

37. Lamb, *Seattle Municipal Water Supply*, 88–90.

38. Cotterill, memoir, 38, box 27, folder 6, Cotterill Papers, UW.

39. *Winston v. Spokane*, 12 Wash. 524 (1895).

40. Wesley Arden Dick, "The Genesis of City Light," (Master's thesis, University of Washington, 1965), is essential to understanding the politics of the Seattle gravity system. Fitzsimons, "Perils of Public Works Engineering," 97–102; "Report of the Fire and Water Committee," drafted by Cotterill, October 23, 1895, 38, box 9, folder 19, Cotterill Papers, UW; RHT, *That Man Thomson*, 68–69; and *Times*, November 9, 1895.

41. A copy of the ordinance is in Cotterill, "Cedar River Gravity Water Supply for City of Seattle, Washington," typescript, 38, box 15. folder 8, Cotterill Papers, UW.

42. *Times*, November 8, 1895; and for differing views on the gravity system, see Fitzsimons, "Perils of Public Works Engineering," 102–8. For McGilvra, see Ivan Doig, "John J. McGilvra," quotation on 3.

43. *Times*, November 7, 1895.

44. RHT, *That Man Thomson*, 69; Bagley, *History of Seattle*, 1: 269; and Cotterill to McGilvra, November 9, 1895, 4806-1, box 1, folder 49, John J. McGilvra Papers, hereafter cited as McGilvra Papers, UW.

45. Cotterill to McGilvra, November 9, 1895, 4806-1, box 1, folder 49, McGilvra Papers, UW.

46. *P-I*, November 10, 1895.

47. RHT, *That Man Thomson*, 69–70; and Bagley, *History of Seattle*, 269–70.

48. *P-I*, November 18, 1895; and for Ammidown, see *Times*, November 21, 1895.

49. RHT to Messers Boone, Shippen, et al., enclosing Cotterill's analysis, 4806-1, box 1, folder 49, McGilvra Papers, UW, and *P-I*, November 22, 1895.

50. *P-I*, November 30, 1895.

51. *Times*, December 4, 1895.

52. See note 59.

53. *Times*, December 6, 1895. See also *P-I* of the same date.

54. Doig, "John J. McGilvra," 181.

55. Some of RHT's difficulties are detailed in Fitzsimons, "Perils of Public Works Engineering," 117–27, though Fitzsimons takes a "presentist" view of RHT's private consulting. See RHT, *That Man Thomson*, 70–71, for his account. For access to T.A. Noble's survey, see RHT to Mr. McMiken, 15 August 1894, 89/1, box 1, book 1, RHT Papers, UW. RHT wrote that he "practically" followed Noble's line, RHT to Thomas Cooper, 7 January 1899, 89/1, box 1, book 1, RHT Papers, UW. RHT's statement is reasonable, for Williams and Scurry made the first survey, on which Thomson's second survey improved. Noble's survey, the third, improved on the first two. Thomson made only slight improvements on Noble's effort, which was probably about the best that could be done, given the instruments of the time. For Bull Run, see Rick Harmon, "The Bull Run Watershed: Portland's Enduring Jewel," *Oregon Historical Quarterly* 96 (Summer-Fall 1995): 242–53.

56. Fitzsimons, "Perils of Public Works Engineering," 120–21; and Cotterill, memoir, 38, box 27, folder 6, Cotterill Papers, UW.

57. *Moran v. Thompson*, 20 Wash. 525 (1899).

58. Ibid., 532.

59. For Humes, see Fitzsimons, "Perils of Public Works Engineering," 125–26, and RHT to D.W. McMorris, 23 December 1898, 89/1, box 1, book 1, RHT Papers, UW.

60. *Moran v. Thompson* 20 Wash. 525 (1899), 538.

61. "Annual Report of the City Engineer to T.J. Humes, December 9, 1899," 38, box 9, folder 19, Cotterill Papers, UW; Fitzsimons, "Perils of Public Works Engineering," 127–40; and *P-I*, April 19, 1899.

62. Charles H. Baker, *Life and Character of William Taylor Baker* (New York: Premier Press, 1908), 178–80, 184–203.

63. *Tracy H. Robertson v. Board of Public Works of Seattle*, filed April 17, 1899, cause 26992, Superior Court, Office of the King County Clerk.

64. *P-I*, April 19, 1899; and, for quotation, see *P-I*, April 28, 1899.

65. RHT, *That Man Thomson*, 75–78.

66. *P-I*, April 27, 1899. The question posed to RHT was "how many gallons of water would flow through a forty-two inch pipe daily, placing the coefficient of the friction inside the pipe at 100?"

67. For quotation, see *P-I*, April 19, 1899. There are many examples of concern over the future pollution of the Cedar River supply, for example, McGilvra's original letter to the *Times*, November 8, 1895. For Baker, see *William Taylor Baker*, 241–42; and for RHT, Fitzsimons, "Perils of Public Works Engineering," 136; and RHT, *That Man Thomson*, 82.

68. *Times*, April 14, 1899.

69. Fitzsimons, "Perils of Public Works Engineering," 137–39; RHT to Thomas Cooper, 12 June 1899, 89/1, box 1, book 2, RHT Papers, UW; RHT to City Council, 3 August 1899, "Water System Miscellaneous," book 1, PSRA; and, for last quotation, "Report" to T.J. Humes, December 9, 1899, 38, box 9, folder 19, Cotterill Papers, UW.

70. Bagley, *History of Seattle*, 1: 270. The extensive correspondence on the watershed issue includes RHT to G.P. Fishburne, 5 March 1908, "Water System Miscellaneous," book 2, PSRA; RHT to W.E. Humphrey, 4 April 1910, 89/1, box 3, book 8, RHT Papers, UW, for quotations; and RHT to J.D. Ross, 8 February 1916, 89/1, box 5, book 15, RHT Papers, UW. See also, RHT, "Sketches," May 8, 1901 entry, 1602-2, box 2, folder 10, RHT Papers, UW.

71. RHT to W.E. Humphrey, 12 March 1910, 89/1, box 3, book 8, RHT Papers, UW.

72. Sources supporting this paragraph and the one following are in Cotterill to R.L. Owen, 31 January 1911, 89/1, box 3, book 9, RHT Papers, UW; RHT to Frederick Sawyer, 11 February 1911, 89/1, box 3, book 9, RHT Papers, UW; *P-I*, March 1, 1911; and RHT, *That Man Thomson*, 82–83.

73. For RHT's view of the cancellation, see *That Man Thomson*, 83.

74. For initial problems, see RHT, *That Man Thomson*, 78–81, although his story about appearing incognito at a plant, the better to correct its faults, may be overdramatized. A more balanced view is in McWilliams, *Seattle Water Department History*, 157–62. For RHT's attention to detail, see RHT to E.W. Cummings, 14 November 1900; and to Henry W. Scott, 14 November 1900, 89/1, box 1, book 2, RHT Papers, UW. Developments from January 1901 are heavily documented. See, for examples, RHT to T.J. Humes, 1 January 1901, City Engineer's Reports, box 1, book 2, PSRA; RHT, Annual Report to John F. Miller, 23 December 1909, Engineering Department Administration, Annual Reports, 1900–1954, box 1, PSRA; L.B. Youngs to J.H. Latshaw, 25 March 1910, Water Department Historical File, box 1, folder Pipeline #1, PSRA; the review of the water system in *P-I*, March 19, 1911, 2nd sec.; and McWilliams, *Seattle Water Department History*, 63–70.

75. RHT to W.J. Woodward, 24 April 1909, 89/1, box 2, book 6, RHT Papers, UW.

76. Quotations are from A.H. Dimock to George W. Dilling, 26 December 1911, Engineering Department, Administration, Annual Reports, 1900–1954; box 1; and McWilliams, *Seattle Water Department History*, 72.

77. *Times*, November 27, 1911; and December 21, 1911. Eventually a bridge replaced the piling and the intake was moved south of Landsburg and the affected area.

78. On Swan Lake and costs, see RHT, *That Man Thomson*, 61. McGilvra assumed that Swan Lake was too low for an adequate reservoir, McGilvra "To the Editor," 28 April 1899, 4806-1, box 2, folder 6, McGilvra Papers, UW. RHT argued that the bottom of Swan Lake, a "black muck," would produce a "vile" taste, and it did, see his paper, "Municipal Public Works," December 31, 1929, 89/1, box 13, folder 5, RHT Papers, UW. For the "real reason," see McWilliams, *Seattle Water Department History*, 87–88.

79. RHT to C.F. Swigert, 20 December 1911, 89/1, box 4, book 11, RHT Papers; UW; and *Town Crier*, hereafter *TC*, December 2, 1911. For the channel change, see RHT [by J.L. Stannard] to J.E. Pearson, 14 January 1909; RHT to G.A. Kyle, 18 January 1909; and L.B. Youngs to RHT, 2 February and 17 February 1910, box 1, folder 13, Water Department Historical File, PSRA. For the railroad's denial, see F.M. D[urgley] to L.B. Youngs, 2 April 1913, box 2, folder 27, Water Department Historical File, PSRA.

80. On the matter of wood stave pipe, see McWilliams, *Seattle Water Department History* 72–73. Among RHT's expressions of faith in wood pipe, see RHT to J.R. Bowles, 6 November 1905, 89/1, box 2, book 4, RHT Papers, UW. RHT was beginning to be disillusioned about wood pipe by the late summer of 1909, see his 28 August letter to St. John David, 89/1, box 3, book 7, RHT Papers, UW.

81. RHT, *That Man Thomson*, 57.

Seattle 3RD St. South From LANORA   513

A view from Lenora Street looking down Third Street toward the rear of the Denny Hotel (later, the Washington Hotel) on the west of Denny Hill, ca. 1896. Also shown are substantial residences that would be moved or razed during the reduction of Denny Hill. *University of Washington Libraries, Special Collections, Warner 3040.*

7
The Regrades

THE REGRADING OF SEATTLE'S DOWNTOWN and nearby streets was the most visible public improvement associated with Thomson, and the most controversial. From 1892 to 1912, the regrades encompassed roughly two square miles, much of it private property. The projects cost millions of dollars, involved dozens of streets, and affected hundreds of individual properties. Regrading leveled a 140-foot hill, left some buildings perched 20 or even 50 feet above lowered street levels, stranded others in deep pits below raised grades, and destroyed structures deemed too difficult or devalued to move.[1]

Regrades exhibited the most visible application of industrial methods for refashioning the urban scene. Contractors utilized huge water cannons to sluice down hills while narrow-gauge engines chuffed through cuts and around hills, hauling supplies in and earth out. Giant sluice boxes moved earth to hollows or into Elliott Bay. Steam shovels, dinosaur-like in proportions, whirred and clanked while gnawing at hills. The big projects— Denny in the north, and Jackson and Dearborn streets at the south of the city's core—were vast undertakings and inhuman in scale. The noise of machinery and dynamite, the fire and smoke from burning houses set alight once they toppled from their perches, and the high temporary wooden bulkheads holding back earth to protect workmen far below, created a landscape at once vivid, garish, surreal, and awesome.

The regrades also were controversial partly because they differed from other municipal improvements such as sewers and paved streets, which usually conferred tangible benefits within a brief time. Sewers banished odors and the bother of private waste disposal, while the paving of roadways eased travel and cleared streets of most mud and dust. Adjacent property holders usually suffered no more than the temporary inconvenience of trenches and street closures. Sewer and street assessments also were usually easy to understand. They were based, normally, on the front footage of each lot facing an improvement, although some lots could be charged more or less. In most cases, costs were clearly related to the benefits to be gained, therefore protests were relatively rare.[2]

Not so with regrades. The major regrades not only forced the relocation or destruction of homes, but also swept away businesses, apartments, schools, and churches, indeed entire neighborhoods. The psychological costs of obliterating peoples' urban anchors were not then well understood. Eminent domain commissions and juries believed that awards for damages were enough. The commissions and juries assessed benefits, too, based on the assumed value of regraded property. The benefit assessments, unlike the per-front-foot costs of paving or sewers, were based on informed opinions about the future value of regraded lots. There could be honest disagreement about something so subjective, but disagreement or no, many lot owners had to pay benefit assessments to help finance the regrading and the necessary new utilities, streets, curbs, and sidewalks. Some property owners were satisfied with their awards or assessments, or at least chose not to complain. Others signed remonstrances and vociferously denounced the assessments before the city council and the courts. Also, regrading was no short-term fix. Contractors on major projects had a year, or sometimes more, to complete the work. The nature of the soil often made regrading and the grading of new streets difficult, physically taxing, and destructive of machinery.

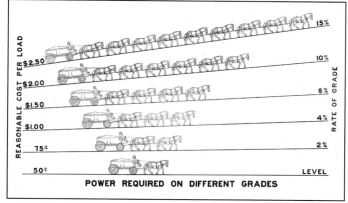

Cost comparisons and horses required for hauling loads on different grades. Though dated late 1913, this graph may have been prepared much earlier. *Seattle Municipal Archives #82.*

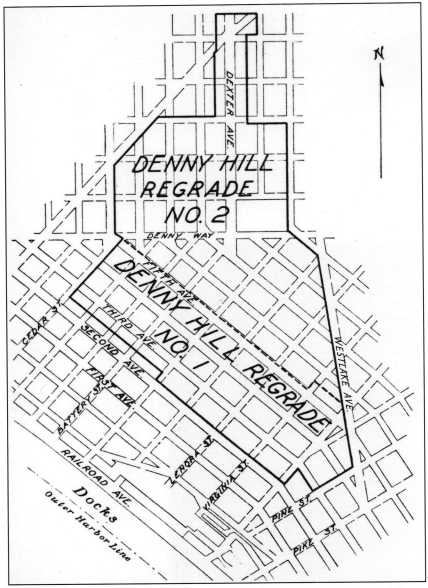

Denny Hill regrades No. 1 (1906–11) and No. 2 (1929–31) were delineated in Von V. Tarbill, "Mountain Moving in Seattle," *Harvard Business Review* Vol. 8 (July 1930). *University of Washington Libraries, Special Collections, UW 27881; courtesy of Harvard Business Review.*

needed more authority, he almost always asked for it or assumed it in ambiguous situations. A contemporary critic, however, denied that Thomson's vision was formed early in his career. "The great regrade projects which have wrought the physical transformation of Seattle were not, in their beginnings, the component parts of one grand harmonious scheme of city building originating in the imagination of Mr. Thomson." Nevertheless, "as this work went forward, the scope of Mr. Thomson's vision widened."[3]

There is some truth in this, but the correct perspective on Thomson's regrade work must be informed by two considerations. After the fire of 1889, the streets in the then southwest part of the city were raised, a program with which Thomson had nothing to do directly, but the improved sanitation and grades were obvious. The earliest pre-Thomson regrades likewise improved street conditions. The second circumstance is Thomson's belief that no matter how important the regrades, they were subordinate to adequate sewage and especially the Cedar River water project.

To turn to the realm of practicality, Thomson and his staff encouraged property owners to submit to regrading for two reasons primarily—first, to ease intraurban horse-drawn transportation, and second, to increase property values along the regraded streets, as well as in other parts of Seattle made easily accessible by the regrades. Thomson or his staff made the case to reluctant property owners—sometimes in person, at other times during public meetings. He described both approaches in his autobiography.

The Second Avenue regrade was one of the early levelings of north-south streets in the urban core. The regrade, begun in 1903, required some heavy cuts, one of them leaving two houses of "a ship captain" high above the new street level. The captain barged into Thomson's office and berated him for ruining his property. He called Thomson "a fool," to which Thomson replied that the captain was "a damned fool," strong language for the dedicated Presbyterian, but it got the captain's notice.

Contractors sometimes asked for extensions of time, and sometimes got them. Meanwhile the costs of business interruption and relocation fell upon the affected property owners.

Thomson's role in all of this was at once determining and severely delimited. His greatest offering to the cause of regrading was his vision of a prosperous Seattle, partly because smooth, level streets would interconnect all sections of the city. The vision demanded determination, persistence, and persuasiveness, all of which he possessed in abundance. His vision also required authority, much of which was granted to him by law and ordinance. If he

Having the captain's attention, Thomson told the skipper to sell his lots on Second and move his houses to Fourth Avenue. The captain, indeed, then unloaded his lots for "a very large sum," but the regrade contractor feared that the two houses could become marooned in the street, interfering with his work, so he refused to allow their removal. The captain appealed to Thomson for help. The city engineer advised him to post a bond indemnifying the contractor if the houses were not moved within ten days. The bond, Thomson declared, "if it says what it ought to say I will give a letter to the contractor directing him to let you move." The corporation counsel (the city attorney) approved the bond, Thomson wrote the letter, and the houses, when moved to Fourth Avenue, "became a very profitable investment, of which the proprietor became very boastful." The captain, however, shunned Thomson thereafter, refusing to acknowledge the good advice that led to the profit. Citing a proverb, Thomson concluded: "Do a man a favor and see what you get for it."[4]

A typical example of the Thomson office's participation in a public meeting occurred when property owners along Jackson Street petitioned for a tunnel under the street to give traffic easy access from Sixth Avenue South to Lake Washington. Regrading in this locality, on the other hand, would involve heavy cuts and fills from about five blocks southeast of the downtown core through Twelfth Avenue, encompassing 54 square blocks of rough, broken terrain with hills and hollows. The ruling grade (i.e., the steepest grade in the section) was a little steeper than 15 percent, or a rise of 15 feet per 100 feet of length. In the horse-drawn era, this gradient practically forbade any teaming over Jackson, thus the local enthusiasm for a tunnel. Interested property owners invited Thomson to discuss it. Thomson worked with a trusted assistant, J.C. Jeffrey, to assemble figures showing that a regrade would

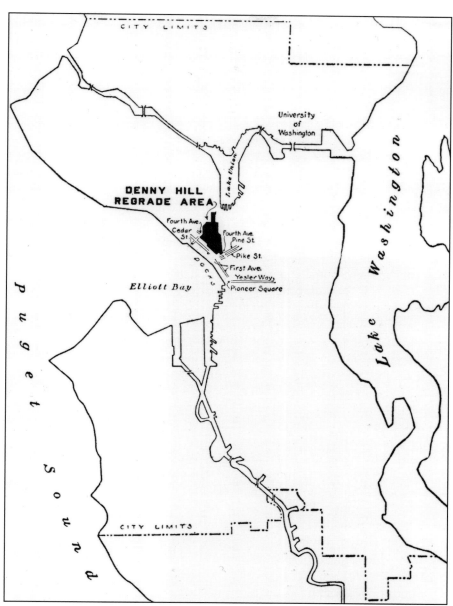

Denny Hill regrade, located north of the commercial-retail core. *University of Washington Libraries, Special Collections, UW 27880;* courtesy of *Harvard Business Review.*

be less expensive and "the benefits vastly more" than what would be provided by a narrow two-lane tunnel. He sent Jeffrey to the meeting with the property owners. "Mr. Jeffrey having a very good understanding of the case, our views were adopted." Shortly thereafter, the owners, many of them absentee, signed a regrade petition, "principally in 1904," that included the required percentage of property.[5]

Both the private and the public meetings reflect Thomson's personal power and his restraints, both institutional and self-imposed. In the private meetings with the ship captain, Thomson dispensed advice based on the captain's assumption that Thomson was controlling events and accurately forecasting increases in property values. In reality, control of the project had passed from Thomson's hands, if it ever could be said to be his exclusively. The law, ordinances, property owners' preferences, court decisions, topography, geology, and technology all strongly influenced project outcomes. On the other hand, Thomson and his staff's promotion of the regrades, and their decisions on the order and importance of each regrade, were, even if not always decisive, significant determinants. In the captain's case, Thomson was correct about the increase in property values. It would not always be so. As for his supposed control of the regrade, Thomson told the captain that if he presented a proper bond, the contractor would allow the houses to be moved on receipt of a letter from the city engineer. Had the contractor objected, Thomson probably would have stood on a clause in the contract allowing him to make changes in the flow of the work, the better to move it along expeditiously. If it would have come to that, Thomson, again probably, would have been on unstable legal ground. But it did not come to that. Contractors usually were in enough difficulty with the Board of Public Works without deliberately antagonizing its chairman. The contractor acquiesced and the captain's houses were moved.[6]

The aforementioned public meeting involved a somewhat different set of circumstances. The owners of a majority of the affected properties had settled, at least tentatively, on the building of a tunnel. Had they affirmed their decision, Thomson could have done little about it except perhaps to delay the work for as long as he could, a course that he was fully capable of taking. Had he done so, the property owners might have mustered the political power to force a showdown. Thomson enjoyed power, too, but he maintained it by using it judiciously, not by squandering it or by inviting conflict at every turn. It was better to try to convince the property owners to accept a regrade than to confront them with a refusal to cooperate. Thus, Thomson sent Jeffrey to the meeting with the property owners, and Jeffrey prevailed. Thomson did not indicate why he did not attend this meeting, only stating that he could not. If he had a scheduling conflict, he could have requested another meeting date. His absence was peculiar, especially because the gathering was held at the home of James T. Ronald, who was responsible for returning him to the city engineer's post following the infamous "Who cut the stick" episode in 1894. Thomson would not have compromised his integrity by attending a meeting at Ronald's house; indeed, he could have believed that he

owed Ronald a gesture, or more than one, in return for past favors. There are several possible interpretations of his decision not to attend, the most plausible being that he wished to avoid a personal dispute with Ronald in case his and Jeffrey's figures were unacceptable. Better to send Jeffrey—then if Jeffrey proved unpersuasive, to fall back on delay until the property owners saw the light. [7]

Thomson carefully pointed out that he was not the first engineer to propose regrades. Indeed, regrading was justified historically. "In the ruins of very ancient cities, we find evidences that the same character of work—that is to say the work of regrading—was carried on before the beginning of history," he wrote in his 1909 report. More to the point, extensive urban regrading was common in the United States. In 19th century Boston, hills were leveled primarily to provide new land around the waterfront, though the regraded hills, too, were redeveloped once they were reduced. At least one early Boston project was, properly speaking, a "regrade." The Oliver Street or Fort Hill reduction began in 1866, reaching completion in 1872 as a combined regrade and landmaking operation. Although the contractors used horse-drawn dump carts to haul away dirt, at least one contractor also employed improved steam shovels to cut down Fort Hill. A railroad hauled earth for the creation of Atlantic Avenue. [8]

How much Thomson knew about the Boston operation is unclear. It is likely that he was more familiar with Pittsburgh's problems over "Grant's Hill" or "the Hump," originally a 116-foot eminence similar to Seattle's Denny Hill in height and proximity to valuable commercial-retail property. The Hump, lowered 10 feet in 1836 and 7 feet in 1847, still presented an obstacle, so in November 1911 authorization came to further reduce it, with a maximum cut of 16.3 feet. The work involved the widening of six "centrally located" streets, along with relaying sewers and the repaving and recurbing of the streets. The effort encompassed 35 acres and involved more than 180 property owners. By about 1914, property owners were spending 7 million dollars on new buildings, with the prospect of another 13 million being committed to new construction. Pittsburgh authorized the 1911 regrade during the same month that Thomson retired, therefore it is possible that Seattle stimulated Pittsburgh more than Pittsburgh inspired Seattle. At any rate, an unpublished record of the Pittsburgh undertaking survives in the Seattle engineering department archives. [9]

What is certain is that one previous Seattle regrade project motivated Thomson—in "about 1883," uncle Harry Whitworth had reworked the "repeat-edly regraded" Front Street (now First Avenue) from Pike Street to Denny Way. The result was "a very great improvement over anything that had been done before." However, the bulk of 140-foot Denny Hill remained. It is probable that the work had been done with more primitive equipment than Boston's earlier Fort Hill undertaking. Picks and shovels, horse-drawn draglines, and horse carts to haul away earth were probably used in the grading of First Avenue (1880), Pike and Union streets (1882), and Jackson Street from Elliott Bay to Lake Washington (1883). Earth from these and other cuts was dumped into hollows or along the bay shore in early efforts to make new land available for commerce. Except for the short stretch of upper First Avenue, the works actually were gradings, not regradings. In Thomson's mind, they were a precedent, but left much to be improved upon. [10]

Thomson also brought urban planning theory into play in defense of the regrades. As he told the mayor, "the city is similar in its requirements to the human system." Elaborating on the organicism then much in vogue in urban thought, he declared, "just as a free circulation of blood is necessary to secure the development of each part of the body, so a free movement of traffic is necessary to develop each portion of the city." The regrades were designed "to enlarge insufficient arteries and to remove… blockades…tending to prevent" the "free flow" of traffic, the city's lifeblood. [11]

Regrading, however much justified by history, prec-edent, and theory, also had to operate within state law, the city charter, Seattle ordinances, and, as will be seen, state supreme court decisions. Washington's legislation and court decisions were derivative, taken from other state and local efforts to regulate relationships between the citizenry and local improvements. This was due to the late entry of both Washington to statehood and of Seattle to full municipal citizenship. It proved advanta-geous to the city, for Seattle inherited a set of procedures tested by time and the courts, and unlikely to be upset by legal challenges. [12]

In brief and in general, the process worked this way. It began with a group of property owners petitioning for the regrade of their street for an agreed-upon dis-tance and conditions. If the owners of 50 percent of the affected properties signed the petition, then property could be charged up to 50 percent of its total assessed value. If the owners of 75 percent or more of the prop-erties signed a petition, they could request a higher percentage, up to 200 percent, as the first Denny Hill

petitioners did. The petition then went to the Board of Public Works, which referred it to Thomson, who served as chairman of the board for most of his term in office. Essentially, Thomson was referring it to himself. After Thomson's office certified that the owners of the requisite front feet of property had signed, the petition went back to the board, which then referred it to the city council. When the council's street committee reported favorably, the council granted the petition, and passed an ordinance setting forth the details of the regrade based on maps and profiles prepared in Thomson's office. The ordi-nance directed the corporation counsel to prepare all the needed legal documents and begin a suit in a Washington State Superior Court, the court of original jurisdiction in such matters. The court then appointed an Eminent Domain Commission to fix the benefits and damages for each property in what was termed a local improvement district (LID). The commission usually consisted of three persons, frequently real estate men familiar with property values in the LID. Once the so-called assessment roll was complete, the court held a hearing at which individual property owners could express their views, as well as real estate and construction people who testified to probable post-regrade values. Then the court could confirm the roll or order modifications. Once confirmed, the roll went to the council, which held its own hearing. The assessment roll could be modified there, as well. Then the council passed a second ordinance establishing the LID, a common vehicle for many improvements, not just regrades, requiring the Board of Public Works to prepare plans and submit bids, and appropriating money, if any, from the general fund. Assuming a successful bid, at that point the regrade passed from the control of the city council and became an administrative matter for the public works board. [13]

This outline ignores, mostly, the political dimensions of regrading. Often a minority of property owners filed a "remonstrance" or protest against a proposed regrade, either because they disapproved of the new grade, or more frequently because they disliked the apportionment of the costs. Either way, the objection was to a cost out of proportion to the benefits received. [14]

The first opportunity to object occurred in the superior court hearing on the assessment roll. Even though they were experienced specialists, the eminent domain commissioners could make what an aggrieved lot owner would perceive to be a catastrophic error in the assignment of damages and benefits. The val-ues established by the commissioners and the state-ments by the construction men as to the worth of the

The Remains of Denny Hill

O.T. Frasch Seattle 620

O.T. Frasch's "The Remains of Denny Hill" and Asahel Curtis's elevated view often are reproduced to illustrate the extent of the Denny Hill leveling. Commodious houses have been lowered far below the original height of Denny Hill, losing their panoramic views in the process. The photographs demonstrate that regrading affected middle-class and elite neighborhoods as well as lower class and transient districts. *University of Washington, Special Collections, UW 6018 (Frasch) & UW 4812 (Curtis).*

buildings to be built on the freshly regraded lots could be no more than educated guesses. Other lot owners, judged to be damaged, could protest that their damages were greater than the amount allowed them. There was always room for interpretation. If the court rejected a lot owner's challenge, the owner could next file a written complaint with the city council in advance of the council hearing. That failing, the owner could go to trial in superior court. Either the lot owner or the city could appeal the superior court verdict to the state supreme court. "No questions come to this or any other court that involve such entanglements and complications as do these assessment cases"—so went a mildly exasperated Washington State Supreme Court decision in 1911. The questions could not "be resolved by reference to equation or theorem." Damages, benefits, and assessments could, in other words, be distributed unevenly based on the best judgment available. [15]

The courts created another field for internecine disputes among property owners in the same LID when they held that, in general, property damaged more than it was benefited could not be charged additional benefit assessments. For example, a court jury awarded one "Smith" $50.00 in damages, over and above benefits, for his property in the Pike-Pine LID, then at the northern edge of commercial development. The city paid Smith the money from its general fund. But when the assessment roll came before the city council, the council charged a new benefit assessment of $345.67 to Smith's property. Smith objected to being, in effect, assessed twice for benefits. He carried the day in both superior and supreme courts. What Smith's case and others meant was that, in practical terms, the owners of severely damaged property received compensation while the owners of greatly benefited property saw themselves as stuck with all or at least a significant part of the costs of improvement. The Washington State Supreme Court deviated from this stand only in special cases, as when benefits and damages were assessed against the same property for distinctly different and separate projects. [16]

As the 1911 statement from the court suggests, the court heard many cases, assessment and others, on appeal from one superior court or another. Some involved landslides or issues of so-called "lateral support." Before reviewing these issues, some words of caution are in order. A relatively small number of cases involving the regrades actually reached the Washington State Supreme Court. For example, the first Denny Hill regrade involved 350 verdicts and "the interests of nearly 800 persons," yet only a few supreme court cases concerned

Denny Hill properties. Those cases were important, of course, but the small number suggests that many potential suits were never brought or that many were settled in superior court, either by a verdict or by agreement among litigants prior to a verdict. As time went on and more precedents were set by supreme court decisions, the proportion of cases appealed to the high court probably diminished.

The assessment cases were not of primary importance to Thomson, however significant they were to the litigators. Neither were those cases brought by one private party against another as a result of changed circumstances produced by a regrade. One example involved the inability to meet a mortgage because of the purchaser's too-optimistic belief in increased property values. Procedural rulings were usually not important to Thomson, although in one instance the court held that he had overstepped his authority. What concerned Thomson the most were judgments against the city resulting from cuts or fills that left property too inaccessible, or worse, judgments for slides that undermined property or spilled onto land. Such judgments were unfortunate because they drove up costs beyond the amount budgeted for a regrade, and these unfortunate incidents could make Thomson, his office, and the contractors look bad. The slide cases were especially difficult because the earth in the regrade areas was comprised of glacially deposited soils, strata that could move independently, causing a slide. The propensity for slides existed apart from regrading, but regrading uncovered soils to the effects of Seattle's persistent fall, winter, and spring rains, increasing the chances for slides. [17]

Two court cases controlled the city's obligation to compensate citizens for damages caused by street work. Both were decided in 1892 before serious regrading began, and though controversial at the time, determined how compensation for regrading would be paid in Seattle. In the first case, the grading of the present Yesler Way at Sixth Avenue caused a slide that undermined a house, outbuildings, and other property at the intersection's southwest corner. The city contended that the property destruction was "consequential" (i.e., not a "direct" or immediate result of the grading) and therefore the municipality was not liable. Furthermore, the city was protected by its acting in the public interest, and besides, the whole episode occurred before the adoption of the state constitution. The court dismissed all of these arguments, finding that "natural justice" to an owner deprived of "lateral support" for his property demanded reasonable compensation. Commonsensical as the decision may appear to a contemporary reader, it flew in the face of long-held distinctions between "direct" and "consequential" damages, and between the heavy liability of a private party damaging another's property and the nearly nonexistent liability of a government under the same circumstances. Justice John P. Hoyt pointed out the majority's deviation in a vigorous dissenting opinion. Among other statements, Hoyt declared that abiding by the majority decision "would compel the proper authorities…to determine beforehand…the amount of soil which would fall from the adjoining lots…and show the same by the most exact profile and figures, and have the damages…determined and paid before they proceeded at all with the improvement." That, of course, is exactly what happened. [18]

The court majority had the last word. Perhaps anticipating radical changes to Seattle's craggy topography, Justice Theodore Stiles wrote that "it would certainly be a great hardship, indeed, if the city could go on with gross recklessness to remove…the only support for the whole hillside." The second 1892 case differed in its details but not in the court's conclusions. In this instance, a property owner sought and received an injunction against the city and its contractor from regrading a portion of Jefferson Street before paying damages. The litigant owned rental houses on Jefferson and on the present Seventh and Eighth avenues bringing her $237 each month, a tidy sum in 1892. The supreme court affirmed that the proposed regrading in an already hilly area would leave the houses and an access alley so high above the streets as to undermine the property's value for rental or resale. This second 3-2 decision, again written by Stiles, admitted that the law once weighed against the citizen who sought compensation for damages resulting from public construction. But the law was changing and in any case the state constitution of 1889 required payment for property taken or damaged. The constitution prohibited any appropriation of property "without just compensation having been first made or paid into court for the owner." When "private property is damaged for the public benefit the public should make good the loss to the individual," Stiles declared. That "always was the equity of the case, and the constitution makes the hitherto disregarded equity now the law of it." The injunction would stand until the property owner's compensation was paid. [19]

Given the precedent set in 1892, it is scarcely surprising that the supreme court upheld the pleas of people whose property was undermined or overwhelmed by slides. The court supported these claims whether or not the damages occurred soon after the regrading or as the result of a slow-moving slide. Except in a few instances, which it later overruled, the court maintained that the city was liable for slides whenever and wherever they occurred, if a regrade was the cause of them. It was of no importance whether or not the damaged property was included in the LID. If a contractor caused the earth to move destructively, the city was responsible because contractors worked under close city supervision, making the city liable for "the wrongful acts of its agents and servants." [20]

The Jackson Street regrade caused some of the most dramatic and continuing slides, which persisted at least until 1923. Thomson would leave office late in 1911 when the rebuilding of streets and utilities along Jackson was under way. Whether he would have handled the situation more effectively cannot be known. [21]

The city fared better when complainants challenged it on procedural grounds. What helped the city here was the fact that the ordinance and law controlling the regrades, and the contracts made under them, were not in themselves experimental, however radical the scope of the regrading. The courts in the states and cities from which Seattle and Washington borrowed their public improvement statutes had generated a body of case law supporting the procedures laid down in those statutes. Thus the Washington State Supreme Court upheld the right of the city to collect a reassessment in order to correct irregularities in the original assessment, or to reassess based on legally imposed changes in its original plans. [22] It upheld the authority of the condemnation commissioners to set the boundaries of the benefited districts, and in general prevented either the city council or the superior courts from adjusting them. [23] It upheld the city's 30-day time limit on filing claims as adequate in and of itself. In a few cases it held that the filing deadline trumped the constitutional guarantee of just compensation for property taken by a government. [24] The *Wong* decision of 1927 overruled those cases, restoring the constitutional protection. [25]

Unfortunately for Thomson and Seattle, the city engineer ran afoul of the supreme court's concern for procedural correctness as defined by a contract. It occurred this way: The contract for regrading a portion of Denny Hill provided for the contractor leaving a slope of 1:1 on private property along the streets being excavated to the new, lower grade. The 1:1 slope meant that the base of the slope (the first number) would be one foot in horizontal measurement for each one foot of vertical measurement (the second number) to the height of each private lot. The 1:1 slope was usual for the area and nothing exceptional. It was in one sense a boon to the

The first Denny Hill regrade involved much more than lowering the hill. In 1906, photographer James P. Lee pointed his camera north along Third Avenue, from near Spring Street. The street itself is impassable. Pedestrians, seen at the right foreground, struggle along a makeshift sidewalk. A remnant of the once-elegant Washington Hotel looms in the far background. The view below, taken on an overcast autumn day, shows at right one system of cribbing used to support wooden buildings until they were lowered to the new street grade. *University of Washington Libraries, Special Collections, Lee 20008 & Lee 20010a.*

property owner because it removed some of his earth. It was made, not for the owner's benefit, but to avoid some of the slides on to the newly regraded public street that would, probably, result from a steeper slope. However, before work could get under way, the state supreme court intervened with its 1908 decision declaring that property held to be damaged could not be assessed additionally based on its perceived benefits. In other words, a damage award assumed that benefits had been considered, and that the damages were greater. Therefore, no additional benefit charges could be levied. Because the Denny Hill assessment roll included the then-standard benefit assessments charged against damaged property, the decision rendered about $67,000 uncollectible. How would the deficit be erased? Thomson looked at those projected 1:1 slopes on private property fronting on the affected streets and came up with the answer—the contractor would cut only ¾ of a foot for each foot of elevation, or in other words, only 75 percent as much as under the contract. It was clever engineering and clever economics. There were only two things wrong with Thomson's brainstorm—it was a violation of the contract and it left the private lot owner holding a very large bag of earth. [26]

To understand why this was so, two matters must be considered. First, all the regrading contracts during Thomson's time included a clause stating that private property owners could have their lots brought down to the new street grade at the same price as the contractors charged the city. Or, to put it another way, the remainder of the earth left on the lot at the 1:1 slope would be removed at, in this case, 27¢ per cubic yard if the property owner elected to have the work done at the same time that the street was being regraded. The second consideration returns to the original 1:1 slope versus Thomson's revised ¾:1 cut. The problem for the lot owner may be visualized by imagining a lot 200 feet deep and 100 feet above the new street grade. With the original 1:1 slope, the contractor would cut away the first 100 feet from the street, plus enough soil from the second 100 feet to create a slope from the new grade to the top of the back of the lot. The remaining soil would then be 100 feet horizontally and 100 feet vertically, or a 1:1 slope. However, under Thomson's program, the contractor would remove only 75 feet from the street, plus enough soil from the remaining 125 feet to create a slope to the top of the back of the lot. The lot owner would then confront a larger volume of earth to be removed, because the horizontal unremoved earth would extend for 125 feet instead of 100 feet. Thomson's solution saved the city the $67,000 in the short run, but threw the burden of making it up on the lot holders who would pay the contractor more for removing the greater volume of earth from their lots.

The contractor stood on a clause in the contract stating that the decisions of the city engineer on all disputes "shall be final and conclusive, subject to the approval of the board of public works." Thomson, though not a direct participant in the suit, was indirectly involved because his judgment and authority were at stake. The court ruled that he had overstepped. It agreed that the language in the contract allowed Thomson to "make such changes as necessary to correct structural defects in the plans…or to oversee engineering difficulties… not foreseen or…correct minor inconsequential omissions or mistakes." The change, however, "was radical instead of minor and inconsequential." It "was made for the sole purpose of eliminating a large part of the cost of the work." The contractor would have to accept a charge based on the 1:1 slope. The contractor sued the city to pay the difference. The contractor won, forcing the city to reassess to raise the necessary money. [27]

While the supreme court honed the laws controlling the regrading, the spectacular work of "washing away a city's hills" went forward. It was a daunting task. Following the First Avenue regrade that smoothed the humps on First Avenue and allowed better passage over the western toe of Denny Hill, came the massive regrading of Second, Third, Fourth, and Fifth avenues and other streets, later known as the Denny Hill regrade No. 1. The designation rather diminishes the extent of the work because the contractors not only knocked down the Denny Hill massif, they lowered the grades on Second, Third, Fourth, and Fifth avenues as well. These major commercial streets rose and fell over a series of humps and hollows making horse-drawn teaming over their length a practical impossibility. Assuming a modest total load of one ton in a horse-drawn vehicle, a 4 or 5 percent grade (a rise of 4–5 feet in a hundred) was the maximum pull for a single draft horse. Taking Fourth Avenue as an example, its original grade against northbound traffic in the block between Washington Street and Yesler Way was 14.8 percent, from Jefferson to James, 10 percent, and from Marion to Madison 8.7 percent, meaning that Fourth was closed to continuous light northbound teaming and that teamsters were forced into southbound travel only. Worse, continuous southbound single-horse traffic was impossible because of steep grades from Union to University. [28]

Of course, heavy loads could be delivered by adding horses or taking circuitous routes. Every delivery address could be served if the load to that point were light, or the horses numerous. But such compromises increased either the expense of hauling, or the potential for abuse of an overworked animal. The new grade on Fourth lessened these difficulties. From Washington north to Yesler the new grade became 4.9 percent, with a steady 4.7 percent from Yesler to Madison. The grade from there to Spring was a gentle 2.29, while the grades southbound from Union past University to Spring were no steeper than 3.92 percent. Thomson accepted the revised grades on Fourth and other streets as "all in the right line," but still they were "excessive" and not "satisfactory to a close student of economics, as related to urban transportation."[29]

These were far from the only improvements under the Thomson program. Fourth and other streets were widened from 66 to 90 feet. The widening of Fourth as well as the cuts to reduce the grade—cuts as deep as 28 feet—demanded the relaying of all the utilities as well as rebuilding the street and sidewalks. The buildings along Fourth were set back and lowered or demolished. The Seattle Athletic Club at the intersection with Cherry Street decided on a different solution. Rather than lower the building and lose their view of Elliott Bay, the own-

ers filled the cut with two new stories beneath the existing edifice. The public and private property involved 40 acres, with a total of 693,000 cubic yards of earth and rock removed. The work, begun in June 1907, took about two years from start to finish.[30] The most drastic regrading occurred on Denny Hill itself. From Pike Street (Pike and Pine, the next streets north of Union, were already regraded), the ruling grade was an impossible 16 percent. Southbound traffic from Wall Street faced a maximum 12.47 percent grade. Such inclines were the stuff of alpinists or residents who traded breathlessness for the spectacular views from their hillside homes. The demolition of Denny Hill produced a gentle 1.38 percent grade from Pike to Virginia, while southbound grades from Wall were scarcely noticeable at 0.6 and 0.7 percent.[31]

Apart from Denny Hill, Jackson Street was the most sensational regrade, already mentioned as the site of the property owners' switch from advocating a tunnel. The Jackson Street regrade well illustrated the procedural complexity of the process. Property owners' initial petition came in on October 11, 1905, augmented by a supplementary petition on December 15, 1906, increasing the percentage of property owners and allowing a charge

A December 1908 photograph of the Jackson Street regrade (in the middle distance) provides some idea of the project's scope. In the foreground, commercial blocks are braced against tumbling into the tideflats. *University of Washington Libraries, Special Collections, UW 1563.*

A 1909 view, looking west through part of the Jackson Street regrade wasteland. The pipe probably feeds hydraulic "giants" busily demolishing heights in the regrade. Fascinated kibitzers and sidewalk superintendents often visited the project sites, as they are doing here. The tower of the GN and NP's jointly operated King Street Station soars in the background above the city and tideflats. *Museum of History and Industry, PEMCO Webster & Stevens Collection 83.10.8131.*

against the property involved up to 200 percent of the assessed valuation. Meanwhile the process went forward with the court trial concluding in October. The Eminent Domain Commission finished its work and filed its report on July 27, 1907. In advance of final approval of revisions under the supplementary petition, the political procedures continued. The council passed and the mayor signed the necessary ordinance in February 1906. For almost a year, the Board of Public Works prepared final plans while court challenges were settled, and then advertised for bids. The one bid was opened on March 9, 1907, the contractor's bonds for the public and private property involved approved in April, and the contract awarded the same month. The city allowed the contractor six months to assemble his equipment and plant, a reasonable time given the complexity and magnitude of the task. An additional two years were granted for completion. The new assessment roll based on the supplemental petition was finally approved October 23, 1907.[32]

The lead contractor, William L. Lewis, was an attorney and property owner in the Rainier Valley area south and east of Jackson Street. His mind had turned away from the law to adapting hydraulic mining or water sluicing to removing the soil for the regrade. In an unpublished paper, Thomson credited W.C. Morse, later a city engineer, with the sluicing idea. Other writers have seconded his notion. Thomson also credited himself with

supporting the sluicing against skeptics, who included bankers unwilling to finance the Jackson Street undertaking. The objections could not have been to the novelty of the hydraulic method for regrading, because it was used on the Second Avenue regrade in 1903–4. On the other hand, the very scale of the Jackson Street regrade was enough to produce a roomful of skeptics. The core of the project involved the destruction or removal of every building along a five block swath of land from the south side of Washington Street through Main, Jackson, King, Weller, and on the north side of Lane Street. And not only buildings, for every fence, shrub, garden, tree, sewer pipe, water main, light and telephone wire and pole, and every scrap of street paving and sidewalk would be destroyed or moved along those five blocks from Fourth Avenue South to Twelfth Avenue South. The core area covered 38 blocks if the filled area within those boundaries is included. Other areas to be filled outside the core brought the total to 53 city blocks, or about 125 acres, not including 678 acres of tideflats south of the regrades. The latter acreage was to be filled two feet above high tide from earth washed down from the regrade's formidable hills. Within the regrade, the deepest cut would be 92 feet at Tenth Avenue South and Jackson, with the most substantial fill being some five blocks west, at 54 feet. Its surface area would include the largest single regrade in Seattle and perhaps in any other city.[33]

Despite the massive projected dislocations of the Jackson Street regrade, Lewis persevered, lined up his financing, and began work under the company name of Lewis & Wiley. Innovations in hydraulics helped to move matters along. In place of the stationary hoses and nozzles often used in mining, the nozzles of each of the four "giants" sat on a ball and socket joint allowing the operators to control them from the rear with long wooden handles. The nozzles could swing horizontally in a full circle, and through a vertical arc of about 30 degrees. The detachable nozzles were from 2.5 to 5 inches in diameter, depending on the desired breadth and force of the stream, which in turn depended on the type of soil that the operators confronted. At first the operators encountered a sandy loam running as deep as 30 feet, and then beneath it, a blue clay subsoil. Here the trouble began, for the subsoil was shot through with stratified glacial deposits of "hardpan"—hard cemented ground, with boulders up to about ten feet in diameter, and rock lenses intermixed with the hardpan. Sluicing alone often failed to dislodge the material. Blasting crews worked with the "giant" operators, mostly veterans of the Alaska gold fields, to apply the most effective combination of explosives and water jets.

The sluicing was unlike mining in other ways. First, there was no retrieving of gold since Seattle's hills contained no precious metals. Second, it was a fully industrialized, around-the-clock operation, designed to reduce the grades on Jackson and related streets in minimum time. It was not a seasonal activity like hydraulicing mining in Alaska or the mountains of the West. Third, it required a lot of water, and the flow had to be not just abundant, but certain. For that reason, and because of the need to protect close-packed urban residents from scouring floods, Lewis & Wiley could not rely on the makeshift dams and flimsy flumes of the mining companies. Instead it contracted for the city to supply water from the disused Beacon Hill reservoir about a mile south of the regrade. Water came down through a specially-built wood stave pipe, providing a pressure of at least 75 pounds per square inch at the nozzles. Lewis & Wiley paid the city $15.00 per million gallons, a good deal even at turn-of-the-century prices, because the water was surplus, thanks to Thomson's foresight and determination in building the Cedar River system. The six to ten million gallons per day, however, were not enough. So the contractors activated the city's abandoned Lake Washington pumping station at Holgate Street, obtaining an added six million gallons or so per day. The contractors paid the city $3,000 per year for the use of the plant, again a fine deal for them, but an

even better deal for Seattle, which was earning nothing on its idle equipment. The pumping station also delivered to the Beacon Hill reservoir.

Still there was not enough water. Lewis & Wiley built an elaborate pumping station in Elliott Bay off Connecticut Street (now South Royal Brougham Way). It was erected on pilings, caulked to prevent flooding at extreme high tide, and equipped with especially designed pumps and inlet tubes. During shut downs, the salt water line filled with fresh water through a connection with the pipe from Beacon Hill. The fresh water kept the wooden stave line wet, and kept out ever-present teredos or shipworms, the wood-eating insects devastating to untreated wood. The huge 24 inch line ran east from Connecticut and crossed under two paved streets and the Great Northern Railway tracks to Fourth Avenue South. From there it turned 90 degrees north in a cast iron elbow. Other twists and turns brought it upgrade to the works. In one of the more daring and ingenious solutions to the problem of getting the pipeline to the regrade, workmen suspended it 22 feet above the new Oregon & Washington Railroad (Union Pacific) passenger station on Jackson between Fourth and Fifth.

At last Lewis & Wiley had the needed water. The Elliott Bay pumping station added a potential 12 million gallons of salt water per day to the fresh water capacity. Using salt water was a mixed blessing, however, for it pitted nozzles, frothed, bubbled, and tended to spray in contrast to fresh water's more compact streams. But because of its greater specific gravity, salt water was effective enough at shorter distances. Lewis & Wiley's salt water source provided more than either of the fresh water sources, well over an astounding 4,300,000,000 gallons. The total sluicing gallonage was an amazing 10,095,179,594, a flood that washed down a total of 3,347,883 cubic yards of earth between the end of 1907 and the beginning of 1910. Horse-drawn scrapers finished off the final foot of the regrade.

In the Jackson Street regrade, there was no option to raise or lower houses and buildings, as on the downtown streets; they had to be destroyed or moved. In the muddy swath, movers competed with the regrade contractors for time and space to do their jobs. When the detritus from the washings began filling the tideflats, it plugged drains coming from buildings on the flats and sewers serving both the flats and the regrades. In the flats, salvageable buildings were raised and wooden box sewers were built extending to the bay. In the regrade area, the movers squeezed salvaged houses onto available lots while the

During the Jackson Street regrade, a bulkhead at Fifth Avenue South and South Weller Street kept fill away from these shored-up apartment houses. *University of Washington Libraries, Special Collections, Lee 20018.*

residents continued living in them. Box sewers connected the relocated houses on high ground with the bay, rigged to temporary bridges and other support.

Filling in the mud flats and creating sustainable slopes in the regraded area was as critical to the success of the operation as the excavation itself. Crews directed the water—carrying soil, rock, and other debris in suspension—into sluice boxes barred in front to prevent large rocks, roots, and lumps of clay from entering. The boxes connected to so-called "mud lines" at the flats. Other crews spread the mixture over the flats, raising its level. Dikes held the muddy mix in place until the liquid evaporated or soaked through into the bay. Crews created relatively steep 1.5 to 1 slopes where necessary on the edges of the regrade and in the fill. Twelve-foot-long boards, each a foot high, ran along the base of the area to be sloped. Heavy stakes braced them on the downslope side. The "giants" shot streams of dirt-laden water over and above the boards. After about 1¼ feet of dirt had precipitated out and was dry, workmen staked another row of boards in place on top of the previous line of fill.

The process was repeated until the wood and earth ziggurat reached the desired height.

It was hard, exhausting labor. Crews worked three eight-hour shifts every day except Sunday, pausing only when an accident or equipment failure forced a shutdown. A man stationed at the entrance to each sluice box or pipe pulled away rocks, tree roots, and other debris too large for the barriers (the "grizzly bars"). Nothing was wasted. Men sledge hammered rocks unwanted by landscapers until they were small enough to pass through the "grizzlies." They hacked and sawed roots, and trimmed other junk to size. The "giant" men worked in all sorts of weather and conditions to play water on the sometimes barely yielding earth. In the fill area, others handled the stave pipe mudlines. Unfortunately for them, it was next to impossible to leave a mudline in place until it had filled its assigned space. Agreements with hard-pressed business owners to raise, or delay razing, of buildings, or the need to build temporary bridges to keep some businesses in operation, required the mudline workers to move their pipes here and there as the occasion demanded. Maintenance was a chore. Metal pipes and wooden sluice boxes could wear through quickly from stone and sand abrasion. Finally an inventor came up with an ingenious solution. The bottoms of the sluices were lined with wooden blocks wedged in place and standing on end, so that the fibers of the grain absorbed and resisted the wear. But even the blocks had to be replaced now and then.

Lewis & Wiley also maintained their own repair shop on the regrade grounds. Industrialized as their operation was, it demanded an average monthly payroll of 111, with the largest at 239. Lewis & Wiley were released from their contract on April 8, 1910, having spent $455,226.64, a small fraction of what this undertaking would have cost a century later. Yet only the clearing was done. The lowered ground yet had to be surveyed, utilities restored, removed buildings resited to new lots, and the widened Jackson and other streets resurfaced. All this took another four years. The project was completed at last in July 1914, more than seven years after it began. As already mentioned, earth slides caused trouble, while lawsuits continued for years afterward. As for the tide-flats, the settling of the new fill played havoc with some bridges, utility lines, and building foundations for years. The area was not brought to its final grade until 1929.

The regrading of Denny Hill itself involved only 99 acres of surface area, an undertaking modest compared to the Jackson Street effort. The destruction of Denny Hill was more poignant, nonetheless. Atop the hill and astride Third Avenue stood the late Victorian Denny (later Washington) Hotel, the epitome of a type of edifice practically gone from today's Seattle landscape. It rose five stories, with a tower, turrets, and a cavernous lobby. The ground floor stood some 150 feet above the surrounding streets—its views of Puget Sound, the Olympics, the Cascades, and the city were the stuff of real estate superlatives. A residential area around the hotel sprouted comfortable Victorian and Edwardian houses for the same reason. The uncomfortable fact that the hill and the ravines to its east impeded easy access to the developing northern part of the city scarcely deterred devotees of the picturesque, then or later. [34] The reduction of Denny Hill involved a series of regrades beginning with First Avenue. Regrading Second Avenue brought down more of the western toe of the hill as it opened another retail-commercial thoroughfare for easier north-south traffic. Regrades of east-west Pike and Pine Streets hacked away at the hill's southern edge.

The Second Avenue regrade became part of the lore of the Thomson era. If viewed in profile south to north,

Second Avenue rose from Pine on an 18.3 percent grade to Stewart, then fell on a grade of 8.3 percent to the intersection with Virginia, then rose again on the same grade to Lenora, then fell again to Blanchard on a 17 percent grade, delineating the especially rough western shoulder of Denny Hill. The up-and-down from Pine to Virginia and from Virginia to Lenora "left Virginia Street a low spot between two peaks," Thomson wrote. "People said it was like a saddle on a two-humped camel." Thomson wanted the saddle cut way down, which meant, of course, that the humps would go, and so would the tons of earth lying below Virginia and the humps. He approached James A. Moore, the dynamic businessman who owned the Washington Hotel, perhaps believing that if Moore would consent to a release of damages, thereby paying a benefit assessment, other property owners would go along. Moore refused because of the expense and disruption involved, as did others. Moore later redeemed himself in Thomson's eyes by paying for the demolition of his great hotel and much else besides, but the best the city engineer could manage in 1903 was a regrade of 11 feet on Virginia, plus enough of the mini-mountain on either side to leave a northbound ruling grade of 4.7 percent and a southbound grade of 3.2 percent. The low point on Second Avenue between Stewart and Lenora thus became the high point, especially when seen from the south at the intersection of Pike or Pine. [35]

This since-notorious "hump" at Virginia remains. As one property owner wrote years later, he was one of "perhaps a hundred owners who pushed the project through the Council" with its more modest regrade, "despite Mr. Thomson. And today we have at Second and Virginia a sort of terrestrial dunce-cap as a monument of our political victory over the engineer in 1903." Even with the hump, Second Avenue was much improved over its length from Yesler Way north to Denny Way. Its easier grades spurred enthusiasm for other regrading, including much more of Denny Hill. [36]

The Denny Hill regrade began under city contract in 1908. Giants did some of the work, a steam shovel some more. Narrow-gauge trains hauled part of the spoil, and landscapers took away stones, just as they were doing on Jackson Street. The Great Northern disposed of about 700,000 cubic yards of earth for fill in its freight yards. About a half million cubic yards went into the ravine and other low areas east and north of Denny Hill. These amounts were scarcely significant considering the additional 5,000,000 cubic yards of material sluiced and shoveled away on city contracts. The water came from

Lake Union, and was sluiced into Elliott Bay. James A. Moore converted to Thomson's cause when he saw property values along the regraded Second Avenue jump despite the "hump," and concluded that he would be better off without Denny Hill. Moore agreed to demolish his hotel astride the line of Third Avenue, dedicate the avenue to the public, and contract for extensive regrading at his expense. Moore's decision was not altruistic, for he correctly believed that his property would be worth more regraded. As soon as the new grades were established well enough, he built the New Washington Hotel (now the Josephinum) and the Moore Theatre on Second Avenue north from Virginia.[37]

The regrading of Denny Hill and of Third, Fourth, and Fifth avenues ended in 1911. Not all of Denny came down. The eastern shoulder of the hill, deemed too expensive to include in Denny Hill regrade No. 1, was not undertaken until the late 1920s. Regrading designed to link the major projects continued until 1915, and minor projects after that time. The physical and legal cleanup work of the major regrades and their links continued for several years. Sources differ on how much earth and rock the contractors excavated on all projects. At the end of Thomson's tenure in 1911 it was about 19,789,200 cubic yards. By comparison, in the colossal engineering undertaken for the Panama Canal, 310,000,000 cubic yards were removed through 1914.[38]

What was the value to Seattle of all this effort? It is a question with no single or simple answer. One place to begin is with a general assessment, and in that regard judgments have varied with time. Before, during, and just after the major regrades, there was some grumbling about the extent and expense. Thomson noted the discontent when he wrote that "some quarters" exhibited "a strong tendency to oppose every regrade which was planned to make a reasonable street level," but he blamed the opposition on inadequate civic-mindedness. "Some people seemed to think that because there were hills in Seattle originally, some of them ought to be left there, no difference how injurious a heavy grade over a hill may be to the property beyond."[39]

Contemporary books unstintingly praised Thomson, based on the conviction that the regrades were essential to the city's future. Welford Beaton's sprightly *The City That Made Itself* (1914) declared the regrades to be "largely the story of one man's dream." In a paragraph dropping the names of Edison, Bell, Marconi, and Morse, Beaton declared that to Thomson "must be given the credit for making over the physical Seattle into a city of present easy lines of communication." For Beaton, the

regrades were "wonderful" yet required "a great struggle" because Thomson "was assailed on all sides by a public that could not grasp the boldness of this conception… But he went ahead, pushing his plans through in a manner that showed that he completely dominated the city government." Writers echoed Beaton's hyperboles into the 1960s, when enthusiasm for such bold public works crested. Historiography followed the trend.[40]

Then judgment began to change. In 1976, Roger Sale's Bicentennial history of Seattle, although sympathetic to Thomson and his "wonderful record," deplored the destruction of Denny Hill and the loss of such "enduring wonders" as exist in the hills of San Francisco. Sale worried about "the potential dangers of setting such people" as Thomson "loose on the landscape," and argued that "one of Thomson's most enduring legacies has been the habit of mind which thinks that all the problems of any city can be solved by more and better engineering."[41] Sale's judgment has reverberated in subsequent histories more friendly to preserving natural topographies.[42]

While criticism of Thomson's "habit of mind" continued, skepticism about his approach to urban problems arose from other concerns, too. Increased awareness of the matters of race, gender, and class, and of the multiplicity of influences on patterns of urban growth and settlement influenced later historical viewpoints. Sensitivity to the fragility of ecosystems as well as to the intrusiveness and frailty of human systems designed to modify or supplant them, led to the rise of environmental history.[43]

These concerns led in their turn to serious doubts about the value or wisdom of the regrades. The heaviest charge against them is their human cost, for they disrupted many lives, fostering confusion at best, and personal anguish and economic ruin at worst. That lives were disrupted is undeniable. In the short run of a decade and a half of the most intensive regrading, people lost houses to destruction or removal, businesses suffered, and many who retained their residences in or away from the regrades were inconvenienced. The enthusiasts of regrading admitted as much at the time. A mostly favorable newspaper review of 1909 recounted the trials of one "Smith" who lived in a rented house with his wife "and a number of children." First, Smith struggled through mud for three blocks to and from the trolley. Then the contractor moved an engine in front of the house to haul away fill, a racket that awakened the baby. Next, the trolley line had to be rerouted still farther away. Grocery and coal deliveries were problematic. As things were returning to normal, the landlord decided to tear down Smith's house and put up an apartment building in response to rising land values. "I'm going to build me a little residence away out on some good car line…where they will never monkey with the grades," Smith promised.[44]

Smith's plight, and the dismay of an African-American family whose house was crushed when it fell from its perch during the Dearborn Street regrade, became the fulcrum for assumptions about class- and race-based motives for regrading. It is fashionable to find class and race bias operating in major public works projects, doubtless because bias was indeed present in some of them. The argument regarding Seattle runs like this: Thomson and other engineers masked their anti-minority and anti-immigrant biases with fine words about improved sanitary, aesthetic, social, and economic conditions while pursuing a nativist, racist agenda. Thomson belonged to the Municipal League of Seattle, founded on May 23, 1910, to fight against "those forces" causing immorality in the city's politics and daily life. Therefore, Thomson favored regrading the western edge of Jackson Street and filling in the tidelands because immoral people lived there. He favored regrading the rest of Jackson Street, and Dearborn Street four blocks south of Jackson, because some transients, workingmen in residential hotels, or African-Americans lived on those streets.[45]

There are several answers to this assumption about Thomson's motives. One is that class and race bias hardly applied to the regrading of First, Second, Third, Fourth, or Fifth avenues, or to other major streets or the necessary cross streets in the urban core. It would be rank absurdity to claim class or race bias for the flattening of Denny Hill. As the 1909 newspaper article had it, Denny Hill residents "have had to move out of fine, sightly houses where they had expected to enjoy the bay view for the rest of their days," although they were receiving such high prices for their property that "they are not objects of unmixed sympathy." Thus regrading in general could not be based on distinctions of race or class unless Thomson was revealing a bias against middle and upper class Euroamericans. Thomson's surviving correspondence and diaries contain many forceful opinions but they do not pander to the biases of his time. One letter from Thomson to a friend and colleague expressing concern about some rough characters abroad in Seattle during the height of the Alaska gold rush is not evidence that the city engineer wanted to destroy the residences and livelihoods of people who were feeding the fires of the city's boom. So far as the Municipal League goes, its historian demonstrated that its middle-class, professional members were united only in opposing elites who used the existing system to dominate city government. Further, Thomson's support of the failed Bogue plan (a city beautiful-city practical conception), charter reform, and municipal ownership all flowed from personal considerations having little to do with the Municipal League. His duties in the engineer's office, then at the Port of Seattle, and next in British Columbia, not to mention his consulting work, left little time for deep involvement in any private organization except his church, at least through 1915. Finally, though Thomson was a teetotaler who lived an exemplary personal life, he was not a moral zealot. His focus was on improving the quality of life through the physical reformation of Seattle, not by leading sinners into paths of virtue. [46]

Absolving Thomson of ulterior motives does not resolve the issue of overall benefit. Some Denny Hill residents were furious because the eminent domain commissioners assessed benefit charges against their property while adjacent or nearby property received damage awards, substantial in some cases. Receiving damages was an added boon to a property owner because of the state supreme court ruling that damaged property could not be assessed benefits, then or in any later reassessment. The *Post-Intelligencer* did not help matters by referring to the damaged property as "The Denny Hill Free List," and suggesting that somehow the damaged property holders gained at the expense of their fellows who were assessed benefit charges. While disappointed property owners were venting their frustration, two important facts were escaping them. One was that the city engineer's office, corporation counsel, eminent domain commissioners, judges, and juries did the best they could to be thorough and fair. The second was that all property was assumed to be benefited, and therefore damage awards, whether great or small, were intended to be over and above benefits and did not presume to cover all costs of removal or relocation. [47]

That regrading was done during the twilight of the horse-drawn era is another consideration. Today when motor vehicles scoot up any grade that can be paved, it is easy to forget how daunting a grade of 4 or 5 percent was to draying. Thomson or someone in his office prepared a card showing the escalating costs of drayage as street grades steepened. On a level surface, one horse could pull a teamster and his load, presumably a gross ton, at a cost of 50¢. A 4 percent grade required three horses and cost a dollar. A 15 percent grade, the ruling grade of Jackson Street, required nine horses and cost five times as much as hauling a load on the level. Thomson claimed that the graphic was based on "Trautwine's Engineers book," then a bible of civil engineering. He also claimed that "a gentleman who had become intensely zealous for the regrade" showed the card to "people in the district… and the result was the undertaking of the Jackson Street regrade." This is an obvious exaggeration, similar to his claim that his winning over John J. McGilvra to a gravity waterworks assured the success of the Cedar River system. On the other hand, Thomson would not have mentioned the card if its effect was nil or negative. The card is a reasonably correct representation of John C. Trautwine's calculations in *The Civil Engineer's Pocket-Book* if the speed of a horse or horses, and therefore of the time and cost of moving a load, are considered.[48]

The irony of the graphic (and of the regrades) is that a decade after most of the heavy regrading was completed, the climbing ability of the motor truck and the automobile rendered them unnecessary. Or, they were unnecessary if they are considered only from the standpoint of reduced grades, and not from any other benefit such as using the surplus soil to fill ravines and raise the tidelands. Arthur H. Dimock noted in 1926 how cars and trucks "made old theories" about horses and wagons "seem very ancient indeed." Gentle grades were preferable, of course, "but the limits have been greatly widened." Dimock cited a street "paved with asphalt on a maximum grade of 12%, on the theory that it would never be used anyway," but the street had become heavily traveled. Indeed, Dimock declared, "the ease and comfort of the lowly pedestrian is a more potent factor than motor traffic in limiting the growth of a business district" and in setting grades. Such rearward vision is almost always perfect. Of course, neither Thomson nor other urban planners of the early 20th century foresaw the democratization of the motor vehicle. How could they, along with predicting rampant suburbanization, long-distance air travel, the shopping mall, and the near-death experience of the passenger railroad and the trolley? The short supply of crystal balls among Thomson and his cohorts permits one historian to pass a judgment both ahistorical and unconsciously elitist. According to him, the affluent residents of condominiums built decades later in the Denny regrade would have been better off had Denny Hill survived. Why? Because the well-to-do would have enjoyed better views![49]

There are other dimensions of what would later be called a cost-benefit analysis. Thomson claimed that rising property values along regraded streets were the major justification for the effort and expense of all the earth moving and its attendant inconvenience. He used an argument reaching back at least as far as Frederick Law

Olmsted, who defended 19th-century park and boulevard development on the same grounds. In general, Thomson was correct. The newspapers of the time heralded rising real estate values. Whether the rising values were because of actual or anticipated regrading or the filling of tidelands, or resulted from the fantastic growth of a city surging from an 1890 population of 42,837 to 237,194 in 1910, are effects impossible to disentangle. It could be argued that the city's phenomenal growth depended in part on Thomson's "ruling passion," to "open and keep open lines of easy communication between the center of the city" and nearby areas "which would become factory centers." In any event, impresario James A. Moore, the huffy ship captain whose two houses were moved from Second Avenue, the owners of "fine, sightly houses" on Denny Hill, and others did well. Property owner C.C. Closson laid out the rationale for the increases in value in a candid letter to the weekly *Town Crier*. "We are not obstructionist speculators," he wrote of himself and other property holders in regrade areas, "but manufacturers of facilities. Hills and tideflats are our raw materials and level land our product. Like other manufacturers we need a reasonable market for our output."

But timing was critical to success in the volatile real estate market. A private suit resulting from the regrades showcased the risks for investors. One Joseph Brinton in 1907 made a down payment on a lot on the west side of Rainier Boulevard, in the middle of the block between Norman Street and Bush Place, about seven blocks south of Jackson Street. He hoped to "make a resale of the lot before any additional payments were required" when the Jackson Street regrade brought the property "into closer touch with the business district of the city," increasing its value. The panic of 1907 soured many investments, including Brinton's. He would have to accept his loss, as well as his "disappointment and withered hopes." Real estate agent Von V. Tarbill wrote that of "the speculators" who bought lots near or on Denny Hill with the intention of flipping them, "it may be said that many of them lost." Those who held their property and paid all of their assessments, "very generally lost money, and some of them lost their entire investment." Those who "sold out early," and owners who improved their properties usually made money. Thomson concurred. Some investors, he wrote, expected values to jump on "the day the regrade was finished, and from then on to continue to advance rapidly. Persons making purchases under that vision, as well as persons holding property under that vision, suffered disappointment." Those failures notwithstanding, "values have continued to increase."[50]

Naiveté, gullibility, bad luck, or other human foibles were not all of the story. State law required the payment of all benefit assessments within ten years, at an interest rate of, usually, 6 percent. Responding to the "prevalent feeling that we have undertaken large improvements too rapidly," Closson wrote that "we are paying for them too rapidly." He argued for "some plan of long-term bonds. This is a matter in which our State laws and charter provisions are unnecessarily crude and work a hardship on many property owners." As Tarbill explained, repayment of assessments began the first year of the regrade, with that 6 percent interest on the unpaid balance. The assessments for a regrade and the necessary post-regrade improvements were vastly more expensive than for, say, street pavement. Yet property owners had to wait several years before improving their properties. Some sold at a loss or defaulted on their assessment payments. The defaulters "were of course subject to foreclosure, and a number of property owners lost their properties completely through foreclosure for assessments."[51]

Still another consideration is the fact that the regrades did not advance all property and even rendered some practically worthless. Thomson's house and lot at 701 Yesler Way is a case in point. The Jackson Street regrade left it perched high above the new street levels, its access to the south cut off by a precipice. Thomson argued that "the grade is injurious to our property by reason of the fact that it separates us from all the southern part of the city and makes us totally dependent upon Yesler Way for access to the city." A worse plight befell property on the east, unregraded shoulder of Denny Hill, where "values slumped to nearly nothing." The situation on Dearborn Street south of Jackson was no better, even though the street was regraded from its western edge through the Rainier Valley. By the late 1920s, most values along the street remained stable or had declined. The situation of a regrade being "an injury to the immediately abutting property rather than a benefit," puzzled Thomson. He was forced to conclude that the Dearborn regrade, though beneficial to property elsewhere, "must be regarded as that value which comes to the community by the opening up of an arterial highway." Then there was the Denny Hill regrade, its second section completed just in time for the nation's slide into the Great Depression. As late as 1976, Roger Sale found the Denny Hill regrade area "a chronically semi blighted area," and despite some positive development, "at its more frequent worst the home of car lots and claims that Jesus Saves placed next to cut-rate furniture and clothing stores."[52]

Where, then, does all this leave the question of benefits? Considered strictly as an entry on the urban financial ledger, the regrades were a gain. That is so, even if the gains belied some of the wilder ambitions for the regrades. It is so, even though the belief of Thomson and others, that the central retail-commercial core would greatly expand under the pressure of a booming population, never entirely come to pass. But as Thomson pointed out in the late 1920s, "all assessments" were "long since liquidated, together with costs of new sewers, water mains, pavements, [and] sidewalks.[53]

Easy grades for the remaining horses, and cars, trucks, and pedestrians, made the downtown area more inviting and helped lead ultimately to the revival of the Denny Hill regrade. Whether or not it is good public policy today for motor vehicles to crowd Seattle's downtown streets, the fact is that they do. Almost everywhere, wheels turn more cheaply because of the regrades. Although the regrading destroyed some actual and potential views, leveling hills opened up other vistas while at the same time filling in unlovely depressions. Finally, there are the tidelands, partly filled from the regrade's spoil. Controversies over their use in some cases, for example, as the home of expensive sports stadia, do not gainsay the fact that the tidelands replaced a nasty, offal-strewn salt marsh. The sometimes bitter struggles over the cutting and filling are long gone, their protagonists dead. The values—economic, aesthetic, and sanitary—remain.

NOTES

1. The regrades were so dramatic that virtually every history of Seattle mentions them. Among the most recently published studies is Matthew Klingle, "Changing Spaces: Nature, Property, and Power in Seattle, 1880–1945," *Journal of Urban History* 32 (January 2006): 197–230, especially 207–16. Klingle is critical of the way that regrading undermined Seattle's natural setting while noting that nature regularly defeated or forced a modification of engineering plans. He links regrading to other efforts to impose harsh conditions on Seattle's poor and dispossessed. In *Emerald City*, the same author links the regrades to Thomson's supposed snobbish and racist moral reformism whose naïve reordering of the city created more anguish than it meliorated, 94, 104, 111–16, 117–18.
2. A rough comparison of all types of complaints against city work is in Office of the Mayor, Adjudication Committee Minutes, box 1, PSRA.
3. *Town Crier (TC)*, August 19, 1911.
4. RHT's discussion of Second Avenue regrade, among others, is in RHT to John P. Hartman, 25 February 1909, 89/1, box 2, book 6, RHT Papers, UW. The quotations are in RHT, *That Man Thomson*, 87–88.
5. Phelps, *Public Works in Seattle*, 15–20; and RHT, *That Man Thomson*, 91. See also RHT, "Sketches," 1904 entry, 1602-2,

box 2, folder 10; and RHT, "In re Seattle Regrades," 1602-2, box 3, folder 5, both in RHT Papers, UW.

6. For Thomson's authority in the matter of overriding contracts, see *Atwood v Smith* 64 Wash. 470, and 473 for quotations.

7. For RHT's ability to delay an improvement when it did not, at the time, fit into his overall scheme, see the testimony of Arnold Zbinden, n.d., Engineering Department, Administrative Services, box 1, folder City Engineering Department, Emerson Report, PSRA. RHT, "Sketches," 1904 entry, 1602-2, box 2, folder 10, RHT Papers, UW.

8. RHT to John F. Miller, 23 December 1909, Engineering Department Administrative, Annual Reports, 1900–1954, box 1, PSRA; and Nancy S. Seasholes, *Gaining Ground: A History of Land-making in Boston* (Cambridge, MA: MIT Press, 2003), 59–71.

9. Anonymous, "Pittsburgh's Hump," c. 1914, box 29, folder "Miscellaneous Data," Engineering Department, Administrative Services Subject Files, PSRA.

10. RHT, *That Man Thomson*, 85; for second quotation, Sayre, *This City of Ours*, 41. See also Buerge, *Seattle in the 1880s*, 6, 106.

11. RHT to John F. Miller. 1 December 1908, box 1, book 4, Engineering, City Engineer's Reports, PSRA.

12. *Parke v Seattle*, 5 Wash. 1(1892).

13. "The Jackson Street Regrade," 1213, Jackson St. et al. Regrade Letters, fiche 1, SMA; *P-I*, May 26, 1907, sec. 2; and O.A. Piper to Carey H. Brown, 27 October 1932, 4818, Grading/Paving, fiche 2, SMA.

14. For examples, see LID 784–814; LID 808; LID 701, Denny Way et al., fiche 1; David Perkins, et al., to RHT, 29 January 1904; and RHT to W.D. Perkins, 4 February 1904, LID 701, Office of the City Clerk, Local Improvement Files, SMA. For inequitable damages, see *P-I*, May 21, 1907.

15. *In re Fifth Avenue and Fifth Avenue South, Seattle, v. Seattle*, 66 Wash. 327 (1911), quotation on 335.

16. *Smith v. Seattle*, 41 Wash. 60 (1905). An important supporting case is *Schuchard et al. v. Seattle*, 51 Wash. 41 (1908). An exception to the Smith and Schuchard cases is *Levy et al. v. Seattle*, 61 Wash. 540 (1911).

17. *P-I*, quoting Scott Calhoun, May 26, 1907, sec. 2. The private case was *Brinton v. Lewis-Littlefield Company et al.*, 66 Wash. 40 (1911). A case that combined a ruling on assessments and on procedure was *In re Westlake Avenue* 40 Wash. 144 (1905). For slide problems, see Robert Graham Hennes, *Analysis and Control of Landslides*, Engineering Experiment Station Series, bulletin No. 91 (Seattle: University of Washington, 1936).

18. *Parke v. Seattle*, 5 Wash. 1 (1892), quotation on 16.

19. *Brown v. Seattle*, 5 Wash 35 (1892), quotations 38 and 41. For the city's taking responsibility for slides, see John C. Scurry to Committee on Streets, 22 August 1888, quoted in *Smith v. Seattle*, 20 Wash. 613 (1899), on 616.

20. An example holding the city harmless, see *Postel v. Seattle*, 41 Wash. 432 (1906), overruled by *Wong et al. v. Seattle* 143 Wash. 479 (1927). For property damaged though not in an LID, see *Johanson v. Seattle*, 80 Wash. 527 (1914). For the city's responsibility for contractors, see *Provine v. Seattle et al.*, 59 Wash. 681 (1910), quotation on 685.

21. Phelps, *Public Works in Seattle*, 27–28; and Matthew William Klingle, "Urban by Nature: An Environmental History of Seattle, 1880–1970," (PhD diss., University of Washington, 2001), 133–34.

22. For examples, see *Frederick v. Seattle*, 13 Wash. 428 (1896); and *Lewis v. Seattle*, 28 Wash. 639 (1902).

23. *In re Westlake Avenue*, 40 Wash. 144 (1905); and *In re Elliott Avenue*, 74 Wash 184 (1913). For a partial exception, see *In re Boyer Avenue*, 79 Wash. 664 (1914).

24. For upholding the time limit, see *Jurey v. Seattle*, 50 Wash. 272 (1908); and *International Contract Co. v. Seattle*, 69 Wash. 390 (1912). For an anti-compensation decision, see *Postel v. Seattle*, 41 Wash. 432 (1906).

25. *Wong et al. v. Seattle*, 143 Wash 479 (1927).

26. *Atwood v. Smith*, 64 Wash. 471 (1911).

27. Ibid., 473 for first quotation; 475–76 for second quotation. For the contractor's suit, *Times*, January 14, 1912.

28. Philip R. Keller, "Washing Away a City's Hills," *World Today* 19 (July 1, 1910): 703–8. For grades, see A.H. Dimock, "Street Grades in Seattle," *Proceedings of the Pacific Northwest Society of Engineers* 3 (May 1909): 2, 723; and for teaming limits, see John C. Trautwine, *The Civil Engineer's Pocket-Book* 19th ed., rev. by John C. Trautwine Jr., and John C. Trautwine III (Philadelphia: Trautwine, 1916), 683–84. The 19th edition repeats the grade and pull calculation of earlier editions.

29. For animal abuse, see Trautwine, *Engineer's Pocket-Book*, 683–84; and Clay McShane and Joel A. Tarr, *The Horse in the City: Living Machines in the Nineteenth Century* (Baltimore: Johns Hopkins University Press, 2007), 46–53. For the new grades, see Dimock, "Street Grades in Seattle," 723. For the RHT quotation, see RHT to John F. Miller, 23 December 1909, Engineering Department Administrative, Annual Reports, 1900–1954, box 1, PSRA.

30. For widening, see A.H. Dimock to George H. Randall, 9 February 1915, LID 1345, fiche 6 and fiche 7, SMA. For Fourth Avenue grades, Dimock, "Street Grades in Seattle," 722. For Fourth Avenue in context, see RHT to John P. Hartman, 89/1, box 2, book 6, RHT Papers, UW. For the athletic club, see Keller, "Washing Away a City's Hills," 708.

31. *P-I*, April 8, 1909, sec. 2.

32. Jackson St. et al. Regrade Letters, fiche 1, 1213, SMA.

33. This paragraph and those following in the discussion of the Jackson Street regrade are based on many sources. Unpublished sources include RHT, "The Seattle Regrades," n.d. but probably in the late 1920s before or about the time the Denny Hill regrade no. 2 began, 89/1, box 13, folder 5, RHT Papers, UW; Oscar A. Piper, in Jackson St. et al. Regrade Letters, fiche 1, 1213, SMA; and, for Second Avenue, RHT to L.B. Youngs, 1 February 1904, box 1, book 6, Local Improvement Letterpress Books 1900–1904, PSRA. Published sources include Phelps, *Public Works in Seattle*, 22; Dimock, "Street Grades in Seattle," 723–24; Bagley, *History of Seattle*, 2:361; Louis P. Zimmerman, "The Seattle Regrade, with Particular Reference to the Jackson St. Section" *Engineering News* 60 (November 12, 1908): 509–11; "The Regrading of Seattle, Washington – I," *Engineering Record* 57 (May 9, 1908): 600–3; "The Regrading of Seattle, Washington – II," *Engineering Record* 57 (May 16, 1908): 637–40; and, for many specifics of the Jackson Street regrade, R.M. Overstreet, "Hydraulic Excavation Methods in Seattle," *Engineering Record* 65 (May 4, 1912): 480–83. Lewis & Wiley used 4,326,689,219 gallons of salt water. Lake Washington provided 3,705,884,623 gallons, and the Cedar River 2,062,605,752 gallons.

34. Dorpat, *Seattle Now and Then*, secs. 50, 53; Roger Sale, *Seattle Past to Present* (Seattle: University of Washington Press, 1976), 75–76; and Peter Donahue, *Madison House: A Novel* (Portland: Hawthorne Books and Literary Arts, 2005), 28–32.

35. Dimock, "Street Grades in Seattle," 722; and RHT, *That Man Thomson*, 89. RHT cited only one other holdout, and wrote that Moore "would not consent to anything." If so, Moore later changed his mind. For a detailed profile of Second Avenue, see *P-I*, August 2, 1903.

36. C.C. Closson, "Seattle's Regrade Projects: A Letter to the Editors of the Town Crier," *TC*, August 26, 1911.

37. RHT, *That Man Thomson*, 89–90; *In re Third, Fourth and Fifth Avenues*, 49 Wash. 109 (1908); *P-I*, May 5, 1907, magazine sec.; and F.H. Whitworth and Catherine Whitworth to RHT, 31 January 1908, 89/1, box 2, book 5, RHT Papers, UW. See also Oscar A. Piper, "Regrading in Seattle North District," n.d., LID 4818, 6th Ave. et al., fiche 1, folder 3, SMA.

38. Phelps, *Public Works in Seattle*, 33, estimated that, by 1914, regrading had moved more than one-eighth of the Panama Canal yardage. David McCulloch, *The Path between the Seas: The Creation of the Panama Canal, 1870–1914* (New York: Simon and Schuster, 1977), chart following p. 465, estimates that the French and American companies moved 310,000,000 yards by 1914.

39. RHT, *That Man Thomson*, 92. For objections, see, for example, "Remonstrance Against Improvement of Denny Way et al." (LID 701), November 10, 1902, box 23, Controller's Files, PSRA.

40. Beaton, 64. For echoes of Beaton, see Bagley, *History of Seattle*, 1: 359–62; Murray Morgan, *Skid Road: An Informal Portrait of Seattle*, rev. ed. (New York: Viking Press, 1960), 167–68; and William C. Speidel, *Sons of the Profits* (Seattle: Nettle Creek, 1967), 269–71.

41. Sale, *Seattle*, for first quotation, 76; for second quotation, 77; and for third quotation, 74.

42. Richard C. Berner, *Seattle 1900–1920*; 135; and Mansel G. Blackford, *The Lost Dream: Businessmen and City Planning on the Pacific Coast, 1890–1920* (Columbus: Ohio State University Press, 1993), 111. Klingle's criticism is noted in note 1.

43. For the race-class-gender triad as it applies to Seattle, see Janice L. Reiff, "Urbanization and the Social Structure: Seattle, Washington, 1852–1910," (PhD diss., University of Washington, 1981). See also Brian J.L. Berry, *The Human Consequences of Urbanisation* (New York: St. Martin's Press, 1973); and Alison Isenberg, *Downtown America: A History of the Place and the People Who Made It* (Chicago; University of Chicago Press, 2004). As with race, class, and gender, it is possible only to scratch the surface of the outpouring of environmental history. For examples see David Lowenthal, *George Perkins Marsh: Prophet of Conservation* (Seattle: University of Washington Press, 2000), especially 404–31; Marc Reisner, *Cadillac Desert: the American West and Its Disappearing Water*, rev. ed. (New York: Penguin, 1993); Andrew Hurley, ed., *Common Fields*; Klingle, *Emerald City*, and Craig E. Colton, *An Unnatural Metropolis: Wresting New Orleans from Nature* (Baton Rouge: Louisiana State University Press, 2005).

44. For Smith, see *P-I*, April 8, 1909.

45. Klingle, "Urban by Nature," 111–17. The damage award to the African-American family "never covered the loss" (p. 135), but damage awards were not supposed to, because all property was presumed to be benefited. See also Seasholes, *Gaining Ground*, 61; and Evelyn Fairbanks, *The Days of Rondo* (St. Paul: Minnesota Historical Society Press, 1990), 181–82. A contemporary depiction of an improvement in Seattle at least

46. *P-I*, April 8, 1909. For the rough characters, see Klingle, "Urban by Nature," 113. For RHT's objection to a Mark A. Matthews crusade, see RHT to Will H. Parry, 4 February 1905, 89/1, box 1, book 3, RHT Papers, UW.

47. *P-I*, May 21, 1907. See also *P-I*, May 22, 1907, sec. 2; and Corporation Counsel Scott Calhoun's defense of the regrade, May 20, 1907, sec. 2.

48. The card is reproduced in Klingle, "Changing Spaces," 209. The card was produced some time before the summer of 1911, see RHT, untitled, undated statement, c. 1911, and RHT to William McLeod Raine, 31 July 1911, both in 89/1, box 4, book 10, RHT Papers, UW. Trautwine, *Engineer's Pocket-Book* repeats earlier calculations regarding horses and loads, 683–84, 685–86, and 687–88.

49. Dimock's observations were not published until 1928, Dimock, "Street Grades in Seattle," 721. Paul Dorpat and Genevieve McCoy, *Building Washington: A History of Washington State Public Works* (Seattle: Tartu, 1998), 170. For a study of the Denny Hill regrade at the beginning of its redevelopment, see Alan Jay Razak, "Redeveloping the Redevelopment: the Denny Regrade" (Master's thesis, University of Washington, 1981).

50. For Olmsted, see Albert Fein, ed., *Landscape into Cityscape: Frederick Law Olmsted's Plans for a Greater New York City* (Ithaca: Cornell University Press, 1968), 157. Newspaper articles on rising property values include the *P-I*, November 23, 1901; and September 3, 1905. For quotations from "ruling passion" to "factory centers," see RHT to Welford Beaton, 9 July 1914, 89/1, box 5, book 13, RHT Papers, UW. For Closson, see "Seattle's Regrade Projects." For Brinton, see *Brinton v. Lewis-Littlefield Company et al.*, 66 Wash. 40 (1911). See also *Kroll's Atlas of Seattle* (Seattle: Kroll Map Company, 1912), 19. RHT, "The Seattle Regrades," 89/1, box 13, folder 5, RHT Papers, UW; and V.V. Tarbill, "Mountain Moving in Seattle," (reprint from the *Harvard Business Review*, Vol. 8, July 1930), 487–88.

51. Closson, "Seattle's Regrade Projects," and Tarbill, "Mountain Moving in Seattle," 487–88.

52. RHT to L.T. Turner, 26 April 1906, 89/1, box 2, book 4, RHT Papers, UW. For "values" quotation, see Tarbill, "Mountain Moving in Seattle," 486. For Dearborn Street, see RHT, "The Seattle Regrades," 89/1, box 13, folder 5, RHT Papers, UW. Sale, *Seattle*, 76.

53. For some of the wilder beliefs in the results of the regrades, see Closson's conviction that the opening of the Panama Canal and the development of the Port of Seattle would result in the development of all regraded and tidelands property, "Seattle's Regrade Projects," or the assertion of L.H. Griffith, a real estate agent, that the retail center of Seattle would shift to Twelfth Avenue and Jackson Street, *P-I*, September 3, 1905. For RHT quotations, see "In re Seattle Regrades," 1602-2, box 3, folder 5, RHT Papers, UW.

in part motivated by anti-Chinese bias on the part of property owners is in *P-I*, August 14, 1902. For "those forces" quotation, see Klingle, "Urban by Nature," 116.

The Milwaukee and Union Pacific shared the Oregon & Washington Station just south of downtown. Shown here under construction on March 27, 1911, the O&W facility later became known as Union Station. The NP and GN's jointly operated King Street Station stands to the west (at left). Built in 1904–6, the tower is modeled on the Campanile di San Marco in Venice, Italy. *Seattle Municipal Archives #52100.*

WHILE HE STRUGGLED with sewers, the water supply, regrades, and related issues, Thomson played a role in three other key elements shaping Seattle's urban fabric—the railroads, the municipal electric light plant, and the ship canal and locks from Lake Washington to Salmon Bay. Taking the railroads first, their serious physical, legal, and emotional tangles with the city and each other began in 1873 when the Northern Pacific Railway (NP) chose Tacoma as its Pacific Coast terminus and later ran a poorly-operated stub train north to Seattle over a badly maintained track, the "orphan road." Thereby it earned the enmity of slighted Seattle. Things scarcely remained stable in the high-stakes world of 19th-century railroading, however, and the NP soon improved its service, at first slowly, then with increasing urgency.[1]

The NP acted because it had to. Seattle never lost control of Puget Sound shipping to Tacoma, nor did it cease to add population, the 19th century's touchstone of urban vitality. By the late 1880s, it clearly overmatched Tacoma, although Tacoma, by virtue of its NP connection, enjoyed a greater national trade. During the autumn of 1889, a surging Great Northern Railway (GN) was headed for Puget Sound, a reality that had been a growing possibility for a few years. The GN's president, the tough, grizzled, and keenly intelligent James J. Hill, played his cards close to his ample paunch, but his choice of terminus was, probably, Seattle. He could not be allowed to conquer that market; so the NP at last ended its rate discrimination against Seattle and dramatically improved its services to the city on Elliott Bay even as it bettered its rolling stock.

In 1891, Hill's Great Northern finally ran trains to Seattle. In 1892, Hill declared the city to be his western terminus, a decision likely to stick barring some unforeseen circumstance. In the depression year of 1893, the GN's tracklayers pounded the line through from St. Paul, breaking the NP's northwest continental railway monopoly. The situation in 1893, then, was this: the GN built its first terminal facilities in the Smith's Cove (now Interbay) area, between Magnolia and Queen Anne hills, located northwest of the city's commercial-retail core. Meanwhile, Hill and his engineers also planned a freight yard and, increasingly likely as time passed, a passenger terminal on the tideflats south of the city's core. Superficially the matter was a simple one—just connect the 3½ miles between the Smith Cove terminal and the tideflats by laying tracks, then build the southern freight yards, and be done with it.[2]

Unfortunately it was not so simple. Hill's problem fractured into two issues, both serious and related, although separate in their solution. The first issue involved how the GN was to reach the southern tideflats,

A 1903 view from Queen Anne Hill, looking northwest across the Smith Cove tideflats (now Interbay) toward largely undeveloped Magnolia Bluff and Fort Lawton (opened in 1900). The Great Northern Railway established its 1893 terminal on Smith Cove. James J. Hill greatly compounded Thomson's infrastructure planning when GN proposed connecting to passenger and freight terminals 3½ miles south, near downtown. *Seattle Municipal Archives #29330.*

land that Hill's agents were busily acquiring. In 1894, Hill got his four track right-of-way, except for a narrower, two track waist on a part of Railroad Avenue along the downtown shoreline. He reached this solution only after a good deal of grumbling, posturing about leaving Seattle, and spending a lot of money on lawsuits and right-of-way concessions. So much for the first issue.

The second issue, the shaping of the GN's tideflat terminals for freight and passengers, was tougher to solve. It involved Thomson directly. In the spring of 1893— while Hill's fight for his tracks was still red hot—the GN asked the city council to approve its plan for the tideflats. Essentially the plan called for tracks south on the same grade as Railroad Avenue, crossing the present First Avenue South and then continuing across Second through Fifth avenues at grade. In other words, the tracks would come in south of east-west running Jackson Street at a fairly high elevation, then cut across all of the intersecting north-south streets, and therefore stand athwart the streets connecting the tideflats to the rest of Seattle. The crossings were to be at grade; i.e., the GN contemplated no bridges or viaducts for either the railroad or streets. The tideflats would not be raised significantly, as later occurred during the Jackson Street regrade, thus the streets would have to ramp up to the rails.

Thomson studied the plans for a month, then dropped his bombshell on May 17. Using words such as "almost criminal" and "homicidal," he condemned the GN plans in terms that no amount of moderate language elsewhere could conceal. His objections drove stake after stake into the heart of Hill's plans. In the first place, the plans would force grades on the north-south streets south of Jackson so steep as to be impossible for teaming. For example, the grades on South Fourth and South Fifth would be over 11 percent, which would bar "heavy traffic between the city and the great mud flat [tidelands] district lying southward," even without the inevitable blockades of freight cars. That and the closing of portions of Second and Fourth "would block business at Jackson Street almost as effectually as with a wall." Second, grade crossings were dangerous, especially in the case of First Avenue, where curvatures would shorten sight lines and be an invitation for accidents. Next, Thomson figured in overhead crossings for the streets involved but found their length to be prohibitive. Furthermore, if the present tideflats grades were fixed by the GN, then the land would be too low for gravity sewage and the future manufacturing area would need to be served by expensive pumping. In addition, granting the GN franchise request would fly in the face of past city efforts to rationalize rail-

road arrangements "in harmony with the general plan," as well as setting a precedent for other railroads to barge in and demand whatever they wanted. The solution, as Thomson saw it, was for the city to compel at least the GN and the NP to form a union terminal company on designated lands. Finally, he suggested that a commission be created to advise the city on the best terminal plan and policy for the city. [3]

The publication of Thomson's report brought forth a stream of denunciations. The city engineer wanted to drive out the GN, he was in the pocket of the rival NP, he should help railroads and not hinder them, the city needed railroads more than an ultimate solution to the sewage problem, and so on. His calls for a joint NP-GN terminal and a commission were ignored, but his negative report had one positive effect, a meeting with the formidable James J. Hill. According to Thomson's memoirs, when Hill arrived in Seattle he went over the tidelands ground with both his franchise proposal and Thomson's report in hand, then asked for a meeting with the city engineer at the office of the GN's local attorney, the ubiquitous, redoubtable Thomas Burke. As a prelude to the late May or early June meeting, Burke told Thomson, "out of Mr. Hill's hearing" how Hill had already commented that he, Thomson, was "no damned fool." The meeting proceeded with Burke present. Thomson and Hill talked for a time, then Hill asked for something more than criticism of his position. What would the city engineer propose instead? After restating the fundamentals of his report, Thomson remembered himself saying that the problem of orienting the GN tracks and the streets north to south would be solved, "if you will cut a tunnel under the city reaching from a block or more north of Pike Street to the tideflats somewhere near South Third Street." When the GN extended its line south to Portland, the tracks then would be properly aligned, with the major tideland streets paralleling the tracks, making streets and tracks free from serious interference with each other. After conferring with Burke, Hill promised to do what he could to "adjust" his terminal situation in the evident belief that he could do what he wished. Then, if Thomson would refrain from agitating the matter, Hill promised, "I will build as you want." [4]

Thomson's account of this meeting has been greeted with complete acceptance, even to the point of minor embellishment, as well as with skepticism and outright rejection. While it is almost certainly true that Thomson did not recall the exact language of each participant after the lapse of half a century, several things indicate that a meeting took place. Further, they indicate that there was a pact not to make permanent improvements on the tidelands terminal grounds except by agreement between Thomson, the GN, the city council, and, if possible, other railroads. The first indication is a lengthy letter from Thomson to Hill dated July 27, 1894. The letter follows a conference with Hill for the purpose of solving the tideflats problem. Thomson's letter was more accommodating than his earlier objections, in part because the council had granted much of what Hill wanted over those objections, although it denied Hill all the track space he desired. In the letter, Thomson conceded the issue of tideflats levels, the council having established future street grades high enough to allow adequate sewage flow. The grades were still too low and should be raised, but for the time being higher street levels "must be treated as impractical and visionary." He also "eliminated from the argument the grave question of interposing further permanent grade crossings over railway tracks." That left the question of grades to and from Hill's Jackson Street property. Thomson found that the grades on South First and South Third remained practically unusable, either by the railroad or by teamsters, short of a radical regrading not then contemplated. "I have no disposition to be captious," he assured Hill, expressing his willingness to "go as far as possible to meet your plans, consistent with the public interest in these streets." But he warned Hill that "unless your depot and warehouses can be placed so as to be a <u>center</u> and not a <u>block</u> to progress in our City[,] I am satisfied to leave to your judgment the question of whether the site is fitted for the purpose." [5]

There is another item of support for Thomson's version of the meetings. Late in October 1899, the Northern Pacific announced plans for a depot along the waterfront—a French Renaissance pile effectively blocking access to prime Elliott Bay property and requiring the city to close four east-west streets across Railroad Avenue. Apparently the NP moved without lining up adequate local support for its project. Hill erupted, once more threatening to move the GN out of Seattle. The NP plan, he thundered, would deprive the GN of its hard-won access to Seattle's waterfront. Hill's allies in Seattle denounced the NP proposal, but Thomson took a different tack. "The question of the Northern Pacific depot is now agitating the J.J. Hill element very seriously," he wrote his friend Daniel H. Gilman in November. The NP had "introduced their proposition so awkwardly that there was little hope for it. I am heartily in sympathy with their proposition, but taking it in the shape it is now, I do not see how they can be helped." Without

Hill's agreement and with the tying up of the waterfront, the NP's plan was doomed. So, attention returned to Hill's proposed tidelands location and the tunnel, a focus made easier because, by 1902, Hill effectively controlled the NP in alliance with the powerful financier, J.P. Morgan. The NP came into camp on the union terminal issue, while Hill moved the terminal to a more suitable location on King Street. He agreed to build what became the Fourth Avenue tunnel as a joint GN-NP enterprise. He also agreed to overcome some grade problems with viaducts built at GN expense. Tunnel construction began in April 1903, with holing through on October 26, 1904. Spoil from the tunnel filled the terminal grounds to their proper height. [6]

Additional corroboration for Thomson's version comes from several other sources. In May 1902, Thomson wrote to Thomas Cooper, the general manager of the GN, that the GN, NP, and the Columbia & Puget Sound (C&PS) should develop a unified plan for tidelands grades and for "joint or friendly use of railroad terminals in the city," and "that I should be inclined to oppose every proposition now pending unless there was some joint action taken by the three roads." (The smaller C&PS built its terminal elsewhere.) In July, J.D. Ferrell, the president and general manager of the Pacific Coast Company, parent of the C&PS, wrote to the NP president that Thomson "seems to be worrying over the problem of our entrance to the city, approach to bunkers, etc. He suggested the railroads get into one bed, then the city will deal with all together." The next month, the NP and GN climbed into that bed. The tunnel as well as the union (King Street) station plans followed, with the station opening in 1906. In February 1906, Hill's son Louis telegraphed the GN's L.C. Gilman that teaming and pedestrian traffic on the waterfront argued against any increased railroad operations. "To avoid increasing this we went to great expense of constructing tunnel at request of City." Finally, Thomson and Hill knew each other well, and in a way impossible without the two having had at least one lengthy conversation. Thomson traded on that relationship in September 1913 when he persuaded Hill to loan $42,000 to the Seattle *Sun*, a short-lived daily in which he was a stockholder. [7]

Thomson remembered how, after the city ordinance affirming the NP-GN agreement was "published January 7, 1903," he "sighed a great sigh of relief," because he could "proceed on other necessary work without being plagued with loud complaints about the railroad franchise." [8] Alas, things did not work quite so smoothly. Both the Chicago, Milwaukee & St. Paul (Milwaukee

Road) and the Union Pacific (UP) were building to Seattle. The Milwaukee Road's track laying in the Cedar River watershed required special care to avoid contaminating the city's water supply, while Edward H. Harriman of the UP could be as demanding as Hill or the NP. Eventually the franchise matters were settled with the two railroads sharing a passenger terminal—the Oregon & Washington (UP) Station (1911). Nor was that all. Taking the NP-GN through traffic off the waterfront did not eliminate local trains and freight switching on Railroad Avenue. As the railroads expanded their operations in Seattle, new franchises and new structures were necessary. Thomson was involved in all of those changes, working with the railroads to mutual advantage. He was uninterested in hostility toward them for its own sake. Yet he was correct, essentially, about his sigh of relief. The Milwaukee Road and the UP were icing on Seattle's generous railroad cake, while the new franchises, bridges, and track alignments, although troublesome at times, were routine vexations. At the end of Thomson's term in office, Seattle was what he hoped for, a major railroad city.[9]

ഔറ

The public light and power issue loomed large for Seattle during Thomson's tenure, though he was never as much at the center of the contest as he was with sewers, water, and the railroads—first, because he was not an electrical engineer, and second, because he hired the dynamic James D. Ross to supervise the city's light and power construction and production. His more limited role was important, nonetheless. A quick study, Thomson learned the basics of electric power production well enough to write intelligibly about it. Ross was an outstanding appointment. A large, dominating, and yet affable man, Ross inspired loyalty among subordinates while he employed his promotional gifts to win sympathy for public power.[10]

The thrust toward a city light plant began in 1890 with the vote to build a gravity water system on the Cedar River. The approved ordinance contained nothing directly about a lighting works but that omission hardly deflected civic interest away from the Snoqualmie River, where private efforts were under way to develop a strictly power proposition, or from the Cedar River, where the city would eventually supplant the company seeking to supply both water and electricity. In 1890, too, it could have been possible to dispute the successful transmission of electricity over significant distances. That argument vanished in 1893 when alternating current lit, spectacu-

larly, the World's Columbian Exposition in Chicago. That same year, the Seattle Board of Public Works voted in favor of a municipal lighting system. Whatever the relative merits of direct and alternating current, alternating current carried the day for long-distance transmission.[11] In 1896 a charter amendment confirmed the Seattle voters' determination to have city-owned light in addition to privately-manufactured illumination. Three years later, Thomson, at the city council's instruction, was at work on a system using Cedar River water to generate power for street lighting.[12]

As the council's initiative suggested, Thomson was not, in the late 19th century, a public power enthusiast. At the same time he went along with movements in that direction. His early investigations of water power installations involved using water, "instead of working horses," to turn machinery—scarcely a novel idea in the late 19th century. His attention shifted to electric power production when his friend, the promoter and genial four-flusher, Daniel H. Gilman, took control of power-production sites at Snoqualmie Falls. Gilman hired Thomson to produce a plan for electric generation, which he did before Gilman lost control of the power sites to Charles H. Baker. Several more investigations followed, all in the Pacific Northwest and British Columbia. Thomson's critical trip was to a power site in the high Sierras on the Bear River above the once hurly-burly mining camp of Dutch Flat, California. There, Thomson and his assistant J.C. Jeffrey—he who would talk the Jackson Street property owners out of their proposed tunnel—examined a power plant that "was the pet of some younger men who…owned and operated it and had built it." The "younger men" showed their Seattle visitors how they had built the plant "to guarantee its long operation and its high efficiency." They carefully installed safeguards "around their transformers, governors, and so forth."[13]

With notes from this visit and others, the two men worked nights to prepare the report delivered to the city council in January 1902. As did any good report, the Thomson-Jeffrey effort considered the three locations most frequently mentioned in the newspapers, but tipped their recommendations toward their favorite site, a dam and plant below the falls of the Cedar River. They designed the dam to raise the level of Cedar Lake enough to provide for electrical generation. Neither man was an expert electrical engineer, however, so they merely "sketched" the location of the elements of the plant and its system, including the necessary distribution facilities. The council accepted the report and called for a bond

James D. Ross. *Seattle Municipal Archives #4059.*

issue to construct the dam and works at this preferred location.[14]

This is where Ross stepped in. Born in Ontario in 1872, he enjoyed the equivalent of what in the 21st century would be a good community college education. After six years of teaching, he joined the gold rushes in northwest Canada and Alaska. He then made his way southward, arriving in Seattle about 1901, during the rising interest in public power. Meanwhile, he had become a self-taught electrical engineer, inveterate tinkerer, and minor inventor. Perhaps on the strength of his talent and the growing interest in applied electricity, he opened an electrical contracting business. After the council approved the Thomson-Jeffrey location, he submitted a plan for the electrical works. In 1902 or 1903, Thomson hired him to supervise the installation of the electrical apparatus. The two men were drawn to each other and formed what was likely a brotherly relationship. For Thomson, Ross was a probable substitute for his family members, all of whom were now dead, aging, or living too far away for easy interaction in the era of train travel. Both Ross and Thomson were dedicated, church-going Presbyterians, and neither smoked tobacco or drank alcohol.

More to the point of their immediate collaboration, both men by then believed in public power for purely pragmatic reasons. Neither countenanced any sort of socialism. They did believe in what Ross would later call "city building"—that cheap public power would attract industry, jobs, and population to the Pacific Northwest. Both accepted the concept of public power providing a "yardstick" of rates against which to measure the fairness of private power charges, especially to residential customers. Both believed in promoting municipal patriotism by showing citizens how well city government, its utilities included, could operate on their behalf. The difference was that Ross would advocate public power as a secular religion, fanatically favoring public utilities while developing a paranoid view of the machinations of private power company executives. Thomson's conversion was slower and less complete. He began work in June 1902 by building a sawmill for constructing a log dam, finding the exact location for the structure, and figuring its precise dimensions. By September he was making

"a trip to Cedar Lake about once a week. The lighting plant is progressing, although a little more slowly than I would desire." On the other hand, it was "well, however, for one to make haste slowly in expending six hundred thousand dollars."[15]

Over the next 2½ years, equipment for the system arrived in fits and starts. Although Ross knew what he was doing, he was at the mercy of inexperienced crews. But the equipment was put together well enough so that in January 1905 the plant began illuminating the city's street lights—lights purchased from the previous private owner, the Seattle Electric Company. While the plant was operating, if not entirely smoothly, Thomson left to study municipal conditions in Europe. After returning, he ordered a complete overhaul of the plant, bringing in a university-trained electrical engineer to supervise the work. In the meanwhile, Luther B. Youngs, who as head of the water department was in overall charge of the dam and powerhouse, had signed up "a very few private customers." Thomson ordered the competition with Seattle Electric "stopped" until the plant was operating to his satisfaction. The delays were matters of circumstances rather than any indifference to public power on Thomson's part. "The work under way this year, is intended simply as a starter" he wrote the editor of *Engineering Record* in 1903. Later the same year, he informed his friend Gilman that "I am giving most of my time to the lighting plant." He halted residential lighting contracts only because the city's power plant was in disorder.[16]

Thomson's enthusiasm for public power, nevertheless, appears to have grown, first, after the initial successful trials of the Seattle plant, and second, following the 1905 trip to Europe. In February 1905—after the plant was up and running but before his trip to Europe—he wrote that he wanted city power to electrify the streetcar lines but that "a great company" (Seattle Electric) would prevent his doing so for the time being. Before leaving for Europe, he wrote Youngs to cooperate with Ross in preparing to expand municipal lighting "service to the uttermost." During his trip overseas, he visited municipal operations and returned satisfied with their value to the citizen. Although he confessed uncertainty about what to municipalize after lighting and water, he had no doubts about municipalization itself. "About the only thing that I can say with reference to municipal ownership," he wrote in October, "is that wherever I found municipal ownership existing, there I found the larger degree of true morals in government." In 1909 he admitted that once upon a time, "I labored under the common delusion that no public utility could be managed successfully, excepting by a private corporation." The success of Seattle's water and lighting systems under competent and honest management had convinced him otherwise. None of this meant open hostility to private power. On the eve of his retirement as city engineer, Thomson wrote that both the city plant and Seattle Electric were "giving excellent service."[17]

The light plant expanded, fueled by bond issues in 1906, 1908, and 1910. A 1910 charter amendment created an independent lighting department, splitting it from the water department. Ross could have expected to be named the first superintendent of lighting because he had moved from general foreman to general manager of the light plant. Instead, Mayor Hiram C. Gill appointed Richard M. Arms, an employee of Seattle Electric, the city's competition. Seattle Electric was controlled by an engineering firm of Stone & Webster, the operator of street railways in Seattle and other cities, and financed by its Boston-based banking syndicate. The tabloid *Seattle Star* soon charged that Gill, in return for Seattle Electric's support, had promised to name Arms to the city lighting post. According to the *Star*, Arms then refused contracts with major local business, and refused to extend service to built-up residential sections in favor of stringing wires to sparsely populated areas. Arms replied that he feared overextending the municipal plant and that in any case, city council policy mandated serving those without private power first.[18] A city council committee investigated. Thomson testified before the committee—as had Ross—that no water shortage existed. The committee found Arms guilty of excessive timidity but not of unlawful conduct. So did an investigating committee of the Seattle Municipal League. No evidence of a conspiracy between Seattle Electric and Gill ever surfaced. In any event, Seattle voters recalled Mayor Gill in February 1911, less due to the lighting department issue than over Gill's unabashed support of an "open town" of gambling, prostitution, and liquor sales. Arms resigned, whereupon the new mayor appointed Ross to head the lighting department.

In his memoirs, Thomson makes light of the charges against Arms, but by then he was estranged from Ross, who had been dead for a decade. All controversy aside, the lighting department was a good deal for ratepayers. In 1901 private firms charged as much as 22½¢ per kilowatt hour. The consolidated Seattle Electric Company charged 20¢ per kwh for residential power, but massive city rate reductions eventually forced the private rate to 9½¢, while the city charged only 7¢. Street lighting

expanded and improved, while rates fell from $86.00 to $54.00 a year for the relatively primitive arc lights, and rates for incandescent fell from $15.00 for the older carbon lamps to $13.80 for the improved tungsten model. The residential rate was considerably less than what residents of other Pacific Northwest cities of comparable size were paying, except for citizens of Tacoma, who also enjoyed public power. All this occurred while a 1905 deficit of $18,877 became a surplus of $103,427 in 1910.[19]

Thomson was implicated, however, in a colossal failure during the lighting department's early years, due to the inability of a basin below his original log dam to hold water. The stage for this misfortune began after a few years of city operation, when it had become obvious that the Cedar River log dam, good as it was, was too low to impound the water necessary to meet the growing demand for power. A temporary expedient, increasing the dam's height with so-called "flashboards," proved to be only that when the 1911 flood that wrecked the city's water pipelines also tore away the flashboards. Meanwhile, Thomson was looking for a good site for a concrete dam. He found it about 1½ miles downstream from the original dam, where the Cedar River ran between two abutments at the head of a gorge. As built, the dam's spillway augmented by flashboards was 1,590 feet above sea level. At that height, or indeed any level above 1,546 feet, water would submerge the original crib dam. The result would have been—had the scheme worked—an enormously expanded Cedar Lake and greatly increased power potential.[20]

The problem lay with what was called the north bank of the basin, a loosely compacted shoulder running west and north of the dam site. Two eminent engineers, Milnor Roberts and Henry Landes, later the president of the University of Washington, studied the site. They reported to Thomson in July 1910 their serious doubts about the ability of the north bank, composed partly of "glacial sediments," to contain water behind the proposed dam. They suggested two or three years of testing for leaks, plus building a long concrete curtain from the dam along the north bank to a secure spot in the basin. If concrete from bedrock to the top of the bank proved impractical, then "it may be sufficient to puddle the slopes of the reservoir where the glacial sediments constitute the embankment."[21]

The Landes-Roberts report was a red flag, one that Thomson could not ignore. In September 1910, he wrote an assistant engineer of his doubts about what he called "the great stone dam" because its amortized cost would drive up power prices. "If there is any means of delaying this work and we can devise any system of storage more economical than that proposed by this great dam, it is our duty to do so," he wrote. Although Thomson did not refer to the Landes-Roberts report it could not have been far from his mind. Then two events forced him to return to the Cedar River site. In November, Seattle voters approved $1,400,000 in bonds for the dam. Secondly, potential alternative sites elsewhere were expensive—$640,000 for one and $1,000,000 for the other, with the costs of a dam, penstock, and power house loaded on top of the costs of acquisition. In November 1911, shortly before Thomson's retirement, he recommended, and the Board of Public Works and the council approved, building a dam at his preferred location on the Cedar River. Still, there were doubts, especially after his successor, Arthur H. Dimock, revealed that Thomson had not made test borings along the suspect bank. Nor had he begun work on a design for a dam. Thomson refuted both these contentions in a 1929 autobiographical statement. He had made test borings, he declared, borings leading to some "apprehension," countered by a belief that "any newly exposed surfaces would in time seal themselves." He asserted that he had made preliminary plans, for to admit otherwise would have been asking for an expensive bond issue without a serious investigation. The final plans, he admitted, were drawn later. [22]

Irrespective of Thomson's or others' doubts, the path to the Cedar River dam, once chosen, led to its construction. Under Dimock, the engineering department designed a concrete dam. The public works board appointed a board of engineers, which, after due consideration of the dam and its site issued a report ambiguous enough to justify any course of action. It did recommend suspending work on the present site until others had been considered, a solution that the public works board rejected on account of the costs and the delay to power production. The public works board's report to Mayor George F. Cotterill concluded that, all in all, the plans for the new basin were "amply safe" and that the suspect bank would seal itself in time. Only Ralph H. Ober, the superintendent of buildings, dissented. Ober recommended suspending "all constructive operations" until the definitive testing of the bank and a complete set of plans and costs were prepared. Cotterill in his turn reported to the council that a "stable and secure dam" could be built. The council voted 5-4 to continue work on the dam, despite continuing concerns about its cost and the north bank. Ross' influence was exercised mostly behind the scenes but it was real. To the lighting superin-

tendent, the ambivalent engineers' report proved that its authors were "lacking the ordinary horse sense" of other people. "The dam should go right ahead," he wrote. [23]

After the dam was completed and the basin began to fill, water indeed spurted from the north bank. In December 1914, engineers estimated the loss at 4,250 cubic feet a day, or some 318,750,000 gallons every 24 hours. In 1915 the engineers raised the water level in the new reservoir. Then "seepages through the north bank surpassed even the direst predictions," raising the height of nearby, ominously named Rattlesnake Lake. Lake waters poured into the hamlet of Moncton, forcing its relocation to Cedar Falls. In 1915 and 1916, Thomson and other engineers reported on the suppurating north bank. Dimock might have commissioned his predecessor to examine the north bank anyway without an appeal from Thomson, but Thomson did appeal. Early in 1915, Thomson was forced out of a job in Canada because of wartime stringency and he was skating close to bankruptcy over his wretched involvement in the failed Seattle *Sun*. He encouraged Dimock to hire him in language detailing his Canadian difficulties, yet equivocal enough to appear that he was not begging. "I believe I can seal that basin," he told his former assistant, "but I shall not ask for the job of consulting engineer thereon unless you should suggest it and work it through the Council." In any case, all the investigators concluded that the bank could be sealed, for a high price in cost and downtime. Meanwhile the lighting department had covered its bets in 1912 with a plant on the east shore of Lake Union designed to use surplus water from the reservoir in Capitol Hill's Volunteer Park. Added bond funds in 1916 provided for the plant's expansion. [24]

Back at the north bank, beginning in 1916 the city attempted some modest sealing, then in 1918 raised the level of the reservoir close to its maximum elevation. Early on the morning of December 23, 1918, the north bank blew out near its northeast corner. Water swept down Boxley Creek, wiping away the town of Edgewick, one or two sawmills, and some tracks of the Milwaukee Road. Nobody died but the physical damage was great. The entire eight-year episode, from Thomson's selection of the site to the Boxley Creek or Boxley Canyon flood, was an unmitigated disaster. Cost overruns drove up the dam construction itself to at least $1,700,000. On top of that, sealing cost another $185,000, damages at Moncton $69,000, and the settlement of the Boxley Creek catastrophe almost $362,000. These were substantial sums at the time and represented practically a dead loss, except for some modest power production.

Well before the final act of the fiasco, Ross was seeking an alternative. In December 1917—a year before the flood—Ross secured the Skagit River north of Seattle for a new power source.[25]

Thomson supported Ross's move, but that wise decision scarcely atones for his initial decision to place a dam at a vulnerable site. The question is, what blame should he bear for one of the region's more egregious engineering failures of the 20th century? In the nature of things, the answer cannot be precise and the best conclusion is that he should assume some responsibility but not all of it. Thomson overrode doubts about the north bank—correct doubts as it turned out, of two respected engineers. He overrode his own concern about the probable cost of the new dam and its impact when he recommended construction of the dam at the place he selected. He continued to support plans for the preliminary investigations, looking toward redeeming the Cedar River plant through the expenditure of still more millions.[26] Otherwise, the failure of the reservoir was a specific, disastrous example of "path dependence"; i.e., of an early decision reinforced by a skein of subsequent choices forestalling alternate possibilities. For that outcome, Dimock, Cotterill, Ross, and their supporters on the city council must share the blame. Failure is often an orphan, but in this instance it had many fathers.

Given Thomson's culpability in the dam matter, what did he do right? Several things. He selected the site for the original log dam—a dam in backup service four decades later. He became a convert to public ownership, remaining steadfast despite the temporary cloud over public power resulting from the Boxley Creek flood. He hired Ross. And he supported the ultimately correct decision to tap the Skagit River for Seattle's new power source.

ഐൠ

In his memoirs, Thomson placed himself at the center of the struggle to build Seattle's ship canal from Shilshole Bay on Puget Sound eastward through Lake Union to Lake Washington. "I secured the $2,275,000 with which to build the canal and locks," he wrote. Then he confounded the still-determined enemies of the canal by outmaneuvering them at a hearing before Secretary of War Henry L. Stimson and Attorney General George W. Wickersham.[27] Thomson's claim of decisiveness before the House Rivers and Harbors Committee was a gross exaggeration, although he did favorably impress Secretary Stimson. In actuality, the dedication of the waterway in 1917 could never have happened without the active participation of dozens of men.[28]

Joining Puget Sound to Lake Washington through the arms of Lake Union was scarcely a new idea. Pioneer Thomas Mercer suggested the scheme in an 1854 Independence Day oration during which he named the smaller Lake Union, for its projected uniting role, and the larger Lake Washington in honor of the first president. The advantages to a unification were obvious. Lake Washington, 19 miles long and an average of 2 miles wide, beckoned as an industrial site and a protected, fresh-water naval anchorage; "the finest body of water in the world for government vessels to lie,"[29] as Thomson put it. The canal was easier proposed than completed. Who would finance the required excavation, who would purchase the property rights along the canal, who would determine the number and location of the locks required to raise vessels above the level of Puget Sound, and who would estimate the volume of traffic needed to justify the canal—all were questions debated through a series of government studies and reports, and private efforts to build a canal or at least part of one. The practical results so far were few, including some preliminary federal government excavation west of Lake Union, and a private cut at the portage between Lake Washington and Lake Union for floating logs down into the latter.

Meanwhile, an ambitious, persuasive former territorial governor (1887–89) argued for another, shorter route from salt water to Lake Washington. Eugene Semple, a compact, bewhiskered visionary with a gift for compelling oratory, wanted to cut a canal from east of present-day Harbor Island to Lake Washington. The canal would run through the tideflats, Beacon Hill, Rainier Valley, and the Mount Baker area. Whether Semple really intended to build a canal is a good question; construction through Beacon Hill a little north of the line of the present West Seattle Freeway involved a cut of up to 370 feet and an expensive lock. What is certain is that Semple planned to use the spoil from the excavation to fill the tidelands lying mostly north of the proposed canal. In

Eugene Semple's "south canal" project got off to an ambitious if shaky start, but ultimately was dropped to the relief of many, including Thomson. *Washington State University Libraries.*

1893 he used his contacts in the state legislature to secure an act allowing, among other things, companies to dig waterways and use the excavated soil to fill tidelands, lands that could then be sold at a price equaling the cost of the fill plus 15 percent. Governor John McGraw of Seattle, although a partisan of the Lake Union project, signed the bill. With capital raised locally and in St. Louis, Semple's company began work in late July 1895. Thomson was among the throng giving an enthusiastic sendoff. Whatever his private doubts may have been, he welcomed any scheme for filling the tidelands. Less than a year later, Semple's firm had filled 70 acres of salt marsh, and two dredges were busy raising still more fill.

Progress on the Lake Washington ship canal, with Lake Union in the background, November 21, 1913. This probably is part of the Fremont cut, connecting Salmon Bay with Lake Union. *Seattle Municipal Archives #6498.*

But all was not well with Semple's scheme, known by 1896 as the "south canal" project. For one thing, landowners along or near the Lake Union, or "north canal," route and their supporters redoubled efforts to secure federal appropriations. Thomson's friend Gilman wrote to his fellow property owner, Thomas A. Burke, of the high hopes for Congressional action. At the same time, he demonized Semple's plan. The Semple canal, "that fake," harmed "the prospects of the Gov't appropriation" for the north canal. Anyone who did not understand the situation "was little short of a fool and the man who couldn't see that it was a fake was an idiot." [30]

The north canal people received the appropriation, while Gilman's letter displayed the earnestness of the north canal group's determination to fight Semple with more than federal funding. Compounding Semple's difficulties, he had launched his project during a severe economic depression when purchasers could not or would not pay his company for filled land. Lawsuits and bitter disputes over various delays hampered the work. Refinancing, reorganization, and the end of the 1890s depression eventually revived Semple's activity. Work on the present East and West waterways of the Duwamish River around what is now Harbor Island went forward, and the canal effort moved to the west face of Beacon

Hill. Giant water cannons sluiced down the hill, as they later would the regrades, with the help of city water.

There was, however, no hope for Semple. City officials who once viewed his work approvingly became alarmed at the prospect of a great ravine thrust amongst Seattle's major north-south streets and utilities. The council refused Semple a right of way. Thomson was aghast at the prospect—"an enormous chasm, which, in ordinary parts of the world, would be styled a canyon…imposing upon the general public the dangers, the costs and the inconvenience incident to descending the side of said canyon or of bridging the same." [31] Semple hung on until May 1905, when he resigned. His successors allowed the canal to die a quiet death while they went forward with dredging, filling the tidelands, and creating Harbor Island. In any event, the south canal scheme was impractical. There was room for only a small turning basin from the East Waterway into and out of the canal. Cutting through Beacon Hill and building the lock would have been expensive beyond any private funds available. While Semple's route from salt to fresh water was the shortest, ships would need to travel through the congested waters of Elliott Bay to reach it. His proposed lock also would prevent the lowering of Lake Washington. Lowering was desirable because it would end the flooding of valuable

Construction of the Montlake bridge, September 12, 1914. The canal's Montlake cut connected Union Bay on Lake Washington with Portage Bay on Lake Union. *Seattle Municipal Archives #390.*

pasture and crop land south of the lake, and stabilize the lake's level.[32]

Attention never wandered far from the north canal, whatever the swings in Semple's fortunes. The emphasis on the north canal shifted for good with the 1906 arrival of Major (ultimately General) Hiram M. Chittenden as the new district engineer of the U.S. Army Corps of Engineers. Chittenden was a career Army man from West Point—ramrod straight, correctly attired, and with a neatly trimmed Van Dyke beard. Although he could hardly be called humorous, and was for good reason worried about his health, he enjoyed a national reputation as the developer of Yellowstone Park, a prominent historian of the American West, and author of lucid reports on various public works projects. Most important, he was a "dedicated, highly intelligent, inhumanly industrious man," who "fixed upon the Lake Washington canal as the most important project in his district."[33]

Meanwhile, sentiment coalesced in favor of the present-day route through Salmon Bay over other possible courses. A final private effort came from the redoubtable James A. Moore, he of the elaborate hotel atop Denny Hill, who obtained congressional and state legislative approval for a canal. Moore's scheme was not as harebrained as Semple's, but unequally unrealizable under private auspices. He gave it up after elaborate maneuvering by Burke, Chittenden, and others. Chittenden was then free to write a report favoring a government canal. He came out for a lock toward the west end of Salmon Bay, although it was rumored that he favored a lock elsewhere on the bay.[34] This would be the only lock, as congressmen had already ruled out a second lock

between Lake Washington and Lake Union's Portage Bay as too expensive. The single lock would reduce the expense of the canal and require the lowering of Lake Washington to end the seasonal flooding of the lands to its south. The lock Chittenden recommended was a twin device—one for large vessels, the other for small craft. He finished his report at the end of 1907.

While this was transpiring, Thomson was taken officially into the north canal fold when the state legislature authorized an assessment district formed from property owners along and around the canal route. Thomson and most north canal enthusiasts were committed to the lock at the west end of Salmon Bay, both because it was the best engineering solution and because it provided for a consistent water level for industrial sites along the bay. But not everyone involved was enthusiastic about that solution, and for various reasons put pressure on Chittenden to move the lock east to the head of the bay. Chittenden capitulated late in 1909 in a reversal displaying the mental and emotional dimensions of the illness, probably a type of multiple sclerosis, that would eventually claim him. The ensuing uproar among advocates of the western site caused him to reverse field again and return in March 1910 to the position he originally held in his 1907 report. Chittenden's confusion gave ammunition to Salmon Bay lumber mill operators, railroads, and Lake Washington property owners who opposed the canal and persisted even after Congress authorized it in June 1910. As Thomson noted to Senator Samuel H. Piles after Piles had shepherded the bill through the Senate, much "of the present trouble has resulted from the fact that at one time, General Chittenden wobbled a little, which gave certain persons" ammunition against the canal. In any event, as Thomson admitted at the time, Congressman William E. Humphrey was the driving political force behind the bill. Thomson's testimony before the house committee on rivers and harbors was, therefore, useful but not compelling.[35]

More to the point was Thomson's intervention with Secretary of War Stimson. Opponents of the canal had asked Stimson's predecessor to block the canal project despite congressional approval, and managed to hold up action for more than a year. They appealed on the ground that the federal government had no authority to tamper with Lake Washington because it "was a fast lake and not navigable water of the United States."[36] Frantically, the canal supporters "raised a small purse"[37] and returned Thomson to Washington, D.C., to state the case to Stimson, now ensconced as William Howard Taft's secretary of war. Reluctantly, Thomson went.

Looking east toward the Ballard locks and the Lake Washington ship canal, June 1921. The locks are named in memory of Hiram M. Chittenden (1858–1917). *Seattle Municipal Archives #1942.*

What, then, was significant about Thomson's role in the development of Seattle's railroads, electric service, and the ship canal? The railroads would have been less attractive and more disrupting had he not countered the demands of the authoritarian James J. Hill for practically unlimited access to whatever space he wanted, on his own terms. Later Thomson won some restrictions on the Union Pacific and the Chicago, Milwaukee & St. Paul railroads that created better alignments within the city and superior sanitary protection in the Cedar River watershed.[40]

His grasp of the electrical situation was less certain, but he did supervise the design and construction of the successful log dam and power house on the Cedar River. He hired J.D. Ross to operate the system, an inspired appointment. His work for the ship canal was less spectacular, although he joined the growing opposition to the absurd south canal scheme. He helped the triumphant north canal effort when he convinced Secretary of War Stimson that local agencies were prepared to carry their share of its costs. He also persuaded the cautious, conservative Stimson about the federal government's authority to intervene in the project because Lake Washington was a navigable waterway. In these three instances Thomson helped to change the face of Seattle, and for the better.

Once in Washington, he was in despair of making a strong case, when he encountered Burke, who seemed to appear as if by some trick of stage magic whenever he was needed. Burke helped Thomson strengthen his case before Stimson and Attorney General Wickersham. At the hearing, Thomson impressed the two cabinet members with the fact "that King Co. had fulfilled every demand" made by the federal authorities. He presented "affidavits showing that there had been commercial navigation from Elliott Bay into the lake" via the Duwamish and Black rivers, although the navigation must have been at flood stage in little more than rowboats. But navigation it was. Thomson won his point, and was back in Seattle by July 6, 1911, returning the unspent balance of his "small purse" to its donor.[38]

Work on the canal soon began and was completed, except for some details, in time for dedication ceremonies on July 4, 1917. It was the product of joint involvement from the federal government, the state, King County, and the city. Its most visible immediate result was lowering the level of Lake Washington some ten feet.[39] The canal did assist commerce on the two lake shores, but industrial traffic, except for fishing boats, declined after the 1920s. Lake Washington's shores became home sites and park land, uses also claiming increasing space along once-gritty Lake Union. The dream of Thomson and several others for a vast fresh water harbor for naval and commercial vessels went unrealized. It is just as well. The Lake Washington canal has become one of the great aesthetic attractions of a beautiful city. When it opened in 1917, Chittenden and Thomson were long gone from the jobs that gave them the leverage to help it through. Chittenden was too ill to attend the Fourth of July ceremonies. A little more than three months later, he died.

NOTES

1. Armbruster, *Orphan Road*, 143–61.
2. Ibid., 163–85; Nesbit, "He Built Seattle," 213–43; and Frank Leonard, "'Wise, Swift, and Sure,'? The Great Northern Entry into Seattle, 1889–1894," *PNQ* 92 (Spring 2001): 81–90.
3. RHT's report was printed in the *P-I*, May 18, 1893.
4. For denunciations, see *Seattle Press-Times*, May 28, 1893. RHT's account of the meeting is in *That Man Thomson*, 50–51.
5. In declining order of belief in Thomson's account of the meeting, see Armbruster, *Orphan Road*, 174–75, 182, and especially 214–15; Klingle, *Emerald City*, 60, 80; Nesbit, "He Built Seattle," 235–36, the supporting citation of which has little to do with the statement in the text about the GN's attempting to enter Seattle; and Berner, *Seattle 1900–1920*, 12–14. The date of the letter, for which see Engineering, City Engineer's Correspondence, box 1, book 3, PSRA, indicates that the meeting RHT describes may have occurred in 1894, and not in 1893, as RHT's memoirs have it.

6. RHT, *That Man Thomson*, 53; RHT to Gilman, 3 November 1899, 89/1, box 1, book 1, RHT Papers, UW. RHT supported an earlier NP effort to close Marion Street between Western and Railroad Avenues, under certain conditions, see RHT to Committee on Corporations, 991688, SMA. For the tunnel and related issues, see Armbruster, *Orphan Road*, 182, 223–24.

7. RHT to Cooper, 26 May 1902, Engineering, Franchise Correspondence, book 1, PSRA; Ferrell to C.S. Mellen, 14 July 1902, box 417, file 913, NP President's Subject Files, Manuscripts Collection, Minnesota Historical Society, hereafter cited as MHS; and Hill to Gilman, 20 February 1906, box 52, folder 11, GN President's Subject Files, MHS. For the *Sun*, see William H. Wilson, "The Rising and the Setting of Seattle's *Sun*," *PNQ* 92 (Spring 2001): 59–70, especially 64. For RHT's admiration of Hill's "intellect," see RHT to Samuel Hill, 1 June 1903, 89/1, box 1, book 3, RHT Papers, UW.

8. RHT, *That Man Thomson*, 56. For his dislike of Harriman, see RHT to D.H. Gilman, 12 May 1906, 89/1, box 2, book 4, RHT Papers, UW.

9. For other railroads entering Seattle, see Armbruster, *Orphan Road*, 188, 231–49. For RHT's cooperation, see L.C. Gilman to L.W. Hill, box 52, folder 11, GN President's Subject Files, MHS. For continuing problems, see RHT by A.O. Piper to A.L. Valentine, 10 August 1911, box 5, book 32, Engineering Department, Local Improvement Letterpress Books 1911–1912, PSRA; Carroll B. Graves to B.S. Brosscup, 29 June 1906, box 31, NP Engineering, MHS; RHT to James Anderson, 11 January 1907, 89/1, box 2, book 4 RHT Papers, UW; RHT to John P. Hartman, 23 August 1909, 89/1, box 3, book 7, RHT Papers UW; and RHT to J.R. Holman, 4 November 1911, 89/1, box 3, book 9, RHT Papers, UW. Protecting the Cedar River watershed presented its own problems, see "Report on Possible Pollution of the Water Supply of Seattle by a Proposed Railway Throughout the Drainage Area," *Engineering News* 56 (August 30, 1906): 238–39; and "Railways and Water Pollution, with Special Reference to the Water Supply of Seattle," *Engineering News* 56 (December 27, 1906): 684–86.

10. For a study of Ross and a Ross bibliography, see chapter 12. For RHT's grasp of electrical engineering, see RHT to City Council, 8 April 1911, 89/1, box 4, book 10, RHT Papers, UW.

11. David E. Nye, *Electrifying America: Social Meanings of a New Technology* (Cambridge, MA: MIT Press, 1997), 37–41; and for AC versus DC power, 145, 195–96, 197–98, 227–28.

12. For RHT's work, see the weekly *Seattle Argus*, hereafter cited as *Argus*, June 17, 1899. RHT's account of electric power developments, besides his memoirs, carries the story to 1930, 89/1, box 13, folder 5, RHT Papers, UW.

13. RHT, *That Man Thomson*, 95–97. For quotation, 95.

14. Ibid., 98. See also "Sketches," 1901 and 1902 entries, 1602-2, box 2, folder 10, RHT Papers, UW.

15. RHT to W. Thomson, 26 September 1902, 89/1, box 1, book 2, RHT Papers, UW. See also RHT, *That Man Thomson*, 99–101.

16. RHT, *That Man Thomson*, 101–3, first two quotations on 103. RHT to John Goodell, editor, *Engineering Record*, 6 May 1903; and to Gilman, 23 November 1903, 89/1, box 1, book 3, RHT Papers, UW.

17. For quotations, in order, see RHT to William Carnes, 18 February 1905; to L.B. Youngs, 5 April 1905, 89/1, box 1, book 3; to E.T. Perkins, 13 October 1905, 89/1, box 2, book 4; to W.J. Woodward, 24 April 1909, 89/1, box 2, book 6; and to Charles Hanes Talbot, 14 October 1911, 89/1, box 4, book 11, all in RHT Papers, UW.

18. For Ross, see RHT to Ross, 21 September 1905; and 4

19. November 1905, 33-1, box 84, folder 13, Seattle, Lighting Department Collection, hereafter cited as LDC, UW.

19. Wesley Dick, "Genesis of City Light, 96–109. For Thomson's testimony, see *Seattle Star*, hereafter cited as *Star*, November 23, 1910. See also RHT, *That Man Thomson*, 102. For rates, see RHT to Charles Hanes Talbot, 14 October 1911, 89/1, box 4, book 11, RHT Papers, UW. For the comparison, see Dick, "Genesis of City Light," 165; and for the surplus, 88.

20. J. Hoover Mackin, *A Geologic Interpretation of the Failure of the Cedar Reservoir, Washington*, Engineering Experiment Station Series, bulletin no. 107 (Seattle: University of Washington, 1941), 8. A different view of the events described here, followed by a largely negative judgment of Thomson and his works, is in Klingle, *Emerald City*, 116–18.

21. Landes and Roberts, "A Report on the Proposed Site for the New Cedar River Dam, with Two Plates," July 12, 1910, box 27, Engineering Department, Administrative Services, Subject Files, PSRA.

22. RHT to D.W. McMorris, 14 September 1910, 89/1, box 3, book 9, RHT Papers, UW. For the lack of test borings, see *P-I*, November 2, 1911; and *Times*, December 2, 1911. For RHT's lack of design work, see *TC*, February 5, 1916. For RHT's refutation, see "Municipal Public Works," December 31, 1929, 89/1, box 13, Folder 5, RHT Papers, UW.

23. "Report of Board of Engineers," May 6, 1912, box 1, Engineering Department, Cedar Falls Power Plant Development and Construction, PSRA. Cotterill to City Council, 11 May 1912; and Ober to Board of Public Works, 6 June 1912, 47779, SMA. The issues of the dam site may be followed in *Times*, November 14, 1912; November 22, 1912; and November 24, 1912. For Ross, see Dick, "Genesis of City Light," 128–30, and, for quotation, 129.

24. *P-I*, December 16, 1914; and, for quotation, Dick, "Genesis of City light," 134. for RHT's appeal, RHT to Dimock, 5 March 1915, 89/1, box 5, book 13, RHT Papers, UW. The reports are in box 2, Engineering Department, Cedar River Construction and Replacement Files, PSRA. RHT's "Report on Methods and Costs of Sealing Cedar River Basin by R.H. Thomson, February 24, 1916," is in 33-1, box 12, folder 12, LCD, UW.

25. The literature on the Boxley Creek flood is extensive. Cost estimates are in the weekly *TC*, December 11, 1915. See also Mackin, *Geologic Interpretation*, 11. On the flood, see Mackin; and McWilliams, *Seattle Water Department History*, 235–39. For RHT's support of Ross, see RHT to Manson F. Backus, 29 May 1918, 89/1, box 6, folder 1, RHT Papers, UW. The Skagit episode is considered in chapter 12.

26. As late as 1920 RHT was urging spending $25,000 for an investigation leading, perhaps, to spending $2,000,000 or more; RHT to a member of the utilities committee of the City Council, 6 November 1920, 33-1, box 95, folder 6, LDC, UW.

27. For quotation, see RHT, *That Man Thomson*, 121; and for the entire canal story as RHT defined it, 113–19, 121–25.

28. This discussion of canal matters depends on Bagley, *History of Seattle*, 1: 371–97; Dodds, *Chittenden*, 130–42, 204; Howard A. Hanson, "More Land for Industry: The Story of Flood Control in the Green River Valley," *PNQ* 48 (January 1957): 1–7; Hynding, *Eugene Semple*; Robert E. Ficken, "Seattle's 'Ditch': The Corps of Engineers and the Lake Washington Ship Canal," *PNQ* 77 (January 1986), 11–20; and, for a contemporary account to the end of 1909, Archibald O. Powell, "The Proposed Lake Washington Canal: A Great Engineering Project," *Engineering News* 63 (January 6, 1910): 1–5. A different view, based on the assumption that both canals were

29. For quotation, see *P-I*, July 7, 1907.
30. Gilman to Burke, 26 April 1896, 1483-2, box 6, folder 2, Thomas Burke Papers, UW.
31. RHT to John H. McGraw, 27 October 1904, 89/1, box 1, book 3; and see also RHT to N.H. Lattimer, 21 April 1906, 89/1, box 2, book 4, RHT Papers, UW.
32. Bagley, *History of Seattle* 1: 387–88.
33. Dodds, *Chittenden*, 130.
34. For the rumor, see RHT to William Hickman Moore, 20 July 1907, 89/1, box 2, book 5, RHT Papers, UW.
35. RHT to Col. and Mrs. M.W. Glenn, 12 July 1907, 89/1, box 2, book 5; for quotations, to Piles, 23 April 1910, to Humphrey, 7 February 1910; and to Piles, 8 February 1910, all in 89/1, box 3, book 8, RHT Papers, UW. For RHT's support of Humphrey, see *P-I*, sec. 2, July 9, 1911.
36. Hanson, "More Land for Industry," 3.
37. RHT, *That Man Thomson*, 122, for "small purse" quotation.
38. Hanson, "More Land for Industry," 3; and RHT, "Sketches," 1911 entry, 1602-2, box 2, folder 10, RHT Papers, UW. The amount returned was $80.00, RHT to J.S. Brace, 6 July 1911, 89/1, box 4, book 10, RHT Papers, UW.
39. Various sources give different levels for the lowering of Lake Washington. The mean level of the lake is listed as 10.60 feet above Lake Union in George Cotterill, "Memorandum upon Lake Washington Canal Project and the Interest of the United States Therein," c. 1908, 38, box 15, folder 9, Cotterill Papers, UW. The lowering mitigated flooding in the tangled waterways south of the lake. The Black River, a difficult stream that both emptied and filled Lake Washington, depending on the season, disappeared. The Cedar River was turned into the lake to compensate for the water lost through the locks, Hanson, "More Land for Industry," 3.
40. Armbruster, *Orphan Road*, 242–43.

Horse team and wagon crossing electric trolley tracks, March 27, 1911. *Seattle Municipal Archives #52102.*

Public and Private Life of an Engineer

THOMSON'S INITIATIVES concerning large projects might seem to belie his intense involvement in the quotidian business of the engineering department and the public works board. In fact, he was as physically and mentally committed to the everyday problems and labors of his department as he was to the grand schemes. He had to be. During the 20 years beginning in 1890, Seattle's population shot from less than 43,000 to more than 237,000.[1]

Those were the United States census figures. Thomson thought the 1910 number wildly inaccurate. "The city...has just suffered a terrible calamity," he wrote to his brother "Willie" in May 1910, "in that when the census enumerators began their work, something like seventy-five or a hundred thousand people... immediately left town." He didn't know where they went, he continued, tongue in cheek. "Possibly they fled to Canada." Various real estate agents estimated the actual population at from 330,000 to 500,000. It was "a shame and an outrage that the government was unable to employ...men" for the census work "who were at least able to add and multiply." Whatever the true population, the growth fueled by gold discoveries in Alaska and the Canadian Yukon, and the consequent expansion of shipping, banking, real estate, wholesaling, manufacturing, and railroading was real enough.[2]

By the end of 1900, when the 1890s depression was a bad memory and the gold rush boom was in full swing, Seattle had almost 65 miles of sewers and more than 105 miles of streets. Both streets and sewers were extending rapidly if not satisfactorily. Sewage spilling into Elliott Bay at the foot of Lane Street, Thomson reported, "will soon be the occasion of public uprising unless some steps be taken to abate the nuisance." The long-completed South Sewer Tunnel had to be put into use, presumably with money from the general fund. The streets were graded but their most common improvement was planking. Public dissatisfaction was expressed toward "the ancient dirt roadway," but there was a financial inability to construct "permanent pavements." The situation had "now come to pass, as the poet Horace said concerning the roads of Rome, 'They ride the more easily, who ride the most slowly.'" Not for nothing had Thomson received a classical education! At the same time he argued that many streets were, in pre-regraded Seattle, too steep to warrant much improvement.[3]

Five years later, Seattle's 105-plus miles of streets had extended to more than 214, with almost 42 miles opened in 1905 alone. "This is really an astounding rate of growth," Thomson wrote. Only a little less than 36 miles were paved, mostly with asphalt, though at the time he endorsed phasing out asphalt in favor of durable wood in residential streets, and brick along business thoroughfares. He changed his mind about wood soon enough. More than 348 miles of sidewalks flanked the streets. About 177 of those were concrete; the rest discredited "unsanitary" wood planking. Sewers underlay all the graded portions of Seattle despite the difficulties with "the peculiarly broken topography of our city." More than 191 miles of distribution mains brought Cedar River water to businesses and homes. By the end of Thomson's service, population growth and annexations forced continued water main laying and required new sewers, bringing the total sewer mileage to almost 359. By then the total graded and regraded street mileage was just over 588.[4]

For Thomson, his city's "astounding" growth had its downside—too few people scattered over too much territory, requiring almost ruinously expensive utilities to serve them. He figured Seattle's population density at 6.35 persons per acre, "less than one-tenth the number of persons often found within the corporate limits" of other cities. He concluded that the city's 58.56 square miles would accommodate a population of 2½ million, a density prevailing "in many of the older cities." The main reason for the low density was the uniform 5¢ street railway fare that allowed homeowners to obtain houses "far distant from the centre of the city at very modest prices," yet reach the commercial-retail core "at the same street car fare as is paid by those living nearer the City centre." The remote population required the same utilities as people "living in the very heart of the City." Streets, water and sewer lines, and electric service had to be extended through sparsely settled areas to reach distant dwellings, to meet the demands from "Improvement Clubs and other interested persons." This helter-skelter expansion offended Thomson's engineering sense of the order and fitness of things, though he applauded the local improvement district (LID) system that made it all possible by the assessment of most costs against benefited property.[5]

If the abundant letters in Thomson's papers are any guide, the radical expansion of street mileage and use generated an enormous correspondence among city officials nationwide. The preoccupation with street surfaces would puzzle or astound later generations accustomed to nearly universal ribbons of concrete or asphalt. Of course, they varied in quality according to specifications and conditions, then as now. The difference is that during Thomson's tenure the paving issue was much more complicated, with concrete and asphalt competing with stone, brick, macadam (a rolled chat sprayed with a binder), wooden blocks, and various patent pavements. So much for an arcadian simpler time in the world of paving. In 1909, Thomson confessed that "the answer to the question, how to build a good road…cheaply, is the most difficult answer I have ever been called upon to attempt." He had "travelled all over the United States three times," and over western Europe "twice," a total of "forty thousand miles, in an attempt to solve this question." He wrote little about stone block except to note its high cost and to argue for sandstone over granite on steep grades because sandstone provided better purchase for horses' hooves. Wooden block paving generally was quiet but short-lived except on little-traveled streets, and was too varied in quality for much generalization. Macadam bound by some sort of bitumen he found both cheap and durable, but laid none of it in Seattle because no proper aggregate stone could be quarried for an "economical" transportation cost. Vitrified, or hard-burned brick, uniformly fired and well-laid, was a durable, if noisy, surface. Concrete of whatever type was noisy, difficult to repair, and hard on horses. As late as 1918 he argued against concrete for those reasons, but if horses were "done away with on the city streets, I would unhesitatingly recommend" concrete as best for autos. Asphalt paving was a good compromise. By the summer of 1910, the city had laid down almost four times as much of it as all other surfaces together. Thomson heralded the future with his comments on concrete and asphalt.[6]

Trash and garbage disposal—ordinarily no electrifying topic—brought down reportorial wrath on Thomson. When he proposed solving the disposal problem by incinerating household and other waste, he was responding to an issue transcending neat administrative boundaries. The Board of Health was responsible for municipal cleanliness, while the Board of Public Works controlled the utilities essential to a sanitary city—the sewers, water supply, and paved streets. The city controlled waste disposal. By 1892 private contractors cleaned up the commercial-retail core nightly; garbage scows dumped the offal far enough away in the bay to prevent it from washing up on Seattle's shores. Householders were supposed to contract with private haulers to remove their waste at night, in closed wagons to prevent aesthetic and olfactory affronts to citizens. The haulers were supposed to dump their carts in a tideflat area that Thomson designated. Fires burned what was combustible, and roaming pigs devoured much of the rest. Alas, practice diverged from the ideal. Some householders did not contract for garbage removal, allowing refuse to pile up in and around their dwellings. Some contractors disdained a long drive to the tideflats and dumped loads wherever they could find a vacant lot, sometimes with the lot owner's permission, sometimes without. Carts were not always as well enclosed as they could have been.[7]

Clearly the situation cried for reform, but it was neither Thomson's assuming command of the situation, nor

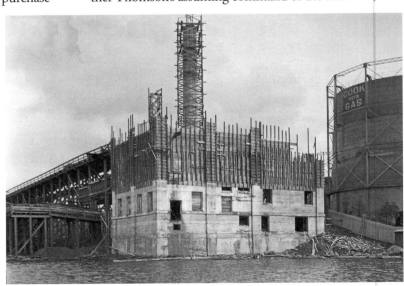

In addition to Thomson's initial "destructor" at the south end of Lake Union, he advocated three more incinerators—No. 2 (north end of Lake Union), No. 3 (Ballard), and No. 4 (south of downtown). Shown here is Refuse Destructor No. 2 under construction, March 16, 1912. *Seattle Municipal Archives #6004.*

his refuse incineration solution, that at first aroused anger in the local press. It was his proposed 1905 trip to Europe to study incineration, sanitation in general, street paving, public transportation, utilities, and port facilities. The weekly *Argus* and the daily *Times* led the charge. Harry A. Chadwick, the publisher and editor of the *Argus*, was a talented wordsmith and businessman who acknowledged Thomson's abilities on rare occasions but who more often condemned him. Chadwick's knowledge of engineering matters was miniscule and his understanding of municipal government minimal, but ignorance was no impediment to his pronouncements on Thomson's work. After plans to send the city engineer abroad surfaced in December, Chadwick denounced them as "ridiculous." He sarcastically remarked that "there are some people who feel that it would be worth something to get rid of Thomson for about four months," but that the expense was too great. Thomson would "visit locations where bathrooms are unknown, where garbage and filth is allowed to rot in the streets" in order to instruct "the most cleanly people" on the planet. Although the United States was "the home of the railroad" he presumed to study European transportation. Europe had no advantage over Seattle in street paving. As for waterfront developments: "Oh, Mama! We have years ago decided on our water front scheme." Yet Thomson, "this barnacle," would "be detached long enough" to assimilate "ideas that can be gathered from any good encyclopedia at practically no cost."[8]

The *Times* echoed Chadwick's outburst. The *Times* publisher, Alden J. Blethen, conceived a venomous hatred for Thomson far surpassing Chadwick's intense dislike. Blethen's attack was far more unsettling because he could spread a daily drumbeat of charges across the front page of the city's largest daily. Both newspapers extended and embellished Chadwick's outburst. In several articles, the *Argus* and *Times* claimed that the cost of the trip was too expensive at $2,000, the information Thomson sought was readily available in publications, and Europe had nothing to teach Seattle anyway. The newspapers charged that paying Thomson up to $2,000

Constructing the furnace in plant No. 2. All four destructor facilities used the Meldrum incinerator principle decided upon by Thomson after his 1905 European inspection tour. *Seattle Municipal Archives #6010.*

expenses above his salary was illegal, while the *Times* asserted that Thomson should stay home and stick to his knitting. The *Argus* cheered when Republican reform mayor Richard A. Ballinger vetoed the council's first attempt to fund the trip on the grounds that the purpose of the ordinance was not stated in its title, but the council quickly amended it to conform to his wishes. Ballinger signed the new ordinance on April 5, 1905. A furious Chadwick sued to prevent Thomson from collecting his expenses but a superior court dismissed the suit while the city engineer was in Europe.[9]

Not everyone denounced Thomson and his trip. The morning *Post-Intelligencer* praised him in an editorial titled "Our Most Useful Citizen." The writer asserted that Thomson's travel would save the city "ten times" its cost. J.W. Clise, a real estate developer, lent his "hearty support" to the venture. Yet Thomson's detractors had a point, even if it was not well expressed; $2,000 was a lot of money in 1905. Trips to Europe took a long time, and Thomson did have work to do in Seattle. Lengthy and expensive trips abroad were not then routine for high-ranking government officials. Although Thomson always maintained that he took the trip at the council's initiative, it is doubtful that the councilmen thought of the idea all by themselves. It is probable, although not provable, that Thomson initiated the plan. It is also likely that the object of his travel was to study refuse incineration and that the other areas of investigation were added to justify his long absence. It is possible that he had already chosen the best incinerator—the Meldrum of English manufacture—and that his incineration study was designed only to confirm what his reading had already suggested. Even granting all that, the trip was worthwhile if for no other reason than he greatly broadened his understanding of all the issues of his work, including municipal ownership.[10]

Thomson left Seattle on April 11 and returned August 29. He traveled through England and Scotland, Belgium, the Netherlands, Germany, France, and England again, studying, observing, photographing, sketching, buying books, maps, and plans, and making extensive diary notes. On the North American continent he visited incinerators at Montreal, Toledo, and perhaps other cities. Well before his return, he was describing incinerators with the English term "destructor" to indicate an incinerator the byproducts of which, such as heat and clinkers, could be sold. It was not all work. Among other diversions, on May 8 he spent part of a day in Glasgow buying jewelry, silverware, and china. There were side trips to the Waterloo battlefield and to the Versailles palace. In Paris he dined with his friend and fellow engineer George Cotterill. But intense study and careful observations were usually the order of the day. Regarding destructors, he confessed "that with all the literature to be obtained, I was unable to get any clear apprehension of the…various destructors until I absolutely sat down beside them and watched their operations for many hours." There was a question whether or not destructors could incinerate American garbage, with its higher moisture content. He concluded that one variant of the Meldrum design built near Manchester "will, without question, burn American garbage." [11]

By August 1906, Thomson was deep in a campaign to build a Meldrum Simplex Destructor under the supervision of an engineer imported from the company. He avoided one issue, reform of the collection system, and successfully opposed another, a competition between the Meldrum and a DeCarie model. Thomson's opinion of the American DeCarie destructor and the DeCarie company was rock-bottom low. "This company has not the slightest conception of the laws of combustion," he told a correspondent. In 1907 crews began building the destructor at the south end of Lake Union. On January 27, 1908, its operators accepted the first load of garbage. [12]

From the beginning the destructor was controversial. Several issues made it so. The destructor had to be built before it was tested, and testing revealed some flaws in the design. For example, the hopper was too small to accommodate all wagon loads, which in any case tended to arrive in bunches, making an even flow of refuse impossible. The high wooden ramp and roadway necessary to elevate the carts above the hopper had open

Wooden ramp to Refuse Destructor No. 2 on the north shore of Lake Union, 1911. *Seattle Municipal Archives #52216.*

railings, allowing trash and garbage to spill from unprotected carts. A temperature of 2,000 degrees or higher was essential for complete combustion, but that temperature could not be reached right away. A health department official, visiting the Lake Union site a little less than a month after, took no account of these difficulties. Acting, he said, on complaints from the neighborhood, he cited the "disgraceful condition" of the dump, where some meat was "raw. Dogs were around the dump helping themselves to the garbage and running away with their jaws full." The same newspaper chronicled a visit the next day from a councilman, who said he was responding to neighborhood complaints. The councilman "found several tons of refuse that had passed through the plant, but which it had failed to destroy." Thomson denounced one of the criticisms—which one is not certain—as "a contemptible political fake." [13]

The *Times* attacked the destructor as part of an ongoing assault on Thomson. Early in April it declared the incinerator "worthless" in a flaring headline. The accompanying story declared that the device burned no more than 60 tons of the some 200 tons collected daily, and did a poor job of burning at that. It announced that the failed crematory would be shut down "within a week." When more than a week passed and the destructor continued to operate, the newspaper ran photographs of items it alleged were unburned after passing through it. The *Times* also consistently overstated the cost of the destructor by $17,000, then a large sum. [14]

Eventually the problems were solved well enough. A reporter for the *Post-Intelligencer* visited the destructor all day early in April and found "not an ounce of coal, oil, or wood" used to prime the furnace. The heat was so intense that few particles and "no pronounced disagreeable odors" came from the 75 foot chimney stack. A representative of the rival DeCarie company, Thomson asserted in July, "visited our plant and held up his hands in utter astonishment to see it burn wet manure without any difficulty whatever, and maintain a temperature of over 2700° F in the combustion chamber." The first destructor's effective operation prompted Thomson to build three more. He hailed them as the heralds of the

Garbage collection in the Capitol Hill area, October 28, 1915. *Seattle Municipal Archives #130431.*

his inability "to attend all the committee and council meetings, or to send enough men to attend all of them to offset the Doctor's political work." Crichton used the destructors only as supplements to land-filling. Thomson's vision of an advanced technological solution for rubbish disposal failed to forecast future development. [16]

Throughout his tenure Thomson was concerned with planning and improvement movements incidentally or tangentially involving the engineering department. An Olmsted Brothers park and boulevard plan grew from previous concerns for preserving and enhancing nature's beauty in booming Seattle. Urban rivalry, especially with Portland, dynamic neighborhood

16 needed to answer the refuse disposal needs of a city of a million. [15]

What really defeated the destructors was not controversy but cost. It was cheaper to dump refuse in landfills, where it could be covered to minimize odors and prevent rodent and insect infestation. Behind that reality lay another—in Great Britain, the destructor was part of a system using the byproducts of incineration, such as heat, to cover the costs of burning. If not all city engineers understood this, Thomson did. He tried to find a market for combustion byproducts, but a combination of a lack of adequate local outlets for clinkers, tin, and glass, plus high freight rates to haul outside of Seattle, doomed his efforts. More than that, he was the victim of a bureaucratic coup when the city council took the destructors from him in 1911, a few months before he left office. His nemesis, Dr. J.E. Crichton, the head of the health and sanitation department, was as resourceful and determined a political maneuverer as Thomson, but with a lot more elective experience. Arriving in Seattle in 1890, he served on the council and as acting mayor before he was named head of the health department. Crichton finessed Thomson when the council replaced the old hit-and-miss scavenger arrangement with a municipal refuse collection system. Thomson thought he knew how Crichton got direction of the destructors. "I am informed that the Doctor has…control of these destructors as a result of having…requested from the city councilmen, the names of…men whom they desired to put to work, and…that they could only be put to work on condition that he managed the destructors." Thomson regretted

The building of Refuse Destructor No. 4, Ninth Avenue South at Massachusetts Street, May 2, 1911. *Seattle Municipal Archives #52108.*

John Charles Olmsted of the famous Olmsted Brothers firm of Brookline, Massachusetts, the landscape planners of thousands of public places, parks, and estates across the country. Olmsted helped to initiate the Seattle park commission's wresting of parks from Thomson's control in 1904. In return, Thomson dangled a city planning job in front of Olmsted in 1910, but instead chose Virgil G. Bogue of New York. *Washington State University.*

associations, a newly energized park board, and the University of Washington's interest in a campus plan combined to realize a plan for the city. John C. Olmsted, a chief partner from the firm's office in Brookline, Massachusetts, arrived in April 1903 to begin the design of a "comprehensive and satisfactory system of parks and parkways" for Seattle,[17] and by the end of June completed a report. The council approved it in October. Using Olmsted's report as a lever, the park board sought increased power.[18]

This is where Thomson entered the planning picture, because any expansion of the park board's power meant a corresponding reduction in the authority of the Board of Public Works. The park commissioners did not try to wrest control of land purchases from the council, but their proposed charter amendments did transfer control of park development from public works to the park commission. Thomson accepted parks and their esthetics but he intended to keep parks in his domain. Although he was not so directly concerned with park funding, he decidedly lacked enthusiasm for the commission's proposed independent property tax levy. The park commission would discover, if they did not already know it, that Thomson was a fierce defender of his prerogatives.

His was an uphill battle, because the council seemed to accept abdicating its spending authority over parks, and because the proposed charter amendment appeared on the March 8, 1904, ballot after a successful petition drive spearheaded by neighborhood improvement clubs.[19]

Thomson nevertheless went to work with what he had. His allies included the other members of the Public Works Board, possibly some employees uncertain of their future with the park commission, and many well-intentioned citizens. His letter denouncing the proposed amendments appeared in the *Post-Intelligencer* on the eve of the vote. His shot across the park commissioner's bow attacked the lack of an external control over the park board's expenditures. He disagreed with large grants of power and fiscal autonomy to unpaid, appointed officials, apparently oblivious to the irony of his own great authority over street and utilities development. He objected to the "compulsory" annual levy of from ¾ to 1 mill on each dollar of property tax valuation. The council's control of park land purchases and park board appointments notwithstanding, he found the amendment "repugnant to good morals" and "repugnant to a democratic form of government." The amendment carried despite Thomson's best efforts, though by fewer than 100 votes, 3,825 to 3,732.[20]

Far from ending the contention between the parks and public works boards, the vote spurred jurisdictional disputes between public works and the newly-empowered park commissioners. In the summer of 1904, Thomson's crews built a sewer that emptied into a park stream. The action enraged one of Olmsted's assistants, who reported the destruction of a small waterway intended for beautification. Whereas Thomson clearly controlled sewers, the park commissioners and their advisors just as clearly controlled park development. There were no easy resolutions to these jurisdictional issues. Nor did Thomson and John Olmsted get along well. Thomson was hardly a backslapping first-namer but he had matured in Indiana, California, and Seattle when these places were not far from their relatively informal frontier stage. On the other hand, Olmsted was an introverted and cultivated New Englander—a shy man who rarely opened up, especially to strangers. He appeared stiff and formal even to himself. Tactically, the two men clashed over extending Stone Avenue north at Woodland Park. Thomson wanted to put a street through the playground area of the park, and, skirting Green Lake, as straight as it could be made, on easy-as-possible grades. Olmsted held out for leaving the playground area inviolate, then passing around Green Lake on curves following the lake's contours. He resented

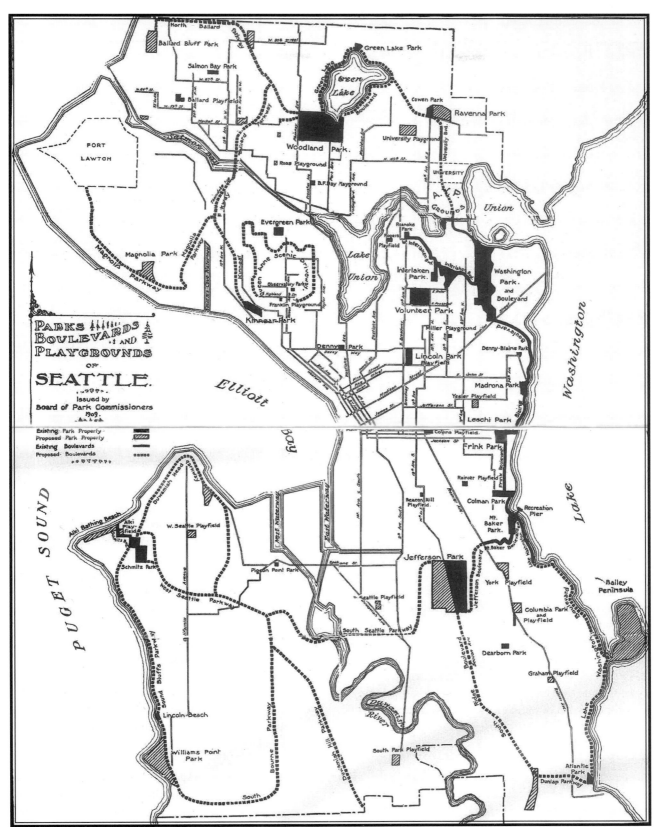

Seattle parks and parkways in 1909, showing the influence of John Charles Olmsted's 1903 recommendations. Thomson had a sometimes contentious relationship with the newly empowered Seattle park commission. *Seattle Municipal Archives.*

what he considered Thomson's interference. "I have the greatest admiration for Mr. R.H. Thomson in his capacity of City Engineer," Olmsted told a park commissioner. "Yet…he might welcome the suggestions of a competent landscape architect when it comes to plans affecting…the city's parks, without implying any doubt as to his ability as a civil engineer." Olmsted won the battle in 1909, but Thomson would remember Olmsted's victory when it came time for him to select a designer for Seattle's comprehensive plan.[21]

Meanwhile, by early 1913, Seattle had 1,267 acres of parks, a vast improvement over the 78 acres of just 13 years before. There were 88 playground acres and more than 15 miles of boulevards, with another almost 10½ miles under construction. Counting the boulevard acreage, the park board controlled 1,580 acres, offering recreational and pleasure driving activity, which was practically unknown in the city of 1899.[22]

Thomson's next involvement with city planning was pivotal. He was an important member of the Municipal Plans Commission (MPC) of 1909, and played the key role in selecting his personal and professional friend, Virgil G. Bogue of New York, to devise the *Plan of Seattle*, published as the MPC's report of 1911. He defended the plan before the public but it was never officially adopted. Instead it went down to a crushing defeat at the polls in 1912.[23]

Understanding all these developments begins with the multiple origins of the Seattle city plan. By 1909 city planning was advancing rapidly under the aegis of the City Beautiful movement, considered by some commenters to be excessively concerned with aesthetics but today generally conceded to involve practical considerations such as traffic circulation, managed growth, and the rational distribution of urban functions. In the Pacific Northwest, rival Portland already had sponsored the Lewis and Clark Centennial Exposition in 1905 and was anticipating a comprehensive city plan. In Seattle, the decision to stage the Alaska-Yukon-Pacific Exposition (AYPE), scheduled to open in 1909 on the then-new campus of the University of Washington, provided some impetus. So did a movement within the Washington State Chapter (WSC) of the American Institute of Architects to develop a civic center and related improvements, plus a comprehensive plan. Thomson's direct involvement in both movements was minimal, though the prospect of the exposition fired his booster aspirations, and he spearheaded the effort to organize a state good roads convention at the AYPE. He enthusiastically endorsed the idea of a comprehensive plan.[24]

From the beginning, what came to be known as the Bogue plan carried within it the seeds of its own destruction. Its supporters, organized into the Municipal Plans League (MPL), secured practically compulsory wording for a proposed amendment submitted to the city council and accepted for inclusion on the March 1910 general election ballot. The virtually mandatory section 8 bound the city to the forthcoming plan. "If a majority of the voters voting thereon shall favor the adoption of said City Plan…it shall be adopted and shall be the plan to be followed by all City officials in the growth, execution and development of said City of Seattle, until modified, or amended at some subsequent election." Only a problematic successful campaign against some aspect of the plan or, perhaps, the whole of it, could prevent its inexorable development. The requirement for implementation went against the grain of previous planning in the United States, including John Olmsted's park and boulevard plan for Seattle. Those plans were to serve as an inspiration and guide, to be developed as circumstances permitted, but their details were not mandated. Flexibility was their key. The coercive language of the Seattle charter amendment originated in the WSC, reflecting a desire to do away with uncertainty and a national legacy of partially completed plans. The solution was to place design professionals in charge of a perceptive plan. Thomson did not originate the language of the proposed charter amendment but there is no evidence that he objected to it.[25]

Otherwise, the proposed amendment provided for a municipal planning commission of 21 members drawn partly from the city council, county commissioners, and various city boards. Other representatives were to be nominated by commercial, professional, and labor groups, and confirmed by the mayor. The amendment allowed the commission to hire as many as three experts to devise a comprehensive plan. It allowed a special tax to be levied for their salaries, staff assistance, and office space. The commission was to meet regularly and frequently, supervise and approve the work of the experts, and submit the completed plan to the city council no later than September 30, 1911. Before the March 1910 vote, commercial and labor groups endorsed the amendment, while the MPL established a speaker's bureau to educate the citizenry about the benefits of city planning. The supporters of planning dealt in abstractions unconnected to the costs, removals, and disruptions required for a concrete plan. There was no serious challenge to the practically coercive language in section 8, and no concerted opposition to planning. The amendment carried every ward, rolling up 13,852 votes in favor, 7,371 opposed, "the largest majority ever cast for an amendment to the charter of the City of Seattle." It was a resounding endorsement of the conception of comprehensive planning.[26]

Thomson was named to the resulting Municipal Plans Commission, a foregone conclusion. He also sat on three of the MPC's eight committees, including its executive committee. In the last position he practically controlled the selection of the expert, his friend Virgil Bogue. He dangled the job in front of John Olmsted, leading Olmsted to believe that he would be one of the three experts selected. He would not be. Thomson not only clashed with Olmsted over planning issues, he also believed that the publicity capacity of the Olmsted firm far exceeded its design capability. Thomson argued that his friend Cotterill, the engineer of the AYPE, "worked out personally" the exposition's design, despite the fact that the Olmsted firm was in charge of the layout. Referring to the Olmsted firm as "certain landscape gardeners" who took "great credit" for the exposition's physical organization, he declared that "the actual credit for the symmetry and beauty of these grounds belongs to Mr. Cotterill." In the event, Bogue's selection had fateful consequences, for Bogue was first and foremost an engineer who devoted his life to conquering landforms. He respected the natural topography when it suited him, for example, in his plans for extending Seattle's park and boulevard system far beyond anything attempted in the Olmsted plan. In other respects, most notoriously his plan for remaking the Denny Hill regrade and relocating Seattle's rail center, he believed in the power of humans to radically reshape the environment irrespective of costs. Bogue arrived in September 1910 and set to work.[27]

Meanwhile the MPC discussed the issue of the scope and extent of the plan. Would it embrace only the city's then-existing boundaries, or would it thrust into Seattle's penumbra, becoming metropolitan in its reach? "After considerable debate" the MPC decided to plan for an area of 150 square miles and a projected population greater than a million. Probably the commissioners responded to the example of Daniel H. Burnham's *Plan of Chicago*, a beautifully crafted metropolitan scheme published the year before. The difference between the Chicago and Seattle situations was one that the MPC ignored at its peril. The commercial-industrial elite of Chicago sponsored Burnham's plan, but, as with other plans of the era, it was not made virtually mandatory. The Seattle plan was made so from the beginning, and now, with the MPC's action, it was made very expensive indeed.[28]

Bogue worked hard, finishing his plan on August 24, 1911, ample time for the MPC to ratify it and then forward it to the city council, a fortnight before the charter deadline of September 30. The plan was metropolitan, but much less beguiling and evocative than the Chicago plan and much more concrete and detailed. Bogue's plan included a greatly expanded park and boulevard system, new recreation areas, new streets and arterial highways, an elaborate waterfront scheme, and a civic center tied to a new railroad passenger entrance to the city. The civic center drew disproportionate attention for several reasons. It centered on the Denny regrade, requiring at least 14 feet of fill to make Bogue's street and railroad grades work out. Its projected land costs alone exceeded Seattle's available debt limit. It would have required the railroads to abandon their newly constructed passenger nexus south of the city core. Its main avenue and connecting streets would have funneled traffic into the center, producing nightmarish jams. It was all very well for the *Plan of Chicago* to parade a gargantuan city hall in Jules Guerin's evocative sketches and paintings; it was unlikely to be built anyway. Yet, if the Bogue plan won voter approval, Seattle's civic center would be. Even the possibility of a later voter rejection of the enormously expensive program would adversely impact property values in and around the site.[29]

For these reasons and more, the Bogue plan met opposition from business, labor, the *Times*, and other organizations. Endorsements were few. Thomson, who worked with Bogue throughout, supported the plan and gave his fellow engineer a ringing endorsement at a testimonial dinner. On another occasion, according to even an unfriendly critic, Thomson bested his friend and mayoral candidate Cotterill during a debate over the location of the civic center, using, to be sure, "a pleasant little story" or some other rhetorical trick to win over the audience. Cotterill, like Bogue, was an engineer who could be presumed to know something about the practicalities of any plan. For the non-professional critics of Bogue's plan, Thomson had nothing but scorn unleavened by humor. He attacked "oratorical engineers" who believed that they could improve on a year of Bogue's labors "in a few minutes of offhand talk." These "advisory geniuses" had failed to find jobs comparable to Bogue's. Neither Thomson's raising the standard of professional exclusiveness, nor any other ploy, worked to turn the tide against Bogue's vision. On March 5, 1912, the voters rejected the plan, 24,966 against, only 14,506 for. It lost in every ward.[30]

The Bogue plan failed for two simple reasons. First, in a preemptive strike against uncertainty or limitation, design professionals mandated a practically compulsory plan. Second, the MPC, probably responding to the sweeping *Plan of Chicago*, insisted on a hugely expensive program. Over the years historians have advanced all sorts of explanations for the collapse of the Bogue plan, ranging from the irrelevant, to the risible, to the bizarre. All of this straining for originality and individuality has advanced obfuscation but not understanding. Bogue's contemporaries saw his plan as well crafted, perhaps, but unacceptable because it was practically required, incredibly expensive, and therefore removed from the participatory politics of planning.[31]

ಶೋಬ್

When not working and planning for Seattle, consulting kept Thomson busy. Consulting with engineering departments in other cities and with private clients requiring engineering expertise was an acceptable way for a public engineer to augment his salary. The permeability of the public and private spheres meant that any conception of "conflict of interest" did not exist, except as it related to bribery and corruption. This reality has caused heartburn in one later detractor, who criticized Thomson for his consulting work with Daniel Gilman while the latter yet retained control of the Snoqualmie Falls powerhouse site. Thomson "seemed oblivious to any conflict of interest" with his job of city engineer, the critic wrote. In fact, however, there was no conflict, as the standards of a century later did not apply in Thomson's era.[32]

During his tenure as city engineer, Thomson consulted for at least 17 private concerns and for at least 13 other municipalities or public enterprises. Portland, Spokane, and Prince Rupert in British Columbia were among the regional cities retaining him. Among private clients, he counted his friend Gilman, the Puget Mill Company, and some residents of Ellensburg who wanted to displace the privately-held water company with a public system. His most adventurous consultation occurred in the late summer and autumn of 1895, when he and two companions journeyed to the Aleutians to survey for sulphur. After landing at Dutch Harbor, they headquartered at nearby Unalaska "and pretty much examined" Unalaska Island. Not surprisingly, they saw "heavy smoke issuing" from Makuskin Volcano on Unalaska and from Akutan Peak on nearby Akutan Island. Where there was smoke, unfortunately, there was "very little sulphur. The sulphur appeared to be extremely fine filmy layers between heavy layers of mud." Within the contiguous United States, perhaps the lengthiest consultation involved Walla Walla. The thriving town in southeastern

Washington retained him in 1904 or 1905 to consult on a new gravity waterworks similar in type, though not in extent, to Seattle's Cedar River project. The association continued at least through the end of 1908.[33]

Consulting was expensive for clients, whether the consulting engineer headed the project or worked with an engineering department or public works board, checking and analyzing plans that others drew up. A century or more of inflation has rendered the charges of the era meaningless; nevertheless a total bill of $1,035.15 for 15 days of Thomson's labor in 1904 and 1905 was a lot when $6.00 for one night's stay in a hotel verged on extravagance, and $1.10 was the most charged for a meal. Thomson went to the heart of the issue with a client who complained of the cost of his review for a proposed waterworks. "The fee for these services is…supposed to be based somewhat upon the value which may be conferred on the system by reason of the experience and information of the person making the examination." In this case, the client would have the benefit of Thomson's 20 years of accumulated skill. Portland "gladly" paid him for a report on their engineer's specifications for a reservoir and trunk pipeline, an exercise saving the city "a great many thousands of dollars, not necessarily that I…knew more than their engineer, but an independent investigation from an outside party" with wide experience usually could produce a savings. Thomson suggested that, after going "over the ground," he and his assistant "sit down with your engineer, and,…for the three of us together to discuss the economy of every proposition contained in the scheme…all in the spirit of the most helpful cooperation." The meeting would benefit from "our diversified experience," as well as "leaving your engineer free at every point of the work, to call upon me for further suggestions and help."[34]

Thomson's Seattle work and his consulting would have claimed most of the waking hours of many men, but he also had plenty of energy to devote to real estate. It was a family tradition to invest in property, although Thomson did less well by it than his Whitworth relatives, or his Laughlin in-laws in California. In 1891 he owned 11 lots and some rural property, while his wife Addie owned a lot in Seattle and a lot and portions of two others in Spokane. He was responsible for taxes and the oversight of 11 more lots, 10 of them in the estate of his sister, Henrietta (Retta) Losee, who died in 1893. By 1900 he had added property in Portland and interests in gold claims in the Nome and Ruby districts of Alaska. In 1909 and 1910, he paid $918.19 in taxes on 31 lots in Seattle plus his rural property, including taxes on 10 lots that were part of Retta's estate. Surely his greatest real estate coup was a gift from John J. McGilvra—a lot in McGilvra's Second Addition with a beautiful view of Lake Washington and the Cascade Range beyond. McGilvra knew that he was dying and wished to make a gift to Thomson, as Thomson phrased it directly if immodestly, for "your esteem of me on account of my making an honest and fearless attempt to better public conditions." Decades later such a gift would have raised cries of conflict of interest, but no such outburst occurred in 1903. Both donor and recipient were men of probity. No *quid pro quo* was suggested or proffered. What Thomson could have done in return for McGilvra was moot anyway, for the city engineer received the deed early in November 1903 and McGilvra died in December.[35]

That windfall aside, Thomson's struggles with his property or the property he managed for others belied the notion that real estate ownership was a smooth highway to wealth. The original Thomson homesite on the bluff at Hanover, overlooking the Ohio River, was a constant headache. Eventually the property sold but the sale merely freed him to concentrate on difficulties with other parcels. Some of sister Retta Losee's estate property moved in 1903; more than seven years later the rest had not. "During all those years, however, I have kept up the taxes and special assessments liens that have been levied against this property, paid from my own income as there is no income from the property which she left, whatever." Recent street and utilities improvements made the charges even more onerous, yet there seemed to be no "movement" toward the lots. In blunt terms, a lot of Thomson's properties were losers. His four cottages in the town of Everett drained his resources, since there were "a thousand vacant houses in Everett," depressing the rental market. He instructed his agent to renovate "those that are empty and rent them for some price. If you can't get thirteen dollars, get twelve, and if you can't get twelve, get ten, but keep them rented." Nor did investments beyond the Puget Sound region turn a profit as quickly as he wished. Two related British Columbia businesses, the Pacific Coast Coal Lands Company and the Red Fir Lumber Company, are cases in point. Thomson's brother, Henry, a stockholder in both, asked Heber to represent his shares. Thomson also became a shareholder and a director in the coal company, while his friend, Seattle attorney John P. Hartman, was assigned stock and assumed a directorship. Hartman tried to right the foundering companies, "and, to his astonishment, he became satisfied" that one of the partners "was attempt-

ing to conduct his business by consulting mediums." Hartman discovered that the partner "even went so far as to bring a celebrated English medium over to New York for the express purpose of advising him how to conduct his business." Thomson advised inquirers to refuse to invest in the company.[36]

The private Thomson was sensitive, and generous with time and money. The private man gave some public hints of his feelings, but not many. While absorbed with the quadruple goals of providing clean water, easy intra-city traffic, effective sewage, and inexpensive utilities, he fought against obtrusive, ugly billboards. His work on the Municipal Plans Commission was not only on behalf of his friend Bogue or the ideal of comprehensive planning, but also for beauty. In 1911 he carefully repeated a standard argument of the late City Beautiful, that the commission did not seek beauty for itself, although "beauty has an intrinsic value." The commission sought a rational division of functions in the city. "One of the crimes against" cities was "to permit saloons, brothels and factories…to come in anywhere and be just as mean as they can about it because of the so-called inalienable rights." Urban sensibility was changing, however, and "we as a people are coming to realize the necessities of the many[,] more than the rights of the few." Thus the first goal was to make the city "sensible," and when that was done, Seattle would be "famed for its beauty" because its physical organization was "useful."[37]

Thomson's private comments reinforced his public statements, and although containing similar intellectual boilerplate they were no less serious. In 1903 he commended the Daughters of the American Revolution for becoming involved in civic beautification. The organization's participation, he wrote, was strong evidence that "we have now reached a time when the residents of the city have become citizens." Following his trip to Europe, he wrote an assistant about plans for new standpipes. Thomson wanted for Seattle what "the old world" offered, constructions of "beauty and stability" because "any structure which is lacking in either, is defective." Beautiful standpipes would bring "pleasure" to "all the thousands of citizens of Seattle" who gazed upon them. Designing a beautiful standpipe would not be easy, he admitted, but the effort to avoid ugliness was worth it. "A public structure without beauty is a public curse." Three years later he informed a correspondent of the "great struggle" world wide to secure "beauty with utility." Street designs that failed to "add beauty to the territory" would "fall short of their complete purpose and detract from the sale value of the land." To ensure that most utilitarian of ends—high land values—street "grades should be established at one and the same time," throughout a neighborhood or development, along "symmetrical lines." Once the plan was settled, individual streets could be developed as needed, in conformity with the plan. These beliefs in the maturity of citizens who appreciated beauty, the esthetically advanced position of Europe, the essential combination of beauty and utility, and the value of drafting a general plan while developing it as circumstances allowed, all were hoary with age in the City Beautiful era. The point here is not their originality but rather that Thomson's vision embraced them. [38]

Thomson was mindful of the costs involved no matter how essential or beautiful public improvements were. To the public, Thomson could appear oblivious to taking on heavy expense, as when he advocated extending the entire waterfront two blocks westward, supported by fill and a new seawall. The brouhaha following this 1909 proposal ignored his suggestions to build the extension in stages and to appoint a commission to examine "all plans" for public improvement, "selecting the approved points of each and assembling them as one harmonious scheme." It also ignored his caution in the same report against a proposed regrading project because of physical and "financial considerations." But such subtleties rarely deterred his critics. In 1913 Thomson— gone from the city engineer's post—advised Seattleites to vote against bond issues unless "vitally needed." Harry Chadwick of the *Argus* unleashed an attack that was ignorant and overly vituperative, even for Chadwick. "As city engineer he had control of everything, excepting the police and fire departments," Chadwick roared, a statement that was news to past mayors, city councils, corporation counsels, comptrollers, and park commissioners. "If there was an improvement or a big bond issue during the time that he was city engineer that he was not the author of," Chadwick thundered, "the *Argus* does not know what it was." Conveniently forgetting park bond issues and improvements, Chadwick moved on to Thomson "the dreamer. He built for the future. The troubles of individuals were nothing to him." The antics of "Czar Thomson" had left Seattle "staggering under a burden of debt," but, sensing the public's alienation, this "dangerous" man issued a conciliatory statement "not worth the paper upon which it is printed." [39]

The private Thomson thought big, certainly, but paid more property taxes and assessments for public works than many other Seattle residents. Though Thomson had the power to determine the speed and direction of the city's growth, it was the successful land developments and rampant population increases which in fact detailed where money had to be spent. "The city is growing…more nearly by explosion than by expansion," he lectured a paving enthusiast in 1909, "and if it were to…make all the improvements demanded this year, we would spend in the vicinity of one hundred millions dollars. For a city of our population and wealth, this expenditure is out of reach." If that were not enough, the paved streets in question would run through a district that "has now been assessed three times for improvement work, each time practically to the 50% limit." Ten months later he complained, "I have been struggling to prevent the city from going forward next year with the rush pace it has kept up." "So far, my struggles have not amounted to much," he confessed, because "citizens are holding meetings in the woods all around, insisting upon millions and millions more being spent," while "the Park Board is asking for two millions to put out in pleasurable amusements." Writing in June 1910, he asked the corporation counsel to have a reliable person appraise the property of one Wittler and determine the damages. "I must admit that Mr. Wittler has, in all things, been most patient and most courteous," he urged. In these and many other instances Thomson was hardly the spendthrift ogre as caricatured. [40]

On the other hand, he was steadfast in his determination to bring his projects to a conclusion. When opposed, he wrote, "I attempt to bear in mind the injunction of Solomon when he said 'a soft answer turneth away wrath.' In making an answer, however, I make no promises to change my mind or to change the nature of the work or to follow any other person's advice. My purpose is always to discover what is the right thing for the community before determining upon this scheme of work, but having determined upon that scheme, to look neither to the right nor to the left until the work shall have been accomplished, using, of course, all due and proper worldly wisdom to avoid dissentions and contentions." Thomson was so determined because he saw the interrelation of his several development goals so clearly. It was a vision he also tempered with such comments as, "I make errors of judgment, make actual mistakes, and manifest other evidences of mortality." Those errors and mistakes nevertheless occurred within a context of development that was itself unimpeachable. It was a vision beyond the grasp of most ordinary mortals. "There is so much crying to be done for the relief of the common people, and they are so blind themselves," he wrote during one of his periodic bouts of doubt about continuing in office. Duty triumphed, however, over leaving the "blind" and the "so few who care" to their fate. He concluded "that it seems impossible for me to quit."[41]

His attitude about the "common people" could not always be concealed behind a mask of bonhomie. In 1906 he wrote to Richard A. Ballinger, the retiring mayor, to thank him "for the kind and fatherly manner in which you, from time to time, talked with me concerning my attitude toward the public." Describing the concern of a man two years younger as "fatherly" was a rare avowal of emotional debt from Thomson. Ballinger's "sincere desire to help a public official,…has placed me under obligations to you, which I can never repay," and only partly repay through "conduct toward the public" following more "nearly along the lines which you desired." Thomson proved his loyalty when he stoutly defended his confidant during the Ballinger-Pinchot controversy (see chapter 10). Ballinger's advice was not always heeded, as when, in October 1909, Thomson received a letter charging "another graft" in the engineering department and threatening a suit to recover alleged illegal assessments. "Your statements are…absolutely without basis in truth, justice, or decency," Thomson shot back. Enclosing the facts of the case, the livid engineer told his correspondent that if he were "any kind of a man,…you will send me a written apology and will tell your neighbors what kind of a fool you have made of yourself."[42]

As the letters to many others suggest, however, Thomson rarely let his temper get the best of him. He was, moreover, a loyal friend to a varied group of men that included Ballinger and Daniel H. Gilman. His close friendship with George Cotterill survived their occasional disagreements, such as the one over the value of Thomson's seawall proposal. He and the legendary Samuel Hill of Maryhill mansion fame were fast friends for years despite Hill's prodigal, adulterous life style, so different from Thomson's own. A fascination with invention and inventors partly explains his close ties to Samuel Lancaster, a road expert and scenic preservationist, and to James D. Ross, his choice to head the electrical department. Friendships with attorney John Hartman and newspaperman Edmund H. Wells were strained at times but survived. These were late 19th and early 20th century friendships, formal by later standards. In letters, Thomson saluted these intimates as "My dear Mr.…." Family and old friends continued to call him "Heber" but he had abandoned that name by the time he became city engineer. Close associates addressed him as "R.H."[43]

In this area of his life, as in others, the private Thomson rarely surfaced. Readers of Henry W. Scott's obituary on November 2, 1907, noted that Thomson was with Scott, an assistant city engineer, "at the time of his death." Scott died in Wenatchee, a train trip of several hours from Seattle. Some readers may have thought it a nice gesture; others may have mused about the *Times'* frequent complaints of Thomson's dereliction of duty. They would not have grasped Thomson's grief. To one correspondent he wrote that "there never was a time when a life long friend was more needed at the dying bedside of another." To a second addressee, the workaholic engineer wrote, "I am not fit, this afternoon, to write a letter containing any detail, as I have just returned from the cemetery, where we have laid to rest, Mr. Henry W. Scott." Almost two years later he reminisced about "Henry W. Scott, a prince among men, now dead and gone to his reward, who did much to aid me in the struggle."[44]

Thomson's human sympathy, usually so well concealed from public view, was privately known to a wide circle. He wrote numerous letters of introduction to friends and acquaintances on behalf of other friends and acquaintances. The practice, common then, has long since been abandoned in favor of informal self-introduction to unknown people. He wrote letters of recommendation for jobseekers, and letters requesting favors for others. His sense of duty and his personal kindness prompted several people to ask for loans and secure them, for Thomson was a soft touch. His correspondence is replete with appeals for the repayment or partial repayment of debt. He asked a widow to "remember that, several years ago, at the time of the sickness and death of your husband, I loaned you a sum of money, used in connection with his burial." He asked for "such portion of the loan as you shall be able to return" within 60 days. Whether or not that loan was repaid, other debtors paid slowly if ever. E.A. Knight, the superintendent of the Walla Walla waterworks, asked for loans while Thomson was consulting with the city on its gravity system. Knight repaid one loan. When repayment on another was not forthcoming Thomson threatened to give the note to a Walla Walla bank for collection. The son of a professional acquaintance in New York state was an apparent deadbeat. The young man sized up Thomson well when he invoked his "dear mother" and his desire "to be a new man." He walked away with $125. That was in March 1910. In January 1911, Thomson was still attempting without success to set up a repayment schedule through the young man's father. Thomson's dunning letters contained such phrases as "I am pressed at the present time for money," statements doubtless true because of the sizeable costs of maintenance, taxes, and assessments on his properties, to say nothing of his obligations to his church and family.[45]

Presbyterianism remained a significant part of Thomson's life. He could write of "the great battle against sin," and how "a merciful Heavenly Father has dealt very gently" with him, "giving increased vitality and increased ability to labor, from year to year." On the other hand, he did not blame the Heavenly Father for his frequent bouts with bad colds or influenza, nor for his poor teeth, nor did he dwell on his self-evident status among the Presbyterian elect. He was too much involved with practical matters and too sensitive to the realities of his position to endorse anti-corruption and anti-vice crusades such as those of his famous, popular fellow Presbyterian, the Rev. Mark A. Matthews, pastor of the First Presbyterian Church. The two were cordial enough, but Thomson's identification with Westminster Presbyterian Church as well as his doubts about the wisdom or efficacy of ministerial crusades prevented an intimate friendship. At the same time he opposed leasing space for city offices in buildings containing "liquor houses," but that was a matter of "public policy" and not one for a crusade.[46]

An active layperson at Westminster, he was in charge of corresponding with a new pastor. His devotion did not preclude criticism of the same pastor, when, years later, the clergyman claimed that some residents were overcharged for their pavement "because someone had blundered or because of graft." Thomson angrily rebutted the assertion, then assailed the minister for charging "by inference" former mayor John H. McGraw with running a house of prostitution. Thomson called on his 29 year association with McGraw to dismiss the charge as "unpardonable," "absolutely false," and one for which there was "no public necessity." Thomson could not "justify the attack" or "cease to resent it." He was equally blunt with the Rev. Matthews when Matthews assumed that Thomson would pay for all the reservations that he had ordered for a Presbyterian banquet if the reservations went unpaid. "I wish it distinctly understood that I positively refuse to become responsible for any plate other than my own, and if it is the duty of the Chairman of the Banquet Committee to pay for the delinquencies of others, I shall immediately transmit my resignation as Chairman of the Committee."[47]

In most voluntary and fraternal settings he was enthusiastic and agreeable. He worked hard and well for the Washington State Good Roads Association, serving as its president in 1910–11. He was an active member of the Pacific Northwest Society of Civil Engineers. He retained his ties to Beta Theta Pi, his college fraternity. Christian Endeavor, the YMCA, and speeches to a variety of religious and civic groups occupied his time and thought. His widespread interests included history, genealogy, and photography.[48]

⁂

Despite all this activity, Thomson left time and affection for his family, the mainstay of his emotional life. For 26 years he, Addie, and the children lived in a house at 701 Yesler Way. "Looking forward to marriage," he had the house built in 1883, two years after he moved to Seattle. Two more children followed James Harrison and Marion Wing; Reginald Jr. on December 26, 1894, and another daughter, Frances Clifton, who arrived on October 22, 1897. The Yesler Way house stood on a large lot (since demolished; the site is now part of the Interstate 5 right of way). Later Thomson moved an old cable car to the lot for the children to use as a playhouse. The home was commodious enough for the family, at least one "hired girl," and Thomson's mother, who lived with them during the last years of her life. As late as 1908, though it had electricity, a telephone, and running water, "we have no water closet connected with the house, we using an earth closet in the yard," explained the man who planned Seattle's water and sewer systems. He confessed that he "did not know that bath and sink water" had to be run through a septic tank. "I am a poor man, and a mechanic," he explained, and would build a septic tank if the city would furnish the plans.[49]

Primitive or not, the house was a refuge and a delight for Thomson. He and Addie were devoted to one another. He doted on his children. "One of my principal joys is the companionship of my little children," he wrote in 1903, although son Harry, as the family called him, was, at 17, well beyond "little." His family life dimmed awhile in 1906 with his mother's decline. During her last days, she was "unwilling for any one except my wife or myself to attend her. This makes it very hard and keeps us entirely exhausted." On November 4 she died. His mother, Thomson declared, "made quick judgments of more worth than those which I could have given after months of consideration." Her death was devastating.[50]

Yet family life went on. Over the years, the Yesler Way house, for all its memories and its convenient location to Thomson's office in city hall, became less and less desirable. This was not so much due to its primitive toilet facilities as to a steady creep of commerce eastward up Yesler Way, making the place less inviting. There were the growing children to consider, too. The neighborhood was not only "deteriorating" in the parlance of a later time, but it was isolated from the University of Washington, where some of them likely would enroll for their post-secondary education. As early as 1905, Thomson intended to build on the Washington Park Addition property overlooking Lake Washington, but the plans fell through. By early 1909, his desire to move was well enough known that a banker asked if he would consider a home loan. "My financial condition does not permit me…to consider either purchasing or building a new home," he replied.[51]

At the end of the year he arranged a move, renting a house at 955 Thirteenth Avenue North (now Thirteenth Avenue East), the second door south of Volunteer Park. In one of several letters, he described the move, and discussed Marion's plans to enroll at the University of Washington. Her trip to the campus would be briefer by 45 minutes than from the Yesler Way home. Thomson's commute was considerably lengthened, for it required as much time to walk to the nearest streetcar as it formerly took him to walk to city hall. Then he needed "30 to 45 minutes, owing to conditions," to arrive at work. Then, too, the house was "a good deal smaller" than the Yesler Way place, "but by using basement, main floor, second floor and attic, each to its utmost, I think we will finally get located." He noted the problem with Yesler Way, which was "more related to business than residence, and therefore our surroundings had become rather unpleasant." The new house was in "a very pleasant location," and family life flourished there. More than a year after the move, Thomson could report that Harry was enrolled at the University of California, Marion was attending her freshman year at the University of Washington, Reginald Jr. was in high school, and Frances, "the happiest and brightest and healthiest of them all," was "coming along."[52]

ॐ

Whether involved with everyday work, bureaucratic infighting, consulting, personal relationships, or church and family, Thomson approached each in a spirit of remarkable candor. He was usually courteous regarding personal relationships, generous to the point of harming his own finances, and a true friend. Presbyterianism meant much to him, but he was most secure, happy, and loving when amongst his family. A little more than a half year after writing about his children and how the family was "quite well," he would begin a phase of life proving as unsettled as it had ever been since his early manhood.

NOTES

1. U.S. Bureau of the Census, *Census of Population: 1950*, 2: pt. 47 (Washington, D.C.: GPO, 1952), 47-8, Table 4.
2. RHT to W. Thomson, 17 May 1910, 89/1, box 3, book 8, RHT Papers, UW.
3. RHT to T.J. Humes, 1 Jan. 1901, report for the year 1900, box 1, book 2, Engineering Department, City Engineer's Reports, PSRA.
4. RHT to R.A. Ballinger, 27 December 1905, report for 1905, box 1, book 3, Engineering Department, City Engineer's Reports, PSRA; and A.H. Dimock to George W. Dilling, 26 December 1911, Engineering Department, Administrative, Annual Reports, 1900–1954, PSRA.
5. RHT to H.C. Gill, 31 December 1910, box 4, Engineering Department, Administrative, Annual Reports, 1900–1954, PSRA.
6. RHT's correspondence on the subject of paving is voluminous. For the difficulty of the question, see RHT to Otto A. Weile, 15 November 1909, 89/1, box 3, book 7, RHT Papers, UW. For a comparison of various types of pavement, see RHT to Thomas F. Mahony, 26 April 1910, 89/1, box 3, book 8, RHT Papers, UW. For wood, see RHT to William B. Chase, 26 August 1901, 89/1, box 1, book 2, RHT Papers, UW. For asphalt and comparative quotation, see RHT to M.T. Maloney, 1 July 1910, 89/1, box 3, book 8, RHT Papers, UW. For concrete, see RHT to I. Lang, 18 June 1918, 89/1, box 4, book 11, RHT Papers.
7. Rockafeller, "Public Health in Progressive Seattle," 115–16; RHT to Will H. Parry, 15 September 1897, 991146, SMA; and *Times*, February 1, 1907, and February 3, 1907, two good articles, despite some exaggeration.
8. *Argus*, December 31, 1904.
9. The arguments may be followed in *Times* February 3, 1905; March 18, 1905; March 20, 1905; March 24, 1905; March 25, 1905; and *Argus*, March 11, 1905. Ballinger's actions are in the March 30 Minutes of the City Council, Record of the City Council, book 4, pp. 164–65, SMA; and a copy of the corrected and approved ordinance in 1602-2, box 3, folder 7, RHT Papers, UW. For the *Argus* reaction, see April 1, 1905; and for the suit, *Argus*, July 22, 1905.
10. *P-I*, December 27, 1904. The Clise quote is repeated in RHT to Clise, March 21, 1905, 89/1, box 1, book 3, RHT Papers, UW. For RHT on the matters he would study, see RHT to the council's committee on public works, 13 March 1905, 89/1, box 1, book 3, RHT Papers, UW.
11. Details of the trip are in expense books that RHT kept for the purpose of noting his activities. For destructors, see Expense Book 1, August 8 and 12; for Waterloo, June 29; for Versailles, July 15; and for Paris, July 15. See also Expense Books 2 and 3, 1602-2, box 1, folder 2, RHT Papers, UW. For quotations, see RHT to Alva Brown, 12 October 1905, 89/1, box 2, book 4. For the garbage burning question, see Melosi, *Sanitary City*, 199. RHT could not complete the report of his trip until 1 July 1907 because of the press of other business. It is reprinted in *P-I*, July 7, 1907.
12. RHT to Meldrum Brothers, 23 August 1906, 89/1, box 2, book 4; and for the DeCarie model, RHT to W.F. Goodrich, 21 November 1905, 89/1, box 2, book 4, RHT papers, UW. See also *Times*, February 1, 1907; February 3, 1907; February 25, 1907; and January 28, 1908.
13. *P-I*, February 25, 1908; February 26, 1908; and RHT to R.F. Dunden, 14 March 1908, 89/1, box 2, book 5, RHT Papers, UW.

14. *Times*, April 2, 1908; April 3, 1908; and April 15, 1908. For the correct cost, see RHT to E. Roche, 5 June 1908, 89/1, box 2, book 6, RHT Papers, UW.

15. RHT, Scrapbook, "Miscellaneous I," article attributed to *P-I*, April 5, 1908, 89/1, box 11, RHT Papers, UW; RHT to G.A. Bading, 31 July 1908, 89/1, box 2, book 6, RHT Papers, UW; and Phelps, *Public Works in Seattle*, 205–6.

16. Phelps, *Public Works in Seattle*, 206–7. For a somewhat different view, see Martin V. Melosi, "Technology Diffusion and Refuse Disposal: The Case of the British Destructor," in Tarr and Dupuy, *Technology and the Networked City*, 206–26. For problems of selling destructor byproducts, see *P-I* February 21, 1908. For the transition to land filling, see *Report of the Department of Health and Sanitation of the City of Seattle, Washington,…nineteen twelve, thirteen and fourteen* (Seattle: Lowman and Hanford, [1916]), which includes reports for 1915. For Crichton and his activities, see Rockafeller, "Public Health in Progressive Seattle," 63–67, 87–94, 107–27. For quotation, see RHT to D. McGuire, 14 August 1911, 89/1, box 4, book 10, RHT Papers, UW.

17. Seattle Board of Park Commissioners, *First Annual Report, 1844–1904* (Seattle: Loman and Hanford, 1905), 44.

18. Wilson, *City Beautiful Movement* 156–57, 159–60.

19. Ibid., 163.

20. RHT, letter in *P-I*, March 6, 1904. For the vote, see *Journal of the Proceedings of the City Council of the City of Seattle*, March 11, 1904, SMA.

21. For the sewer, see Wilson, *City Beautiful Movement*, 218. For Olmsted in Seattle, see Joan Hockaday, *Greenscapes: Olmsted's Pacific Northwest* (Pullman: Washington State University Press, 2009), 8–11, 37–100. *Greenscapes* is a detailed, highly readable, beautifully illustrated analysis of John Charles Olmsted's work with the city, private clients, and the AYPE, in the context of his other activities in the Pacific Northwest and elsewhere. See also Wilson, *City Beautiful Movement*, l5l, l64–66, and, for quotation, 218–19.

22. *Eighth Annual Report of the Board of Park Commissioners for the Calendar Year 1911* (Seattle: Smiley, [1912]), 9, 23.

23. See the excellent summary of the Bogue plan in Mansel Blackford, *Lost Dream*, 111–24.

24. For Portland, see Carl Abbott, *Portland: Planning, Politics, and Growth in a Twentieth Century City* (Lincoln: University of Nebraska Press, 1983), 36–48, 57–61. For RHT, the AYPE, and good roads, see RHT to William Carnes, 9 July 1907, 89/1, box 2, book 5; and to W.W. Campbell, 26 April 1909, 89/1, box 2, book 6, RHT Papers, UW. An example of his support for comprehensive planning is in RHT to Gill, note 5. For the AYPE, see the pictorial studies by Nicolette Bromberg, *Picturing the Alaska-Yukon-Pacific Exposition: The Photographs of Frank H. Nowell* (Seattle: University of Washington Press, 2009); Shauna and Brennan O'Reilly, *Alaska Yukon Pacific Exposition* (Charleston, SC: Arcadia, 2009); and Alan J. Stein and Paula Becker, *Alaska-Yukon-Pacific Exposition, Washington's First World's Fair: A Timeline History* (Seattle: HistoryLink, 2009). Two issues of the *PNQ* (Winter 2006/2007 and Spring 2009) feature articles on the AYPE.

25. Quoted in Wilson, *City Beautiful Movement*, 216. See 216–17 for support for this and the next paragraph.

26. Quoted in Ibid., 217.

27. *P-I*, November 17, 1909, local news sec.; and RHT to Paul C. Murphy, 4 June 1909, 89/1, box 3, book 7, RHT Papers, UW.

28. Wilson, *City Beautiful Movement*, 217–20, and for quotation, 217.

29. Ibid., 221-24, 226. For the Chicago plan, see Thomas S. Hines, *Burnham of Chicago: Architect and Planner* (New York:

Oxford University Press, 1974), 341; and Carl Smith, *The Plan of Chicago: Daniel Burnham and the Remaking of the American City* (Chicago: University of Chicago Press, 2006), 41, 80, 147.

30. For working with Bogue, see RHT to V.G. Bogue, 5 April 1911; and to Francis W. Grant, April 13, 1911, 89/1, box 4, book 10, RHT Papers, UW. For the dinner, see *Times*, sec. 1, November 20, 1910; and a transcript or reconstruction of RHT's address in 89/1, box 6, folder 9, RHT Papers, UW. For Thomson and Cotterill, see *Times* February 4, 1912. For other quotations, see Wilson, *City Beautiful Movement*, 226; and, for a review of the issues, 221–26. See also Wilson, "How Seattle Lost the Bogue Plan: Politics versus Design," *PNQ* 75 (October, 1984): 171–80.

31. For a review and analysis of reasons for the failure of the Bogue plan up to its publication date, see Wilson, "How Seattle Lost the Bogue Plan." Since then at least two more explanations have been advanced. Norbert MacDonald, in order to reach his conclusion that "there never had been a major commitment to planning in Seattle" has to ignore Thomson's work, the Olmsted plan, and the practically mandatory nature of the Bogue plan, omissions that would be laughable if they did not distort reality as voters saw it then, and as MacDonald's readers deserved to see it in his *Distant Neighbors: A Comparative History of Seattle and Vancouver* (Lincoln: University of Nebraska Press, 1987), 72–74, and for quotation, 74. Richard Berner's analysis in *Seattle, 1900–1920*, is equally curious. Despite the enormous publicity given to the Bogue plan, Berner found that Seattle's newspapers almost completely failed to give the plan any publicity during the closing days of the campaign for its adoption. This failure led to its defeat. To reach his conclusion Berner adopts a reductionist theory of public issues in Seattle: they stand or fall on the volume of major media publicity given them, especially in the final week or so of the vote that decided their fate. Park bonds, however, passed, although they also received significant opposition and little late publicity. To explain their acceptance, Berner abandons his model for another explanation, that parks were acceptable to Seattleites, but the civic center was not. Even stranger is his notion that a substitute civic center, though it contained no public buildings, was developing on the north edge of the commercial-retail district. No collection of buildings, there or elsewhere in the city, remotely conformed to the civic center idea. See pp. 105–6, 122, 128, 135–36, 139, 141–52.

32. Fitzsimons, "Perils of Public Works Engineering," betrays no understanding of the earlier unconcern, for examples, see 42, 68, n. 48, and for the quotation about RHT, 117. See also Henry Petroski, *Engineers of Dreams: Great Bridge Builders and the Spanning of America* (New York: Alfred A. Knopf, 1995), 44–45.

33. For Portland, RHT to P.D. Clarke, 6 March 1911, 89/1, box 4, book 10; for Spokane, RHT to George W. Armstrong, 15 December 1910, 89/1, box 3, book 9; for Prince Rupert, RHT to William Manson, 1 May 1911, 89/1, box 4, book 10; for Puget Mill, RHT to Puget Mill Co., 11 June 1898, 89/1, box 1, book 2; for Ellensburg, RHT to O.W. Ball, 31 August 1911, 89/1, box 4, book 10; for the Aleutians, RHT, "Sketches," 1895 entry, 1602-2, box 2, folder 10; for Walla Walla, RHT to H.H. Turner 15 April 1904, 89/1, box 1, book 3; RHT to E.A. Knight, 9 March 1905, 89/1, box 1, book 3; and to Knight, 1 December 1908, 89/1, box 2, book 6, RHT Papers. UW. The general matter of consulting is based on the study of all of RHT's diaries, diary notes, and correspondence, 1892–1911, but does not include casual advice or endorsements for which RHT charged a modest fee or none at all.

Once in a great while RHT would refuse a consulting job, for reasons not clear in his letters of refusal, which cited the press of other business, see, for example, RHT to L.P. Fisher, 17 March 1900, 89/1, box 1, book 2, RHT Papers, UW.

34. An expense sheet included in RHT to R.P. Reynolds, 11 November 1905, 89/1, box 2, book 4, is revealing of price levels at the time of RHT's submission of his bill. His most expensive day cost $22.50. A two-day stay in a hotel cost $9.50. A Pullman berth and meals cost $4.30. Any meal costing more than 50¢ was expensive. For quotations, see RHT to William Manson, 8 April 1911, 89/1, box 4, book 10, RHT Papers, UW.

35. RHT, Excelsior Diary, 1891, 1592, box 1, RHT Papers, UW. For Retta's death, see RHT, "Sketches," 1893 entry, 1602-2, box 2, folder 10, RHT Papers, UW. For 1909 and 1910 taxes see the lot lists and taxes due in 89/1, box 3, book 8, RHT Papers, UW. For the McGilvra gift, see RHT to McGilvra, 3 November 1903; and to Mayor Olney, 1 January 1904, 89/1, box 1, book 3, RHT Papers, UW. In an issue involving property and a potential conflict of interest, RHT was pushing a sale of a client's property to the city while he was also city engineer. He appears, however, to be acting as an honest broker and concealing nothing about his consulting relationship, see RHT to Pope & Talbot, 28 December 1899, 89/1, box 1, book 2, RHT Papers, UW.

36. For the Indiana property, see RHT to Rodgers Brothers, 20 December 1902, 9 March 1903, and 2 September 1903, 89/1, box 1, book 3, RHT Papers, UW. For the sale of the Losee property, see RHT to P.P. Dabney, 5 March 1903, 89/1, box 1, book 3, RHT Papers, UW. For Losee property quotation, see RHT to P.P. Boyd, 8 September 1910, 89/1, box 3, book 9, RHT Papers, UW. For the drain, see RHT to D.H. Glass, 4 September 1909, 89/1, box 3, book 7, RHT Papers, UW. For the number of houses, see RHT to Smith and Hansen, 5 February 1908, 89/1, box 2, book 5, RHT Papers, UW. For the quotation, see RHT to John Hansen, 13 June 1912, 89/1, box 4, book 11, RHT Papers, UW. For the British Columbia company names, see RHT to D.C. Wilson, 16 March 1911, 89/1, box 4, book 10, RHT Papers, UW. For brother Henry and John Hartman, see RHT to S.N. Wilson, 31 March 1911, 89/1, box 4, book 10, RHT Papers, UW. For quotation, see RHT to H.C. Thomson, 15 October 1910, 89/1, box 3, book 9; and for details on company operations, see RHT to H.C. Thomson, 16 March 1911, 89/1, box 4, book 10, RHT Papers, UW.

37. For billboards, see, for example, P-I, October 6, 1904. For quotations, see P-I, April 2, 1911, sec. 2.

38. For DAR, see RHT to Mrs. Horace Phillips, 22 September 1903, 89/1, box 1, book 3, RHT Papers, UW. For assistant, see RHT to H.W. Scott, 11 October 1905, 89/1, box 2, book 4, RHT Papers, UW. For street grades and plan, RHT to H.C. Gage, 9 December 1908, 89/1, box 2, book 6, RHT Papers, UW.

39. RHT to John F. Miller, 23 December 1909, Engineering Department, Administration, Annual Reports, 1900–1950, PSRA; Times, January 2, 1910; John Lamb to Cotterill, 2 January 1910, 38, box 5, folder 4, Cotterill Papers, UW; and Argus, November 29, 1913. For a more reasoned criticism of RHT, see TC, November 29, 1913.

40. For the paving enthusiast, see RHT to N.H. Latimer, 29 January 1909, 89/1, box 2, book 6, RHT Papers, UW. For "struggling to prevent" quotation, see RHT to Samuel Hill, 12 November 1909, 89/1, box 3, book 7, RHT Papers, UW. For Wittler, see RHT to Scott Calhoun, 15 February 1910, box 4,

case file June to December 1910, Law Department, Correspondence, series I, PSRA.

41. For Soloman's injunction, see RHT to W.T. Hall, 5 October 1910, 89/1, box 3, book 9, RHT Papers, UW. For "make errors" quotation, see RHT to Goodwin Real Estate Company, Inc., 2 May 1908, 89/1, box 2, book 6, RHT Papers, UW. For "so much" quotation, see RHT to William Carnes, 18 February 1905, 89/1, box 1, book 3, RHT Papers, UW.

42. RHT to Ballinger, 22 March 1906, 89/1, box 2, book 4; and RHT to P.J. Casey, 2 October 1909, 89/1, box 3, book 7, RHT Papers, UW.

43. For the friendships with Hill and Lancaster, see William H. Wilson, "'Names Joined Together as Our Hearts Are,' The Friendship of Samuel Hill and Reginald H. Thomson," PNQ 94 (Fall 2003): 183–88. For strains in the Hartman and Wells friendships, see Wilson, "Rising and Setting of Seattle's Sun." Close as he was to Samuel Hill, for example, he addressed Hill as "Mr.," see RHT to Hill, 23 January 1905, 89/1, box 1, book 3, RHT Papers, UW.

44. P-I, November 2, 1907; and to J.R. Taylor, 4 November 1907, 89/1, box 2, book 5, RHT Papers, UW.

45. Letter of introduction for Samuel Hill, RHT to Harvey W. Wiley, 29 November 1911, 89/1, box 4, book 11, RHT Papers, UW. For a letter of recommendation, see RHT to C.W. Fairbanks, 7 January 1907, box 2, book 5, RHT Papers. Requested favors are in RHT to A.L. Walters, 18 January 1906, box 2, book 4; and RHT to R.A. Ballinger asking for Chittenden's promotion to brigadier general, 30 September 1909, box 3, book 7, RHT Papers, UW. For debt repayment, see RHT to Edith P. Nelson, 30 October 1902, 89/1, box 1, book 3; RHT to Knight, 1 December 1908; 89/1, box 2, book 6; RHT to Knight, 25 March 1909, 89/1, box 2, book 6; RHT to Knight, 14 June 1909, 89/1, box 3, book 7, RHT Papers, UW. For the young man, and for quotations, see RHT to Dan Ward, 6 April 1910, 89/1, box 3, book 8; and RHT to Francis G. Ward, 10 January 1911, 89/1, box 3, book 9, RHT Papers, UW. For "I am pressed" quotation, see RHT to Knight, 25 March 1909, 89/1, box 2, book 6, RHT Papers, UW.

46. For "great battle" quotation, see RHT to J.M. Wilson, 14 November 1902, 89/1, box 1, book 3; and for "Heavenly Father" quotation, RHT to Minard Brown Sturgis, 20 March 1906, 89/1, box 2, book 4, RHT Papers, UW. For one of many references to serious illnesses, see RHT to C.E. Fowler, 21 January 1903, 89/1, box 1, book 3; and for teeth, RHT to William Carnes, 30 March 1905, 89/1, box 1, book 3, RHT Papers, UW. For Matthews, see RHT to Will H. Parry, 4 February 1905, 89/1, box 1, book 3, RHT Papers, UW. Matthews' biographer is Dale E. Soden, The Reverend Mark Matthews: An Activist in the Progressive Era (Seattle: University of Washington Press, 2001). For opposition to leasing, see RHT to Francis W. Grant, 18 November 1909, 89/1, box 3, book 7, RHT Papers, UW.

47. RHT to J.M. Wilson, 16 October 1910, 89/1, box 4, book 11; and for Matthews, RHT to Matthews, 26 May 1909, 89/1, box 3, book 7.

48. For the good roads association, see William H. Wilson, "'Names Joined Together as Our Hearts Are,'" 185–89. For the PNSCE, see RHT to Major C.W. Kutz, 24 May 1909, 89/1, box 2, book 6, RHT Papers, UW. For Beta, see RHT to James T. Brown, 6 May 1903, 89/1, box 1, book 3, RHT Papers, UW. For Christian Endeavor, see RHT to William Hickman Moore, 20 July 1907, 89/1, box 2, book 5, RHT Papers, UW. For YMCA, see RHT to C.M. Rood, 25 September 1905, 89/1, box 2, book 4, RHT Papers, UW. For speeches, for example, see RHT to C.B. Yardell, 29 January 1910, box 3, book 8, RHT Papers,

UW. For history, see RHT to Bureau of National Literature and Art, 4 March 1903, 89/1, box 1, book 3, RHT Papers, UW. For photography, RHT to Taylor, Taylor & Hobson, 5 August 1903, 89/1, box 1, book 3, RHT Papers, UW. For genealogy, "A Brief Statement of the Ancestors of … Magdelene … Thomson," 89/1, box 4, book 11, RHT Papers, UW.

49. For quotation, see RHT, "Sketches," 1883 entry, 1602-2, box 2, folder 10, RHT Papers, UW. For the last two children, see RHT, "Sketches," 1894 and 1897 entries, 1602-2, box 2, folder 10, RHT Papers, UW. For the "hired girl" quotation and incidental information, interview with Sally Hepler, June 15, 1999, and January 5, 2000, hereafter Hepler interview; and RHT to Sunset Telephone Co., 21 December 1909, 89/1, box 3, book 7, RHT Papers, UW. For "water closet" quotation, RHT to J.E. Crichton, 1 April 1908, 89/1, box 2, book 5, RHT Papers, UW.

50. For "principal joys" quotation, see RHT to E.G. DeWald, 28 May 1903, 89/1, box 1, book 3, RHT Papers, UW. For "unwilling" quotation, see RHT to Herbert Thomson, 3 November 1906, 89/1, box 2, book 4, RHT Papers, UW. For his mother's death, RHT to "Dear Brother Laughlin," 4 November 1906, 89/1, box 2, book 4, RHT Papers, UW. For his evaluation of his mother, see RHT to F.G. Strange, 27 November 1906, 89/1, box 2, book 4, RHT Papers, UW.

51. For building on the McGilvra lot, see RHT to J.D. Ross, 14 September 1905, Cedar Falls Electric, vol. 1, book 2, PSRA. For "financial condition" quotation, see RHT to J.R. McLaughlin, 25 January 1909, 89/1, box 2, book 6, RHT Papers, UW.

52. For house quotations, in order, see RHT to Frank W. Laughlin, 18 December 1909, 89/1, box 3, book 7; RHT to Mrs. H.E. McCulloch, 18 December 1909, 89/1, box 3, book 7; and RHT to H.C. Thomson, 18 December 1909, 89/1, box 3, book 7, RHT Papers, UW. For the new house and family matters in this paragraph and the next, see RHT to H.C. Thomson, 16 March 1911, 89/1, box 4, book 10, RHT Papers, UW.

ON NOVEMBER 7, 1911, Thomson resigned from the city engineer's post. His letter of resignation noted that he and Mayor George W. Dilling had discussed his leaving and that he was being offered the job of chief engineer of the newly-formed Port of Seattle. In Thomson's judgment, "securing the construction of a safe and commodious harbor, is now of greater importance than any other work." He wrote "that my affections are with the city and that I ask permission to take this step only because I believe it will be advantageous to the city." It may have been that Dilling had decided not to reappoint Thomson, but it certainly was true that Thomson was "very weary" and longed "most earnestly for some rest from the incessant grind," as he had written in March 1909. This was not his only expression of discontent with aspects of the job, yet he always found some compelling reason to stay on. It is not certain why he chose to leave in 1911, beyond Dilling's presumed decision. Some inferences may be made. He was 55 in 1911 and had been on the job for almost 22 years, with his greatest work behind him. He took two new jobs in 1911–12, the port commission's post for a short time, and the superintendence of a provincial park in British Columbia. Both offered a fresh start, a relatively clean slate, and a respite from the less appealing tasks of being the city engineer. [1]

Nor was this the first time he had sought, or been tempted by, another position. He wanted an engineering job on the Panama Canal although he had "no serious thought" of it happening. "Nevertheless, if

East Waterway, looking north from Hanford Street, 1915. At left is Harbor Island, site of F.A. Ayers' failed terminal plan, which Thomson opposed while serving with the Seattle Port Commission. *Seattle Municipal Archives #740.*

one does not seek to enter when the waters are moved, nothing can be done." The waters moved several more times, with no more result. In 1904 or 1905, he and friend Samuel Hill planned an unspecified project, for which Thomson would have opened a separate consulting office while retaining his city post. While Mayor Ballinger would allow the usual sort of consulting, "when he learned I was negotiating for a room he came to me and set his face against the matter like a rock," Thomson complained to Hill. Ballinger made two points to the crestfallen engineer—if he opened an office he could not prevent his assistants from doing likewise, which "would work havoc in an office heretofore free from scandal," and in that case he would have to resign from his city job. Thomson gave up the proposed consulting work. In June 1908, he delivered a lecture on municipal improvements "to a representative body of businessmen" in Portland, resulting in a "shaking up" such as Portland had never witnessed. A real estate man wrote him: "No public speaker who has appeared before an audience in this city since I have lived here has ever succeeded in arousing the enthusiasm that has permeated the Community since your memorable oration of the 11th." The real purpose was to woo him to work for three years at a "handsome salary," superintending "the general development of the city" of Portland, but he said no, having before him a prospective offer from Tacoma, as well as doubts about leaving his Seattle post. The Tacoma job, for whatever reason, did not materialize either.[2]

In 1909 came other opportunities. By June of that year, the former mayor, Richard Ballinger, now Secretary of the Interior in the William Howard Taft administration, announced his intention to appoint Thomson as Chief of the Reclamation Service. Ballinger's announcement was naïve because it gave the incumbent, Frederick H. Newell, and his supporters time to build a backfire. A lengthy article in the January 13, 1910, *Engineering News* praised Newell and accused Ballinger of attempting to politicize the Reclamation Service. Ballinger, in fact, had doubts about the legality of some of Newell's cooperative activities with private "water users associations," doubts supported by an opinion of the U.S. Attorney General. Beyond that, he was suspicious of Newell's executive ability. For his part, Thomson did "not know that I would be well adapted to this position and have very grave doubts as to my accepting the offer," doubts reinforced by nearly unanimous urgings that he stay on in Seattle. None of this made any difference. By the time that the *Engineering News* article appeared, Ballinger was

embroiled in the Ballinger-Pinchot controversy over the validity of some coal land claims in Alaska and widely denounced as an enemy of conservation and the manservant of large development interests. In the spring of 1910, Ballinger gave up his plan to appoint Thomson. Though a joint congressional investigating committee's majority report cleared him, Ballinger was a liability to the Taft administration. He resigned in March 1911.[3]

The Reclamation Service was a sideshow in the national theater and Thomson probably would not have accepted the appointment to head the service had it been offered. The attack on his friend Ballinger, however, infuriated him. Thomson had no use for Gifford Pinchot, Ballinger's chief tormenter. Pinchot—then Chief of the Forest Service—a few years before had frustrated for a time Thomson's hopes of gaining control of the Cedar River watershed. Thomson intended to allow the "original owners" to log the property that the city would purchase, then re-forest the land "on the most scientific basis." He "had several personal interviews with Mr. Pinchot," including one during "which it seemed to be agreed that he would consent" to the city taking over lands in the watershed. "He made a date when he was to go with me to the land. However, when the time came he broke faith with me and did not go." This was not the only time that Pinchot broke an appointment to avoid a potentially unpleasant confrontation. Later, Thomson "found from the office force that there was no intention to let the City or any other person control that timber if the Forestry Department could help it." In writing to Secretary Ballinger in November 1909, Thomson asserted, "your thousands of friends throughout the country are incensed at the infamous and wicked attacks made upon you, and that you know that they are ever ready to refute them." He complained to Congressman William E. Humphrey of the "extreme disloyalty of many government employees to the head of their department and their willingness to peddle pure gossip, with malicious purpose." As for Pinchot, he was "guilty of criminal conspiracy to defame the character of a public official." Because of the tying up of Alaska, "the commerce of Seattle is actually suffering." To another correspondent he wrote of the "bitter and indecent fight against Secretary Ballinger" made by "Socialists," who wanted to retain control of Alaska lands forever through "short term leases of ten-acre tracts."[4]

Thomson's friend Samuel Hill made the other, more attractive and less controversial 1909 offer. Hill was interested in a large tract in central Oregon originally deeded to a wagon road company as a land grant. The manager of the vast property dangled it before Hill and others. Thomson told Hill, if they could find someone to make a down payment, then "I would be willing to quit the City of Seattle and give my time exclusively to the management of the proposition." In another letter to Hill he supplied a personal motive for his interest. "This long office confinement is telling on my reserve vitality." Thomson's hopes for release from the office grind went unrealized. Despite Hill's considerable charm, persuasiveness, and involvement in a multitude of enterprises, he lacked the funds to purchase the huge tract. Forming a syndicate was his only hope, but hope was dashed when a group of St. Paul investors associated with the Great Northern Railway bought 799,664 acres for $6 million. It was the largest private land deal in the country up to that time. Thomson's hopes went out the door with Hill's. There probably were other job possibilities for the engineer during this period, which all fell through for one reason or another.[5]

There would be the right combination of circumstances in 1911, however, to relieve Thomson of the "incessant grind" if not from "office confinement." Many duties having nothing directly to do with engineering had borne in upon him. One of these was civil service. Thomson praised the civil service requirements for "keeping the Council's fingers out of every contract and out of all employment of labor," and for thus maintaining the city council as a group capable of an impartial examination of citizen complaints. Nevertheless, the civil service examinations themselves sometimes posed problems. His assistant Charles J. Moore wrote about an excellent worker who had no contact with the public and yet was required to spell 20 words in English. The worker left the examination room "and we have not seen him since." In words reminiscent of New York's famed district leader George Washington Plunkitt, Moore pleaded for "a little common sense" in the civil service examination. "In the case in question, we do not care what a man's opinion may be of the reformed spelling book, the effect of the Sun on the solar system, or the state of art in ancient Egypt. What we want is results."[6]

A related problem involved state and city limits on public-works labor to eight hours per day. In some cases it was possible to dodge the requirements, but there was no getting around them "in the matter of street grading," though "to keep a horse standing in the stable five days on account of rain, and then to allow him to work but eight hours on the sixth day was little short of idiotic." Thomson thought that men should be made of sterner stuff. "Out of regard for their delicate health," male state and city employees were limited to eight hours per day, he wrote to his friend John Hartman and several others early in 1911. Women, on the other hand, were "by law compelled to work ten hours per day in all their labor." Nothing could be done about the men but he thought it "a special injustice" to "women and girls" and therefore "a matter of common decency" to amend the law.[7]

Many of Thomson's tasks were demanding and time consuming. Near the end of his tenure he oversaw a workforce of more than 200, requiring continuous close supervision of his staff. As chairman of the Board of Public Works, he often served as the conduit to other members in matters of administration and public relations. He was himself a master of public relations, taking city officials on tours of the Cedar River dam and power house. Giving testimony in court during the many suits over city improvements claimed enormous amounts of his time and the time of his assistants. In 1906 he prepared a favorable report on a municipal street railway system at the behest of the city council. He appended an elaborate analysis from an engineering firm in support of the system. A spirited bond issue campaign followed, with a Municipal Ownership Party favoring the bonds and the *Times* vigorously opposing them. The proposition lost at the polls in September. Attending city council meetings was important but a thief of time, as was lobbying state legislators. It was little wonder, despite his robust appearance, that he fell ill under pressure from this hectic schedule. The symptoms varied, but to Thomson and the doctors of the day they were all in the category of "grip," a catchword for everything from a heavy cold to mild influenza. In 1905 he complained of being "confined to the house" and "weak as a cat." Two years later he was in bed, and in the autumn of 1909 again "was in bed," this time "with my eyes bandaged" under an "acute attack of Grip." These instances are examples of a malady that struck as often as two or three times a year.[8]

Of course, there were compensations. National recognition came through articles in the widely-read *Saturday Evening Post* and other magazines. The *Post-Intelligencer* continued its usually favorable review of Thomson's work. One article in the *P-I* prompted Thomson to write to a brother about those who "have so faithfully served with me," including the deceased Henry W. Scott, "a prince among men," and J.C. Jeffrey, "who by his very boldness helped me to do much to put forward a difficult scheme," a probable reference to his winning property owners over to the Jackson Street regrade. Finally, "for fourteen years, I have had a little stenographer to sit by and stand up for the truth." Katharine Stream's only known photograph, dated 1895, shows a serious-looking young woman in a prim shirtwaist, whose hair is fastened in a bun. Appearances aside, she was humorous, intelligent, and industrious. She produced reams of Thomson's letters and reports on the typewriter and handled much other office business. He trusted her completely. When he was ill, she wrote letters on his behalf, and when he took a second trip to Europe in 1908, he authorized her to sign his checks. He could not have worked as effectively as he did without her mastery of his duties and procedures. The Thomsons treated her practically as a member of the family.[9]

Attacks on him, especially from the *Times*, generated letters of support. Few incoming letters survive but their content may be assumed from Thomson's replies. To a group of correspondents, he replied that it was "necessary for me to protest against giving control of all public utilities to certain corporate interests." He opposed using the utilities "for personal profit," and therefore was forced "to withstand the intrigue and malice of those who would absorb as their own, all those rights which I believe belong to the people." To another correspondent he declared that "I have absolutely no apologies to make for my conduct, because I know full well that the uproar was made simply because I insisted upon that which was right." During the first decade of the 20th century, a grand jury extensively investigated private and public activity, including the engineering department. Its March 1910 report handed up indictments and criticized some city and county agencies. Its thorough investigation of the engineering department found mistakes and work retarded for reasons beyond its control, "but no evidence of corruption or graft, and the efficiency of the department is commendable."[10]

In July 1911, Councilman Albert J. Goddard accused Thomson of serious misconduct. Other than general claims of inefficiency and extravagance, Goddard's most damning charge was that the city engineer enabled contractors to make exorbitant profits by rigging contracts. Thomson wanted a joint investigation by the chamber of commerce, commercial club, the Rotary Club, and the Municipal League, as "representatives of the public," but the council's department efficiency committee undertook the review. In a follow up statement, Goddard claimed that Thomson overreacted to his charges. He had not accused Thomson of dishonesty, as Thomson claimed. He had instead accused Thomson of incompetence and manipulating contracts, not of dishonesty, a distinction without a difference. Thomson also accused Goddard of having political ambitions, which Goddard denied.

As far as his charges were concerned, Goddard insisted they were "matters of common knowledge to every resident of this city and need no investigation to establish their truthfulness." Nevertheless the council committee insisted on evidence. A parade of former councilmen followed. They testified that the council's street committee heard recommendations for and objections to each regrade; that while Thomson's views carried considerable weight, grades almost always were adjusted to satisfy the greatest number of property owners; that the engineering department sometimes exercised poor judgment in the opinion of others; that the matters of cuts and fills usually were left to the engineering department, but that at least two councilmen worked with the department to balance cuts and fills on projects in their wards; that public clamor for a regrade overrode Thomson's objections on one occasion and the council's on another; that contractors' handling of some projects was open to criticism and that the finished product was Thomson's responsibility, however, the council could have defeated any or all regrade projects as they came before that governing body.[11]

There was no evidence for Goddard's pet propositions, that cuts and fills were incorrectly completed or designed, or that contractors received favorable treatment. The hearings ended after Thomson resigned, leaving Goddard without a target. Had they unearthed any criminal action, the evidence of wrongdoing could have been presented to a prosecutor, but nothing came of it. Thomson continued to believe in the hearing's political purpose. "Mr. Goddard, a member of the city council, has been very anxious to be elected mayor, and has chosen to try and exalt himself by abusing me," he told a correspondent. "The whole thing has fizzled out so completely that it is mostly forgotten here in town now."[12] If Goddard was as ambitious as Thomson believed, his aspirations were frustrated; he never became mayor.

Thomson did become the chief engineer of the Seattle Port Commission despite a display of public opposition. The opposition came after an open meeting of the port commission on September 28, 1911. Chairman Hiram M. Chittenden asked for a budget amount "put in with the specific idea that we could get Mr. Thomson" for "that sum." A Mrs. Annie Lindsay heatedly opposed Thomson as a spendthrift, who was no better than any number of other engineers who would work for less. The contentious Commissioner Robert Bridges also angrily criticized Thomson and supported Thomson's erstwhile assistant and long time friend, George F. Cotterill. A number of leading Seattleites, including Thomas

Burke, praised Thomson. The third commissioner, C.E. Remsberg, voiced no preference. Whether or not they were moved to action in response to Thomson receiving support from Chittenden and some of Seattle's elite, the city engineer's opponents organized a mass meeting at the Dreamland dance pavilion for Sunday afternoon, October 1.[13]

Exactly who was behind the meeting was obscure, but many of the attendees understood it to be an anti-Thomson assembly. In any case, that was the way things turned out. Thomson attended, and was called with others to sit on the speaker's platform. Cotterill, pleading a previous engagement, did not appear. A series of speakers supported Cotterill for the port commission post. Applauded when he moved to the platform, applauded when he rose to speak, and applauded again for his talk, Thomson spoke briefly at the end of the lengthy burst of speechmaking. Then, after giving Thomson "a near-ovation," the meeting endorsed Cotterill on a rising vote. Only 20 or 30 people remained seated. The straw vote, however, had no influence on the commission when they met the next day (October 2,

chronologically before Thomson's official November 7 resignation from the city engineer post). Commissioner Bridges vigorously opposed Thomson as he had in the past, probably because of Bridges' identification with labor and Thomson's opposition to the eight-hour day. Chittenden and Commissioner Remsberg voted for Thomson, while Bridges cast for Cotterill. Over Bridge's objections, Thomson's salary was set at $7,500, the same as he received for his Seattle engineer post. After the vote, Bridges pledged his support for Thomson and assured the public that the commissioners would work in harmony.[14]

Thomson believed that the partisanship of the pro-Cotterill Sunday gathering had redounded to his benefit. "I find that there are great many persons who deeply regret the manner in which they were unwittingly drawn into the Sunday meeting," he told a fellow Seattleite. Although he did not say so directly, he may have believed that the blatant packing of the Sunday gathering influenced Commissioner Remsberg in later voting in his favor. Yet it should have been disquieting that a public meeting so obviously rejected him. Granted, Thomson

East Waterway in 1914, looking north towards Lander Street, former tideflats now filled in after Thomson's city regrade projects. *Seattle Municipal Archives #73.*

was appointed and reappointed to get things done for Seattle and not to win a popularity contest. Whether fairly or not, his opponents had persuaded a large number of people to register their distrust of him, apparently on the grounds that he was personally responsible for high municipal taxes. One of his opponents at the port commission meeting where he was selected reminded the commissioners that they "would have to answer to the people" for their decision. But all this was lost in a wave of accolades for the departing city engineer. The Board of Public Works presented him with an inscribed resolution praising his tenacity, integrity, and successful conclusion of many projects. More than 200 prominent men attended a banquet in his honor at the Seattle Commercial Club. It was a ceremonial occasion typical of the era, with speeches extolling the work of the honored guest. Thomson acknowledged them all, praising his assistants and explaining the need for undertakings such as the Cedar River waterworks and the regrades. He acknowledged, too, the imperfections of the work, declaring that, while he spent $40,000,000, he wished he had been able to spend $75,000,000. Perhaps Joe Smith, a crusading, gadfly newspaperman and politician, best summed up Thomson's career. "We have had crooked money on one side and Mr. Thomson on the other," he declared. "Mr. Thomson may have made mistakes, but think of the mistakes he saved us from making." [15]

Despite the declarations of goodwill and the auspicious sendoff, Thomson's new tenure at the port commission lasted a mere four months. Its brevity is all the more remarkable because Chairman Chittenden and Thomson were friends, and the commission itself was established after a long public ownership campaign. Thomson's and the Municipal Ownership Party's campaign for a municipal street railway system, though defeated, was a landmark along the way. He was close to the core of the group pressing for a state port law and a municipal port district ordinance, gathered port information during his travels, and helped to draft the Port District Act of March 1911. The success of the port legislation and approval by King County voters that September rested on nonlocal causes as well—particularly the long national and global tradition of public port ownership, and the pending completion of the Panama Canal with its promise of greatly expanded Asian trade. Thomson's formal assumption of office came in December 1911. There were the usual problems of settling into new office surroundings and adjusting to the personalities of the commissioners and others, difficulties made easier by the presence of assistant Katharine Stream. For his office staff he rec-

ommended Paul P. Whitham of Seattle's public utility department, who was hired, and became his successor. Beyond Whitham and three draftsmen, he saw no need for any other full-time employees. [16]

With his staff in place, Thomson began drafting a comprehensive harbor development plan. Good sense required it, and there were plenty of port proposals to adapt from, including Bogue's elaborate and not-yet-rejected plans. Most important, the Port District Act required a specific plan before the commissioners could ask the people for a bond issue. The elaborate plan included facilities at Smith Cove on the north edge of the waterfront, a terminal and other developments along the East Waterway of the Duwamish River between Harbor Island and Seattle, ship and rail yards at Salmon Bay, a marina and pier at the central waterfront for small cargo and passenger vessels (the "mosquito fleet"), and improved ferry service on Lake Washington. Chittenden estimated the complete cost at $3,000,000, but nobody in authority, including Thomson and Chittenden himself, thought it prudent to ask voters for that sum. The commissioners instead settled on $500,000, an amount enabling them to build one large pier in the hope that its success would impress the public and lead to future winning bond votes. [17]

While this work advanced, the commission became embroiled in a Harbor Island controversy, or what Chittenden would later call the "Harbor Island Episode." It was both long and bitter, beginning in December 1911 and not ending conclusively until June 1913, after Thomson had left the commission. The uproar began when R. F. Ayers, an advertising vice president of the Bush Terminal Company of New York, offered to construct a version of the Bush terminals at Harbor Island. At the time, the Bush complex in New York was the country's best and most elaborate. Ayers insisted that the citizens of Seattle would have to approve a bond issue to cover the cost of the terminals, and that the commission had to pledge its full cooperation. Alden J. Blethen used both his personal influence and the *Times* to push the plan. The *Post-Intelligencer* backed it as rabidly as the *Times*. Thomas Burke and other prominent Seattleites mobilized their influence. In an atmosphere of near hysteria, a majority of voters became convinced that the "Bush terminals" would make Seattle the west coast's premier port and that opposing the plan was municipal treason. The emotionally charged atmosphere smothered the skeptics. But the problems with Ayers' plan were severe. The Bush Terminal Company itself was not involved in the project. Ayres was representing mostly himself and was practically without capital. Also, as Thomson pointed out to Burke, complying with some of Ayres' demands would violate both the state constitution and the statute creating the commission. Despite all that, public enthusiasm became so fevered that the best Chittenden could do was insert clauses in the $5,000,000 bond issue requiring the Ayres group to provide a personal bond before beginning construction. The bond proposal passed on March 5, 1912, in the midst of a circus-like promotion. Eventually, however, the New Yorkers could not raise their bond after being granted delays, and the entire program reverted to the commission. In June 1913, the voters approved a $3,000,000 bond issue allowing the commission to proceed.[18]

Thomson resigned shortly after the Ayres bond issue passed in 1912. Regarding the reasons offered for his resignation, later historical judgments have less credence than the contemporary ones. One historian of the port has declared that Thomson "was forced to resign as chief engineer for the Port when General Chittenden learned that he had originally tried to strike a deal with Ayers, by which Thompson [sic] would throw his support to the terminals project in exchange for a financial interest in the project."[19] This historian offers no evidence for his assertion. His contention seems to be a highly imaginative misconstruction of Chittenden's statement that he "hesitated to give full credence" to a critical economic analysis of the Ayers plan that Thomson prepared for him. Chittenden had reservations because, "Mr. Thomson's informant was shown to have been trying to get in on the ground floor in New York with the Terminal people, and, failing in that, was now doing all he could to injure them."[20] Note that it was Thomson's informant, not Thomson, whom Chittenden accused of attempting to involve himself in the Ayers scheme. Furthermore, Thomson rebuffed Judge Thomas Burke's demand that the commission knuckle under to the wishes of the New York group. After citing difficulties with the constitution and the law, Thomson struck a note both friendly and firm. "Now, Judge," he wrote, "you know that for thirty years I have been struggling to build up Seattle, and am willing to go the limit to make the town, but," he continued, the Ayers proposal was "a 'strong arm proposition'" containing "a flavor or an odor…which, to say the least, has been offensive from the time it was first sprung." It was unnecessary for Thomson to write such a letter to a vigorous partisan of Ayers and a man so powerful locally, unless Thomson thought it essential to put a deeply held conviction on the record.[21]

Thomson also had a published explanation. He outlined a dispute with Chittenden over how best to publicize the port, with Thomson wishing to appoint people who knew the language and commodities at "foreign centers of trade," who would steer goods to Seattle, while Chittenden wanted to rely on "maps and pamphlets" to be distributed by "ship officers" in their travels. The other commissioners believed nothing needed to be done because trade would flow to Seattle with the opening of the Panama Canal. A dispute over publicity was scarcely a reason for resigning, and Thomson makes no direct claim that it was. However, he offers no other reason for leaving the commission.[22] One inference from his comments is that perhaps there was something else in play between the two strong-willed engineers, Thomson and Chittenden.

A contemporary surmised as much. The vitriolic Harry Chadwick of the *Argus* confessed that Thomson "has not taken *The Argus* into his confidence, gentle reader" (little wonder, that!) but speculated "that he resigned because he found that Gen. Chittenden had ideas of his own, and that the astute engineer discovered that he was not selected to be the whole port commission."[23] Chadwick's guess was close. Thomson had no illusions about running the port commission, but was frustrated by the commissioners' squabbling. Moreover, he did have trouble with Chittenden. Possibly one source of difficulty sprang from a statement of Chittenden's presented in explanation of his vote for Thomson. Chittenden argued that a salary of $7,500, Thomson's present remuneration, was not excessive. Thomson, he said, "could easily make twice or three times this sum in outside work," but the engineer had "agreed to" devote "his time exclusively to" the commission, thereby demonstrating his disinterest in "purely mercenary" matters. That was not the way the monetarily-pressed Thomson saw things, although his sideline consulting activity during this period appears to have been only limited to one three-day investigation, and payment for work performed possibly before he took up his port commission tasks.[24]

Thomson nevertheless told George McAneny, a prominent New York politician, that his appointment carried with it the opportunity of doing some consulting work. It would have been practically unthinkable for Thomson to surrender his consulting option, given his heavy financial obligations. Chittenden's statement may have been an instance of the mental confusion and indecision first publicly displayed when the major agreed to move the site of the Salmon Bay locks, then

Developing the East Waterway channel and ground required extensive sluicing and dredging, 1913. *Seattle Municipal Archives #6409.*

later reverting to his original (and final) decision about their location. In September 1911, after the first port commission had won election, Thomson received word of Chittenden's belief that Virgil Bogue of the Bogue plan fame wanted to become Seattle's city engineer. The idea of Bogue's surrendering a lucrative private practice in New York for a job in a provincial city was ludicrous. Chittenden also believed that Archibald O. Powell, a prominent civil engineer, should be made engineer of the port, while Thomson would be a consulting engineer. Thomson claimed that he could not keep his city engineership while serving another public entity, but in any case Chittenden's suggested salary of $3,000 was unattractive. By early the next month, Chittenden had flip-flopped and was backing Thomson. Chittenden's mental gyrations and his partial paralysis after physical exertion were probably symptoms of relapsing-remitting multiple sclerosis, a disease then undiagnosed. [25] Whatever their origin, these periodic confusions and disabilities were disheartening to his associates and could not have made Thomson's job any easier.

The overriding reason for Thomson's resignation was simple—the port commission job brought no relief from long hours in the office, controversy, and press criticism. He had to get out. Fortunately for him he had a choice. "I am under definite obligations to remain with the Port until at least...April and at that time, am obligated to decide whether I will continue with the Port" or accept another offer at "more than twice the salary" of the port commission. In fact, the new British Columbia salary was precisely twice, $15,000, at a time when Canadian and United States dollars circulated at par. If neither salary seems much more than a pittance today, when Thomson went to Victoria to discuss the position in October 1911, the round trip boat fare was $3.50, with $1.25 added for a stateroom. Lunch on board was a whopping 85¢. When purchasing a commodious house in a pleasant Victoria neighborhood, he paid the "outrageous price" of $9,000. Yet, his comments make it clear that the large salary and five-year contract were not his overriding considerations. "My heart will ever be with Seattle," he wrote from Victoria, "but...my physical strength was so run down that I felt it an absolute necessity for me to take to the mountains for a time to recover myself." To another correspondent he confided that his exhaustion "compelled me to leave Seattle for awhile, that I might live in the woods and regain my fighting edge." As late as August 1913, he wrote about how he was "attempting to avoid all nerve strains of every class and kind." [26]

Although his serving more than three years as the first superintendent of Strathcona Park on Vancouver Island had its own "nerve strains," it was a much better mix of office work in Victoria and time in the field. Arriving in March 1912, he soon settled into surveying and planning a program for the park. The park itself was a practically undeveloped, rugged, right-angled triangle of about 480,000 acres, isolated in the middle of the island. Jagged mountains, crashing waterfalls, tumbling creeks, breathtaking valleys, and dense forests complemented the park's centerpiece, Buttle Lake. The lake's terrain was familiar to Thomson because it was riverine like Cedar Lake, a hollow formed by a river and smaller streams flowing into it, with a narrow throat at its foot allowing the river to flow onward. More than that, Buttle Lake was beautiful, some 18 miles long by a ½ mile wide. On bright, calm summer days it was a sparkling mirror of the surrounding slopes and mountains.

The Strathcona work plunged Thomson into an administrative and contextual situation very unlike his surroundings in Seattle. He was directly responsible only to Thomas Taylor, the provincial minister of works, and not to a mayor and a bevy of councilmen. There was no jostling for bureaucratic position with other department heads. Nor did he have to cope with bickering commissioners, as at the Port of Seattle. When Taylor decided an issue, that was it. [27]

A broader context involved rural park development as it had evolved in North America up to that time, with antecedents and practices far removed from the kind of planning that Thomson had practiced before. The founding of Yellowstone Park in 1872 provided one inspiration for future park development on both sides of the Canada–United States border. Yet it also supplied an excuse for creating subsequent park parcels without ecologically sound boundaries. When British Columbia's parliament formally established the park's boundaries in March 1911, Strathcona's arbitrary limits were based primarily on the availability of land, leaving many scenic features partly or entirely outside the park limits. There were relatively few "glamour" or "nice" animals, such as elk, deer, and bear, for tourist viewing; indeed, there was not much regard for wildlife preservation in British Columbia at the time. Despite all that, Thomson plunged ahead with plans for Strathcona's development. Characteristically, he did not think small. He threw himself into the work, planning tourist access to Strathcona by a road network, building internal roads and trails, selecting sites for hotels and other amenities, working with Canadian and U.S. railroads to publicize the park, and devising ways to improve the stock of animals and fish. He contacted park superintendents in the United States, traveled to Yellowstone on at least one occasion, and probably had at hand the latest edition of his friend Chittenden's *Yellowstone National Park: Historical and Descriptive*.[28]

Thomson's diaries demonstrate his close supervision of park work. They are sprinkled with comments about foremen and their camps, such as "meet Ben Lewis on trail at end of work. Everything dead. Men all fired because they had to get drunk," or, regarding another foreman, "go over his work. Tell him to pick up trash better," or "I go up the lake to Urquarts [*sic*] camp.—About 7 ½ miles. Find camp in good order. Work progressing well." For all his effort and his close relationship with Taylor, Thomson worked under several constraints. The British Columbia economy was booming in 1912 when he became park superintendent, but the next year it collapsed, bringing appropriations down with it. From time to time, Thomson left the park to consult and report on harbor and utilities work in British Columbia cities and towns. The work was part of his job, but it stole time, energy, and thought from Strathcona. He developed a friendship with G. Corey Wood, whose provincial parliamentary seat centered on a town near the park. When Wood wanted to alleviate unemployment in the town by recommending "none but A1 men" for park jobs, Thomson complied. Other limitations involved criticism of his hiring a few U.S. citizens (he may have hired as many as six during his first year), but the number was not large when measured against an average of 100 or more workers during a construction season. Critics leveled other complaints about his U.S. citizenship, his selection of subordinates, his abilities when measured against those of Canadian engineers, and his high salary, "$3,000 per annum more than the prime minister of Canada." The complaints availed little, but the outbreak of World War I in August 1914 effectively finished Thomson's work. By October, the Canadian Army had confiscated "practically all" of his pack animals, and crewmen were entering military service. The war increased the resentment against a highly-paid alien. According to Thomson, "I had either to become a British Citizen or withdraw. I withdrew." He negotiated a financial settlement, returned to Seattle in August 1915, and wound up his provincial commitment from there. [29]

Historians' judgments against Thomson and other park superintendents of his era are often severe. They attack park development plans, such as Thomson's, for their arrogant presumption that they could pick and promote different species of animals based on tourist desires or other reasons. They argue that no one in Thomson's era understood the beneficial role of predators in nature, and instead destroyed them. They fault men like Thomson for failing to comprehend how encouraging "nice" animals led to overpopulation and the destruction of their food resources, resulting in catastrophic diebacks. This manipulation of animal populations, plus the rearrangement of foreground fauna along tourist roads and paths, to say nothing of the roads themselves, created a landscape of contrivance. Tourists reached this fraudulent display by incongruous modern means, the railroad or the automobile.[30]

There is some merit to these strictures, but such views misunderstand the sociopolitical climate in which Thomson worked. Tourists, as every park superintendent knew, were essential to the parks for their direct spending as well as for their support of government funding. Killing predators was thought essential to wildlife management in that era, which was yet to experience the irruptions and diebacks that plagued later times. Had British Columbia followed Thomson's plan after the war, the province would have had an imperfect park but one superior to what it did develop. Instead, the emphasis shifted to resource exploitation; not until the 1980s did the provincial government agree to curtail mining and logging. Some of Thomson's trails were restored, but with no acknowledgment of their origin. His integration of scenic preservation, wildlife management, road and trail development, intra-park visitor accommodations, and tourist promotion remained largely unrealized. But for Thomson personally, the time was well spent. "He enjoyed being out in the woods in Strathcona," his granddaughter later recalled. "That was one of the most enjoyable events of his career."[31]

Not so enjoyable were two of his other causes running parallel in the Strathcona years—his suit against Alden J. Blethen and the *Times*, and his participation in a failed effort to sustain the *Sun* as an alternative to the dominant *Times*. Taking the suit first, it resulted from years of the *Times*' virulent criticism of Thomson. Blethen recognized that a successful newspaper depended on a talented staff, entertaining features, thorough local coverage, excellent layout and design, and the resulting circulation and advertising revenue. He was a man of conviction, daring, and intense personal loyalties who hired first-rate reporters and editors. He was also an incredibly pugnacious, bigoted, mean-spirited man, whose venomous attacks on people he disliked passed the bounds of reason. Just why he gave so much space to unremitting, distorted assaults on Thomson is unclear. Undoubtedly, Blethen's fondness for gambling and liquor, and Thomson's disdain for both, had something to do with it. Their differing personal preferences are not, however, an adequate explanation. What appears to be at the core of Blethen's hatred is the difference between influence and power. Blethen

certainly had influence through the *Times*, although the extent of his influence is debatable. Without question, Thomson had power. One demonstration of his power was his survival. Though he heartily disliked "open town" tolerance of gambling, prostitution, and unrestrained liquor trade, he served in the city administrations that supported it, as he served in other city administrations with varying degrees of "closed town" policies. Though a Republican, he retained his job during Democratic administrations. His power, theoretically unlimited regarding Seattle's physical development, was circumscribed by his own restraint and external circumstances. Nevertheless, power it was.[32]

There may have been a trigger to Blethen's wrath. It could have been a water department decision to cut off the supply to the editor's house when he was found watering his lawn in violation of city rules. The water was not restored until the enraged newspaper man paid a fine. Or it could have been Thomson's refusal to change the grade of a regrade in front of Blethen's house. It might have been Thomson's staying power, since Blethen may have exacted a promise from William Hickman Moore, mayor from 1906 to 1908, to fire Thomson. In any event, Moore not only did not fire Thomson, he referred to the city engineer as "the brains of the administration." The *Times* thereafter ran a series of cartoons showing a diminutive Thomson popping out of the head of a resigned or somnolent Moore. The newspaper's attacks on Moore, too, were as provocative as those on Thomson.[33]

A catalogue of the *Times*' accusations against the city engineer and refutations of them requires a book in itself, so only a few of the more egregious misstatements can be noted here. The *Times* asserted that Thomson merely followed the Cedar River plans of Benezette Williams, with the near-fatal omission of Swan Lake from the scheme. In fact, Williams came to Cedar River only after he abandoned Rock Creek as a source. Thomson's final conduit survey was very different from Williams', while Swan Lake was omitted because of costs. The *Times* blamed Thomson for the "hump" in Second Avenue, when reluctant property owners who refused greater assessments were the real culprits. Any and all regrading difficulties were laid at Thomson's door. The city's first incinerator was "worthless," a blatant distortion of the facts. What infuriated Thomson the most was a charge lodged on the front page and then later in one of Blethen's "speckled" editorials, so called because they were laced with bold-face type inserts, that he had favored certain contractors, especially on the Denny

Hill regrade. The *Times* claimed that on the Denny project Thomson "personally and individually, profited by this misappropriation of money—either as a stockholder himself, or through some 'dummy' who has held stock for him." It was the last straw for Thomson, who rode herd on contractors, and who could be merciless when they fell behind on their work and asked for time extensions. Because Addie feared for his physical safety, Thomson did not file suit until they were in Victoria.[34]

He filed four lawsuits, asking a total of $175,000 in damages. The *Times'* attorney successfully delayed the first three suits, but the fourth, for $75,000, came to trial on April 26, 1915. It was a popularly attended litigation, with the courtroom crowded to capacity. On the fourth and final day, "the few additional spectators who squeezed in sat on the floor or stood in serried ranks about the walls." The gist of the *Times'* defense was that the articles and editorials were printed without malice or the intent to defame, and were fair comment on the actions of a public official. Further, its attorney insisted that Thomson was not damaged because he held high-paying jobs throughout, and left the port commission for a post paying double the port commission salary. The judge, however, held that neither malice nor overt damages need be proven, only the truth or falsity of the statements made. The suit came down to a July 20, 1913, editorial in the *Times* made after Thomson brought the second of his four suits. In that screed, inspired by Blethen if not written by him, the *Times* charged "that after he had helped skin the people of Seattle to the limit, he thought he would find other fields in which to aggrandize himself—and so went away to another country." Citing criticism of Thomson in British Columbia, the editorial speculated that Thomson had brought the suits to confuse the issue in British Columbia and keep his job. The editorial noted anonymous letters, "probably inspired" by Thomson asking the *Times* to attack him, with "the implication" being "that we don't dare." Nevertheless, the *Times* would continue to attack the "semi-criminal" Thomson, as in the past, "exposed his nefarious and outrageous plans in robbing the taxpayers of Seattle in more ways than the Denny Hill robbery."[34]

The "Denny Hill robbery" alluded to the undeniable fact that his former assistant and continuing partner in an investment company, J.C. Jeffrey, had formed a partnership with another man to do engineering work. The partnership, after adding others, became the firm that made the successful bid on the Denny Hill regrade project. It was then bonded; in effect certifying that it was capable of performing the work. After that, it sub-contracted the job to an experienced enterprise, grossing $200,000 in the process. But the *Times* attorney could offer no proof of Thomson's involvement. Nor could he prove that Thomson's changes of the slope on the Denny Hill "spite mounds" (see chapter 7) was an attempt to benefit the contractor, or, indeed, anything more than an effort to deal with a reduced budget and avoid a new assessment against the affected private property.

Because the *Times* could not prove the editorial claims, the jury had an easy task. It awarded Thomson $15,000, far less than the amount asked for, but enough. Blethen sulked: "I was prepared for an adverse verdict when I saw that the jury was so largely composed of women, who are naturally unacquainted with public affairs," he wrote on learning of the verdict. A month and a half later, Blethen was dead.[35]

From another perspective, no amount of money would have assuaged Thomson's hurt at being so mercilessly and falsely accused. He did put on a brave front to sympathetic friends. "If I were to take time to answer all the untruths concerning me in the city press, daily and weekly," he wrote as early as 1901, "I think I should have to neglect public duties." To a husband and wife he wrote: "Don't let the villainous assault of Col. Blethen weigh on your minds at all." To a correspondent he declared that "were it not for the companionship of the Blessed Saviour" he could not "have so calmly borne the great volume of vituperative abuse which has been heaped on me." Blessed Saviour or not, the attacks were painful. To another correspondent he wrote about how well his "revolution" in public utilities had progressed, "with the exception, that that old son of evil, who publishes the *Seattle Times*, has to pour out some of his lying venom on the scheme" from time to time. "The ravings of the *Times* are not based on any element of truth" and were "all paid for at a good figure," he wrote in 1906. Later he commented on the *Times'* statements, so "outrageously false" that he "refused to be annoyed by them." But of course he was more than annoyed. "I am not acquainted with anything more brutal or more cowardly than the actions of an unprincipled editor who always has the opportunity of vilifying those who have no possible means of making full reply."[36]

By the time of the judgment against Blethen, Thomson was embroiled in the most disastrous investment of his life, the collapse of the *Seattle Sun*, founded to be a rival to the *Times*. The *Sun* began publishing on February 3, 1913, after raising money from Thomson and other investors. Its editor, Edmund H. Wells, was a skilled newspaperman and promoter, but also a spendthrift. Soon his free-spending ways began to undermine what was an attractively formatted paper featuring good national and local coverage. For his part, Thomson knew Wells and believed in his probity. He may have known of Wells' lavish lifestyle but assumed that it would not carry over into business. Unfortunately it did, although whether a prudently-run paper would have survived in the tough competitive environment is problematic. Soon Thomson was caught in a downward spiral of endorsing note after note for the *Sun* and pledging more and more of his real estate holdings as collateral. His only outside financial coup was securing a $42,000 loan from James J. Hill, the Great Northern railroad baron. In return, Hill received $50,000 in bonds and a promissory note signed by Thomson and others.[37]

Not even his legal bout with Blethen brought so much distress as the financially faltering *Sun*. "There has nothing entered my life that has caused me more worry than this matter," he exclaimed. On December 30, 1914, the paper published its last issue under Wells' direction. By then the creditors had closed in, scooping up parcel after parcel of property pledged to unredeemed notes. The largest outstanding debt was to the corporation formed following Hill's death to deal with miscellaneous matters in the tycoon's estate. Protracted negotiations and delays ensued, but at last in 1922, Thomson and Addie surrendered their remaining property save for their house in Canada, their home at 1636 34th Avenue, and their beloved "Broomgerrie" summer place in the Yoemalt section of Bainbridge Island. The surrendered property was badly in arrears for taxes and assessments, and they had paid no principal or interest on a refinanced Hill note for three years. They were lucky to escape bankruptcy.[38]

⇜❧⇝

The conflict with Blethen and the failure of the *Sun* typified, in their way, Thomson's post City of Seattle years. These were nevertheless productive years, if not always pleasant. For the Port of Seattle, he and his staff worked out the first plan of development, and had the pleasure of seeing the ill-advised "Bush terminal" scheme collapse. The port job promised, however, to entangle him still more in politics and editorial controversy. He had had plenty enough; therefore he chose the British Columbia option.

At Strathcona Park, he gloried in a return to the outdoors. He carefully built a blueprint for the park's development according to the best practices of the day. He escaped neither politics nor newspaper controversy, but their effects were lessened by his time spent in the woods.

Relatively little resulted from his work at the port or in the park, but the efforts were by turns demanding and invigorating, leaving him ready for fresh challenges.

NOTES

1. RHT to Dilling, 7 November 1911, 89/1, box 4, Book 11, RHT Papers, UW. For the possible non-reappointment, see *TC*, September 23, 1911. For quotations, see RHT to H.C. Thomson, 3 March 1909, 89/1, box 2, book 6, RHT Papers, UW. For other expressions of discontent, see RHT to F.A. Hill, 31 August 1905, 89/1, box 1, book 3; and RHT to F.G. Jordan, 7 August 1906, box 2, book 4, RHT Papers, UW.

2. For Panama Canal, see RHT to W.E. Humphrey, 28 January 1904, 89/1, box 1, book 3, RHT Papers, UW. For the aborted project, see RHT to Hill, 23 January 1905, 89/1, box 1, book 3, RHT Papers, UW. For first quotation about Portland, and possible Tacoma job, see RHT to Mayor Linck, Tacoma, 15 June 1908, 89/1, box 2, book 6, RHT Papers, UW. For second and third quotations, see RHT to George W. Kummer, 23 June 1908, 89/1, box 2, book 6, RHT Papers, UW. For fourth quotation, see Jas. O. Rountree to RHT, 15 June 1908, 89/1, box 6, folder 1, RHT Papers, UW.

3. For the public announcement, see RHT to Minard Brown Sturgis, 21 June 1909, 89/1, box 3, book 7, RHT Papers, UW. For RHT's prior knowledge of the announcement, see Ballinger to RHT, 19 April 1909, 15, box 13, folder 19, Richard A. Ballinger Papers, hereafter cited as Ballinger Papers, UW. *Engineering News* 63 (January 13, 1910): 46–48. For Ballinger's doubts, see Ballinger to RHT, 28 May 1909, 15, box 13, folder 17, Ballinger Papers, UW. For "not know" quotation, see letter to Sturgis, above. For urgings to stay on, see RHT to M.A. Matthews, 21 July 1909, 89/1, box 3, book 7, RHT Papers, UW. For Ballinger's giving up on appointing RT, see *Portland Oregonian*, May 19, 1910. For the Ballinger-Pinchot controversy, see James L. Penick, *Progressive Politics and Conservation: The Ballinger-Pinchot Affair* (Chicago: University of Chicago Press, 1968); and for Pinchot's role, Char Miller, *Gifford Pinchot and the Making of Modern Environmentalism* (Washington, D.C.: Island Press, 2001), 206–38.

4. For RHT's probable non-acceptance, see RHT to Minard B. Sturgis, 4 September 1909, 89/1, box 3, book 7, RHT Papers, UW. For the watershed control from the Forest Service's viewpoint, see Klingle, "Urban by Nature," 139–43. For "scientific basis" quotation, see RHT to Findley Burns, 4 February 1909, box 2, book 6, RHT Papers, UW. For Pinchot's breaking faith and Forestry's determination, see RHT to James Sloss, 25 April 1910, 89/1, box 3, book 8, RHT Papers. RHT was communicating with Pinchot on the issue, see RHT to Pinchot, 6 February 1905, Cedar Falls Electric Plant, 1904–1911, book 2, PSRA. For Pinchot's making an appointment and failing to keep it on another occasion, see Robert W. Righter, *The Battle over Hetch Hetchy: America's Most Controversial Dam and the Birth of Modern Environmentalism* (New York: Oxford University Press, 2005), 67. RHT to Ballinger, 27 November 1909, 89/1, box 3, book 7, RHT Papers, UW. RHT to Humphrey, 12 March 1910, 89/1, box 3, book 8, RHT Papers, UW. RHT to George W. Tibbetts, 29 January 1910, 89/1, box 3, book 8, RHT Papers, UW.

5. For first quotation, RHT to Hill, 24 October 1909, 89/1, box 3, book 7; and, for second quotation, RHT to Hill, 12 November 1909, 89/1, box 3, book 7, RHT Papers, UW. For

details of the transaction, see Wilson, "'Names Joined Together as Our Hearts Are,'" 190.

6. RHT to Warren Olney, 11 January 1904, 89/1, box 1, book 3, RHT Papers, UW; and Moore to RHT, 15 April 1909, Engineering Department, City Engineer's Reports, book C.J. Moore No. 1, PSRA.

7. For RHT's attitude against hours-of-work limits, see *Seattle Union Record*, August 27, 1904. For dodging some of the hours limits, see *Times*, May 20, 1906. For "horse" quotation, see RHT to James A. Moore, 18 July 1908, 89/1, box 2, book 6, RHT Papers, UW. RHT to John P. Hartman, 7 January 1911, 89/1, box 3, book 9, RHT Papers, UW.

8. For the 200 staff and his salary of $7,500, see RHT to J.M. Preston, 1 May 1911, 89/1, box 4, book 10, RHT Papers, UW. For RHT's multiple duties, see his annual reports, and, for specifics, the following: RHT to "Mr. Walters," 14 February 1905, 89/1, box 1, book 3; RHT to L.B. Youngs, 18 July 1908, 89/1, box 2, book 6; RHT to D.W. McMorris, 7 October 1909, 89/1, box 3, book 7; and three letters from RHT to A.H. Dimock, 14 November 1910, 89/1, box 3, book 9; and 30 and 31 March 1911, box 3, book 9, RHT Papers, UW. For court cases, see RHT to J.R. Bowles, 6 November 1905, 89/1, box 2, book 4; RHT to Smith & Hanson, 13 April 1907, 89/1, box 2, book 5; and RHT to D.W. McMorris, 10 May 1911, 89/1, box 4, book 10, RHT Papers, UW. For the municipal campaign and defeat, see Berner, *Seattle, 1900–1920*, 111–12. For samples of *Times* opposition, see September 2, 1906, and September 5, 1906. For the related dam and power house, see RHT to George Kinnear, 16 July 1909, 89/1, box 3, book 7, RHT Papers, UW. For RHT before the council, see *P-I*, July 31, 1906; and Berner, *Seattle, 1900–1920*, 110–12. For lobbying, see three letters from RHT to Cotterill, 28 January 1905, 89/1, box 1, book 3; 6 February 1907; and 13 February 1907, both in 89/1, box 2, book 5; and RHT to Ralph Nichols, 27 February 1907, box 2, book 5, RHT Papers, UW. For illnesses, see RHT to G.H. Plummer, 20 February 1905, Cedar Falls Electric Plant, 1904–1911, book 2, PSRA; Katharine Stream to E.P. Kendall, 13 August 1907, 89/1, box 2, book 5; RHT Papers, UW; and RHT to G.E. Morley, 3 November 1909, box 3, book 7, RHT Papers, UW.

9. "Who's Who – And Why," *Saturday Evening Post* 182 (November 20, 1909): 23; and Richard A. Ballinger, "Seattle: A Metropolis Built in a Single Generation," *American Review of Reviews* 39 (June 1909): 714–20, especially 718. RHT to W. Thomson, 21 June 1909, 89/1, box 3, book 7, RHT Papers, UW. For Katharine Stream, see RHT, "Sketches," 1908 entry; 1602-2, box 1, folder 10, RHT Papers, UW; Stream to "Dear Mrs. Thomson," 9 August 1912, 89/1, box 4, book 11, RHT Papers, UW; and item no. 130344, Fleets and Facilities Department "Imagebook" Collection, SMA.

10. For quotations, in order, see RHT to Goodwin Real Estate Company, Inc., 2 May 1908, 89/1, box 2, book 6, RHT Papers, UW; RHT to Alexander Myers, 31 July 1906, 89/1, box 2, book 4, RHT Papers, UW; and *P-I*, March 6, 1910.

11. Goddard's charges and the investigation are in "In the matter of the investigation by Department Efficiency Committee of Charges against Mr. R.H. Thomson and the Board of Public Works," Engineering Department, Administrative Services, box 1, PSRA. For RHT's proposed investigative structure, see RHT to Chamber of Commerce et al., 11 August 1911, 89/1, box 4, book 10, RHT Papers, UW. For hostile reactions to RHT, see *Argus*, August 19, 1911; and *TC*, August 19, 1911. RHT's accusation against Goddard is in an undated statement, 89/1, box 4, book 10, RHT Papers, UW. For Goddard's

denial, see Goddard to Mr. President, filed August 14, 1911, in "investigation." For the committee's work and other testimony not included in the transcript, see *P-I*, November 3, 1911; November 17, 1911; and November 24, 1911.

12. RHT to C.F. Swigert, 20 December 1911, 89/1, box 4, book 11, RHT Papers, UW.

13. *P-I*, September 29, 1911.

14. For "near-ovation" quotation from the hostile *Times*, see October 2, 1911. See also *P-I*, October 2, 1911; and October 3, 1911.

15. RHT to John Edwin Ayer, 10 October 1911, 89/1, box 4, book 11, RHT Papers, UW. RHT incorrectly remembered the outcome of the meeting as unanimously in his favor, see autobiographical statement in 89/1, box 6, folder 3, RHT Papers, UW. For the hostile quotation, see *P-I*, October 3, 1911. For the resolution, see 89/1, box 6, folder 1, RHT Papers, UW; and *P-I*, December 2, 1911. For the banquet and Joe Smith quotation, see *P-I*, December 9, 1911.

16. For RHT and the port commission, see Padriac Burke, *A History of the Port of Seattle* (Seattle: Port of Seattle, 1976), 27, 29. RHT was a pallbearer at Chittenden's funeral, Dodds, *Chittenden*, 205. For the establishment of the port commission, see replies to the circular letter from Hamilton Higday to Scott Calhoun, et al., 3 January 1918, 38, box 7, folder 14, Cotterill Papers, UW. For hiring, see RHT to Chittenden, 14 December 1911, 89/1, box 4, book 11, RHT Papers, UW.

17. Hiram M. Chittenden, *The Harbor Island Episode* (Seattle: author, 1915; retyping, 1917), 72–73.

18. Ibid., 72–73. Burke, *Port of Seattle*, follows Chittenden, 34–39.

19. Burke, *Port of Seattle*, 39.

20. Chittenden, "Harbor Island Episode," 37.

21. RHT to Burke, 7 February 1912, 89/1, box 4, book 11, RHT Papers, UW.

22. RHT, *That Man Thomson*, 128. See also 128–29.

23. *Argus*, March 16, 1912.

24. For RHT's frustration, see autobiographical statements in 89/1, box 4, folder 2; and box 6, folder 3, RHT Papers, UW. For quotation, see *P-I*, October 3, 1911. For consulting, see RHT, "Sketches," 1911 entry, 1602-2, box 2, folder 10, RHT Papers, UW. For a consulting payment, see RHT to George H. Tilden, 12 December 1912, 89/1, box 4, book 11, RHT Papers, UW.

25. RHT to George McAneny, 18 December 1911, 89/1, box 4, book 11, RHT Papers, UW. For Chittenden's indecision, see RHT to Scott Calhoun, 13 September 1911, 89/1, box 4, book 10, RHT Papers, UW. Chittenden's partial paralysis after exertion is well documented. See Dodds, *Chittenden*, 138–39; and RHT to R.A. Ballinger, 30 September 1909, 89/1, box 3, book 7, RHT Papers, UW. My daughter, Margaret Wilson, a neurology nurse, is the source for statements about Chittenden's condition. Ms. Wilson cautions that his condition cannot be known with absolute certainty. RHT maintained friendly relations with the commissioners, and a positive attitude toward the commission. See RHT to Chittenden, 28 January 1913, 89/1, box 5, book 12, one of many later letters. See also RHT to Paul P. Whitham, 27 August 1914, 89/1, box 5, book 13; and to W.N.G. Pace, 6 November 1913, box 5, book 12, RHT Papers, UW.

26. RHT to McAneny, note 25. For par circulation, see RHT to Arctic Club, 26 May 1913; and to W.R.B. Willcox, 14 September 1913, both in 9/1, box 4, book 11, RHT Papers, UW. Expenses are in RHT notebook, "Diary of Business Expenses and Related Material," 89/1, box 13, folder 4, RHT Papers, UW. For the "outrageous price" quotation, see RHT to C.C. Michner, 6 August 1912, 89/1, box 4, book 11, RHT Papers,

UW. For "heart" quotation, see RHT to Sydney Strong, 17 May 1912, 89/1, box 4, book 11, RHT Papers, UW. For "exhausted" quotation, see RHT to J.D. Ross, 3 December 1912, 89/1, box 5, book 12, RHT Papers, UW.

27. For more information on RHT in British Columbia, see William H. Wilson, "Reginald H. Thomson and Planning for Strathcona Park, 1912–1915," *Planning Perspectives* 17 (2007): 373–87; and two papers with the same title, "Reginald H. Thomson and the Opening of Strathcona Park," in author's possession.

28. For *Yellowstone National Park*, see Dodds, *Chittenden*, 19–21.

29. For close supervision, see RHT, diary, 1913, in order of quotation, 22 July, 22 April, 25 April, 1602-2, box 1, folder 8, RHT Papers, UW. For the economy, see Jean Barman, *The West Beyond the West: A History of British Columbia*, rev. ed., (Toronto: University of Toronto Press, 1996), 176–201. For consultations and reports, see, for example, RHT, "Sketches," 1913 entry, 1602-2, box 2, folder 10, RHT Papers, UW. For Wood, see RHT to Lewis Casey, 16 April 1914, 89/1, box 4, book 13, RHT Papers, UW. For criticism, see Thomas Taylor to Christian Sivert, 23 September 1914, GR75, British Columbia Department of Public Works and Railways, Semi-Official Correspondence Outbound, 1909–1915, vol. 9, British Columbia Archives and Records Service. For quotation, see Strathcona Park – Miscellaneous Articles Relating to…, [vol. 1] 11, and see also 24–27, 36–37, BCARS. For RHT's leaving British Columbia quotation, see Wilson, "Thomson and Planning," 383. Diary entries from 1914 through March 16, 1916 cover RHT's final work, departure, and completion of tasks, RHT diaries, 1602-2, box 1, folder 8, RHT Papers, UW.

30. For critics, see Wilson, "Thomson and Planning," 382–83.

31. Ibid., 383–84; and Hepler interview.

32. For Blethen, see Sharon A. Boswell and Lorraine McConaghy, *Raise Hell and Sell Newspapers: Alden J. Blethen and The Seattle Times* (Pullman: Washington State University Press, 1996). For RHT's dislike of open town policies, see RHT to C.J. Moore, 15 February 1898, 89/1, box 1, book 1, RHT Papers, UW.

33. For water, see *Argus*, June 11, 1898. For a "brains of the administration" cartoon, see *Times* October 11, 1909. For other comments and analyses, see *Argus*, August 2, 1930; and Boswell and McConaghy, *Raise Hell*, 150–54.

34. The *Times*' assertions, in the order mentioned, are in the issues of April 2, 1908; October 3, 1911; and, for lengthy quotation, August 15, 1911. For a few of RHT's numerous letters to or about contractors, see RHT to C.J. Erickson, 2 October 1908, LID 1310, letters, fiche 2, SMA; RHT to James A. Snoddy, 11 April 1910; and to William Hickman Moore, 30 June 1910; 89/1, box 3, book 8, RHT Papers, UW. For answers to the *Times* assertions, see *P-I*, December 14, 1915. The best coverage of the trial is in the *P-I*, April 27 – May 1, 1915.

35. Boswell and McConaghy, *Raise Hell*, 148–53.

36. In the order cited, all in 89/1 and all from RHT, are, to Mr. Ronald, 18 September 1901, box 1, book 2; to Col. and Mrs. M.W. Glen, 26 October 1905, box 2, book 4; to Edward Lincoln Smith, 7 October 1911, box 4, book 10; to M.H. Allen, 27 August 1906, box 2, book 4; and to Winlock W. Miller, 1 December 1911, box 4, book 11, RHT Papers, UW.

37. Wilson, "Rising and Setting of Seattle's *Sun*." See also RHT to Wells, 3 May 1908, and 6 May 1908, 89/1, box 2, book 6, RHT Papers, UW.

38. For quotation, see RHT to George A. Virtue, 30 December 1914, 89/1, box 5, book 13, RHT Papers, UW. See Wilson, "Rising and Setting of Seattle's *Sun*," for details of the paper's failure and RHT's debt.

A FORAY INTO POLITICS marked Thomson's return to his familiar Seattle setting after working in British Columbia until August 1915. In January 1916, he filed for a three-year term on the city council. Others had encouraged him to run for political office in the past. Mayor William Hickman Moore, a Democrat who won a narrow victory at the head of the Municipal Ownership Party in 1906, suggested Thomson for the Republican nomination in the 1908 race. From its wording, Moore's statement indicates no trial balloon coming from Thomson himself, and in any case the engineer was uninterested.[1]

During the second decade of the 20th century there was some enthusiasm, unfulfilled, for converting Seattle to a commission or city manager form of government. Though Thomson freely offered suggestions for the reform of city government, he was leery of the city manager plan. "Several persons," he wrote to a correspondent, had "spoken to me about the position of City Manager." He loved Seattle but doubted "very much if the town" wanted "the 'iron hand' in control that the papers talk about." What the public desired in the abstract and what it required in practice, he noted, were "often" not the same. He was certain that if he were truly in charge of Seattle's government he could operate efficiently and effectively, "but I expect that my life would have to be well insured."[2]

Several names, Thomson's included, were put forward for commissioner when Chittenden resigned his post on the Seattle Port Commission in October 1915. The *Times* quickly supported Thomson in an editorial bearing the name of Clarance B. Blethen, a son of the late Alden Blethen. This endorsement coming less than three months after Thomson's victory in his libel suit against the *Times* would be "a great shock to many," Blethen admitted. The engineer was the best man for

The driver of a Ford pauses at Seventh and Dearborn as a flusher sprays the trolley tracks and street. By 1920, motor vehicles were well on the way to eventually replacing horses on city avenues. *Seattle Municipal Archives #1723.*

the job, and by supporting him the newspaper demonstrated "its freedom from the laws of feud and the rules of vendetta." The next morning the *P-I* joined its rival: "Thomson by all means!" If the candidate could not "afford to give the non-salaried service required," why then not make him city manager, "Seattle's paramount need." Thomson's reply to the *P-I* endorsement was an adamant refusal to throw his hat in the ring. Although he "noted" the newspaper's editorial "with pleasure," he was "not an applicant for any public office. Under no circumstances can I permit my name to be used as a candidate for the position suggested." The brief letter gave no reason for Thomson's decision, but the bitter disputes within the port commission, coupled with the lack of salary, certainly were considerations. His friendship with Chittenden, despite the previous exasperation with his fellow engineer, would count against him because commissioners Remsberg and Bridges had lined up against Chittenden in the past. Moreover, they would appoint Chittenden's successor in October, giving the appointee the inside track in the December elections. It was a situation best avoided.[3]

A run for the Seattle City Council was different. Three months after declaring he was "not an applicant for any public office," Thomson filed for the job. His filing was no about face, for real threats to municipal ownership had emerged. A 1914 charter revision, though defeated, could be interpreted as anti-Seattle City Light in its attack on the civil service. The 1915 state legislature adopted legislation requiring the Washington Public Service Commission to decide whether a municipal corporation could compete with a private one. It also passed bills limiting cities in transferring funds or physical property among their agencies. The measures were intended to hobble municipal railways and other city-owned services. Referenda would overturn these legislative measures and others in the general election of November 1916, but that outcome was not vouchsafed to Thomson in January. Sitting on the city council would provide Thomson with a platform for attacking the laws and promoting their repeal. He noted to his brother Henry, "for the purpose of being in a position where I could do some work in protecting some of the utilities which I designed and secured for the city, such as our waterworks and our city lighting plant, I ran for the position of Councilman."[4]

The *Post-Intelligencer* coordinated his filing for the position with a favorable review of his engineering work, while the rest of the daily press endorsed him too. The weeklies, *Town Crier* and *Argus*, harsh critics in the past,

also chimed in. Endorsements were not necessarily tantamount to election, though Thomson need not have worried. The *P-I*'s headline comment that he and the colorful mayor, Hiram C. Gill, were "regarded as almost certain winners" proved correct. Gill, once recalled in 1911 as mayor because of his "open town" or pro-vice stance, but elected again in 1914, was re-elected in 1916 on his promise to continue reforming the city, however gingerly. Thomson stood on his record of civic service, campaigning very little. The only electoral activity worth mentioning in his diary occurred on January 22 when the staunch Republican showed up at a "Democrat meeting for candidates." His consulting and church activities received more diary space than that. In the primaries he ran behind only his friend and former mayor, William Hickman Moore. The March 1916 election confirmed his victory.[5]

Named to the utilities, street, and finance committees, he soon learned that their demands plus council meetings were a sink of time. In the ten days of April 3–12, a heavier schedule than usual found him working "all day" on council business on April 3, spending the morning and afternoon of April 6 in committee meetings, and returning to a committee meeting on the afternoon of April 7. On the 10th, committee and council meetings, plus a conference with city officials, took most of the morning and all of the afternoon. Another committee meeting occupied the morning of the 12th. Not surprisingly, given his committee work, his concerns included the growing crisis over the street railway's service and its liquidity. Street problems and city purchases also came within his purview. These issues were not unique to Seattle, but the city was not any the less a crucible of conflict.[6]

Thomson's private schedule during those ten days also accented his return to consulting and involvement in family life. On April 4, a day free of council and consulting demands, he and Addie left early for their Broomgerrie resort home on Bainbridge Island, taking with them "1/2 Dozen Rhododendrons, and two kinds of willows" to add to their plantings. They returned home, where their daughter Marion arrived "with ulcerated tooth." Thomson arranged for a dentist to extract a molar. Two days later, after morning and afternoon committee meetings, he spent the evening working on bridge plans with two other engineers. Consulting occupied the following day, both before and after a finance committee meeting. The next day, a Saturday, was taken up with consulting. Engineering again filled an evening following committee and council meetings. On the 12th, after a morning spent on "street troubles," he was in an afternoon conference on city engineering problems.[7] It was a busy life.

A month after this rush of city business, Thomson replied to an invitation from the tabloid *Seattle Star*. The *Star* assumed that after two months in council harness, "he has had time to get warmed up," and could inform its readers "what he considers are the city's real problems." True to his letter to brother Henry during the election period, the new councilman led off with his concern about the extent of the state public service commission's influence over private and public utilities. (As noted above, later successful referenda against the bills limiting municipal corporations would eliminate that issue for the immediate future.) He next turned his attention to "the most important matter before us"—equal and economical rail access to existing and prospective industrial sites. He wished to end the tangled railroad switching practices along the waterfront and elsewhere, and to assume the development of new industrial locations that would become available with the opening of the soon-to-be completed Lake Washington ship canal.[8]

The next paragraphs in the newspaper article covered the topic of "cheap power," especially for encouraging industrial growth. Thomson strongly suggested an end to competition, with the city acquiring the facilities of the local private power company as a means of ending "duplication" and thus lowering costs. Then he dealt with the contention between the city and the street car company over several issues, although he did not go into specifics. "There is heavy work to be done in this matter," he admitted. Next he took up the issue of the leaking north bank of the Cedar River in the area of the new concrete dam, a "matter now being considered by competent men," including himself, although he did not specifically mention his involvement. He believed in "the sealing of this porous tank without the expenditure of any stupendous sum." (As related in chapter 6, the bank sealing proved a failure, leading to the devastating 1918 Boxley Creek flood.) After coming out in favor of a retirement system for "faithful servants of the city," he wrote that the "greatest need" was for the council to conduct itself to "inspire confidence" in "would be investors" and the "public." Finally, he called for "harmony" and "good humor" in the conduct of business, even with those who disagreed with council positions.[9]

Later if not sooner, Thomson would live to see fruition of much, though not all, of what he believed essential. Meanwhile, city council activities, church, family, and consulting filled his days until April 1917 and the

U.S. entry into World War I. He was, at 61, well past military age, but the war effort piled added obligations on his already busy career. This involved, first, his membership on the King County Council of Defense, a branch of the Washington State Council of Defense. Supervising 87 local councils, the latter organization was charged with promoting the war effort. Second, Thomson actively participated in a search for a new source of electric power, on the Skagit River north of Seattle—a search intensified because of wartime needs and restrictions. Third, he wrote an extensive report on the mounting rail distribution crisis in Seattle brought to a head by the war. Fourth, he pressed for city ownership of the private streetcar system, which was in serious straits because of wartime inflation and manpower shortages.

Historians have not been kind to the defense councils. The National Council of Defense, begun as a prewar industrial and resource coordination agency, was largely powerless and ineffectual in that activity. It was, however, the inspiration for state defense councils, their county branches, and the local offshoots of the county organizations, some 184,000 in 1918. These groups raised money for the war effort through Liberty Bond sales, encouraged food conservation, organized women to knit sweaters for servicemen, and engaged in other patriotic activities. Later critics have deemed all this as relatively harmless if a little naïve and fatuous. Violations of civil liberties, such as forced Liberty Bond purchases, the persecution of people suspected of disloyalty, and hostility to any dissent, were another matter. A tendency among historians in viewing the World War I domestic front is to highlight the most grievous radical actions among the councils of defense, and lump them together with the militant responses of vigilante groups. Even a nuanced survey of excesses, including tarring and featherings, denuding suspected disloyalists, whippings, and murders, bristle with such phrases as "wartime hysteria," "fanatic nationalism," and "ethnic hostility," while condemning "certain people" able to "act out fantasies that could not be performed in ordinary circumstances."[10]

Against this backdrop, the activities of the King County Council of Defense were tame indeed. It did investigate "persons accused or suspected of disloyalty," but took no action other than to exonerate the innocent and report "others" to constituted authorities. It did issue a "patriotism questionnaire" to educators, but turned the results over to educational institutions for any response. Fundamentally, on the other hand, "the council and its auxiliaries constituted a body of citizens organized for the general welfare." It helped to end a streetcar workers' strike, organized patriotic speakers (the "Four Minute Men"), gave assistance to "needy families" of men serving in the armed forces, and promoted food conservation. It aided the military draft by providing the medical and dental treatment necessary to remove disqualifications from those men who otherwise were able to serve, and it maintained a training camp to prepare men for the non-commissioned grades. It provided each group of draftees with "lunches, candy and cigarettes." At war's end, the council participated in welcoming events for the returning troops. The members paid dues, held fund raisers, and solicited contributions to finance all these activities.[11]

Harold Preston, a prominent attorney, headed the 18 member King County council. Besides Thomson, the members included judges, leaders of conservative labor organizations, housewives, and others, as well as Thomson's old bureaucratic nemesis, Dr. J.E. Crichton. The council's work appealed to Thomson's interest in community involvement and his penchant for donating to needy people or good causes. Preston or others may have asked him to join because of his work with the Red Cross. There was, besides, no question about his strident patriotism. In a January 1918 interview following a trip east, he said, "from Omaha east the only thought is of the war and how to win it." Perhaps he was contrasting fervent eastern patriotism with the radical labor movement and socialist anti-war activity in the West and Pacific Northwest, however overrated that threat proved to be to the war effort. There were "some traitors" located "in high places" and "in low, even as Judas was with the twelve," he averred. The traitors should not be deceived by their gentle treatment: "Mollycoddle notions will soon fade, however, and a service of lead will be given instead of comfortable internment." His statements were of the sort common at the time, showing how much a careful, responsible man could be carried away by wartime emotion.[12]

In any event, he need not have worried about "traitors" because a largely self-appointed group of vigilantes, with the cooperation of the mayor and the police, rode herd on anyone suspected of unpatriotic motives. These respectable businessmen—the Minute Men—lumped radicals of any sort with alleged draft dodgers, "slackers" who bought insufficient quantities of Liberty Bonds, enemy aliens, presumed spies, and a raft of others. Their investigations led to so many arrests that local jails could hold no more. Eventually the Minute Men were absorbed into the American Protective League, a national vigilante group having Department of Justice

sponsorship. Minute Men activity led to a few convictions and imprisonments, but contributed much more to individual losses of livelihood and the erosion of civil liberties.[13] What is important to remember about the King County Council of Defense, on the other hand, is that almost all of its patriotic activities were constructive. Thomson might have questioned whether the best interests of the country were served by America's participation in the war, but nothing survives in his writing to indicate any serious wrestling with the issue. If he had had such thoughts, the declaration of war ended whatever interior debate he may have had.

☙❧

The investigation for a new location to generate electric power and lighting had antedated the war, but wartime industrial and other needs spurred a new sense of emergency. Early on, Thomson and other municipal power enthusiasts had argued that the log dam and expanded power plant on the Cedar River were inadequate. Their efforts led to adding the ill-advised dam, but did not end there. Other supplementary sites were under consideration. In the meantime, the lighting department's J.D. Ross believed it imprudent to wait until new proposed dams were built, the equipment installed and tested, and all brought on line. Thus, in 1912 the lighting department opened a small, reserve hydroelectric plant on the eastern shore of Lake Union. The plant depended on water from the overflow pipe, or penstock, from the municipal reservoir in Volunteer Park. Ross added an oil-fired steam generating plant two years later. The facility produced electricity well enough, though at a higher cost than the Cedar River powerhouse. The cost of operating an oil-fired plant would have enormous consequences during World War I, when the lighting department strained to supply power to booming Seattle.[14]

Meanwhile, Ross and others, Thomson included, searched for other dam and power plant locations. Leading places included the so-called Hebb site near present-day Mud Mountain Dam, some 38 miles southeast of Seattle, and Lake Cushman on the Olympic Peninsula. Thomson favored the Hebb site because it allowed for shorter transmission lines and avoided a possible but certainly expensive submarine cable under Puget Sound from the Lake Cushman location. In 1912, voters approved the purchase of both sites, with the Hebb location receiving more votes. Ross advocated the Lake Cushman location because of its lower development costs, but a 1914 vote to transfer funds to condemn the site fell short of the needed three-fifths

In the 1910s, J.D. Ross established back-up hydroelectric and oil-fired steam generating plants on the east side of Lake Union. *Seattle Municipal Archives #117501.*

majority. Meanwhile, a skein of power development efforts followed—with the Tacoma municipal plant adding capacity, and the Stone & Webster-owned Puget Sound Traction, Light & Power Company developing new capacity and buying or obtaining permits for new power sites. Ross was becoming increasingly desperate over Seattle's municipal power agency being "bottled up" by its competitors. That fate was unlikely, but the private company did hold some of the best power-development locations. Thomson had a solution to Ross's problems. He proposed buying all of the Puget Sound company's power production and transmission facilities, thus creating a city power monopoly. The enormous expense involved, however, gave even some municipal power advocates pause. Thomson prudently refrained from introducing an ordinance to the council.[15]

Events soon moved Ross to consider—actually, to reconsider—the Skagit River, about a hundred miles north of Seattle. The private power company had locked up most power sites surrounding Seattle, including the Hebb and Cushman locations. It held a federal agriculture department permit for the Skagit, too, under a subsidiary, the Skagit Power Company. Ross began

a campaign to wrest the river from Skagit Power. He cross-filed on the Skagit, but nothing came of it until the United States entered World War I.[16]

The war proved a godsend for Ross. As an historian of Seattle municipal power put it, new shipyards appeared "virtually overnight." New manufacturers, almost a hundred of them, sprang up in 1917 alone. The city's population soared by 60,000. As the lighting department strained to keep up with demand, Ross belabored the fact that the department increasingly relied on its steam plant, fired by fuel oil, to meet increasing power obligations. Fuel oil stood high on the government's list of scarce resources, but saving fuel oil by closing the steam plant to convert to wood or coal would deprive the shipyards and their linked industries of power during the conversion process. In essence, Ross put it up to Secretary of Agriculture David F. Houston and other officials—either live with a fuel consumption crisis and the threat of a power failure, or revoke the permit held by the Skagit Power Company. On December 22, Secretary Houston revoked the private company's permit, noting that it had done little at the site since a permit was first issued in 1913.[17]

Gorge Intake on the Skagit River, January 12, 1926. The Gorge Dam project began in 1921, with the first electricity delivered to Seattle by 1924. *Seattle Municipal Archives #2191.*

Thomson helped in winning the revocation, although the extent of his indirect influence is uncertain. He happened to be on the east coast on personal business (to be discussed later) while Ross was pressuring the federal government to act against the Skagit Power Company. Ross wanted Thomson to interview Secretary Houston and the chief engineer of the Forest Service. Thomson's reply was optimistic about the revocation, although he believed that his intervention was unnecessary. Thomson responded as he did because he had an ear to the ground. Apparently, a talk on December 18, 1917, with Washington's senators, Wesley Jones and Miles Poindexter, reassured him. Nevertheless, on December 20 he spent "all day with Jones & Poindexter in re. City of Seattle acquiring Skagit River Power site." He met with Poindexter again the next day and also visited the Forest Service, although it is not clear from his diary whom he saw.[18] If these conferences did nothing else, they confirmed Thomson's commitment to municipal ownership.

Revoking the private company's permit cleared only the first hurdle to a city power plant on the Skagit. Before the city could receive bids on a $3,000,000 council-authorized bond issue, the federal government intervened to stop the process. The government, fearing competition in the financial markets, prohibited all borrowing other than its own, except by authority of the Capital Issues Committee, a small but significant cog in the vast civilian bureaucracy created to advance the war effort. The November 1918 armistice ending the war eventually mooted the committee's work, but the timing of the war's end was unknown to Thomson or other public power advocates at the outset. Thomson worked hard and well to gain approval for construction on the Skagit. With Mayor Ole Hanson, city attorney Hugh Caldwell, and fellow councilman Cecil B. Fitzgerald, he went to San Francisco in June 1918 to appeal to a subcommittee of the Capital Issues Committee. (Hanson would later gain fleeting if unjustified fame in the postwar era as the man who ended Seattle's so-called general strike.) Despite his penchant for self-publicity, Mayor Hanson's interest in the city's wartime problems was genuine, and he probably suggested the trip. At first Thomson was unenthusiastic. "Day ruined by Mayor et al wanting to go to San Francisco," he wrote in his diary on May 28. However, the four men left Seattle on June 4. After a morning strategy session, the group met with the subcommittee during the afternoon of June 7. Thomson spent the following "morning on a letter to Committee to put in writing our oral arguments." Then he took a trip north to the Mark West community to visit in-laws and check on the family burial plot at Healdsburg, finding it in "shameful condition." On the 11th, he returned to San Francisco to discover "our report in poor shape." He rewrote it, but the next day found it to be "in worse shape than ever." He fired the stenographer, rewrote the report, and presented it to the subcommittee. Whether because of the report's delay, opposition from Seattle business groups, or concerns about pre-empting federal ability to borrow, the subcommittee postponed the request.[19]

Mayor Hanson did not give up. He arranged for the same foursome to visit Washington, D.C. They left on July 16, 1918, a rare sweltering day in Seattle when the temperature in their railroad car reached as high as 102 degrees. They arrived in the capital on July 22, also in searing summer heat. Thomson, Hanson, and an advisor met with Charles Hamlin, the chair of the Capital Issues Committee, during another scorching day. "Rather cold reception for so hot a day," Thomson noted in his diary. The doughty engineer took the "cold reception" as a signal that he should get to work. For the next two and a half days, he shaped his own and Ross's material into a report, then went with the others to the Capital Issues Committee to "present case." Then he left town to examine nearby railroad yards. While Thomson was away, the committee accepted his report's position that only the Skagit River site could supply the needed power for Seattle, but the committee also demanded concessions, such as an agreement that the city would interconnect its lines with those of the private company for the duration of the war. When Hanson and Fitzgerald wrote a letter conceding the point, the Capital Issues Committee gave its approval. The battle with the federal government over the Skagit was finished. With the war's end less than four months later, all the federal

The Newhalem powerhouse of the Gorge Dam project, with Mount Ross in the distance, 1935. *Seattle Municipal Archives #16720.*

restrictions were lifted, allowing Ross to proceed with his plans for developing the Skagit River.[20]

ഇന്ദ്രജ്ഞ

Another of Thomson's wartime efforts involved rationalizing freight distribution in Seattle. As with the debate over power generation, the railroad switching issue had emerged long before the war, but wartime demands focused it sharply. The railroads inhibited national and international shipping through Seattle in two ways—first, by charging fees every time a shipment crossed to another's tracks, and second, by refusing to sell any of their portside property, which forced the Port of Seattle into condemnation proceedings in order to have the land necessary for its operations. The second problem was at last overcome. On the other hand, in regard to the first difficulty—the onerous switching charges—the Port of Seattle tried to deal with it by creating a port-owned belt line from one end of the waterfront to the other. Belt lines switched freight cars from one road to another at cost, and were common in several other cities. One was publicly owned, with the others operated under some form of private ownership, usually by the railroads themselves. Seattle's port commissioners took matters into their own hands because neither the Great Northern nor the Northern Pacific wished to create a belt line for the city, despite the commissioners' urging. GN's policy was to "string it along and avoid offense if possible," but also there was not "the slightest possibility of…agreeing to anything of the kind." From 1915 through 1917, the port commissioners attempted to establish their own belt line along the waterfront. To do so, they needed not just a majority vote but a super-majority of 60 percent in order to transfer funds from another project. Four times, voters confirmed the belt line but not by the necessary percentage. In the March 1917 election, however, voters rejected it altogether, leaving the commissioners to create a separate fund for the belt line. Opponents of the line, seeing an end run around the public's decision, sued in the name of one of their number. They won before the state supreme court in August 1917. [21]

Soon, however, the railroads adopted the common user principle along the waterfront and dropped some obstructive charges. They did so for two reasons. First, by the summer of 1917 they experienced snarls in war-time freight traffic (which would lead to federal takeover and operation of the rail lines in December). Second, the city council, as well as the port commission, kept pushing for a solution. The city council had become involved in the matter when it granted the port commission a right-of-way for the anticipated belt line. This November 1915 ordinance, of course, did not have any effect because the port district voters disapproved funding for the line. Thomson was involved in bringing the railroads to agreement, although he refused to collaborate in any effort to coerce them into accepting the belt line on the port's terms. The port's insistence on pressuring the railroads stemmed from the anti-capitalist attitude of Robert Bridges, who was elected president of the port commission on Chittenden's resignation. Tall, hulk-ing, craggy-faced, and often overbearing, Bridges could be a formidable opponent, especially when he believed himself to be fighting battles for the "people" against selfish private interests. Thomson refused to be a party to Bridges' notions. Thomson later recalled that he "was charged with being an enemy of the City. I said I was an enemy of foolish proposals." [22]

Instead, Thomson asked if he could work behind the scenes in persuading the railroads to agree on joint ownership of a line. Thomson's thinking, however, went beyond current issues to include the creation of a work-able makeup and breakup yard for the railroads. He envisioned a freight yard with the capacity to allow the sorting of cars between railroads and trains, so that each train with more than one destination could drop off its last car or cars as it arrived at each intermediate stop. An effective makeup and breakup yard would avoid much shuffling at those way points. Once Thomson had an agreement in hand, the city council granted the railroads a new track, plus the contingent use of the track space originally set aside for the port. After the port's effort to build its own belt line failed in the Washington State Supreme Court, the railroads built and operated tracks on the common user principle, using the area east of the East Waterway (east of Harbor Island) as a "pioneer" makeup and breakup yard. [23]

Although the new plan was an improvement over the old arrangement, it scarcely solved the problems of railroad service in Seattle. Nor could it, given the attenuated strip of tracks, the multitude of piers, and the fragmented ownership of businesses along the water-front. Even before the dust had settled on the common user track issue, the Washington State Public Service Commission in October asked Thomson to prepare a report on rationalizing rail operations in the Puget Sound region. He worked long and hard on the project, spend-ing part or all of at least 39 days gathering information, and writing, revising, and presenting his report to state and railroad officials. The federal takeover in December slowed Thomson's progress but he was able to visit rail arrangements and associated port facilities in Norfolk, Charleston, Baltimore, Chicago, Newark, Brooklyn, New Orleans, Galveston, Los Angeles/San Pedro, and Montreal. He also garnered reports from additional cit-ies, including Boston and Philadelphia. He incorporated the findings in a 52-page typewritten report with volumi-nous appendices and maps, and submitted the completed report to the public service commission early in 1919, recommending new makeup and breakup yards to ease existing congestion and confusion. So far as Seattle was concerned, the railroads did expand and reorganize their existing rail yards to some extent, but the problems of crowded switching and inequitable charges continued. [24]

The fate of the street railway system also demanded Thomson's time and attention. He favored municipal ownership of the major line, a Stone & Webster property. For years, the city and the traction company butted heads over what riders claimed was inferior equipment and poor service. The company argued that the 5¢ fare, required under its franchise, failed to cover all of its operating costs and other franchise obligations. Wartime inflation and a manpower shortage worsened the company's situation. Competition from private busses and automobiles, the "jitneys," had emerged as soon as motor vehicles became reliable and relatively inexpensive. At first unregulated, some of these conveyances ran along the heavily used streetcar lines, scooping up passengers before the railcars could arrive. Others operated opportunistically, having no fixed routes but running wherever passengers might be or want to go at given times of the day. A 1915 bonding requirement cut the jitneys from some 550 to about a third of that number. Still, the remaining vehicles stole revenue from the traction company.[25]

Thomson proposed a municipal buyout of the company during a May 1918 meeting of the company president, Mayor Hansen, and the city council. The proposal was possibly the first public suggestion of a buy out, but Thomson's subsequent role in the city's takeover was marginal. He did support the ultimate purchase price of an agreed upon $15,000,000, a huge sum at the time. This was $3,000,000 more than the company originally asked for, and anywhere from a third to two-thirds more than the opponents of the deal considered fair. In any event, Seattle's voters overwhelmingly approved the transaction in a November advisory vote. Final approval awaited a clearance from the state supreme court, which came early in 1919. In March the council approved the sale, to be paid for with city bonds. The bonds were to be redeemed, principal and interest, in installments. Thomson favored the sale at the $15,000,000 price because of wartime exigencies and because he believed in municipal ownership, not in municipal confiscation. He was too much the investor himself to accept the notion of a municipality wringing the last dime out of a private concern, no matter how disliked it was. As it happened, the city almost certainly overpaid. On the other hand, the transaction was completed, advancing municipal ownership. Charges of fraud, cronyism, and bribery surrounded the sale, charges never brought to trial. Thomson was not implicated in any of them.[26]

World War I brought other challenges. When Reginald Jr. ("Rex") enlisted in the Navy, the war personally came home to the Thomson family. The conflict also piqued Thomson's continuing interest in inventions, no matter how exotic or remote their possible use in warfare might be. Late in January 1918, he met a "Mr[.] Lord in re. machine to kill Germans." The machine, whatever it was, never replaced conventional means of destruction. In the same year, he enthusiastically promoted a patented device to raise sunken ships with the idea of patching and deploying them for wartime use. Thomson cited the "great numbers of ships" lying in the waters off Washington and Alaska awaiting service, "not by construction but by resurrection." Despite his efforts, the ships remained in limbo along with the killing machine.[27]

Thomson also became involved in the critique of a model housing development in Bremerton, to be built in connection with the naval base there, some 15 air miles west across Puget Sound from downtown Seattle. In late September 1918, his friend George Cotterill and others prevailed on Thomson to take a boat trip to the site. The trip and consultation resulted in a "new scheme" for Bremerton, one designed by Cotterill. Opposition arose in Washington, D.C., however. Its source, according to Thomson, was the nationally acclaimed landscape architect Frederick Law Olmsted Jr., since June the manager of town planning for the U.S. Housing Corporation, another wartime agency. What Olmsted wished for was "a Model Mayor in a Model Town, with Model Water and Light and Sewage all separate from the herd," and having nothing "to do with any existing town or city." Thomson met with Olmsted twice, and with other housing corporation officials from time to time throughout most of October. Thomson and others thought they had neutralized Olmsted's influence and received backing for 287 free-standing units in the northwest corner of Bremerton. In the words of one analyst, the curvilinear streets of the Cotterill project "responded to the terrain," producing a sense of "designed harmony" lacking in the rest of the city. In any event, the November 11 armistice ended the project and the land later was developed on the locality's prevailing grid pattern.[28]

In the midst of these wartime perturbations, two prominent Seattleites, George Donworth, an attorney and judge, and Lawrence Colman, a businessman and fellow investor in the defunct *Sun*, asked Thomson to run for mayor. This occurred on January 17, 1918. "I say no," Thomson retorted. The decision was a wise one. Assuming he could have beaten the hyperactive Ole Hanson for the post, Thomson's conscientious performance of his duties would have tied him to city hall and the responsibilities of the mayor's job for a $7,500 yearly salary. His current council pay was $3,000 a year—about the average household income of the era—but he supplemented that amount with a variety of consulting jobs paying much better than the $4,500 difference between the council and mayor salaries. Of course, the consulting work often required travel away from Seattle. The unfriendly *Seattle Union Record* noted that he missed 68 of 163 council meetings during a period of almost two years—March 12, 1917, to February 17, 1919. During that time, he was away for long periods, partly on state, county, or city business, but also in private consulting out of town. On the other hand, most councilmen also held outside jobs or interests, although usually not requiring an absence from the city. Whatever the merits of the argument, Thomson was elected for a second three-year term to the city council in March 1919. [29]

The second term proved no easy time. Two holdover issues from the war years vexed the council: Ross' construction work on the Skagit, and the correct fare for the municipally-owned streetcars. The second problem was the more complex, involving theories of transportation and social benefit not easily agreed upon. Thomson argued that the city's interest and principal payments, as well as the maintenance, operation, and improvement of the streetcar system, should be met at the farebox, at least until the purchase bonds were retired. To put it another way, he wanted riders to pay the bonded debt to the former private owners of the street railway. A 7¢ and later a 10¢ fare, he thought, could manage it, provided that the city efficiently ran the lines. He rejected the opposing view, that a low fare, say 3¢, would increase ridership from residential to business districts and thus stimulate retail sales and other commerce. If a deficit remained, according to the opposing view, it could be made up with higher real estate taxes, which would fall chiefly on those benefitting from the increased business. Eventually the fare rose to 10¢, although municipal transit issues continued to bedevil Seattle politics for years. [30]

Concerning the Skagit project, Thomson believed that Ross was spending too much money on the new dam and its associated structures and should be reined in until better accounting controls were set up. Nobody on the council agreed with him, and the work went

forward. Thomson also advocated raising city light rates by about 20 percent. The council concurred, but Mayor Hugh Caldwell vetoed the measure on the grounds that the council should have worked closely with Ross before presenting the new rate structure. Moreover, Thomson proposed cutting the salaries of many city employees by 15 percent, effective March 1921. He cited needed relief for Seattle taxpayers as justification. His draft ordinance went nowhere. [31] Whatever their merits, Thomson's proposals for slowing or stopping work on the Skagit, higher streetcar fares and electric rates, and lower municipal salaries were scarcely popular. Some of them, such as the curbing of Skagit work and raising streetcar fares, were the favored schemes of some business people, but Thomson apparently acted on his own convictions irrespective of the popularity of these issues with any individuals or groups. Some of his stands in the postwar period, however, cannot be reconciled with his enthusiasm for municipal ownership, his expressions of sympathy for people in difficult economic straits, or his personal generosity. The unifying theme sprang from his belief in municipal economy at all costs. [32] He may also have been disgusted with politics as an apparent one-way conduit for increased costs and higher taxes. This much is certain: he decided not to run for reelection in 1922.

Thomson had an even better reason not to continue on the council—his financial situation. In 1922, he and Addie reached an understanding with the United Securities Corporation, the company founded by the James J. Hill heirs. The Thomsons agreed to surrender their mortgaged property not claimed by others, thus satisfying a note that Thomson and other investors gave to Hill in return for a $42,000 loan to the now defunct *Sun*. Free from serious debt for the first time in seven years, Thomson could turn to his most lucrative occupation, serving as a consulting engineer. From time to time, he had consulted with cities in British Columbia as an adjunct to his work in Strathcona Park, [33] and had hung out his shingle as a full-time consulting engineer on his 1915 return to Seattle. He continued his consulting work throughout the late 1910s and 1920s as much as other interests and obligations permitted. "My work here drags along slowly," he had told his son Harry in 1916. "I am doing as well as anybody else that I know of in this line, but that is not very much to brag about." [34]

He may have resisted bragging, but if Thomson was not doing well, he certainly was staying busy. In 1916 he held 12 consultantships, a number dropping as low as 4 and not exceeding 11 until after he left the city

A view down Second Avenue South from the Smith Tower, June 11, 1929. In the middle distance, the King Street Station tower stands adjacent to the joint railway arrangements strongly influenced by city engineer Thomson years earlier. *Seattle Municipal Archives #3455.*

council in 1922. Then the number jumped to 18 in 1923, rose to 26 in 1925, dropped to 15 in 1926, and did not rise above 7 after 1927. Some of the consulting jobs were brief, involving nothing more than preparation for a court appearance or two, but others continued year after year, such as a waterworks project for the city of Bellingham and a flood control project for King and Pierce counties. Some involved travel, and all demanded strict attention. Some reports were carefully detailed and closely reasoned, such as his 1925 report to a city council committee regarding the feasibility of rail rapid transit. He recommended against rapid transit because of Seattle's relatively low population concentrations and potential ridership. [35]

One of Thomson's most demanding and frustrating if ultimately rewarding jobs involved designing and supervising the construction of a sewer for the hyperenergetic, imperious Charles H. Frye of the Union Stockyards and president of the Frye Company meat packers. Any belief that sewer construction was a simple matter of applying

technical competence to a specific problem not too far removed from a generic situation would be disabused by a study of this job. The episode began in 1923 when Frye realized the need to improve drainage south of the stockyards and his packing plant located opposite one another on Sixth Avenue South and South Walker Street. Frye knew that Thomson had designed a sewer and done other work for a competitor, the James Henry Packing Company, located nearby in the sprawling reclaimed tidelands south of the commercial-retail district. He asked Thomson to design a sewer from Holgate Street, one block north of Walker Street, past the stockyards, then south one more block to tie into a trunk sewer underneath South Lander Street. [36]

Thomson designed the sewer, submitted a request for an ordinance from the city council, obtained the ordinance, negotiated approval from the Board of Public Works, secured agreements from most of the abutting property owners (principally the Great Northern Railway) to pay their proportionate share of the cost, and received bids on the work in September 1925. The delay stemmed partly from the need to remove a construction trestle from Sixth Avenue.[37]

After the work began in 1925, the city engineer's office raised an objection—a portion of the sewer was liable to settling and required a special foundation not provided for in the original contract. During May 1926, Thomson, Frye and the contractor conferred with James D. Blackwell, the city engineer, and others from the engineering department. All agreed on additional support work on a 300-foot section of the sewer near South Lander Street to prevent or mitigate settlement. Nevertheless the city persisted in requiring a $20,000 bond to cover this small portion of work costing less than $11,000 in total. Thomson thought that the repeated demands were "silly," "ridiculous," and "in the nature of practical jokes," but they were serious enough. The GN ignored them. Frye responded differently, for the city's demands raised his ire, not a difficult thing to do. The angry meat packer accused Blackwell of "personal animosity" and repeated his promise to fix the sewer in case of its failure because "I am more interested in the proper function of that sewer than anyone else in the city." Finally the city accepted the sewer.[38]

Meanwhile Frye decided to extend the sewer from Holgate three blocks north to Connecticut Street (now South Royal Brougham Way). Pushing this new sewer through to completion was almost as exasperating as finishing the original. A new agreement among the property owners and another contract were necessary before the work could proceed. So was another ordinance. At first the city wanted a sewer, as Thomson sarcastically noted, "big enough to carry sound steamboats." Once that matter was adjusted, the city council approved the ordinance on April 15, 1926. When the GN decided to add some tidelands blocks to the area to be drained, Thomson and the engineering department agreed on a larger size sewer. Then the city's sewer specialist, who had already protested the ordinance, presented a new objection. Although the sewer was larger than the one required by the ordinance, he declared it was not big enough. In any case, he said, the new, larger size required another ordinance. Thomson wrote to the principal assistant city engineer, "who finally passes on things," and got an agreement affirming the existing plans. To the vice president of the GN he wrote that the city's sewer specialist, "as usual," had "muddied all the water relating to the Sixth Ave. South sewer," but the agreement with the specialist's superior had overcome the "stupidity" of the specialist. The city accepted the second sewer in November.[39]

Thomson's private activities, though sometimes having their own anxieties, often provided a sense of accomplishment and a refuge from the demands of his work. His interventions on behalf of friends and acquaintances continued. An eastern Washington homesteader in danger of losing his land, a hopeful quarry owner wanting to sell sandstone, job applicants, and a Strathcona Park workman who invented saw filing and setting tools all received his help. He continued to loan money despite the financial drain of the failing *Sun*. He gave advice. When a niece wrote him about opportunities awaiting her attorney husband in Alaska, he urged the couple to remain in Virginia or, at most, to relocate to a western town in the contiguous United States. He raised endowment money for his alma mater, Hanover College. His greatest effort went into saving the house and lot of Daniel H. Gilman's widow. Gilman, skilled at promoting shoestring ventures, borrowing money, and living well, left his wife with little more than debt. He had borrowed from Thomson, too. Thomson was willing to allow Mrs. Gilman to retain a house and lot in the Smith Cove area in return for deeding the remainder of Gilman's property to Thomson's Hoosier Investment Company. In 1916 the land had virtually no value, but Thomson would do "something more than what might be called ordinarily fair" for the widow of his spendthrift friend.[40]

When Thomson returned to Seattle from British Columbia in 1915, he lived and worked for a time out of the apartment he maintained at the Silvian, located at 914 East Harrison Street in the Capitol Hill area. In May he rented a downtown office on the fifth floor of the ornate Alaska Building. At the end of August, he and Addie moved to 2827 Broadway North (now East) north of Roanoke Park. In July 1916, Addie superintended a move to 2454 Harvard Avenue North (now East), a block west and four blocks south of their previous Broadway location. In April 1920 they began a search for a house—to purchase this time—finally settling on a place at 1636 34th Avenue in the Madrona neighborhood, where they lived for the rest of their lives together.[41]

It is unclear how he managed to purchase a house and also move to a new office in the Seaboard Building while pleading near poverty to the United Securities company run by J.J. Hill's heirs. Addie signed the notes to secure the $42,000 for the *Sun* from Hill; therefore, all of her financial resources, including her interest in the Laughlin holdings in California, were presumably vulnerable to forfeiture. The 34th Avenue house and the Broomgerrie acreage, again presumably, could have been taken as well. The Thomsons apparently decided to stop paying taxes and assessments on most of the property not pledged to other *Sun* creditors, conserving their resources to buy the 34th Avenue house, develop the Broomgerrie retreat, and continue the consulting business. United Securities was willing to settle for the other properties, perhaps because of the expense and adverse publicity involved in hounding a prominent Seattle citizen and his wife to recover every possible penny.[42]

Thomson accepted the difficulties and personal hazards inherent in consulting work, including delays, slow payments, accidents, and exposure to bad weather. His determination and sturdy physique carried him through when adversity struck, including a serious automobile accident in 1923. On June 5 he and a younger associate, Weinard T. Tolch, were traveling by car with Tolch at the wheel. When returning from a consulting project in Eugene, Tolch tried to pass two trucks about 1½ miles south of Albany, Oregon. The car skidded and Tolch lost control. They plunged down a steep bank and the vehicle rolled over on the two men, killing Tolch outright. Thomson survived, "much bruised" and with "some ribs broken." Injured though he was, Thomson saw to the embalming of Tolch's body, then accompanied it on the next day's train to Seattle. His recovery was slow. For six days he was practically bedridden, before being able to dress and sit up for a few hours. He did not return to the office until June 19, and then only briefly. He visited a consulting site on the 22nd, and resumed traveling on the 29th. Periods of rest and receiving callers were interspersed with his work. At age 67 his injuries were an ordeal for even as strong and dedicated a man as Thomson was.[43]

During these years he remained active in the Westminster Presbyterian Church, leading prayer meetings, attending the cornerstone laying for a new church building in 1923, and in 1924 donating $2,500 toward retiring its construction debt.[44] His service on the board of Whitworth College continued, as did his presentation of speeches and less formal talks. In 1920, for example, he served as the toastmaster at the Beta Theta Pi's Seattle banquet.[45] Katharine Stream, his loyal secretary of many years, continued with him intermittently after his return to Seattle in 1915. He could not provide her with full-time work, and within two years she was looking elsewhere for jobs. From time to time, she took dictation and assumed other tasks, but his last diary reference to her was in July 1921. Other women worked for

him in the years afterward, but his mention of them was routine. None replaced "Miss Stream" in his trust and confidence.[46]

His home life centered on Addie, with concern increasingly focused on her health and moods as they both aged. After arriving in Victoria in 1912, he had commented on how easy it was for him to meet people but how "much harder" socializing was for Addie, "who cannot move about much" and "has not made any great body of acquaintances." Four years later and back in Seattle, she suffered from sciatica, but was "very happy running about and taking care of her little plants" at Broomgerrie. In June and July 1927, he and Addie took an extended trip east, mainly to attend the 50th anniversary of his Hanover College graduation where he was a speaker, but also to see the sights, including Niagara Falls. Addie handled the trip well, but back in Seattle on October 19 she experienced a "very hard heart attack," or at least that was Thomson's diagnosis. Whatever the unsettling episode actually was, Addie recovered. In April 1929, Thomson noted in a visit to Broomgerrie "with Addie. Everything beautiful and Addie happy as a child 3 years old." In August the Thomsons celebrated their wedding anniversary: "46 years sweet companionship with sweet, patient Addie." During the next year, however, Thomson was "home all day with Addie. Dear girl very frail."[47] The "dear girl," nevertheless, recovered to live many more years.

The Thomsons' moves had slowed the education of their children, but with no apparent concern to Thomson whose own college graduation was delayed for two years. Frances, the youngest and perhaps his favorite, in 1912 was enrolled in a Victoria high school and "working like a tiger" to get off probation. Four years later, she still was in high school, this time in Seattle. In June 1921, she graduated from the University of Washington, and in December became engaged to Edward Porep. They married in September 1923.[48] Marion graduated from the University of California at Berkeley in 1916 and began a public school teaching career. After teaching away from Seattle for a few years, she returned to the city. In 1928 she and her father jointly purchased a new two-door Chevrolet.[49]

The career paths of the two sons contrasted considerably. In 1912, James Harrison ("Harry") graduated from the University of California at Berkeley with a degree in civil engineering. For a time he superintended the construction of Samuel Hill's idiosyncratic concrete mansion high above the Columbia River in Klickitat County, Washington. Next he worked for a San Francisco electric power company, producing designs that his father found "very creditable indeed." He returned to Seattle in 1917 to join his father's consulting business, but left the next year to work for the Standard Oil Company in San Francisco. Later that year, he came to Seattle to marry, but returned to California to work and live.[50]

Reginald Jr. ("Rex") led a less directed life, one that his father indulged for many years. When the Thomsons arrived in Victoria, they kept Rex out of school because their son, who inherited his father's height genes, was "standing six feet four in his stocking feet and weighing about 175 pounds," and did not "fit in well with the infant class." Soon, Rex was dispatched to the Oregon Agricultural College where he took some courses, including one in blacksmithing. Although Rex wished to board a Pacific steamer, his parents sent him to Berkeley High School where he would be near California relatives and friends. Rex, however, returned to Seattle to complete high school in 1916. His father expected him to enroll at the University of Washington that fall, but Rex instead went to Alaska to work in the famed Treadwell gold mine near Juneau. After an April 1917 cave-in, resulting in a flood of seawater that wrecked most of the mine, he returned to Seattle. America's involvement in World War I gave Rex a new purpose; he enlisted as an electrician, serving on the cruiser *Saratoga*. On July 29, "the *Saratoga* put out to sea," Thomson recorded in his diary. "Addie[,] Harry and I stood at Broomgerrie" watching the ship "and poured out our prayers." The *Saratoga* steamed to Norfolk, Virginia, where a December letter from Rex disclosed that he was in the Marine Hospital there. "Addie determines to go at once," Thomson wrote. In what resembled a home front scene from the Civil War, the parents rushed to their stricken son's bedside. Fortunately, they found him much improved, but then it was Addie's turn to collapse. While she remained indisposed, Thomson went to Washington, D.C., to promote the belt line project. After the November 1918 armistice, Thomson pulled strings to have Rex discharged from the Navy, which he was in December. Following further adventures, Rex went to California, married, and appeared to settle down. By 1926, however, he wanted to return to Seattle and join the office of another consulting engineer. That effort failing, he returned to California where two years later he divorced his wife. That ended the elder Thomson's indulgence of his namesake. In 1929, when Thomson received a telegram "from Los Angeles saying a girl wants to marry Rex," he responded—"wire to forbid." But the time was long past when parents could control their offspring in those matters. Thomson

became reconciled to Rex's second spouse but his first wife remained a favorite with him and Addie.[51]

ℰℭℜ

In 1930 Thomson could look back on a varied, successful career, a long and happy marriage, and a rich if not invariably satisfactory life with family and friends. At 74, he was at or past the age when most men were retired, even in the days before comfortable pensions and social insurance. Yet he next plunged into one of the most active and challenging periods of his life, beginning with a return to a post held long ago, that of city engineer.

NOTES

1. Twenty years before, the city council had been transformed into a non-partisan, unicameral body. For the charter change, see Rex Roberts, "A Study of the Growth and Expansion of the Seattle Municipal Government" (Master's thesis, University of Washington, 1942), 50. For RHT's filing, see *P-I*, January 11, 1916. For Moore's suggestion, see *P-I*, October 3, 1907. See also *Argus*, October 16, 1915.
2. For enthusiasm for structural reform, see M.A. Matthews, "Commission Government for Seattle," *TC*, September 6, 1913; Matthews, "In Moving Up to Better City Government," *TC*, September 20, 1913; and James J. Callaghan, "A Basis for Better Things All Around," *TC*, September 27, 1913. For an example of RHT's suggestions, see RHT to A.H. Dimock, 26 March 1914, 89/1, box 5, book 13, RHT Papers, UW. For quotations, see RHT to George McMonagle, 16 March 1914, 89/1, box 5, book 13, RHT Papers, UW.
3. For Chittenden's resignation, see Dodds, *Chittenden*, 195. For support of RHT, see *Times*, October 8, 1915. *P-I*, October 9, 1915. For RHT's letter, see *P-I*, October 10, 1915. For disputes, see Dodds, *Chittenden*, 193–95.
4. For issues in 1915, see Berner, *Seattle, 1900–1920*, 191, 203–4, 221–22. For quotation, see RHT to H.C. Thomson, 4 April 1916, 89/1, box 5, book 15, RHT Papers, UW.
5. *P-I*, January 16, 1916; *TC*, February 12, 1916; *Argus*, February 19, 1916; for quotation, see *P-I*, January 11, 1916; RHT, diary, 1916, January 22 (quotation); January 18, and January 26 entries, 1602-2, box 1, folder 8, RHT Papers, UW; and *Argus*, February 26, 1916.
6. RHT, diary 1916, April 6–12 entries, 1602-2, box 1, folder 1, RHT Papers, UW; and Berner, *Seattle, 1900–1920*, 264–70.
7. RHT, diary, 1602-2, box 1, folder 8, RHT Papers, UW.
8. *Star*, May 15, 1916.
9. Ibid. RHT mentioned several issues although he generally avoided specifics. See also Berner, *Seattle, 1900–1920*, 264–70.
10. A summary of writing on the defense councils is in Ronald Schaffer, *America in the Great War: The Rise of the Welfare State* (New York: Oxford University Press, 1991). For council activities, see 18–19, and for the national council's inefficiency, 41–43. Quotations are on 25 and 26.
11. For "patriotism questionnaire," see Berner, *Seattle, 1900–1920*, 231. Other quotations are from C.H. Hanford, ed., *Seattle and Environs, 1852–1924* (Chicago: Pioneer, 1924), 1: 351–52. For the activities of local councils, see also Merion and Susie Harries, *The Last Days of Innocence: America at War, 1917–1918* (New York: Random House, 1997), 75–76, 178–89.

12. Berner, *Seattle, 1900–1920*, covers wartime repression in Seattle, 229–57. Thomson's remarks are in *P-I*, January 11, 1918. An excellent review of wartime expressions is in Richard Slotkin, *Lost Battalions: The Great War and the Crisis of American Nationality* (New York: Henry Holt, 2005), 213–39.

13. Berner, *Seattle, 1900–1920*, 230–32, 252–59.

14. Dick, "Genesis of City Light," 148–49.

15. "Copy of Report of the City Engineer," 33-1, box 84, folder 20, LDC, UW; and RHT to L.D. Lewis, 28 August 1912, 89/1, box 5, book 12, RHT Papers, UW. RHT was willing to obtain both sites, however, RHT to A.H. Dimock, 9 July 1912, 89/1, box 4, book 11, RHT Papers, UW. For Ross and his problems, see Dick, "Genesis of City Light," 145–58, and, for quotation, 153; and William O'Dell Sparks, "J.D. Ross and Seattle City Light, 1917–1934" (Master's thesis, University of Washington, 1964), 15–18.

16. Sparks, "Ross and City Light," 15–18.

17. For industrial and population growth, see Ibid., 16. My discussion of Ross's solution to his dilemma follows Ibid., 26–65.

18. The exchange of telegrams is quoted in Sparks, "Ross and City Light," 27–28. See RHT diary, December 18, 20, and 21, 1917, 1602-2, box 1, folder 1. RHT Papers, UW.

19. For the Skagit project developments, see Sparks, "Ross and City Light," 15–16, 48–52; and Berner, *Seattle, 1900–1920*, 263–64. For RHT's role, see RHT diary, 1602-2, June 6–7, 1918, and, for quotations, June 9, 1918, box 1, folder 1, RHT Papers, UW. For RHT's recording of Hanson's interest, RHT diary, 1602-2, January 28, April 9, and May 14, 1918, box 1, folder 1, RHT Papers, UW. For RHT's studies of the Skagit, see RHT diary, April 16, 17, 18, 19, and 20, 1918, box 1, folder 1, RHT Papers, UW.

20. RHT diary, July 16, July 23–August 3, 1918, and, for quotation, July 25. One version of RHT's report on the Skagit is RHT to Manson F. Backus, 28 May 1918, 89/1, box 6, folder 1, RHT Papers. See also Sparks, "Ross and City Light," 53–54.

21. For the port commission's problems and related issues, see RHT "Public Service Commission of the State of Washington: Report of R.H. Thomson on the Necessity of the Coordination of the Freight Terminals of the Railways Reaching Puget Sound," January 13, 1919, 5 (1592, 1602, 89-5) addition pt. 2, 53–80, RHT Papers, UW; and Burke, *Port of Seattle*, 48, 60–61. For the attitude of the NP as interpreted by the GN, see L.C. Gilman to C.R. Gray, 19 August 1913, and, for quotations, Gray to Gilman, 26 August 1913, 6042, Belt Line – Union Terminal Co., folder 3, GN President's Subject Files, microfilm, MHS.

22. For Bridges and the port, see Burke, *Port of Seattle*, 60–62. RHT, autobiographical statement, 140–46, for quotation, 142, 89/1, box 6, folder 3, RHT Papers, UW.

23. RHT, autobiographical statement, quotation, 146, 89/1, box 6, folder 3, RHT Papers, UW.

24. The statement about RHT's labors is based on RHT diaries, October 31, 1917 through January 20, 1919, 1602-2, box 1, folder 1, RHT Papers, UW. Compare *Kroll's Map of Seattle* (Seattle: Hanford, 1920), with the suggestions for yards in RHT's report, 5, "Coordination of Freight Terminals," RHT Papers, UW. For continuing problems, see Burke, *Port of Seattle*, 70–71; and Richard C. Berner, *Seattle, 1921–1940, From Boom to Bust* (Seattle: Charles Press, 1992): 153, 180.

25. For the company and the jitneys, see Berner, *Seattle, 1900–1920*, 319, 238–40, 264–70, and 318–20; and Berner, *Seattle, 1921–1940*, 72–77.

26. For RHT's proposal, see Berner, *Seattle, 1900–1920*, 265. For the transaction and charges, see Berner, *Seattle, 1900–1920*, 268–70; 319–20; and Berner, *Seattle, 1921–1940*, 72–77. A parody of RHT's position, although not a hostile one, is in *TC*, June 5, 1920. A slanted view of RHT's stand on the purchase of private property is in *Seattle Union Record* (hereafter *UR*), March 1, 1919.

27. For the machine, see RHT diary, January 24, 1918, 1602-2, box 1, folder 1, RHT Papers, UW. For the ship raising device, see RHT, "Copy of Letter sent to Senators Miles Poindexter and Wesley L. Jones, and to Congressman John F. Miller, May 11, 1918," 48-70-76, box 6, folder 28, Henry Suzzallo Papers, UW.

28. RHT diary, September 28, 1918, 1602-2, box 3, folder 1; and for quotations, RHT, "Sketches," 1918 entry, 1602-2, box 2, folder 10, RHT Papers, UW. For meetings with Olmsted, see RHT, diary, October 9 and 10, and for meetings with others, October 14, 17, 18, and 20, 1602-2, box 3, folder 1, RHT Papers, UW. For the quotation from the analyst, see Charles Eugene Talmadge, "The Growth of the Puget Sound Naval Shipyard and Its Influence on the City of Bremerton," (Master's thesis, University of Washington, 1983), 54 for map, although it lists E.T. Miscke as "Town Planner," and for quotations, 56. For Olmsted, see John J. Pittari Jr., "Practical Idealism: Frederick Law Olmsted Jr. and the Modern American City Planning Movement," (Ph.D. diss., University of Washington, 1997), 144–63 for wartime planning. For RHT's "Model" quotation, see RHT to Cotterill, 10 October 1918, 38, box 8, folder 2, Cotterill Papers, UW.

29. RHT diary, 1602-2, box 3, folder 1, RHT Papers, UW. For rates of pay, see *The Charter of the City of Seattle: Adopted… March 3, 1896, as Amended in 1900, 1902, 1906, 1908, 1910, 1911, and 1912* (Seattle: Lowman and Hanford, 1912), 15 (council), and 90 (mayor). *UR*, March 3, 1919. For others' outside interests, see Bagley, *History of Seattle* 3: 538–9 (William Hickman Moore); 289–90 (Alpheus F. Haas); and 939–40 (Robert B. Hesketh).

30. On fare setting, see Berner, *Seattle, 1921–1940*, 58–61. For the 3¢ or free fare idea, *TC*, September 10, 1921. For RHT and fares, see *UR*, June 9, 1920.

31. For Skagit issues, see Berner, *Seattle, 1921–1940*, 50–55. RHT's attitude on the Skagit is in *UR*, January 21, 1921. For raising lighting rates and related issues, see *UR*, June 9, June 11, June 14; and June 15, 1920. The pay reduction for city workers is in *UR*, January 1, 1921.

32. Municipal economy was not a new idea with RHT, see RHT to Howard M. Findley, 2 July 1914, 89/1, box 5, book 13, RHT Papers, UW.

33. Wilson, "Rising and Setting of Seattle's *Sun*," 67. For consulting see, for example, RHT to Thomas Taylor, 23 February 1914, 89/1, box 5, book 13, RHT Papers, UW.

34. RHT to J. Harry Thomson, 4, April 1916, 89/1, box 5, book 15, RHT Papers, UW.

35. The consulting jobs are compiled from RHT's diaries and "Sketches," the later "Sketches" usually listing more work per year than the diaries. Some consultations were brief, while others, such as consulting on the Bellingham water works, lasted for years. For RHT and rapid transit, see RHT to Rapid Transit Committee, 89/1, box 13, folder 5, RHT Papers, UW.

36. For Henry see, for example, RHT diary, 1923, September 18; for similar or the same work for Frye, see July 13 and 24; and for work on the new sewer, November 20, 1923, 1602-2, box 1, folder 10, RHT Papers, UW. For other information, see 89/2, box 1, folder 14, RHT Papers, UW.

37. Frye and the GN also agreed to pay any costs not collected from other property owners, see Frye to L.C. Gilman, 15 March 1924, 89/2, box 1, folder 17. Other information is in folder 15, RHT Papers, UW.

38. For the conference and Frye quotations, see Frye to C.B. Bagley, 20 May 1926; for RHT quotations, see RHT to Frye, 19 May 1926, 89/2, box 1, folder 19, RHT Papers, UW. For city approval, see RHT to W.H. Tiedeman, 2 July 1926, 89/2, box 1, folder 21, where other incidental information is located, RHT Papers, UW.

39. For first quotation, see RHT to Frye, 29 March 1926, 89/2, box 1, folder 18; and for the remaining quotations, RHT to L.C. Gilman, 2 July 1926; and for the city's acceptance, see RHT to Frye, 24 November 1926, box 1, folder 21. For other information, see folders 18 and 19, RHT Papers, UW.

40. For the homesteader, see RHT to Charles A. Babbitt, 29 July 1912, 89/1, box 4, book 11. For the quarry owner, see RHT to C.J. Moore, 8 May 1914, 89/1, box 5, book 13. For the park workman, see RHT to A. Champeaux, 30 June 1913, 89/1, box 5, book 12. For a loan, see RHT to George McMonagle, 16 March 1914, 89/1, box 5, book 13. For other assistance, see RHT to George F. Cotterill, 3 December 1912, 89/1, box 5, book 12; and to J.G. Watts, 6 February 1915, 89/1, box 5, book 13. For the niece, see RHT to Mrs. Homer Stiles, 28 February 1916, box 5, book 15. For Hanover, see RHT to Harry Mansfield Waggoner, 89/1, box 5, book 13. For Mrs. Gilman, see the following letters from RHT to James Bothwell, 14 February 1914; to J.C. Jeffrey, 13 July 1914, both in 89/1, box 5, book 13; and, for quotation, to L.C. Gilman, 17 February 1916, 89/1, box 5, book 15. All of the above are in RHT Papers, UW. Gilman was heavily in debt, see "Agreement Between Creditors" August 23, 1907, regarding debts of D.H. Gilman, for $62,307.85, 221-3, box 5, folder 10, Manson Franklin Backus Papers, UW.

41. Thomson's moves may be followed in "Sketches" for the years 1915–20, 1602-2, box 2, folder 10; and, for more detail, in the relevant diaries in 1602-2, box 1, folders 8 and 10, RHT Papers, UW.

42. Wilson, "Rising and Setting of Seattle's *Sun*," especially 66–67. For RHT's pleading near poverty, see, for example, RHT to John J. Toomey, 14 May 1917, 89/1, box 5, book 15, RHT Papers, UW.

43. The accident is in *P-I*, June 6, 1923. For quotation, see RHT diary, June 6, 1923, 1602-2, box 1, folder 10, RHT Papers, UW. For his recovery, see RHT diary, June 7–29, 1923, 1602-2, box 1, folder 10, RHT Papers, UW.

44. For the church, see RHT diary, 1918, 1602-2, box 1, folder 9; 1923, box 1, folder 10; and 1924, box 1, folder 11, RHT Papers, UW.

45. For Whitworth, see RHT to John P. Hartman, 3 November 1913, 89-1, box 5, book 13, RHT Papers, UW. For speeches, see RHT diary, January 15, 1918; and January 4, 1920, 1602-2, box 1, folder 9, RHT Papers, UW.

46. For Stream, see, for example, RHT diary, December 25, 1913, 1602-2, box 1, folder 8, and July 11, 1921, 1602-2, box 1, folder 10, RHT Papers, UW. See also Stream to Edmund S. Meany, 3 July 1918; 106-70-12, box 34, folder 5, Edmond S. Meany Papers, UW. For other stenographic assistance, see RHT diary October 23, 1923, 1602-2, box 1, folder 10; and June 6, 1930, box 1, folder 12, RHT Papers, UW.

47. RHT to W.L. Thomson, 17 September 1912, 89/1, box 5, book 12, RHT Papers, UW; to J. Harry Thomson, 4 April 1916, 89/1, box 5, book 15, RHT Papers, UW. RHT diary, June 1–July 19, 1927, 1602-2, box 2, folder 1, RHT Papers, UW. For RHT as a speaker, see Frank S. Baker, *More Glimpses of Hanover's Past, 1827–1986* (Seymour, IN: Graessle-Mercer, 1988), 123. For Addie, see RHT diaries, October 19, 1927, 1602-2, box 2, folder 1; and April 4, 1929, 1602-2, box 2, folder 1; August 29, 1602-2, box 2, folder 1; and August 10, 1930, box 2, folder 12, RHT Papers, UW.

48. RHT to "Dear Brother," 30 September 1912, 89/1, box 5, book 12; RHT to H.C. Thomson, 4 April 1916, 89/1, box 5, book 15; RHT diary, December 16, 1921, 1602-2, box 1, folder 10; and RHT diary, September 12, 1923, box 1, folder 10, all in RHT Papers, UW.

49. RHT to George Beecher, 5 November 1915, 89/1, box 5, book 13; to H.C. Thomson, 4 April 1916, 89/1, box 5, book 15; and RHT diary, February 8 and February 12, 1928, 1602-2, box 2, folder 1. RHT Papers, UW.

50. RHT to Emma C. Walker, 9 May 1914; 89/1, box 5, book 13; for quotation, RHT to J. Harry Thomson, 4 April 1916; 89/1, box 5, book 15; RHT to H.C. Thomson, 4 April 1916, 89/1, box 5, book 15; RHT diary, April 16, 1917, 1602-2, box 1, folder 9; and "Sketches," 1918 entry, 1602-2, box 2, folder 10, all in RHT Papers, UW.

51. Rex's career may be followed in his father's letters and diary entries, which are too voluminous to include here. For quotations, in order, see RHT to "Dear Brother" 30 September 1912, 89/1, box 5, book 12; RHT diary July 29, 1917, 1602-2, box 1, folder 9; RHT, "Sketches," 1917 entry, 1602-2, box 2, folder 10; RHT diary, December 6, 1917, 1602-2, box 1, folder 9; and RHT diary, box 2, folder 1, all in RHT Papers, UW. For Rex's first wife, Jean, see, for example, RHT diary, August 7, 1939, 1602-2, box 2, folder 4, RHT Papers, UW.

12
Return to City Engineering and the Fight with J.D. Ross

ON AUGUST 20, 1930, at eight in the morning, 74-year-old Reginald H. Thomson went back to work as the city engineer. Appointed by Mayor Frank Edwards and unanimously approved by the council, he greeted his chief assistant, Oscar A. Piper, then plunged into a round of conferences, meetings, and decisions. Edwards' call came after William D. Barkhuff, the incumbent city engineer, died of injuries resulting from a car accident. This was not the first time Thomson had been asked to resume his old job. Two years earlier, in 1928, Edwards ran against Mayor Bertha K. Landes, soundly defeating her after a campaign noted for heavy spending on his behalf, his personal attacks on Landes, and his steadfast avoidance of most substantive issues. On taking office in March, he requested the resignations of all department heads save those of the fire chief and the Superintendent of Lighting ("City Light"), James D. Ross.[1]

W. Chester Morse, a respected engineer, was serving as city engineer when Edwards was elected. Edwards did not make any new appointment immediately, leaving Morse an opportunity to speak to Thomson. Thomson informed his diary on June 2, a Saturday: "Morse calls early, wants me to see Edwards and accept position of City Engr—I decline." Morse, knowing he was "slated to go," resigned the next Monday. The wording of the diary entry suggests that the job was Thomson's to "accept," but it is probable that Edwards had already settled on William D. Barkhuff. In any case, Barkhuff's name and those of several other prospective department heads went to the council, precipitating a row. Barkhuff, the superintendent of streets, was believed by some to be unqualified by experience or leadership to head the department. After a good deal of squabbling, the council confirmed Barkhuff on June 25. Thomson left his reasons for refusing consideration for the job unrecorded, but they are evident. He enjoyed a lucrative if declining consulting practice that would have to be curtailed or abandoned, he would have opposed a fellow engineer already suggested for the position, and he would have to serve under Edwards, a political novice with a reputation for bumptiousness and questionable judgment.[2]

By 1930 things had changed. The unfortunate Barkhuff was deceased and Mayor Edwards wanted Thomson. Edwards had overcome questions about his somewhat murky past in the Seattle entertainment business and other fields to win a landslide re-election. He was a family man who lacked intellectual gifts but who comported himself well, dressed in style but without flash, and who had made no serious mistakes. He and the council locked horns on occasion but that was scarcely a novelty in Seattle politics. For his part, Thomson's reputation for getting along with mayors of varying temperaments and political persuasions was well deserved. Besides, by the summer of 1930 the Great Depression was a reality and no time for optimism about the future of consulting engineering. The engineering department welcomed him back. The *Times* reported that Thomson's "return to his old job was an almost gala affair, with many floral tokens that banked his office and greeting handshakes from several veteran attachés of the engineering department." Thomson wisely declared there would be no immediate changes in personnel or organization. He thought it "somewhat natural" to return to his former post, "but I have been out of touch with city projects and improvements so long,...that I shall have to take it a little slow and depend largely upon my staff until I can catch up with the work."[3]

Thomson was right to "take it a little slow," because it was not too much to say that Seattle had been transformed in the 19 years since he had left the engineering office. Most obviously, the population had soared from about 240,000 when he resigned in 1911 to more than 366,000 when resuming the job in 1930. The city had grown by natural increase and migration, pushing against boundaries essentially the same as in 1911. Cars and trucks jammed the streets. Expanded municipal railway and bus service, pervading the city by 1930, matched the increasing density. Concrete and asphalt paving replaced macadam, while street lighting, under Ross's direction, was vastly improved. The city thrived economically as a great port and commercial hub, but not as an industrial metropolis. Much of the city's industry of the early 1910s

In 1930, Thomson looks up from a Seattle map during his second stint as city engineer. *Museum of History and Industry, Seattle Post-Intelligencer Collection 19865.435455.*

had been either linked to commerce or was "outpost" industry, doomed to replacement or curtailment as improving transportation networks brought products from regions with competitive advantages. To cite one example, the employees in foundries and machining, a prototypical "heavy" industry, numbered 1,230 in 1909, but only increased to 2,193 in 1929, a gain of less than 1,000. Obviously the 1910 vision of a vast industrial base combining iron and steel production with manufacturing would not be realized. Perhaps it was just as well, because Seattle's combined domestic and foreign trade of 1910, approximately 1,530,000 tons, boomed to 8,362,579 tons in 1930, a commerce relatively free of industrial pollution and contamination. A dark underside of unemployment and low wages dimmed this comparatively happy scene even before the full impact of the Great Depression, yet Thomson could be optimistic about his return to the engineering department.[4]

His optimism faded soon enough. A devastating conflict with his old friend James D. Ross would be at the core of it—a conflict that led to Ross's dismissal, a charter amendment victory of Ross over Thomson, Mayor Edwards' recall, Ross's reinstatement, and Thomson's forced resignation. The story has not been told before from Thomson's perspective. To do so, it is necessary to explain, first, the Thomson-Ross friendship; second, Ross's place in the firmament of public power; and finally, the circumstances of the political upheaval in Seattle.

James D. Ross was one of Thomson's few intimate friends. Thomson hired Ross to build the Cedar River dam, and in 1911 Ross became superintendent of the lighting department (see chapter 8). Together they worked to strengthen the department in Seattle power production from a mere supplier of street lighting to a successful competitor with the Puget Sound Light &

James D. Ross at his desk, circa 1930s. *Seattle Municipal Archives #112341.*

Power Company for industrial, commercial, and residential customers. Their personal relationship proved brotherly, united by religion and abstemiousness. Ross was, like Thomson, a Presbyterian eschewing liquor and tobacco. Like Thomson, Ross loved the outdoors. They remained close and committed to public utilities after Thomson left the city for the port commission and Strathcona work. "You are all right," Thomson wrote from Canada at the end of 1912. "May God bless you and all those carrying on the struggle." In late September 1914, Thomson deeded some Bainbridge Island property to Ross "for 1$\frac{00}{}$ and interest in one of his patents. Hope to make something grand." Nothing "grand" came of the patent but the exchange affirmed Thomson's fascination with inventions and his friendship with Ross. Although Thomson was too busy for heavy socializing outside his family, the childless Rosses dined once or twice a year at the Thomsons.[5] The relationship cooled in the late 1910s, after Thomson was

elected to the city council and criticized Ross's spending on the new Skagit power site. It is unlikely that Thomson tried to undermine Ross's authority by his criticism or the failed effort to raise the lighting department's rates. Rather, Thomson attempted to secure a sound financial footing for the city's electric utility. Given Ross's developing cast of mind, however, Thomson's motives would have mattered little.

During and after the Ross-Thomson friendship, Ross's star rose dramatically, both locally and nationally. Ross learned from Thomson's ability to showcase the Cedar River and other projects, catering to politicians' desire for successful public works while largely keeping his own counsel and controlling his bureaucratic domain. Indeed, Ross soon out-did Thomson himself in this regard. Large-framed, gregarious, persistent, a showman, and an engaging speaker, Ross usually captivated the public and enough politicians to have his way. To get the mayor and council to support building a dam on the Skagit, in 1918 he organized a trip to the tumbling, untamed river, with its deep canyons and narrow throats of rock, ideal for dam sites. Mayor Ole Hanson and the councilmen returned to Seattle, dazzled by the prospect of a perfect power source. Nevertheless, Ross by no means always got what he wanted in the short run, having to surmount many obstacles before his great Diablo powerhouse came on line in the autumn of 1936.[6]

Ross got his way often enough in no small measure because of his concept of "city building"—with cheap power firing visions of electric house-currents costing practically nothing and industrial electricity even less. "City building" through electricity was not original with Ross, but its widespread acceptance only made it all the more plausible for Seattle. The idea of a nearly effortless home life and the promise of relative ease and cleanliness in manufacturing proved seductive. After all, Puget Sound Traction, Light & Power had charged residential customers 20¢ a kilowatt hour when city power came on the scene in 1905, but competition from the lighting depart-

ment forced rates down to 7¢ per kilowatt hour by 1912. Of course, the "city building" idea was too pat; Seattle and the Pacific Northwest suffered from locational disadvantages, particularly distance from raw materials and major markets. Those limitations became more apparent in retrospect than in Ross's early years, so "city building," helped by Ross's infectious optimism, survived the post World War I economic depression and the erratic operation of his first pre-Diablo Skagit powerhouse.[7]

Ross was borne along by national developments involving both private and public power. Though private utilities pioneered the technology and organization of electric power production and distribution, they treated electricity as a commodity, like automobiles or wheat. They were in the business of producing and selling electricity for profit, and the more profit the better. Despite rates that reformers considered high, the electrical industry expanded enormously and attracted huge investments while rapidly integrating larger functions. Among other activities, large electrical firms created holding companies, to "hold" the stock of smaller companies, which they bought and unified into interconnected systems with standardized technical and managerial arrangements.

Some large-scale managers, notably the innovative Samuel Insull of Chicago, funneled investment by pyramiding holding companies on holding companies. The operating companies had to make profits for the stockholders of the ultimate holding company. The view of Ross and many others was that such tactics defeated the real purpose of power—to provide a public service, thus "public power." Electricity, of course, would not be free, any more than other public services such as mail delivery or trash collection. Public power needed to make enough money to pay all the expenses associated with the production and distribution of electricity, and to replace depreciated facilities and equipment. Public power also required responsible operation in order to attract investment—i.e., the selling of bonds in the financial markets for expansion and improvement, just like for private businesses. Unlike a business, however, public power did not need to earn a profit over and above all expenses. Therefore, it could sell power for less, encouraging industrial expansion and lowering the household cost of living.[8]

Little wonder, then, that municipal public power boomed in the late 19th and early 20th centuries, the era of the Seattle lighting department's founding. According to one historian, "the rate of increase of public systems was more than twice as fast as private companies. By 1912 there were 1,737 public power systems and 3,659 private companies in operation." Even though public systems

Diablo Dam on June 23, 1936, situated four miles up the Skagit River from City Light's earlier Gorge Dam. The dam was constructed in 1927–30 and began delivering electricity to Seattle when facilities went on-line in 1936. *Seattle Municipal Archives #14680.*

Crowded tour boat behind Diablo Dam, August 1931. *Seattle Municipal Archives #2350.*

20th centuries, but their defense had lost much of its force by the 1920s.[9]

Ross gained local prominence and national notice by expanding the Seattle lighting department when other public utilities faltered or failed after about 1912. Combining skill, dynamism, and vision, Ross stood the private power argument on its head. He ingratiated himself with the city council so well that the council usually did his bidding, meanwhile holding itself aloof from interference in the lighting department. True to his abstemious personal life, he lived comfortably and without ostentation on a modest salary. He concerned himself with employee well-being, adopting a version of the corporate welfare programs popular in the 1920s. He promoted the use of new electrical appliances in homes, just as the private power companies did, and matched private power's advertising efforts with illustrated annual reports and brochures proclaiming

usually were located in smaller places and never replaced private companies in most great cities, it was a time of optimism for public power. The optimism did not last. During the 1920s, municipal systems declined in number and percentage of output, producing less than 5 percent of the national total by 1932. There were several reasons for the decline. Some private companies enjoyed economies of scale because of their connection to large power grids. Private utilities often led in research and technological innovation, and in advertising and public relations. They reduced rates, sought legal relief, and intervened in politics whenever they believed those moves helpful or necessary. They attacked public power, and whether or not the advocates of public power thought the criticisms valid, private power's strictures had some merit. In the days when public power was municipal power, private utilities argued that interference from city politicians caused corruption and inefficiency. Public power, among other sleights-of-hand, paid no taxes. To remain popular among citizens, public power systems set rates too low to finance timely investment in new equipment, or to pay salaries high enough to attract top-flight talent. Finally, public power was socialism, which was bad, while private power was private enterprise, which was good. The defenders of public power challenged all of private power's assertions, but with little practical effect. They strongly defended municipal socialism in the late 19th and early

J.D. Ross meticulously orchestrated visitor activities on the Skagit River. Here, tourists take a thrilling ride on the Diablo incline in 1935. *Seattle Municipal Archives #16711.*

the department to be "Your City Light and Power," or "City Light" for short. Ross reinforced his persuasiveness with a lobbying organization, first called the "Patrons of City Light," and later, the less inosculated "Friends of City Light." In 1926 he began public tours of the upper Skagit area, where visitors viewed the first hydroelectric plant (Gorge Dam; completed 1924), then proceeded to the Diablo Dam and powerhouse site (construction began 1927). While enjoying the magnificent mountain scenery, tourists stayed in cabins and were well fed. At night, the nearby Ladder Creek falls were artificially "illuminated in all the varying colors of the rainbow." City Light charged only enough "to cover bare cost" for the excursions and shows.[10]

Ross planned the "minutest details" of the plantings, a small zoo, and other features of the Skagit tour arrangements. "Please do not pick flowers," a 1930 brochure commanded, "they are needed for seed and to beautify the Skagit." He would not, however, let an opportunity pass to ingratiate City Light with tourists: "If you are a plant lover, leave your request, and we will go further back in the hills and get your plant at the proper season." Ross's conception of a public power grid spanning the west coast was breathtaking for the time. He used the forum of the 1928 Public Ownership League of America conference to

shed any taint of provincialism and become "a statesman for public power." In a speech before that group, certain to be well publicized, he advocated a "Superpower" 300,000 volt (or higher) line from Seattle to Los Angeles, uniting all the Pacific Coast municipal systems into a great grid. In time, public hydropower from the Columbia and Colorado rivers would link with his proposed system to overwhelm private power, which was, he said, nothing more than a stockjobbing venture anyway. Not surprisingly, Ross came to the favorable attention of two nationally known advocates of public power, Senator George Norris of Nebraska, and the governor of New York, Franklin D. Roosevelt.[11]

Unfortunately, there was a darker side to Ross. Accusations that he was building his own "machine" were not far-fetched. Although he looked after employee welfare, he demanded unswerving support and loyalty from underlings in the lighting department. Defending himself against a charge that the lighting department offices were technologically backward and relying too much on handwork, he declared he "went into the question of machine accounting a year ago," finding the cost to be "about 50-50, machine vs. hand work." Therefore he "gave the preference to hand work on account of giving citizens employment where efficiency is equal."

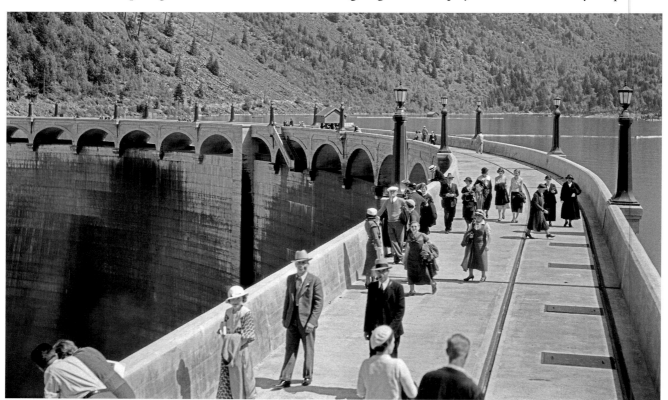

On a pleasant day in 1935, tourists enjoy a walk on the Diablo Dam causeway. *Seattle Municipal Archives #140425.*

Left unsaid was the obvious fact that these employed "citizens" and their families had a stake in the future of the lighting department. Employing "citizens" in this manner left Ross open to charges of payroll padding and inefficiency. A comparative analysis of the 1929 annual reports from City Light and the municipally-owned Tacoma plant found gross revenues per employee to be $545.00 for Seattle, versus Tacoma's robust $800.00. The Tacoma works—similar to Seattle's—generated 907,000 kilowatt hours per employee, much better than Seattle's 358,000 kWh per employee. Seattle's cost per kWh was 0.82¢; Tacoma's a mere 0.33¢. Caution must be used in extrapolating from such figures, but they suggest Ross was not especially concerned with reducing expenses. His effective publicity and self-promotion efforts, while defensible on the grounds of advancing public power, were not cheap either. Ross was not indifferent to the bottom line, but he could make exceptions to frugality, as when he preferred to buy trucks from a City Light customer. In a ham-handed manner, he attempted to punish a department store, a customer of the rival Puget Sound Light & Power Company. In a letter, he urged his employees at the beginning of the 1928 Christmas season to boycott the business. In Ross's mind, such a letter served as an order, not a request. The effort backfired, although Ross survived the episode. [12]

Ross's worst administrative failure proved to be his inability to delegate authority, often even for the most trivial tasks. Nothing could be too insignificant to catch and claim his interest and intervention—one example being his over-involved planning of the Skagit tours. As his workforce expanded to 1,020 employees scattered throughout City Light operations, he could not possibly keep up with all the details. His management style and demand for loyalty bred a lack of initiative among subordinates. Another outcome of his internal preoccupations was the fact that outsiders could have difficulty getting his attention about matters of moment to them, but of no immediate concern to the Superintendent of Lighting. He could not or would not switch attention to them or authorize subordinates to deal with these matters. While fond of chastising others for retarding his projects, Ross's own neglect was to blame for some delays. The inattention to moving lighting department construction forward while he was distracted by unrelated issues could be aggravating to the others involved. [13]

Ross's engaging presence masked other less appealing personality traits. Biographers and a historian favorably inclined toward Ross have noted his "ruthless intolerance" toward those he considered opponents, and his "self-righteous and paranoid" reactions. There was an air of "pomposity and presumption" about him, as well as "a thought pattern that tended to view the world in conspiratorial terms." Ross laid many of his setbacks at the door of private power—the "power trust" as he called it. It is not too much to state that Ross saw the "power trust" around every corner and under every bed. Far from rendering him ineffectual, his paranoia enhanced his political awareness. He combined his mania with a consummate skill at bureaucratic infighting, aided at times by statements bearing what could be charitably described as a distant relationship to the truth. A case in point concerned Ross's addition to the Cedar Falls generating machinery. Ross claimed a total cost of $475,000 for a pipeline from Cedar Lake and for the new generator. In 1919 the council authorized the expenditure and gave the job to Ross, "in violation of the plain terms of the City Charter" placing all public engineering in the hands of the city engineer. The council acted as it did because Arthur H. Dimock, Thomson's successor, "admitted that he could not do the work" for the figure Ross named. As things developed, neither could Ross. In 1921 the bill for the improvements reached $740,000, or $265,000 more than Ross's original estimate. Ross possibly did not intend to deceive the council, but was only self-deceived. Or he could have been using a not-unheard of bureaucratic trick to lure a legislative body into committing itself to a project, then later revealing the real costs. In any event, the episode did nothing to strengthen Ross's record for the accurate calculation of costs and his reputation for veracity. [14]

None of Ross's less winning traits appear to have concerned Thomson when he resumed the city engineership in 1930, nor, for that matter, in the years just before he took the job. In 1928, Thomson had written to Ross asking for information for "certain big manufacturers." These business interests were considering a move to Seattle and wanted, among other things, an "electrical plant which will be free from all influence of Stone & Webster." In 1929, Thomson asked Ross to go with him to the Ballard neighborhood in Seattle, where an investor had developed a machine "able to generate a certain amount of electrical current by gravity." Apparently Ross had sent a subordinate to see the device, but the inventor claimed that the visitor "did not grasp the mechanics of it." Therefore Ross himself should go. Thomson noted that if the machine were "any good," the city should "secure the rights" to it because "I would not our friends, the enemy," that is, Puget Sound Light & Power, to "get the control of it for the territory." The machine probably worked about as

Thompson (left) at a Diablo project gathering in 1930, talking to one of the dignitaries. *Seattle Municipal Archives #2286.*

well as other inventions in which Thomson was interested, because nothing more was heard of it. In 1930, a week after resuming his old job, Thomson spoke at the dedication of Diablo Dam on the Skagit River. Accepting the dam from the contractors, he praised Ross, "whose zeal and vision has made this hour possible," reminding his audience of the time 25 years ago when he and Ross completed the first Cedar River project. That effort cost $580,000 and resulted in a 3,000 horsepower plant, whereas the Skagit construction, when completed, would produce "more than 100 times" that output. Yet it was "but one step in the great scheme of development" backed by an investment of almost $30,000,000, a growing customer base, and rising revenue.[15]

Thomson's remarks likely were his last public praise of Ross. And, if Ross listened closely, which he probably did, he would have heard a shot across his bureaucratic bow. Thomson accepted the dam "as the head of the department responsible for Engineering work in design

and construction," a clear warning to the ambitious Superintendent of Lighting that Thomson, not Ross, would have the final say about the design of the forthcoming Diablo powerhouse. Thomson's cautionary statement was necessary, for Ross had already made it plain that he wanted to control the powerhouse project and, indeed, all future City Light engineering. Ross had done so despite the engineering department's repeated pledge to cooperate fully in the design of the powerhouse. Ross's argument was, essentially, that no matter how closely the engineering and lighting departments cooperated, the lighting department was responsible for the results. Therefore, City Light should control the engineering of all of its projects with an eye to the most effective future operation. Ross's claim will be considered later.[16]

Another issue had arisen by this time. Early in 1929, Mayor Frank Edwards proposed an efficiency review of all city departments, with lighting first. The council unanimously approved. Perhaps Edwards was disturbed by the high costs of the Skagit development, or by Ross's forays into municipal politics including the department store boycott fiasco, or by rumors of flagrant inefficiencies in the lighting department despite its ability to turn a profit. Whatever the council and Edwards' concerns might have been, the accounting firm of Lybrand, Ross Brothers, & Montgomery (LRBM) conducted the review. On January 22, 1930, LRBM submitted a 30-page typewritten report on the lighting department. Because the report was highly critical, not to say condemnatory, of City Light operations, some observations must be made in Ross's defense. As LRBM recognized, City Light existed in a competitive situation not conducive to sweet reasonableness on its part, however desirable an amenable attitude was in conducting municipal affairs. The quickly expanding lighting department had outgrown its administrative structure too rapidly to allow an easy adjustment of its organization. The existing systems of control—supervision partly by the mayor and council, partly by the Board of Public Works, and partly through the device of a budget ordinance—

The calm before the storm—Thomson, Mayor Frank Edwards, and J.D. Ross stand at center (3rd, 4th, and 5th from right) in front of the steel plate wye for the Diablo penstocks, October 20, 1930. *Seattle Municipal Archives #4438.*

were inadequate. All three organizations, the mayor's office, the council, and the board, were too subject to political meddling. LRBM's solution called for a drastically reorganized department headed by a single commissioner, or by a board directly responsible to the mayor.[17]

Otherwise, LRBM found Ross to be overwhelming himself with details, failing to delegate authority, and allowing competing and overlapping functions among subdivisions. The results of Ross's management style included a general ledger posted only through February 1929, as of the end of May that year, no inventory of warehouse holdings for more than six years, and subsidiary ledgers radically out of balance with one another. The situation was bad enough that that state examiners came in to put matters right. Elsewhere, too many subdivisions were

involved with customer relations. Billing and collecting policies were lax. Of the residential accounts reviewed by LRBM, almost 23 percent were past due by two to six months, or "in a few cases" longer, while the reviewed business accounts were almost 50 percent past due.[18]

Ross's rambling response failed to endear him to anyone save those already convinced of the unimpeachable rectitude of the lighting department. He denounced "enemies," who "always twisted" any report on his department. Ross admitted mistakes and praised the integrity of LRBM, but declared that most of City Light's problems originated outside his department due to the political intervention of the council, inefficiencies of the engineering department, and the unfair competition and "political intrigue" of Puget Sound Light & Power. These entities imposed a large "amount of useless expense" on City Light, "a staggering one beside which the losses within the department pale into insignificance." Only a mobilized "public opinion" had saved his department from outside interference in the past. Ross scoffed at LRBM's suggestion of a cooperative arrangement with private power, pending its buyout. "There is no use trying to compromise. It would only last a month." Ross promised to study the report and to implement many of the suggestions, however, his leading remedy for City Light's problems was to change the city charter, giving him control of all his department's engineering. "My plea is for greater authority in organization. I think that should rest with me."[19]

Ross claimed that LRBM had "urged that the work of the Department of Lighting now being done by the City Engineer's department be placed with the Department of Lighting," a statement having little relation to the truth. The LRBM position was that the "charter provision" giving all engineering work to the engineering department "as applied to this utility has not always been conducive to the best results," a critical statement but hardly a declaration that the charter should be changed. Ross's continued distortion of the LRBM report at last produced a response from the accounting firm. It came in the midst of the superheated political atmosphere surrounding Mayor Edward's dismissal of Ross, to be considered shortly. On March 9, 1931, LRBM wrote to Edwards and the council about statements "to the effect that we have unqualifiedly recommended the transfer of certain engineering functions and facilities from the City Engineer's Department to the City Light Department," calling such statements "a misquotation of our reports." The LRBM letter, referring to the lighting department analysis and other reports, argued for a consideration of structural changes in Seattle's administration, but also pointed out that "major savings under the present form of city government were obtainable" without basic charter reform. The letter concluded: "We believe that hasty interference with the charter system of checks and balances would be dangerous, and we did not and do not recommend the proposed transfer of engineering functions so long as the general organization of the city remains as outlined in the charter." The letter came too late; the political maelstrom surrounding Ross's dismissal swallowed it.[20]

On March 9, 1931, Mayor Edwards dismissed Ross, one day before citizens were to vote on a charter amendment granting Ross his sought-after control of City Light's engineering. Preliminary polls indicated that the amendment was doomed to defeat, but vot-ers, enraged over Ross's firing, swarmed to the polls and passed it by a bare majority. Terminating Ross surprised the citizenry, but as usual in such seemingly sudden developments, there was a deep background. Initially, Mayor Edwards and Ross hit it off. In January 1928, Edwards thanked Ross "for the fine large basket of spring flowers with which you welcomed me into the mayor's office." In October of that year, Edwards appointed Ross to the committee in charge of a dedication of the new civic auditorium. For his part, Ross expressed his "deep appreciation" for "the strong support of Mayor Frank Edwards." As recently as a year before his dismissal, Ross wrote to a friend, and to Edwards himself, praising the mayor's commitment to City Light.[21]

But Ross, however unintentionally, was slowly undermining the mayor's confidence in him. Secure in his local and national standing, Ross confidently exerted his accumulated power and prestige. Some of his forays into Seattle politics and his management problems, already noted, disturbed Edwards. A stunning display of Ross's influence occurred when another one of his organizations, the Citizen's Municipal Utilities Protection League, bullied the council into placing the referendum on the March 10, 1931, ballot to vote on transferring City Light's engineering from engineering to lighting. The council earlier refused to submit the referendum, but the league and Friends of City Light began organizing a petition drive to place the measure on the ballot, and the council caved in to the pressure. Edwards, a stickler for municipal economy in the deepening national depression, opposed any measure that appeared to duplicate services and increase city staff. But there was a philosophical difference, too. Edwards was pro-business and probably became tired of what he considered Ross's ranting against the "power trust," which was, after all, a business.[22]

Thomson strode into this worsening personal situation with a complaint of his own against Ross—that the lighting superintendent was negligent in securing power line rights-of-way from the Diablo powerhouse. Therefore, Thomson's engineering department could not let contracts to build the power lines. The irony for Thomson was this: he sprang the trap that wrecked his opposition to Ross's charter change and, a short time later, destroyed Thomson's own job.

Thomson, usually careful and politically astute, would not have challenged Ross in the manner that he did, except for the fact that the lighting superintendent drove him to exasperation over issues involving the Diablo powerhouse. Several powerhouse matters had emerged

Construction of J.D. Ross's Diablo powerhouse, May 19, 1935. *Seattle Municipal Archives #14200.*

department preferred air cooled transformers because of occasional low temperatures at Diablo, while the lighting department wanted water cooled transformers because of lower cost, sturdier construction, and better performance on hot days. When Thomson conceded the issue to Ross if he would assume responsibility for water cooled transformers, Ross did so. Thomson was not so generous when Ross went to the council with a request to put City Light's own field crews to work on Diablo-related projects. Thomson reminded the council that the city charter allocated the work to his engineering department and the council agreed. Nor did he accede to Ross's request to turn over the complete operation of the Diablo Dam to Ross in advance of the engineering department's completing some auxiliary work for which it was responsible.[24]

These disagreements between two strong-willed men increased when Thomson discovered that Ross had failed to secure significant tower and right-of-way easements necessary for installing power lines. Thomson had reason to be irritated. Beginning with ordinance 51989, adopted on November 12, 1926, the council "authorized and directed" Ross to begin acquiring rights-of-way for two transmission lines from Diablo to the south substation

before Thomson came on the scene. Some were settled by then, but two key disagreements remained. First, Ross's dream of a one floor powerhouse was pure Ross, ambitious, untested by precedent, and calculated to stun visitors with a dramatic display of soaring windows and mighty generators rising far above floor level. It was also pure Ross in its disregard of such details as the placement of auxiliary equipment, the location of stairs, or the added expense of burrowing into a rock face to build the wider single-floor space required to accommodate all the needed apparatus. Not surprisingly, the engineering department favored a more conservative design—a two-floor model it considered more appropriate to a large powerhouse. Among other things, the engineering department argued for greater control of vibration, better placement of equipment, and lower costs, while its design still allowed for impressing the visitor with giant machinery. Thomson settled the dispute when he told Ross that the Diablo powerhouse would be a two-floor design, and that was that.[23]

The second contention involved whether the transformers would be air or water cooled. The engineering

Ross's grand generators, intended for dramatic effect as well as function, May 6, 1937. *Seattle Municipal Archives #14857.*

in Seattle. Other ordinances strengthened and extended Ross's authority; still others gave the corporation counsel control of portions of the work, especially for easements for the steel towers, but Ross remained in overall charge. Technically, everything should have been within the purview of Thomson's department because it involved surveying and planning for placing the huge steel towers, unquestionably engineering work. The probability is that the council saw the problem primarily as one of land acquisition. Additionally, the lighting department for years had done "practically all" its own wiring extensions within the city, at the acquiescence of the engineering department. Perhaps the council viewed transmission lines in much the same way. Nevertheless, four years after Ross was first directed to proceed, large portions of rights-of-way had yet to be secured, and some secured portions were not cleared. In another portion—where the council instructed Ross to obtain a 100-foot right of way—an inadequate 75-foot-wide strip crowded a road. Worse from an engineering point of view, the lighting department planned for uniform 600-foot spacing between towers—unnecessarily close for open ground, but sometimes too far apart over broken ground.[25]

With evidence of Ross's inattention to right-of-way matters, Thomson made a fatal move that he surely later regretted. He approached Mayor Edwards, requesting him to ask Ross for an accounting of his stewardship. On February 19, 1931, Ross answered the mayor. He conceded that not all of the right-of-way was ready, but some of the response was Ross at his worst—stating untruths and accusing others. For example, he blamed unsecured tower locations on demands coming from the engineering department, although these requests resulted from the engineering department's concern for better tower spacing. Ross identified the "original width" of right-of-way as "a width of seventy-five feet," a statement not true. He suggested that a contractor could skip over unsecured tower locations and that a temporary wooden pole line could bypass a yet-to-be cleared area. To Thomson, Ross's reply was mostly nonsense. In a statement to the Board of Public Works, of which Ross was a member, Thomson disagreed point-by-point with almost everything in the Ross letter. For example, he disputed Ross's notion that a wood pole line could readily be built around a heavily timbered area, while also pointing out that this temporary line of "more than nine miles" would consist of a more vulnerable single line. The temporary line as proposed by Ross ran as far as 4 miles away from the permanent route, in order to avoid the clearing needed to build a double line "of 7.4 miles"

on steel towers. Thomson also scoffed at Ross's belief that all of the right-of-way could be secured by September or October 1931. He pointed out that several pending condemnation suits were yet to be tried, some condemnation processes still needed to begin, one stretch of right-of-way would be hotly disputed, and that the court dockets were crowded. It would be "very injudicious to let any contract until we have the entire right of way secured," about the end of 1932, "so that we can guarantee the contractor that when he goes on the ground he will have no interference."[26]

It would be naïve to suppose that Mayor Edwards did not have a copy of Thomson's letter to the Board of Public Works, since Thomson's papers contain Ross's original letter to the mayor. Five days after Thomson wrote his letter, Edwards fired Ross. Before noting the results of that event, we must pick up the thread of Ross's effort to secure his charter amendment where we left it, at Ross's less-than-honest statement that LRBM advocated the transfer of lighting-related engineering to City Light. Ross made other statements seriously at variance with the truth. The most generous remark to make about them is that Ross was driven to desperation as opposition to his program intensified. The respected Municipal League advised against the change because Ross might use his new department to increase his use of political patronage and build a powerful political machine. Other opponents, including Edwards, Thomson, much of the business community, and most of the daily press, pointed to increased public payrolls and duplication of services. Thomson insisted that centralizing engineering not only saved money but allowed the engineering department to integrate all city engineering activities because it understood their interrelationships. Besides, he argued, if the lighting department could have its own engineering staff, nothing prevented any other public works department from requesting the same. All these arguments resonated with a tax-paying electorate suffering the increasing financial burdens of the Great Depression. Clearly, Ross had overreached himself. Whether he would have otherwise conducted an honest campaign cannot be known, but in desperation he instead made other wild charges, such as a claim that the engineering department was dominated by refugees from private power. Thomson readily refuted Ross's assertion, showing that no engineer in his department was previously employed by a private power company. Ross had the effrontery to claim that his amendment would end the duplication of engineering work, while Thomson easily demonstrated how it would increase duplication.[27]

Then Edwards fired Ross, a day before the vote on the amendment. The burden of his dismissal letter damned the delays in acquiring the transmission line right-of-way. Edwards' action was stupid at best, resurrecting his reputation for bumptiousness and confirming views that he was something less than a mental giant. Several circumstances should have given Edwards pause. For one thing, Councilman Oliver T. Erickson had fallen out with Ross over the costs of the Skagit development and had run in the city primaries as an anti-Ross candidate. He garnered enough votes to appear on the general election runoff, but two pro-Ross candidates soundly thrashed him. Whatever the outcome of Ross's amendment, Erickson appeared to be finished, as indeed he would be. For another matter, Edwards allowed emotion to rule him, not a wise situation for a politician. At a time when he needed to take a calculated look at his options, his accumulated grievances against Ross swayed him. Perhaps it is true that some businessmen at a pre-election party taunted Edwards that Ross, not Edwards, was the real power in Seattle, and that Edwards fired Ross to demonstrate where authority lay. It makes a nice story. It is doubtful, however, that anyone even as shallow as Edwards would have committed such a blunder had he not already been convinced of Ross's incompetence by such evidence as the LRBM report and Thomson's letter. In any event, Edwards' emotions blinded him to the fact that Ross's charter amendment was going to fail, if he left Ross in office. Even Ross himself believed that it was doomed.[28]

Finally, Ross's self-depiction as an embattled David contending against the "power trust" Goliath, however misleading, was persuasive to voters with no reason to be charitable toward big business during the Great Depression. On the morning of election day, the *Post-Intelligencer* quoted the deposed lighting superintendent as declaring, "the real influences behind my removal are the power trust and Councilman Oliver T. Erickson." Ross's statement reawakened suspicions of Puget Sound Light & Power, and perhaps other like utilities, spending heavily on Mayor Edwards' behalf. Such a connection remained unproven. Large anonymous funding did flow on Edwards' behalf during his successful campaign against Bertha Landes, but Edwards denied knowledge of the source or sources, and no clear evidence of its provenance ever surfaced. Besides, the "power trust"—if it was as conniving and shrewd as Ross believed—would hardly have directed Edwards to fire Ross on the eve of such a critical election. Luckily for Ross, his charges against the "power trust" did not have to be proved in

the atmosphere of shock, surprise, and anger that followed his ouster. If doomed councilman Erickson had Edwards' ear—which was unlikely—that was additional proof of Edwards' political fatuity. When Edwards dismissed Ross, an emotional electorate suddenly shed its fear of higher municipal costs and gave Ross his own engineering corps. The charter amendment passed, 27,893 to 25,911, or a majority of 1,982 of the 53,804 votes cast.[29]

Talk of recalling Mayor Edwards began at once. The mayor, accused of dismissing Ross for false charges, hardly helped his cause. Edwards asserted he would have fired Ross sooner or later, but if he had waited until after the election he would have been accused of "personal neglect" and being afraid of Ross's "political strength." Edwards scarcely would have fared better had he waited, although he would have had the satisfaction of seeing the Ross amendment fail. Recall petitions were gotten up and circulated after being modified by the corporation counsel. By the end of April, enough voters signed. Early in July, the recall forces won a legal battle when the state supreme court ruled in their favor. On July 13, voters decisively removed Edwards, 35,659 to 21,839.[30]

One more act in the drama remained to be played out, with overwhelming consequences for Thomson. Robert H. Harlin, the pint-sized and pugnacious president of the city council, had a majority of votes in hand before his formal election by the council to succeed as mayor. He let it be known that not only would he reappoint Ross, but he would make a "clean sweep" of the Board of Public Works and other appointive offices at city hall. Even though Harlin's election came on a bitterly contested council vote of 5-3, his program was a done deal. Ross "already was giving orders on City Light departmental matters" before his reinstatement. After Harlin's election, the council healed its division and unanimously approved the reappointment of Ross. A flurry of resignations from the Board of Public Works left only Thomson and one other member of the board clinging to their jobs.[31]

Thomson asserted his innocence of wrongdoing and his determination to remain in office. "I'm sitting still and waiting, tending to my own business and going ahead with my work," he told the press. "I don't know what the new administration will be or what it will do, but I'm not going to resign." Harlin was not listening. Edwards and his "business" oriented mayoral administration had been an anathema to him. Harlin was a former coal miner, president of the Washington State United Mine Workers, and an official of the state's federation of labor. On the day of his election, he told the remaining

J.D. Ross wins the fight—he sits surrounded by congratulatory flower arrangements on the day of his reinstatement, July 15, 1931. *Seattle Municipal Archives #5120.*

members of the Board of Public Works to resign or be removed by 5 p.m. on July 15. Only Thomson remained in office at the end of the day. Harlin held off dismissing Thomson, but there was no doubt of his intention to do so. On July 16, following "a short conference" that morning with Harlin, Thomson reversed his stand. "The mayor and I are on good terms but he will have my resignation today." At 75 years of age, Thomson returned to private life. [32]

℘〇℃

Thomson's departure leaves several matters to be sorted out. The first concerns the Diablo powerhouse and other engineering disagreements. From the perspective of years, it is evident that either Ross's design or Thomson's would have worked well. When it finally came on line, Ross's revised one-floor plan did the job. The engineering department's two-floor design was tried and true, especially for plants of Diablo's size, so it would have functioned effectively also. The fact that both were possible solutions does not trivialize the argument between the engineering and lighting departments because they represented different thinking about the role of design in large public works. Either of the transformer types—air or

water cooled—also worked well in various applications. [33] Similarly, there were valid arguments coming from both sides over the locus of City Light's engineering. Despite Ross's claims, the engineering department handled its job well before the charter change, just as the lighting department did its own work creditably in the aftermath of the amendment revision. The real question was whether or not the original engineering arrangement should have been disturbed on the basis of undemonstrated claims of greater efficiency and organizational coherence, and here Thomson had the better arguments.

A second issue involves what Thomson intended to achieve by dropping the right-of-way dispute into Mayor Edwards' lap. He left no surviving record of his thoughts on the matter, but some inferences may be made. The first is that he surely did not intend for Edwards to dismiss Ross. Thomson had to be aware of Ross's iconic status as the man who brought cheap electric power to the city, however much that reputation was based on the public's tolerance of his bureaucratic high-handedness and a misconception that Ross was minding the store at City Light. What Thomson most likely desired was calling mayoral attention to Ross's dilatory pursuit of the right-of-way purchases, followed by Edwards' giving

Ross a thorough talking-to. Then Ross would stop his meddling in engineering department business and devote himself to securing the right-of-way. Thomson was profoundly and deservedly alienated from Ross over the Diablo dispute, and over Ross's demand for his own engineering. Thomson may have been aggrieved, too, because Ross showed no gratitude for Thomson's appointment of him years before to the Cedar River job, the springboard for Ross's later achievements. Thomson may have been jealous of the younger man's rise to local prominence and to national fame among public power advocates. None of these probabilities and possibilities adds up to anticipating Ross's removal. Unquestionably, Thomson's life would have been easier without Ross, but he was no stranger to controversy and bureaucratic infighting. Therefore, the verdict is that he wanted Ross disciplined, but not dismissed.

But if Thomson understood Ross's place in the Seattle political scene, he certainly misread Mayor Edwards. When he requested Edwards to ask Ross for an accounting of his right-of-way stewardship, Thomson in effect aligned himself with the mayor and became hostage to Edwards' subsequent actions. Therefore, Thomson's blunder was his unwillingness to have it out with Ross in some other forum such as the city council or the public works board. Indeed, by appealing to Edwards, Thomson could appear to be going over the heads of both the council and board. On the other hand, Edwards seemed to have shed his earlier volatility and rashness; he apparently could be counted on to behave responsibly. Proper action could have involved calling Ross in and telling him to get busy on the right-of-way project and otherwise behave. Or the mayor could have confronted both Ross and Thomson, telling them to bury the hatchet, come up with a plan to settle the right-of-way business, and bring it before the public works board for transmission to the council. That Edwards instead fired Ross was evidence that Thomson did not take an accurate measure of the mayor.

A fourth issue concerns the right-of-way condemnation, the pivot of the entire episode. There is no doubt of Ross's dereliction of duty. About that, Thomson was right, but being correct was one thing, being astute about seeking a remedy was another. For his part, Ross responded to Edwards' principal charge with dissimulation. "This is absolutely wrong," he declared, "for I recently asked the mayor and city engineer to push the transmission line. It can go ahead if they are willing it should." Ross's declaration was correct as far as it went, for he had in so many words asked for the work to pro-

ceed. The lack of progress, however, begged the question of Ross's inattention to securing the right-of-way, and of letting a contract when so much remained tentative about the project's status. In an expanded statement, Ross insisted that only a "small portion" of the needed property remained in private hands. He was not telling the truth, but even with his version of reality conceded, a lot of the ground acquired had not been cleared and much of it not brought up to a new standard of a 150 foot width. The courts, he asserted, "have been giving the awards rapidly," but if that were so, why was so much as even a "small portion" of the right-of-way unavailable after almost 4½ years? Ross was on slightly firmer ground when he said that the Diablo powerhouse would not be ready for two years, and that the transmission line would require but one year to build. Diablo would not open until five years later, but again, the question was not whether the line work could proceed in a timely manner, but whether Ross had done his job. He had not. [34]

The chair of the council's utilities committee, Philip Tindall, a Ross supporter, did not help matters. He asserted that Mayor Edwards' charges were "utterly baseless" because "the acquiring of the transmission line right of way was in the hands of an agent appointed by the city council, and not by Ross, and that agent has saved the city $500,000 by his handling of the work. This, despite the fact the city engineering department has thrown monkey wrenches into the machinery." Tindall was correct when he said that an agent (actually, two agents) was appointed by the council, for neither Ross nor anyone else had the authority to appoint people to act for the city in land acquisition. The 1926 ordinance's wording was different from what Tindall remembered, for it employed the agents "under contract to assist the Superintendent of Lighting, and under his direction and supervision to negotiate for the purchase of the property and property rights" needed. Thus Ross was still in charge and the agents were responsible to him. Concerning Tindall's claim about the engineering department throwing "monkey wrenches," only engineering's request for flexible spacing of line towers seems to fit this comment. Far from being a hindrance, it would have made the finished transmission line cheaper and safer. [35]

Harlin's showdown with Thomson remains to be considered. Harlin was "surprised and shocked" when Edwards dismissed Ross. He pointed to City Light's national reputation and called Ross's dismissal without a hearing "very unfair." [36] Since Thomson precipitated Edwards' action, Harlin could not have been much pleased with the city engineer. He may or may not have known about Thomson's opposition in earlier years to eight-hour daily limits on city construction work, or Thomson's more recent, if failed, attempt to reduce many city employee salaries. If he did, this knowledge would have strengthened his unfavorable view. Whether Harlin was justified in forcing out all of Edwards' appointees is another matter. His decision appears as emotion-laden as Edwards' firing of Ross, the significant difference being that Harlin had the support of the council and probably much of the electorate. Had Thomson resisted Harlin's request for his resignation and been fired, it is unlikely that any public groundswell of protest would have followed. In other words, Harlin could safely apply a different standard to Thomson's dismissal than he invoked during the Edwards-Ross brouhaha. He could fire Thomson without the "investigation" and hearing that he considered necessary before Edwards removed Ross because there was not much opposition to this course. Thomson could take little comfort in the outcome. He was forced back on his own resources at an advanced age when his only recourse was to return to consulting. His age and the worsening economy made steady independent employment increasingly out of reach. Before considering Thomson's consulting jobs, a look at his other major city engineering activities in 1930–31 is in order, the beginning business of the next chapter.

NOTES

1. For RHT's record of appointment matters, see RHT diary, August 18–December 13, 1930, 1602-2, box 2, folder 12, RHT Papers, UW. See also *Times*, August 20, 1930. For an analysis of the Edwards campaign, see Sandra Haarsager, *Bertha Knight Landes of Seattle* (Norman: University of Oklahoma Press, 1994), 207–28. For Edwards's campaign and actions, see Berner, *Seattle, 1921–1940*, 103–13.

2. RHT diary June 2, 1928, 1602-2, box 2, folder 1, RHT Papers. For the quotation, see *P-I*, June 3, 1928, and, for resignation and new appointment, *P-I*, June 5. For Barkhuff's qualifications and opposition to him, see *P-I*, June 7 and June 23. For his confirmation, see *P-I*, June 26.

3. On Edwards, see Berner, *Seattle: 1921–1940*, 121–26. For quotations, see *Times*, August 30, 1930.

4. Population figures are in Berner, *Seattle, 1900–1920*, 62; and Berner, *Seattle, 1921–1940*, 205. Figures cited here allow for some undercounting. For the physical development of Seattle, see Phelps, *Public Works in Seattle*, for example, 102–7. For demographic development, see Calvin F. Schmid, *Social Trends in Seattle* (Seattle: University of Washington Press, 1944), chart 13, p. 65; chart 14, p. 73; chart 26, p. 98; and chart 46, p. 132. Compare Berner, *Seattle, 1900–1920*, tables on 28, 29, with Berner, *Seattle, 1921–1940*, table 7, p. 170, for industrial growth. Tonnage figures are in Berner, *Seattle, 1900–1920*, chart 152; and Berner, *Seattle, 1921–1940*, table 5, p. 166. For unemployment see Berner, *Seattle, 1921–1940*, 16–18, 293–94.

5. Wesley Arden Dick, "Visions of Abundance: The Public Power Crusade in the Pacific Northwest in the Era of J.D. Ross and the New Deal" (PhD diss., University of Washington, 1973), 233. RHT to Ross, 3 December 1912, 89/1, box 5, book 12, RHT Papers, UW. RHT diary, September 28, 1914, 1602-2, box 1, folder 8, RHT Papers, UW. For socializing, see RHT diaries, July 26, 1913; October 18, 1914; August 27, 1916, 1602-2, box 1, folder 8, and March 6, 1918, 1602-2, box 1, folder 9, RHT Papers, UW. There is no mention of socializing after 1918.

6. Paul C. Pitzer, *Building the Skagit: A Century of Upper Skagit Valley History, 1870–1970* (Portland: Galley Press, 1978), 31, 44–45, 59.

7. Dick, "Visions of Abundance," 243–52; and David E. Nye, *Electrifying America: Social Meanings of a New Technology, 1880–1940* (Cambridge, MA: MIT Press, 1990, paperbound ed. 1992), 1–28, 185–286.

8. Nye, *Electrifying America*, 168–84.

9. Ibid., for quotations 179. See also 172–76, 179–80, 182, and 261 for the advantages of private companies and their arguments against public power. See also Dick, "Genesis of City Light," 167.

10. Sparks, "J.D. Ross," 140; Dick, "Visions of Abundance," 255, 260–61; the *Annual Report* of the lighting department for 1925 and 1928; and, for quotation, a brochure advertising Diablo Dam, 1930. See also Linda Nash, "The Changing Experience of Nature: Historical Encounters with a Northwest River," *Journal of American History* 86 (March 2000): 1624–27.

11. For first quotation, see Nash, "Changing Experience of Nature," 1625. For second quotation, see the Diablo Dam brochure. For third and fourth quotations see Dick, "Visions of Abundance," 255. See also Sparks, "J.D. Ross," 9, 140–60. For Norris and Roosevelt, see Dick, "Visions of Abundance," 254, 264, 265–73; and *P-I*, March 10, 1931.

12. Sparks, "J.D. Ross," 128–32, 162. Ross, "A Discussion of the Report of Lybrand, Ross Bros. and Montgomery Concerning the Department of Lighting, Seattle," January 30, 1930, in 33-1, box 127, folder 22, LDC, UW. An unsigned, undated analysis of Ross's discussion is in 89/2, box 4, folder 4, RHT Papers, UW. It is not written in RHT's style, although he used it in the battle with Ross over City Light's engineering amendment. See Berner *Seattle, 1921–1940*, for trucks, 126; and for department store, 119.

13. Sparks, "J.D. Ross," 110; and analysis of the Ross's discussion in 89/2, box 4, folder 4, RHT Papers, UW. For Ross's indifference to others' problems, see Thomas J. Sheehan to Frank Edwards, 30 April 1930, 33-1, box 87, folder 7, LDC, UW. For blaming others, see Sparks, "J.D. Ross," 164; and Ross, "Present Status of City Light," January 7, 1931, written for the *Seattle Star*, 33-1, box 87, folder 5, LDC, UW. For construction problems, see W.D. Barkhuff to Ross, 1 April 1930, 33-1, box 87, folder 15, LDC, UW.

14. For quotations, in order, see Sparks, "J.D. Ross," 110; Dick, "Genesis of City Light," 186; Nash, "Changing Experience of Nature," 1627; Dick, "Genesis of City Light," 131; and Sparks, "J.D. Ross," 169. For Cedar Lake facilities, see "Unit Number 5 at Cedar Falls," no author or date, in 89/2, box 4, folder 4, RHT Papers, UW. There is some ambiguity in the figures, so the lesser figure is used. Elsewhere RHT listed the cost at "About $900,000.00," RHT to Members of the Utilities Committee, 6 November 1920, 33-1, box 95, folder 16, LDC, UW.

15. RHT to Ross, 4 May 1928; and RHT to Ross, 25 October 1929, 33-1, box 95, folder 16, LCD, UW. "Talk of Mr. R.H.

Thomson given at Diablo Dam, August 27, 1930 at the time of its dedication," 1602-2, box 3, folder 5, RHT Papers, UW.

16. RHT, "Talk," note 15. Ross was present and spoke, *Times*, August 28, 1930. For engineering department cooperation, see W.C. Morse to Ross, 7 May 1927, 33-1, box 85, folder 9; W.D. Barkhuff to Ross, 6 December 1928, 33-1, box 85, folder 12; and Barkhuff to Ross, 26 February 1929, 33-1, box 85, folder 13, LDC, UW. For Ross's desire for control, see his annual reports for 1929 and 1931, 33-1, box 124, folder 7, LDC, UW.

17. Berner, *Seattle, 1921–1940*, 119–20. Lybrand, Ross Brothers, & Montgomery (LRBM) to Mayor and City Council, 22 January 1930, 33-1, box 121, folder 7, LDC, UW.

18. LRBM, note 17.

19. "Discussion," note 12.

20. For Ross's claim, see City of Seattle, Department of Lighting, *Annual Report: Year Ending December 31, 1929*, 7, obviously prepared after the LRBM report. For quotation, see LRBM report, note 17. For LBM letter, see LRBM to Mayor and City Council, 9 March 1931, 33-1, box 87, folder 8, LDC, UW. For Ross's dismissal, see Edwards to Glen Smith, 9 March 1931, 33-1, box 87, folder 8, LDC, UW.

21. Edwards to Ross, 11 January 1928; and Edwards to Ross, 29 October 1928, 33-1, box 87, folder 2, LDC, UW. For Ross quotation, see City of Seattle, Department of Lighting, *Annual Report: Year Ending December 31, 1928*, 33-1, box 124, folder 7, LDC, UW. For Ross's 1930 praise, see Sparks, "J.D. Ross," 169–70.

22. Sparks, "J.D. Ross," 161–81; and Berner, *Seattle, 1921–1940*, 128–29.

23. The interdepartmental and other correspondence on the Diablo powerhouse is voluminous. Key letters on powerhouse design are Ross to RHT, 23 September 1930; unsigned 1 October 1930 memorandum on Ross letter, both in 89/2, box 4, folder 3, RHT Papers, UW; and RHT to Ross, 27 October 1930, 33-1, box 85, folder 16, LDC, UW.

24. For transformers, see Ross to RHT, 13 December 1920, 89/2, box 4, folder 3, RHT Papers, UW. For field crews, see RHT to Ross, 1 November 1930, 33-1, box 85, folder 16, LDC, UW. For the dam, see RHT to Ross, 10 December 1930, 33-1, box 85, folder 16, LDC, UW.

25. All ordinances are dated from the mayor's signature. They are 51989, 56187, 60309, and 60428, SMA. For quotations, see the unsigned analysis of the Ross discussion, note 12. See also the analysis, "Status of Seattle-Diablo Transmission Line Right-of-Way," n.d. but 1930, 89/2, box 4, folder 1, RHT Papers, UW.

26. Ross to Edwards, 19 February 1931; and RHT to Board of Public Works, 4 March 1931, 89/2, box 4, folder 4, RHT Papers, UW.

27. Sparks, "J.D. Ross," 161–65; and RHT radio interview, station KJR, 7:15 to 7:30, March 9, 1931, 89/2, box 4, folder 4, RHT Papers, UW.

28. For Erickson, see Sparks, "J.D. Ross," 66.

29. For quotation, see *P-I*, March 10, 1931. For the amendment, see *P-I*, March 11, 1931.

30. For the modification, see *P-I*, March 29, 1931. For the campaign, see Berner, *Seattle, 1921–1940*, 297–300; and Sparks, "J.D. Ross," 170–81.

31. For "clean sweep" quotation, see *Times*, July 14, 1931. The *P-I* forecast a "complete housecleaning at city hall," July 14, 1931. For "giving orders" quotation, see *Times*, July 14, 1931.

32. For RHT quotation, see *Times*, July 14, 1931. For Harlin, see *Times*, July 14, 1931. For RHT's resignation, *Times*, July 15, 1931.

33. J.E. Atkinson to Ross, 18 December 1930, 33-1, box 102, folder 2, LDC, UW.

34. For first quotation, *Seattle Star*, March 9, 1931. For expanded statement, *P-I*, March 10, 1931.

35. For quotation, see *P-I*, March 10, 1931. For ordinance quotation, see 52129, approved December 9, 1926, SMA.

36. *P-I*, March 10, 1931.

An ungraded section of Denny Hill towers above the Sibbella Court apartments in this 1929 view along Fifth Avenue, the eastern edge of the original Denny regrade. The massif's obstructive presence negatively impacted real estate values and hindered orderly residential and commercial development. *Seattle Municipal Archives #3582.*

13

More Engineering and the Later Years

For Thomson, returning to the post of city engineer in 1930 was similar to sitting down in a theater during the middle of a movie. He did not use that metaphor but conceded as much when saying he would only gradually insert himself into daily operations. He needed to retrace the projects and activities in front of him to their beginning and to understand the planned ending point. The most demanding and frustrating proved to be the Diablo imbroglio, but Denny Hill regrade No. 2 was almost as exasperating. Thomson had had nothing to do with the planning of the second take-down of Denny Hill; the contract "was awarded late in 1928, calling for completion in the fall of 1930." The projected completion date proved to be much too optimistic.[1]

Understanding Thomson's problems with regrade No. 2 begins with a brief look back at Denny Hill regrade No. 1. That effort involved roughly 24 blocks, from Pine Street at the southeast to Cedar Street on the northwest, and from approximately Second Avenue on the southwest to Fifth Avenue to the northeast (see Denny Hill regrade map in chapter 7). Thus, the first regrade occurred in an awkwardly angled street pattern, where the rectilinear block pattern coming up from the downtown commercial district broke to follow the curve of Elliott Bay, shifting from north-northwest and south-southeast to northwest-southeast. The break point was between Pine and Virginia streets on the south. At the north, another directional break came at Denny Way, with the streets shifting to a direct north-south pattern. So far as regrade No. 2 was concerned, this left about 20 blocks north of Denny Way to be lowered in the north-south street grid, with the heavier work south of Denny Way involving some 17 blocks of the northwest to southeast streets. These 17 blocks formed a rough triangle with Fifth Avenue as a base on the southwest, and with Denny Way and Westlake Avenue forming a northeast-pointing apex. What all this meant in a nutshell was that Seattle's growing automobile traffic north of downtown had to shoulder around the remnant cordillera of Denny Hill, using Westlake Avenue to run north toward Lake Union or to turn east on Denny Way or some other convenient street. A lesser traffic stream ran through the first regrade or to the west of it.[2]

This created undesirable situations from three different perspectives. The first was grounded in the fact that, originally, a regrade of the entire Denny Hill area was deemed too expensive to be undertaken all at once. The first regrade was therefore not necessarily expected to be the last and, so long as uncertainty about the future remained, its property "values slumped to nearly nothing," and "the remainder of the hill became a very cheap and undesirable residence section." A "cheap and undesirable" area close to downtown was not in itself new to any American city, but the remnant's rugged status precluded the hope of any real urban improvement for the time being. Second, a real estate analysis blamed the existing regrade's halting redevelopment and stagnant property values on the "undesirable" and less-than-sightly unregraded section on the east. The first regrade was supposed to improve traffic communication with the developing sections to the north and to some extent it did, but with the heavier traffic moving to the east around the ungraded portion of the hill, the anticipated benefits were only partly realized. The analysis, however, did not consider the fact that booming Seattle was deconcentrating, with sizeable retail sections developing some distance to the north and east of the city core. Therefore, the downtown retail section had already practically reached its northern limit.[3]

The third situation involved the fears of downtown Second Avenue merchants who saw the retail district edging east toward Third or even Fourth avenues. For this they blamed the eastward flow of traffic. They demanded a street cut through the first regrade to provide direct access between their First and Second avenue area, Lake Union, and districts beyond. They refused to admit that Seattle's attenuated shopping district bred its own inconveniences, and that the commercial district's expansion of a block or two east was in response to consumer desires for a more compact retail core. In the nature of things, a north-south thoroughfare slicing through the directionally canted streets of the regrade

Reduction of Denny Hill adjacent to the Sibbella Court apartments on Fifth Avenue between Lenora and Blanchard, October 16, 1929. *Seattle Municipal Archives #3689.*

in the old and new regrade districts. Furthermore, few people in the prosperous 1920s foresaw the most blighting effect of all—the Great Depression.

When Thomson took his post in August 1930, regrade No. 2 already was far behind schedule. In theory, it should not have been. As its apologist, real estate agent V.V. Tarbill, explained, matters should have gone smoothly and quickly because "one contract" included "everything, removal of dirt, paving of streets and sidewalks, sewers, water-mains, and even cluster lights for street lighting." According to Tarbill, this enlightened planning arrangement contrasted with the old days when all the contracts "were handled separately in the usual haphazard fashion," resulting in delays and retarded redevelopment. The trouble with this new scheme was that the general contractor holding the "one contract" parceled out the specialized work to subcontractors, who were responsible to the general contractor for earth removal, street and sidewalk paving, and other improvements. The arrangement was typical of large construction projects in which the general contractor functioned as the supervisor, coordinator, integrator, and continuing inspector of the subcontractors' work.[5]

would have produced numerous tiny triangular blocks, each difficult to develop and producing its own traffic nightmare. Because of the disruptions that would be caused by this potential development, landowners in the first regrade successfully fought the cut-through street. It probably was just as well, because the result would have choked First and Second avenues with still more traffic, to no benefit of the merchants. What everyone could agree on, though, was that the Denny Hill remnant should come down. So it did. The immediate result was that the low-income residents of the blighted residential area had to move.

As things turned out, there was no significant retail development in either the first or second regrade districts, no significantly better street connections with the northern parts of the city, and no halt to the gradual incorporation of Third and Fourth avenues into the retail district.[4] The results did not occur as any of the proponents of regrade No. 2 hoped. Had they analyzed their situation more thoughtfully, perhaps they could have foreseen some of the difficulties in making improvements

The conveyor system and a shovel operating south from Fifth Avenue and Battery Street, May 17, 1929. *Seattle Municipal Archives #3429.*

So far so good. But the downside was that the Seattle engineering department could not intervene directly with a subcontractor who was falling down on the job; the city itself only had contracted with the general contractor. Therefore, a city sidewalk inspector could only report poor concrete work to his superiors—he lacked authority to correct the problem on the spot. The engineering department could complain to the general contractor, who then could discuss the problem with the subcontractor. The general contractor remained ultimately responsible and could suffer severely if the city refused to grant him extensions of time or withheld release and final payment. On the other hand, the general contractor, if pressed too hard, could throw up the contract and sue, leaving the city with an unfinished project and an administrative mess.

The issue was not just theoretical, as one example illustrates. The subcontractor responsible for disposing of spoil was operating self-dumping scows especially built for the project. Each of these giant scows held 400 cubic yards of dirt and debris coming off the end of a conveyor belt. Then a tug towed a loaded scow into Elliott Bay. At the designated dumping location, tanks on one side of the vessel were opened to flood with seawater, intentionally unbalancing the scow. It then flipped over, dumping its load. The momentum of the roll-over pushed the tanks high out of the water so that they drained. The underside of the scow, now on top, was a duplicate of the section just emptied and underneath. The scow was now ready for the return trip. While the towing, dumping, and returning of one scow was underway, a second identical scow received its load from the end of the conveyor system. When the first scow arrived for reloading, a tug towed the second scow into the bay to the designated dumping spot. That, at least, was the way the process was supposed to work. [6] It did not always work that way.

The subcontractor took advantage of nights and foggy times to dump the scows too close to shore, rather than spend 43 minutes traveling three-eighths to one-half mile into the bay and back. Dumping inshore brought protests from the Port of Seattle and the Army Corps of Engineers. A month after he took office, Thomson warned the general contractor to stop the illegal dumping or the city would put an inspector on each scow, at the general contractor's expense. Thomson's threat was extralegal, but apparently ended the practice. [7]

The general contractor could have done more to handle this and other subcontracting issues, but he had his own problems. The schedule called for work to begin on September 25, 1928, but various difficulties

Denny Hill regrade No. 2 was supposed to be an organizational and technological advance over the first regrade. Two self-dumping scows hauled spoil away from an extensive conveyor belt system built for the project. Thomson returned to the office of city engineer after arrangements for the regrade were made, but he vigorously enforced dumping rules after close inshore overturning of some loads violated them. *Seattle Municipal Archives #4074, 4076, 4077, 4078, 4080, 4081.*

delayed serious efforts until May 1929. The assessment roll on which the contractor's work depended was not completed until December 31, 1929. A cold snap in January 1930 and high winds interfered with scow dumping in the bay. The urban development built up around the remnant of Denny Hill caused the greatest difficulties. Some hotels and apartments dotted the first regrade area, even if the overall realty development there disappointed early expectations. Consequently, the narrow confines of the cordillera in regrade No. 2, surrounded as it was by retail and commercial buildings, prevented heavy blasting, or the use of noisy, chuffing, grinding steam shovels and narrow gauge steam engines and cars. Sluicing also was unacceptable, since spoil from the earlier regrade already filled hollows and covered nearby tidelands. The only solution for disposing regrade No. 2's detritus was to deposit it in Elliott Bay, the task of the self-dumping scows. The conveyor belt

system to the scows was installed in place of impossibly noisy trains, but this required a break-in period and failed now and then. Four electric shovels, quieter than the steam variety, seemed to serve well, but nevertheless were supplemented by one steam shovel and, for a time, a gas-electric shovel. Furthermore, the widening of Sixth Avenue and the lowering of historic Denny Park were not part of the original plan and adjustments had to be made to include them. Heavy rains, laggard house removal, unanticipated strata of material difficult to excavate, and other problems meant that the work was not completed until August 1931.[8]

Meanwhile the Great Depression struck. The worldwide economic collapse would practically end commercial construction for the rest of the 1930s (as did World War II in the early 1940s, when only the most essential construction occurred). Property values in both regrades slumped or stagnated at best, blighting the hopes of

Before and after views of the Denny Hill regrade No. 2, completed in late summer 1931. Note the Sibbella Court apartments at center left in both photographs. *Seattle Municipal Archives #139483.*

most property owners. The losses would be poignant because they mocked the inflated values of the late 1920s. To quote realtor Tarbill's article again, lots on the Denny Hill remnant "worth $2,000 to $4,000 before the [second] regrade was imminent, with no buyers in sight, have sold for from $20,000 to $40,000 a lot since the regrade was assured." He cited a large lot on Fifth Avenue across from the second regrade that "sold for $65,000 before the regrade was a certainty." After regrade No. 2 "was assured," the lot turned over four more times, rising in value from $135,000 to $200,000, a soaring index "of what the average real-estate buyer thinks as to the probable effect on values of Regrade Number Two." Tarbill also recounted the story of what eventually became his own property on Third Avenue between Virginia and Lenora streets in the first regrade. In 1897, the then house and lot at this location went for $3,500. During the first regrade the lot sold for $10,000, later for $25,000. Tarbill paid $50,000 for the improved lot for his real estate office in 1927. "Late in 1929, an offer of $75,000 was refused"—Tarbill should have taken the money and run. [9]

As far as Thomson was concerned, he only felt responsible for keeping the vast project moving along as best he could. (When he came into office, regrade No. 2 already was well underway and he would resign more than a month before its completion.) There is no doubt, however, that he favored the second regrade. He had supported carefully planned public works in and around Seattle all his life, even when costs outran the city's short-term ability, or willingness, to pay for them. In 1929, for example, he submitted one of the several schemes presented for regrading Yesler Hill to reduce its height. He had a personal interest in lowering Yesler Hill because the Jackson and Dearborn regrades left his Yesler Way house perched high above the new grades, cutting it off from easy access to the south part of the city. The Department of Public Works did not accept his proposal, probably because of its high cost and conventional

Construction of the Aurora Street bridge, March 6, 1931, looking north across Union Bay to the Fremont district. Woodland Park lay at and beyond the crest of the hill. *Seattle Municipal Archives #4819.*

handling of slopes by a grid street pattern only slightly modified. In any case, the adopted plan proved too expensive for the presumed benefits. In 1942 the city council repealed the 1930 ordinance permitting the Yesler Hill regrade, formally killing a program already doomed by the depression and World War II. [10]

Thomson inherited another controversial project—the northerly extension of Aurora Avenue on a high bridge over Lake Union. The crossing, some two blocks east of the ship canal leading west to the Hiram M. Chittenden Locks, was not in itself a matter of much debate, but its path north of the bridge certainly was. A straight line north led to Woodland Park, an aptly named preserve of almost 188 acres of dense foliage. The engineering department chose a straight line slicing through the park, dividing it approximately in half. The council approved this direct route, but dissident citizens garnered enough signatures to place a referendum before the voters on the November 1930 ballot. The dissidents argued for a northeasterly diagonal from the Lake Union vicinity to Stone Way, thence to West Green Lake Way. Their proposed route would lead around Green Lake, located adjacent to the northeast side of Woodland Park. This route, they believed, would be less desecrating to park land, prevent a steep incline between the bridge and the park, and be less expensive. On the other hand, proponents of the city's original plan, Thomson included, believed the direct route would save travel time and distance, be more easily built, be safer, do no significant damage to an "unimportant" part of the park, and avoid the real estate jobbing certain to follow when cutting a major street through a residential area. After a lengthy and bitter debate, the direct route won, 37,374 votes to 29,087. [11]

With the passage of years, it is not difficult to judge the wisdom of building the direct route. While Aurora Avenue indeed bisects Woodland, it divides the park roughly into the zoo and mostly passive recreation on the west, and athletic fields and passive recreation to the east. Foot bridges across Aurora Avenue appear little used,

Aurora Avenue in Woodland Park, March 10, 1936. *Seattle Municipal Archives #30749.*

since park patrons seem to prefer to approach and enjoy the park on one side or the other. The drive through Woodland's trees also provides a restful break from Aurora Avenue's otherwise intensely urban portions. The drive—from the bridge, through the park, and for some distance north—provides some two miles of stoplight-free movement.

Regarding the proposed alternate that the dissidents supported, a northeast diagonal from Aurora Avenue to Stone Way was built as an exit street. This eventually helped make Stone Way a commercial street from the diagonal north to the southeast edge of Woodland Park. Had a main Stone Way route been built, the ¾ of a mile north on Stone Way from the diagonal portion would have required four stoplights. Stone Way would have been steeply graded, with expensive over- and under-passes, plus another stoplight on Green Lake Way North before meeting West Green Lake Way. Heavier traffic on West Green Lake Way would have degraded the environment around the south end of Green Lake more than the existing, less used, but still busy street. Of course, nobody on either side of the 1930 debate foresaw the huge increase in traffic of later years, or an elongated, widened Aurora Avenue extending through Seattle's expanded city limits and far beyond. From the perspective of later years, the cut through Woodland Park was justified.

ॐ

Rightly or not, Thomson lost the city engineering job in July 1931. By then, private consulting work had dwindled due to the depression. Most jobs coming his way around this time were minor, such as reservoir work from 1929 into 1932 for the town of Cle Elum east of the Cascades, a two-day court appearance for

Standard Oil in 1933, and a day in court for the Great Northern in 1934.[12] The bread and butter of his later years came from three government sources—a lawsuit by the Spokane, Portland & Seattle Railway against the State of Washington, work for the Washington Toll Bridge Authority, and efforts on the part of the Joint Commission on Inter-County River Improvement. The decades long inter-county flood control work, between King and Pierce counties, proved the most important for Thomson.

Twisting rivers lay to the south and east of Seattle, running through relatively flat terrain with few natural barriers against damaging freshets sweeping down from the Cascades. The main streams in this sparsely settled, but economically significant, area included the Puyallup and the interconnected White/Green/Duwamish river systems, which coursed through farming country and past small towns before flowing into Puget Sound. The White River, "a rather straggling stream," flowed north in often shallow channels to join the Green River, while the Green itself emptied into the Duwamish River, and the Duwamish debouched into Elliott Bay at what later was called the East and West Waterways on either side of Harbor Island. Stockmen and farmers tampered with the White River from time to time, but without changing its basic course. The nearby Puyallup River flowed northerly in its own twists and bends, until running westward to Puget Sound at Tacoma. This arrangement of stream flows survived until November 1906, when heavy rains plus a warm Chinook wind melted snow in the Cascades, sending water, mud, gravel, and trees thundering down the White River until they blocked a northern turn in the river. A lake grew at this point, then water broke into a small southerly branch, locally called the Stuck River, with the new torrent crashing into the Puyallup River near the town of Sumner. Silt from the redirected White River raised 1,000 acres of swamp land by as much as five feet. Once the flow met the Puyallup River, it "wrought great damage all along the Puyallup down to Tacoma," a straight line distance of about eight miles.[13]

The mischievous White River became a political issue because its lower reach, formerly in King County, had changed course and flowed through Pierce County after 1906. Neither county wanted to deal with it and its potential for future destruction. The river, indifferent to political boundaries, posed an ever-present threat of returning to its old channel in King County or cutting still another path, causing further damage. Years of wrangling over the responsibility for handling the White and lower Puyallup followed, during which time the

The untamed White River in 1912. *Seattle Municipal Archives #5938.*

rivers remained relatively quiescent. In 1913 the state legislature enabled both counties to deal with the White and lower Puyallup situation. Early in 1914, the counties contracted to have the lower White River contained in its present course, angling northwest, turning south, and then emptying into the Puyallup. To reach that goal, a later annual report noted, "bank protection should be so strengthened as to permanently confine the waters to the channel and prevent inundation of adjoining lands." King County, free of the menace of flooding, agreed to pay 60 percent of all costs; Pierce County, 40 percent. The commissioners of the Inter-County River Improvement Commission undertook the work.[14]

According to a later annual report, "at the very beginning little thought was given to the difficulties which would arise" in keeping the White River within its banks. This insouciant attitude reigned briefly, despite the prescient words of Hiram Chittenden—"It is easy enough to <u>assume</u> that the work to be done will be final and will solve the problem," he wrote in 1913. "That has never been the case anywhere else and it will not be here. Whatever fund is raised," he further cautioned, "it is bound to fall below what is really necessary, and the certainty of breaks in the work now and then must be accepted." The joint board at first believed the main White River would take care of itself, while they concen-

trated on confining its redirected lower course within the new channel, and taking the kinks out of the crooked lower Puyallup. When dredging was completed, the lower Puyallup was shortened by 1.64 miles to a little less than 6 miles in length. But the commissioners then discovered they no longer had the luxury of having stable ancient river banks, sealed by sediment and thus resistant to washouts. The freshly cut course of the White River and the newly dredged Puyallup River now flowed faster, knifing into the "raw" banks of "loose earth," carrying large quantities of silt and gravel that settled out lower down, raising the stream bed at those points, and threatening to overflow crumbling banks. Within a year, the commissioners began reinforcing the banks, but the new river courses proved no more tractable than the old.[15]

Engineers tried but failed to contain the streams. First, they employed concrete slabs along the most vulnerable banks, but floods in 1917 and 1919 destroyed the work. The rushing water undercut their slabs and at the same time washed them out from behind. The slabs lost footing, fell into the raging water, and the freshly exposed earthen banks caved in. The concrete slabs in the river beds—now no more than so much junk—had to be cleared out later. As early as the summer of 1919, the commissioners hired Thomson to consult with their chief engineer. Thomson suggested deeper footings and higher walls, plus rock riprap and brush mattresses placed alongside and below the "toe" of each slab, to prevent flood water from undercutting the slabs and rolling over their tops. During his tenure from 1919 through 1929, Thomson worked as a consultant with the chief engineer to improve the survival rate of the concrete barriers, but the efforts could not cure the problem. They also built retards of brush and log cribbing at critical points out from the banks of the White River to force the recalcitrant stream into its center line and keep it there. The devastating 1933–34 flood wrecked "a great number" of the retards, leaving remnants "standing in the middle of the stream when the river washed behind them," a result "far more damaging than had there been nothing there at all." Other methods of holding the banks were tried, with no more success.[16]

Thomson left the project at the end of 1929, but returned as consulting engineer in 1933. By then the joint commission was convinced of Chittenden's observation of 20 years before—that the available funds could never entirely contain the river. On June 6, 1933, the joint board resolved that only a storage dam upstream on the White River would handle the problem. The flood of 1933–34, perhaps the worst since Euroamericans had occupied the area, lent urgency and enthusiasm to the solution—the Mud Mountain Dam. On July 28, 1934, Thomson noted in his diary that he addressed a "crowd on reasons for Mud Mountain Dam. Well received." The project was not so well received by the Army Corps of Engineers, reluctant to commit funding on a cost-benefit basis during the depression. Congress approved the program in 1936, but construction challenges and World War II slowed the work. Partially completed in 1946, the dam staved off serious flood damage that year. Mud Mountain Dam was finished in 1948, and has worked well since. In 1950 the Corps of Engineers completed still more strengthening and the levying of a portion of the lower Puyallup.[17]

Thomson's role in the effort to contain the rivers proved significant. He suggested substantial improvements in the revetment-style concrete banks, which worked well enough, even during floods. The retards were less successful, but there was no way of knowing whether they would work without trying them. In any case, as Chittenden forecast, there was never enough money to do everything that needed to be done. Thomson suffered frustration in failing to solve the problem of the maverick White River. Engineering was rarely an absolute success, and, in this case, his work pointed toward as final a solution as it was in the power of mortals to achieve.

℘℧℆

While Thomson struggled with the recalcitrant White River, a drama unfolded some 80 miles east of Vancouver in tunnel number five on the Spokane, Portland & Seattle Railway (SP&S) route along the north side of the Columbia. Shortly after 5 a.m., January 10, 1936, a five man powder crew working on a state highway tunnel site between the SP&S railroad tunnel and the Columbia River was ready to begin work. The winter morning was damp, chilly, and dark, except for the beams from their flashlights as they walked to the west portal of SP&S tunnel five.[18]

If they reflected on the start of the day, the five could have thought it eerie—the darkness, the recent hard rains turning the work area into slippery rocks and mud, and the deep cold water of the Columbia flowing unseen only a few yards away. They probably did not reflect, for it was a workday like any other. They were fortunate to have jobs in the midst of a severe economic depression.

Entering the SP&S tunnel's west portal and walking east was the quickest and indeed the only reasonable way to reach their work site at the east end of the highway tunnel, a burrow laying roughly parallel to the railroad tunnel, with the Columbia lapping on the other side. Walking along, they heard and saw "a considerable drip" of water coming through part of the railroad tunnel's arched ceiling. A piece of concrete about a foot long lay on the tracks. More water and concrete spalls dropped while they walked. Believing a portion of the ceiling was collapsing, the foreman sent a crewman back through the tunnel to alert the railroad watchman. Another man returned to warn the foreman of the construction company. Meanwhile, more water and concrete came tumbling down, accompanied by cracking and rumbling sounds. Half an hour after the powder crew first observed the structural failure, part of the roof and its overburden crashed to the tracks in two successive caveins, filling the western part of the railroad tunnel. About 65 feet of ceiling had fallen, leaving some 200 feet of tunnel intact. There were no deaths or injuries. Westbound trainmen, notified of the danger, brought their engine and cars to a halt outside the tunnel's eastern portal. Frantic crews worked 11 days to unblock the tunnel. Soon, trains were diverted on improvised tracks through the highway tunnel, while the SP&S labored to rebuild the roof of tunnel five, which would be out of service for four months.[19]

The contractor's bonding company sent Thomson to the scene for a full report. Then almost 80 years old, the doughty engineer arrived at the site only five days after the collapse. Tunnel five and the adjacent highway tunnel were located near Underwood in the Columbia River gorge at a massive promontory called Owl Point. From some vantage points, the basalt formation resembled the head and body of the nocturnal bird. Little did Thomson realize he would visit the scene four times and be directly involved in issues surrounding the collapse for almost 2½ years. On Thomson's first visit, he "entered a scene of great nervous activity." Steam shovels, bulldozers, and laborers from the railroad and the highway contractor swarmed over and around the tunnels. They were cleaning debris and throwing down rocks, fallen trees, and soil from the steep hill above, trying desperately to impose a low angle of repose on the bluff to prevent another slide. They also were working frantically to finish the highway tunnel so that trains could detour through it. Thomson questioned anyone he could in an effort to understand the cause of the collapse, but few of the workers responded to someone they probably considered a nosy, querulous, white-bearded old man. Nor was anyone willing to stop working so that some elderly busy body could examine the undisturbed evidence of the tunnel collapse. Nevertheless Thomson, with an agility belying his age, clambered around, above, below, and inside the tunnel to get at the reason why the ceiling failed. He needed three more visits totaling four days to get his information. At least four other engineers and two photographers also visited the site, either with Thomson or independently.[20]

The investigations and analyses eliminated three possibilities for the implosion—exhaust gasses from steam locomotives, vibrations from trains, or blasting at the site of the highway tunnel, some 100 feet or so from the railroad's burrow. That left two probable causes. One was poor construction of the tunnel arch itself, causing a gradual weakening over the years and eventual failure. The other was the north wall of a deep cut west of the western portal of the highway tunnel. This north wall, closest to the rail tunnel, was about 15 feet at its deepest. Any movement of the north wall could destabilize the high bluff up to its top, causing a massive slide and pulling support away from the railway tunnel's south wall and roof. If the tunnel itself were poorly built, that would be the railroad's problem, irrespective of any highway construction activity. If, however, the highway contractor dug out a cut that buckled, leaving the bluff vulnerable

to a slide, then the railroad had a grievance against the state or its contractor.[21]

Thomson argued that the weakened ceiling of the railroad tunnel caused the collapse. He found, at the point of its failure, that there was no rock over the tunnel, only loose material admitting water into the ceiling. The ceiling could have held if well constructed, but in fact the concrete arch was secured only by rotting timber. The straight walls of the tunnel had cured before the arched ceiling was built, thus there was no bond between walls and roof. Given these circumstances, the roof of the tunnel in the collapse area admitted water, sand, and stones over time, with sand and stones wedging against the concrete to admit more water, sand, and stones. The heavy rains early in 1936 had forced a final failure. The opposing view was that the highway cut near the railroad tunnel robbed the entire bluff of its longtime support against the hard basalt at the river's edge. That is, the highway cut sliced through softer material between the rail tunnel and the river, leaving the rail tunnel vulnerable to movement of the north face of the highway cut. Even a small movement would trigger a slide, which in turn would allow the south wall of the rail tunnel to bulge outward just enough to cause the collapse of the ceiling. A few of the eyewitnesses said they saw the north wall move and a crack appear between the highway cut and rail tunnel. Thomson scoffed at those statements. If the wall of the highway cut moved enough to cause a tunnel ceiling 100 feet away to fail, he reasoned, then surely the activity of steam shovels and bulldozers, which included throwing debris into the highway cut, would have buckled the cut's north wall. The north wall, however, appeared intact. On the other hand, he later admitted that the railroad crews would not have torn down the south wall of the rail tunnel unless it was cracked by soil movement away from the wall. Had the south wall of the tunnel displaced outward as a result of movement in the north wall of the highway cut, then, of course, that movement could explain why the ceiling lost its support and fell. Thomson was in a quandary.[22]

The railroad solved Thomson's dilemma in part when it brought suit against the state in July 1937. The trial began in Thurston County Superior Court in March 1938; Thomson testified on June 2. Thomson's focus had long since shifted from defending the contractor's bonding company to defending the state. The judge instructed the jury that the railroad had to prove that a slide induced by the highway construction, and no other factor, caused its tunnel to fail. Two days after Thomson's testimony, the jury handed up a verdict in favor of the

SP&S, awarding it $119,554.19 plus accrued interest. The railroad had proved its case. Obviously the jury was unimpressed by Thomson's testimony.[23] The state did not appeal, but the state auditor refused payment on a technicality, forcing the railroad to argue its case before the state supreme court. At last, in May 1939, it won its right to be paid.[24]

From the perspective of the engineers' reports, it appears unlikely that any one incident caused the tunnel to collapse. Thomson based his reasoning for a poorly constructed, weakened ceiling on hours of careful study informed by years of experience. A well-built tunnel encased in rock or other permanent material, with sides and ceiling forming a monolith, could have been damaged by a slide such as the railroad alleged, but its failure would have been unlikely. The jury decided otherwise, and that was that. Perhaps the indisputable lesson from the lengthy legal struggle was the hoary one of asking experts and finding disagreement.

∞⃝

By the time the tunnel five matter concluded, Thomson was deeply involved with consulting for the Washington Toll Bridge Authority (WTBA), specifically in the building of its daring pontoon bridge across Lake Washington, east from Seattle to Mercer Island. He also became involved with the boring of dual tunnels through Seattle's Mount Baker ridge, which would link the floating highway bridge with Seattle south of downtown. The projects were approved at the end of 1938 after years of controversy over the type of bridge to be built and its location, or whether there should be any bridge at all in deference to ferry service and its linked businesses.[25]

In March 1937, the state legislature finally cut through the muddle by creating the WTBA, with exclusive control over the financing, locating, construction, and operation of all state toll bridges. One of the WTBA's obvious, if undeclared, purposes was to assume responsibility for the Lake Washington span and to wheedle federal funding for it—money then funneled through the Public Works Administration. In no way did the shift from any possible private, city, or county funding to state control mean that the bridge was a sure thing. It meant only that the opponents and supporters of the bridge shifted their sights to the WTBA and to the state highway department, in charge of the bridge's design.

For its part, the WTBA established a four-man Board of Consulting Engineers, naming Thomson as one of the members. At 81, Thomson was accustomed to controversy, a good thing since the engineering questions concerning the bridge involved fundamental problems. He was also interested in the broader economic and infrastructure issues surrounding the bridge. In 1938 he was a member of the 40th annual convention of the Washington State Good Roads Association that unanimously and enthusiastically endorsed the project. This endorsement rebutted all of the claims against the bridge—that it would be expensive (it was a toll bridge, after all), impede navigation and aviation, adversely affect private property, and benefit only commercial interests. The Good Roads resolution pointed to the savings in time and lives of an improved Lake Washington area road system, the sound if unusual method of construction, the stimulation of the labor and materials markets, the benefit to commerce, and, ultimately, the positive economic gain for the entire state. On other occasions, Thomson spoke in favor of the bridge or attended pro-bridge meetings.[26]

Thomson's primary duty, however, was not to defend the bridge or counter its opponents, but to help get it built. In 1937 he spent a day on a lake steamer scouting out routes for the bridge with members of the consulting group and Lacy V. Murrow, the director of highways. Another day passed in driving around Lake Washington for the same purpose. Other days involved conferences to firm up the location decisions. Thomson made a signal contribution to the project when responding to a respected engineer, who claimed that reinforced concrete was a fatally flawed material for the pontoons supporting the "floating" portion of the bridge. "So far as I know," the engineer wrote, "there is nothing that will protect ordinary poured concrete from the action of our water for any length of time except a covering of copper." This engineer, Thomson pointed out, had only issued a blanket condemnation; he did not specify a brand of concrete, a mix with any type of sand or stone, "nor the character of the curing, nor any element of manufacture or construction." Thomson promised a "thorough investigation" of the concrete issue. In the autumn of 1937 he revisited a portion of the original Cedar River waterworks—the concrete gate chambers built in 1900 below the original log dam. When reconstructed in 1935, the crews discovered that the existing concrete retained its satisfactory condition despite 35 years of submergence. In 1937, when this concrete was struck several times with a "steel rod, it gave forth a ringing sound, as though striking granite." Although Thomson admitted that the concrete reservoirs in Seattle needed repairs after a quarter century of service, he blamed their partial failure on the previous inadequate knowledge of concrete linings.

In the two decades after the Lake Washington Floating Bridge opened, traffic increased dramatically as seen in this view taken July 19, 1960. The span proved the catalyst for vast population growth on Mercer Island (visible in the distance) and the east side communities of Bellevue, Kirkland, and Redmond. *Seattle Municipal Archives #63709.*

Later reservoirs begun in 1909 and 1911 were sound, and indeed appeared stronger in 1937 than when built. So did a 1912 reservoir in Victoria constructed under Thomson's supervision while he served as the Strathcona Park superintendent. Finally, he investigated experimental concrete pontoons submerged for 25 years in salt water and found no deterioration. Other experts accompanied Thomson on these investigations and agreed with his findings.[27]

Thomson's studies confirmed that concrete pontoons would work. As built, 25 pontoons, most of them 350 feet long, 60 feet wide, and 14½ feet deep, were anchored to the bed of Lake Washington by an elaborate cable system. The pontoons supported the four-lane highway in the 6,620 feet of its "floating" section. Opened in 1940, the bridge worked well, but unfortunately did not "last long beyond the life of the youngest citizen of the state," as the Good Roads resolution declared it would at the time. On November 25, 1990, a storm sank eight pontoons while the bridge was undergoing renovation. The

failure was not the fault of the pontoons, but rather of the contractor and the state supervising agencies. For different reasons, they allowed too much water to accumulate in the pontoons, leaving them vulnerable to sinking in bad weather. When rebuilt, the replacement pontoons and deck incorporated improvements based on the experiences of a half-century.[28]

Otherwise, during his tenure Thomson closely followed the design and construction of the bridge. Although he concurred in its development generally, he was cautious about the long, continuous span of pontoons. To further stabilize the structure, he suggested that two piers be built on either side of the bridge's draw span. The suggestion was not adopted, in part because of the enormous expense involved in sinking four piers to bedrock, hundreds of feet below the lake surface. Whether the piers, if built, would have mitigated the 1990 damage is unknowable. Meanwhile, he carefully observed the construction of the twin tunnels in Mount Baker ridge. When a slide occurred at the west portal,

Thomson angrily blamed both the engineer and the contractor. This matter was peaceably settled and the bridge and tunnel were drivable by June 18, 1940, and formally opened on July 2, 1940. Thomson also studied plans for the first Tacoma Narrows suspension bridge, the famous "Galloping Gertie." The film of Gertie's collapse on November 7, 1940, remains today as one of the most widely viewed disaster documentaries of all time. Although Thomson visited the site after the breakup, his involvement in Gertie's construction and its subsequent problems was much less extensive than his work on the Lake Washington span.[29]

℘ℂℛ

Meanwhile, Thomson's private life slowed because of his and Addie's age and his declining income, but nonetheless he remained active and busy. The big event of 1930, other than his return to the engineering office, was the birth on November 16 of the only grandchild he would know well, Sarah Caroline Porep, whom the family called "Sally." She was the apple of her grandfather's eye. He noted the baptism of "little Sally" one Sunday when she was five months old. On another Sunday, Sally and her parents visited the Thomsons when the child was nearing her first birthday. "Sally laughs heartily when she pulls a handkerchief off my head and I boo at her," Thomson told his diary.[30]

Sally's birth prompted changes at Broomgerrie. For years, the Thomsons resided in what was little more than a framed tent at their Bainbridge Island retreat. They gradually made improvements until it had a floor, roof, and partial wooden walls with movable canvas between the walls and roof for light and ventilation. It had a sink but no indoor toilet. Their granddaughter later recalled it was "very primitive always, and yet they seemed to enjoy it." But it would not do for Sally, so Thomson "had two Norwegian carpenters on the island" build a summer house for her and her parents, complete with a fireplace. This may not have been the best move financially; less than five months later Thomson noted in his diary, "Cash running low," a rare statement of financial distress, at least since the *Sun* debacle. In any event, Broomgerrie remained the family's summer retreat for many years, with no one enjoying being there more than Addie. At Broomgerrie she grew specimen plants and trees, including "an oak tree from her parent's ranch in California," and plants from Thomson's area of Indiana, until the place resembled "an arboretum." Addie suffered from angina and "would be in bed most of the winter, and really not very well." She tended plants on the sun porch

of their Seattle house and looked forward to taking them to the island. Soon after arriving with her new plantings, "she'd be out working in the garden, and she had a hired hand that helped her with the heavy work." She tended flowers, gave teas, and enjoyed herself generally. Then it was back to Seattle and the life of a semi-invalid.[31] Addie also may have suffered from Seasonal Affective Disorder, or SAD, a mental depression caused by a lack of sunlight during wintertime in northern latitudes, a syndrome not identified until years after her death. In any case, relatively little could be done during her lifetime for her heart condition or the symptoms of light deprivation.

Aging took its toll on Thomson, too. In April 1933, he slipped and fell on the bedroom floor, landing on his right hip. The incident broke no bones but confined him to a hospital for two days. He was home on the 18th, but unable to dress himself, "a slow job" until the 28th. The next day he decided to close his Seaboard Building office for three months. But he did not reopen it until August after paying part of the "back rent" and moving to a lower floor. In the meanwhile he returned to work, helped by a regular "rub" from a Dr. Ford. When he complained about Ford's fees, the doctor explained that the treatments were responsible for his restored health. On August 29, he and Addie celebrated their 50th wedding anniversary at Broomgerrie, along with Addie's sister Annie, daughters Frances and Marion, granddaughter Sally, and a friend of theirs. Harry sent a $20 gold piece, while Rex and "Billie" sent a photograph of themselves in a "fine frame." Thomson was in a celebratory mood. "To tease Addie I wear a pair of pumps with extreme hi [sic] heels." But work, however minor, could not be ignored. He had testimony to present in court the next day, so he returned to Seattle on the boat that evening. His health continued on its uneven course. During March and April 1937, he suffered from a "carbuncle," a cluster of pus-filled boils on his back and left shoulder. Marion helped by changing compresses. A series of tests at a clinic followed. "Dr. reports there is not definite showing of Diabetes but owing to my age thinks I should begin a new Insulin use." The insulin treatment, whatever it was, began a few days later. Fortunately it caused no apparent ill effects. By 1939 a combination of aging, reduced income, and limited work, mostly consulting for the inter-county flood control program and the bridge authority, led him to close his office on June 2. "There being very little work I felt that I could do as well at home as in the office and also save rent."[32]

In November 1940 a cold developed into influenza. Thomson tried to fight it off but a series of relapses sent him back to bed. On December 30 he was "in bed very sick," and "bitterly disappointed" because he could not attend the New York meeting of the American Society of Civil Engineers (ASCE), where he was awarded an honorary membership. On January 31 he felt well enough, with Marion's assistance, to attend a meeting of the ASCE's Seattle section where he received recognition as one "who conceived the future of Seattle and who moulded its development." The honor softened his attitude toward the ASCE, which he once described as "the most cold-blooded organization of engineers in the country." He returned to work the next month, but only by a great effort of will. In March, a doctor "says my heart is very irregular and very weak—My foot and ankles much swollen." While in Victoria in June, he suffered another bad fall, but again with no broken bones. In August 1942 he spent almost two weeks in bed and in September complained of back pains, which Dr. Ford's treatments scarcely relieved. Gaps in his diary keeping had always occurred, but now they grew to encompass months at a time, although such events as family birthdays, conferences, and the 1946 birth of his second grandchild, to Rex and his third wife, merited mention. In October 1944, with Addie by then in a nursing home, he left their house for apartment #409 at 2404 42nd Avenue North. Although he moved, he was reluctant to give up the house where he had lived with Addie and later with Marion, too, for so many years. [33]

Despite his infirmities, he fared better than many contemporaries his age or even people considerably younger. In January 1930 his "old friend" and erstwhile assistant Charles J. Moore died. The next year Samuel Hill passed away. Famed regionally for his Good Roads work and the Maryhill mansion high above the Columbia River, Hill had at one time been one of Thomson's closest friends. They became estranged since 1920 over a reservoir that then councilman Thomson wanted built in Seattle's Volunteer Park, overlooking Hill's massive poured concrete mansion. Hill defeated the plan but alienated Thomson. "I have had one of the most serious blows which has ever come to me in the loss of my friendship for R.H. Thomson," Hill wrote to their mutual friend Edmond S. Meany, the noted Northwest historian and University of Washington professor. Thomson's reaction was unrecorded, though he did accept the provision in Hill's will naming him an honorary pallbearer. In 1932 he attended the funeral of Clarence B. Bagley, the early, invaluable historian of Seattle. In 1939, Frederick Mears died. Mears, a fellow engineer formerly with the federal Panama and Alaska railroads, was active in Seattle during his later years. J.D. Ross also passed from the scene in 1939. On September 6, 1940, death came to Thomson's son-in-law, Edward W. Porep. Frances's husband suffered from heart trouble and was unwell, but his death was a blow. Soon afterward, Samuel Lancaster, an old Good Roads associate, paid Thomson a visit. "Samuel Lancaster tells me of the unhappy death of Samuel Hill, and of his suffering." Early in January 1941, Addie's sister Annie died. Neither of the Thomsons could attend the funeral, but Rex's first wife Jean sent "a very dear letter" describing "Annie's last hours." Then Lancaster, the bearer of news of Hill's "suffering" died, followed by Asahel Curtis, the famed photographer who preserved many of Seattle's public improvements on film. On December 6, 1944, Thomson's brother-in-law, Frank Laughlin, "passed away." [34]

Throughout this grim chronicle of loss, he still had Addie. Although in a nursing home, she remained lucid. Thomson regularly telephoned and visited her, on at least one occasion bringing new books for her to read. On the evening of June 8, 1945, when he had almost finished moving out of their last home, she fell and broke a hip. An ambulance took her to a hospital where she died late the next morning. She was 89. Her granddaughter remembered that the Thomsons "were very, very close and happy. And he was just devastated when she passed away." Addie's funeral came on the 12th. On June 16, Thomson noted: "Sell house & lot at 1636 – 34 Ave. Seattle for $7000.⁰⁰[.]" [35]

Through the years, Thomson continued to attend meetings and give speeches. Beta Theta Pi banquets were a favorite when he was available and felt well enough to attend. In 1936 he spoke at a Beta banquet at the University of Washington, probably for the last time, though he attended another banquet ten years later. Other speeches during the 1930s included those to the King County Republican women, the associated clubs of Seattle's north end, and the federation of Seattle women's clubs. Attendance at meetings and conferences, except those associated with his work, became fewer as the 1930s advanced. In 1931 he attended the Presbyterian General Assembly in Pittsburgh. For years afterward he remained an active layman, though he continued to believe in the fallibility of men of the cloth. In 1937 he noted "a loud sermon" from the pastor of Westminster Presbyterian Church. "Says he hates the name Fundamentalist and the name Modernist. I am persuaded that regardless of his talk he is only an opportunist." The next year, the pastor compared

Jesus Christ and Abraham Lincoln. Though Thomson admired Lincoln, the pastor's comparing of the martyred president to Christ left him "very heartsick." "A Year of Hard Times" was his reminiscence about 1932, yet his commitment to the Republican Party on the state and national levels was not any less because of the advancing Great Depression. "There was little work done during the year. Everyone seemed depressed—cowed by fear." He deplored the Democratic victories of 1932 and 1934, and Franklin D. Roosevelt's triumphant reelection in 1936 was viewed no better. "Election day," he wrote in his diary. "The Mongrel Democrats sweep the country." His last diary entry regarding politics came in 1940—he put in a "Vote for Wilkie [sic]," who ran a strong if losing race against Roosevelt.[36]

Biographical and autobiographical writing became major preoccupations in the 1930s and 1940s, pursuits sandwiched between bouts of ill health and the demands of consulting. In 1930 he wrote an account of John B. Shorett's interest in the development of West Seattle and the Duwamish Waterway and mailed it to Shorett. In his diary on May 17, 1933, Thomson noted: "Write my record from birth to graduation." Three years later, with the determination typical of him, he was learning to type, and in 1938 completed five typed copies of his cousin Frederick H. Whitworth's "statement of how they made the first authentic City Surveys." Not until giving up his downtown office in 1939, however, did he became actively involved in narrating his personal and family history. By late the next year, he was writing and rewriting his "biography." The work involved abstracting from, and reflecting on, his diary entries from 1877 to 1932. His summaries and emendations are invaluable because many records covering his city engineering years are lost.[37]

The writing of his memoirs got underway as a serious, focused project after a "committee" of 18 attorneys, Shorett included, asked Thomson to "dictate" his reminiscences "in an informal manner just as though he were talking to a friend." Some time in 1945 he began dictating to two typists, whose services he had used in preparing consulting reports. It is likely that members of the group put Thomson in touch with William M. Read, a classics professor and director of the University of Washington Press, and Charles M. Gates of the university's history department, a Pacific Northwest specialist. Before the end of October, he made an informal contract through a publication committee member of the press, George Milton Savage of the university's English department. Savage probably introduced him to Grant H. Redford, then in his late 30s, who had just joined

the English department. Savage probably also brokered a fee of $300 for Redford's editorial assistance—in 1945 a generous payment to an academic. By January 1947 the manuscript was complete and Thomson had a three-paragraph contract. Later that year the manuscript was set in type but, for reasons not clear, the production process halted. Thomson expected the book to appear in 1947. The press's failure to bring it out surely disappointed him. When *That Man Thomson* at last was released in 1950, a year after Thomson's death, it was basically as Redford noted, "R.H. Thomson's report in his own words as city engineer." However, the book's focus had narrowed from Thomson's original understanding of what it would be, perhaps because of production costs, or because of Thomson's reluctance at his advanced age to meet all of Redford and Read's requests for information. On the other hand, Redford was well aware of the exclusion from the manuscript of what Thomson had written about his childhood and youth, his pre-Seattle sojourn in California, his brief tenure as engineer of the port commission, and his trip to Europe in 1905. Therefore it was rather disingenuous of Redford to write, "time and Mr. Thomson's health did not allow time for 'the full report.'"[38]

Otherwise in his last years, Thomson enjoyed life as much as declining energy and the debilities of age allowed. His 90th birthday came on March 20, 1946, but the big celebration occurred on Sunday, March 31. "Happy group of 105 in to greet me on my 90th birthday," he wrote. In the months ahead he continued to write cards and letters, as well as occasional diary entries. He was the subject of a feature interview on page three of the *Times* that November. He reminisced about being "the most cussed man in Seattle," and "laughed heartily" over negative reactions to his city-making. When remembering those times, "his eyes sparkled and a mischievous smile crept over his face." He declared, "I love a good fight. Still have them occasionally." The man who was "only 90" continued his consulting and also took "walks, and an occasional run." Indeed, as his granddaughter remembered, "he was a great walker. He took me on walks. He walked until a week before his death." Yet he slowed still more, giving up diary keeping after 1947. In early 1949 he suffered a cerebral hemorrhage and four days later, on the morning of January 7, died at home. His simple will left the residue of his estate to his four children. Frances he named executrix. His beloved granddaughter, Sally, received his fire opal stickpin and a silver napkin ring engraved "Meeda," a keepsake from a sister long dead.[39]

The obituaries noted his engineering achievements, professional activities, consulting work, and other hallmarks of a busy, fully engaged life. Other tributes and memorials followed. Finally, *That Man Thomson* was published, a little more than a year after his death. Reset with line drawings added and other alterations made, its publication was honored with a reception in the elegant Pacific Northwest Room at the University of Washington's Suzzallo Library. Redford's contributions included his graceful if not entirely truthful introduction as well as his reorganization and editing of Thomson's text for clarity and emphasis. *That Man Thomson* recounted events from the author's perspective, especially as the intervening years altered his viewpoints. Nevertheless, it remains an original source for any study of the physical reconstruction of Seattle during Thomson's years as city engineer. Other recognition followed, including the naming of a new junior high school in his honor in 1962. The formal dedication occurred in 1964, and as late as 1969 the students observed a "Thomson Day." In 1963 the ground-breaking ceremonies for a new sewage treatment plant honored Thomson as the man who chose the location as the outfall for the North Trunk Sewer. In 1993 the Seattle section of the ASCE established a scholarship in Thomson's name. [40]

What Thomson would have thought of all this cannot be known. As with most human beings, he cherished recognition, but also "it was part of his personality that he didn't think that any one of those projects that he worked on should be named for him." When the possibility of using his name for a public work or other structure had emerged, "he just said no," his granddaughter remembered. "It just wasn't part of his ambition." [41]

But ambition itself Thomson possessed in abundance. It was an ambition to overcome natural obstacles in providing for a healthful, full urban life. It was an ambition to provide city dwellers with "clean air and good food," together with "an abundance of water, fuel, and light," capped by "as perfect sanitation as the inventive mind of man can provide." All of this depended in one way or another on improved transportation, both internal and external. It depended, too, on a city's ability to reach out and gather in the products of its region. His ambition saw no limit to urban growth, for when a city developed "new centers of congestion," it also demanded "new means of access" in an unending effort to maintain its unfettered internal movement even as it expanded. [42] His ambition accepted no limits to the trade and markets on which cities thrived, and therefore no limits on the development of land, sea, and air routes. His ambition

willed the defeat of the human enemies of expansion, who would limit abundant urban living. He had, indeed, taken both boy and man out of Hanover, Indiana.

NOTES

1. Tarbill, "Mountain Moving in Seattle," 486. The project was completed on December 9, 1930, "Seattle Completes Denny Hill Regrade No. 2," *Western Construction News* 5 (January 25, 1931): 49.
2. Tarbill, "Mountain Moving in Seattle," 484.
3. Ibid., 486.
4. Ibid.
5. Ibid.
6. Ibid., 487; and "Denny Hill Regrade No. 2, Seattle, Washington," *Western Construction News* 5 (July 25, 1930): 354; and RHT by Oscar A. Piper to Commissioners of Lincoln Park, attn. John W. Eagan, 9 December 1930, LID 4818, 6th Ave., et al., fiche 2, folder 2, SMA.
7. Tarbill, "Mountain Moving in Seattle," 487; Mayor John S. Butler to City Engineer, attn. D.W. McMorris, 6 September 1930, fiche 3; J.R. West to RHT, 3 January 1931, fiche 1; and RHT by L.R. Andrews to George Nelson and Company, 19 September 1930, fiche 3, folder 2, LID 4818, SMA.
8. "Denny Hill Regrade No. 2," 351–54; W.F. Way, "Handling Earth by Belts," *Engineering News-Record* 105 (November 27, 1930): 838–40; George Nelson and Company by Edwin H. Flick to Board of Public Works, 9 September 1930; fiche 3, folder 2, LID 4818, SMA; RHT by O.A. Piper to Board of Public Works, 29 September 1930, fiche 3, folder 2, LID 4818, SMA; and D.W. McMorris by O.A. Piper to H.W. Carroll, 24 August 1931, fiche 1, folder 3, LID 4818, SMA.
9. Tarbill, "Mountain Moving in Seattle," 488.
10. RHT, *That Man Thomson*, 127, 130–32. For Yesler Hill, see Photograph Collection, images 1 through 6, of which RHT's is 5. The voluminous correspondence includes City Planning Commission to City Council, 10 June 1925, Comptroller File 100373; W.D. Barkhuff by O.A. Piper to City Council, file 124810; and the engineering department's general file, 2608-02, fiche 1, SMA.
11. *Report of the Department of Parks, City of Seattle, 1923–1930* (Seattle: 1930), 170; *Argus*, September 22, 1930 (quotation); and October 4, 1930. *Times*, October 27, 1930; and October 28, 1930. For the vote, see *Times*, November 5, 1930.
12. RHT diary, August 30 and 31, 1933, 1602-2, box 3, folder 2 (Standard Oil); and diary, September 26, 1934, 1602-2, box 3, folder 3 (GN), RHT Papers, UW. For Cle Elum, see RHT diaries, January 2, 1930; October 6 and 31, 1931; and May 28, 1932, 1602-2, box 3, folder 2, RHT Papers, UW.
13. Invaluable for general information on the rivers and the later Mud Mountain Dam is Dorpat and McCoy, *Building Washington*, 257–84. For quotation, see "Annual Report of the Chief Engineer for the Year Ending December 1938," 62, box 6, King County Board of Commissioners (hereafter KCBC), UW. See also "Annual Report of the Engineer, Inter County River Improvement for Year Ending December 1935," 62, box 6, KCBC, UW.
14. For quotation, see "Annual Report, 1938," note 13.
15. For first quotation, see ibid. Chittenden to Harold Preston, 27 June 1913, 62, box 1, KCBC, UW. For dredging, see "Annual Report, 1935," 62, box 6, KCBC, UW. For "raw" and "loose earth" quotations, see "Annual Report, 1938," note 13. For the bank reinforcement in 1915, see "Chief Engineer's Annual Report for the Year 1926," 62, box 6, KCBC, UW.

16. For RHT's work, see RHT, "Supplement to the Chief Engineer's Annual Report for the Year 1946," 62, box 6, KCBC, UW. For retards, see "Annual Report, 1926," and "Chief Engineer's Annual Report for the Year 1927," 62, box 6, KCBC, UW. For quotation, see "Annual Report 1938," note 13. RHT at first believed that eventually the White River would "return again to its old course," a development necessary for "a sufficient current in the Seattle waterways to reasonably cleanse them," RHT to A.H. Dimock, 29 July 1914, 89/1, box 5, book 13, RHT Papers, UW.

17. "Resolution," 62, box 1, KCBC, UW. RHT diary, 1602-2, box 2, folder 3, RHT Papers, UW.

18. Statement of E.G. Berg, January 14, 1936, 89/2, box 4, folder 8, RHT Papers, UW. Other members of Berg's crew made statements corroborating Berg's.

19. Ibid., for quotation. See also office of the County Clerk, Clerk's Minutes, Thurston County, Washington, Records of *Spokane, Portland & Seattle Railway v. State of Washington*, dept. 2, vol. 3, case 17190, Thurston County Court House.

20. For quotation, see RHT, draft letter to Curtis Harold, 19 March 1936, 89/2, box 4, folder 8, RHT Papers, UW. See also undated "Memorandum by Mr. R.H. Thomson with Reference to His Visits to SP&S Railway Tunnel No. 5," and "Report on the Collapse of SP&S Tunnel No. 5 near Underwood, Washington, J.C. Stevens," n.d., 89/2, box 4, folder 8, RHT Papers, UW.

21. A comprehensive examination of all the issues is in "Memorandum from Mr. Duffy" to G.W. Hamilton, May 10, 1938, 89/2, box 4, folder 9, RHT Papers, UW.

22. See sources in note 20; and RHT to J.A. Davis, 7 May 1938, 89/2, box 4, folder 8, RHT Papers, UW.

23. For RHT's record of his testimony, RHT diary, June 2, 1938, 1602-2, box 2, folder 2, RHT Papers, UW. See also Thurston County Superior Court, Appearance Docket Fee Book, 164, case 17190, Washington State Archives, and Clerk's Minutes, note 19.

24. *State ex rel. Spokane, Portland & Seattle Railway Co. v. Yelle*, 199 Wash. 70 (1939).

25. Dorpat and McCoy, *Building Washington*, 35–36, 120–25, contains information summarized in this paragraph and below.

26. Resolution to the WTBA by the Washington State Good Roads Association, October 17, 1938, in 1602-2, box 3, folder 10, RHT Papers, UW. See also RHT diary, February 16 and 20, 1937, 1602-2, box 2, folder 3, RHT Papers, UW.

27. RHT diary, August 20 and 24; August 26 (steamer trip); August 27 (auto trip); August 14 and August 28, 1937, 1602-2, box 2, folder 3, RHT Papers, UW. See also RHT to L.V. Murrow, 3 September 1937, 71-3, box 2, folder 6, U.W. Experiment Station Correspondence (hereafter ESC), UW. The engineer is quoted in RHT to Lacy V. Murrow, 1 October 1937, 71-3, box 2, folder 9, ESC, UW. See also "Appendix A" and "Appendix No. 2" of the 1 October 1937 letter; and Arthur G. Smith to Luther E. Gregory, 27 October 1937, 71-3, box 2, folder 9, ESC, UW.

28. Dorpat and McCoy, *Building Washington*, 123–24. For quotation, see note 26.

29. RHT to Consulting Board et al., 24 June 1938; and to Lacy V. Murrow, 27 June 1938, 71-3, box 2, folder 6, ESC, UW. For ventilation concerns, see RHT to Charles Andrew, 7 March 1939; and Andrew to RHT, 11 March 1939, 71-3, box 2, folder 6, ESC, UW. For RHT's anger, see RHT to Charles E. Andrew, 6 October 1939, 71-3, box 2, folder 13, ESC, UW. RHT and others went across the bridge on June 18, 1940, see RHT diary of that date, 1602-2, box 2, folder 4, RHT Papers, UW. For the Tacoma bridge, see Albert F. Gunns, "The First

Tacoma Narrows Bridge: A Brief History of Galloping Gertie," *PNQ* 72 (October 1981): 162–69; Dorpat and McCoy, *Building Washington*, 128–31; and Richard Hobbs, *Catastrophe to Triumph: Bridges of the Tacoma Narrows* (Pullman: Washington State University Press, 2006). RHT visited the site on November 7, 1940, see RHT diary for that date, 1602-2, box 2, folder 4, RHT Papers, UW. For RHT's work on the bridge, see RHT diaries, January-March 1939; and January-April 1940, 1602-2, box 4, folder 2, RHT Papers, UW.

30. RHT diaries, November 16, 1930; April 26, 1931, and November 1, 1931, 1602-2, box 2, folder 2, RHT Papers, UW.

31. All quotations except "Cash running low" are from the Hepler interview. See RHT diary, April 25 and September 8, 1931, 1602-2, box 2, folder 2, RHT Papers, UW.

32. For RHT's fall and return to health, see RHT diary, April 16, 18, 28, and 29; May 9; and August 29, 1933, 1602-2, box 2, folder 2, RHT Papers, UW. For the wedding celebration, see RHT diary, August 29, 1933, 1602-2, box 2, folder 2, RHT Papers, UW. For 1937 health problems, see RHT diary March 11 and 25, and April 9 and 10, 1937, 1602-2, box 2, folder 3, RHT Papers, UW. For closing the office, RHT diary, June 2, 1939, 1602-2, box 2, folder 4, RHT Papers, UW.

33. For influenza, see RHT diary, November 30-December 31, 1940; for quotation "in bed" December 30, 1602-2, box 2, folder 4, RHT Papers, UW. For "bitterly disappointed" see RHT to George T. Seabury, 21 January 1941, and, for the citation, 89/1, box 6, RHT Papers. For "cold blooded" quotation, see RHT to W.E. Humphrey, 11 January 1904, 89/1, box 1, book 3, RHT Papers, UW. RHT diaries, March 18 and June 9, 1941; August 17–29; and September 16–18, 1942, 1602-2, box 2, folder 5; and, for lack of entries, October 26-December 31, 1942, 1602-2, box 2, folder 5, RHT Papers, UW. For 1946 entries, see RHT diary, January 18 and March 20, 1602-2, box 2, folder 6, RHT Papers, UW. For the move, see RHT diary, October 21, 1944, 1602-2, box 2, folder 5, RHT Papers, UW.

34. For Moore, see RHT diary, January 27, 1930, 1602-2, box 2, folder 2, RHT Papers, UW. For Hill, see Hill to Edmund S. Meany, 11 November 1920, Box 73, 106-70-12, Meany Papers, UW; and RHT diary, March 1, 1931, 1602-2, box 2, folder 2, RHT Papers, UW. For Bagley, see RHT diary, February 29, 1932, box 2, folder 2, RHT Papers, UW. For Mears, see RHT diary, January 13, 1939, 1602-2, box 2, folder 4, RHT Papers, UW; and Katharine Carson Crittenden, *Get Mears: Frederick Mears, Builder of the Alaska Railroad* (Portland: Binford and Mort, Publishing, 2002). For Porep, see RHT diaries, June 11 and 14, 1940; and September 6, 1941, 1602-2, box 2, folder 4, RHT Papers, UW. For Lancaster's visit, see RHT diary, September 18, 1941, 1602-2, box 2, folder 4, RHT Papers, UW. For Annie's death, see RHT diary, January 7, 1941; and for Jean's letter, January 11, 1941, 1602-2, box 2, folder 4, RHT Papers, UW. For Lancaster's death, see RHT diary, March 4, 1941; and for Curtis's, see March 13, 1941, 1602-2, box 2, folder 5, RHT Papers, UW.

35. For visits, see RHT diary, January 27, February 28, and March 12, 1945, 1602-2, box 2, folder 5. For Addie's fall, see June 8, 1945; and for her death, see June 9, 1945, 1602-2, box 2, folder 5, all in RHT Papers, UW. For "very close" quotation, see Hepler interview. For the sale, see RHT diary, June 16, 1945, 1602-2, box 2, folder 6, RHT Papers, UW.

36. For the Betas, RHT diary, February 1, 1936; 1602-2, box 2, folder 3; and November 14, 1946, box 2, folder 6, RHT Papers, UW. For the Republican women, see March 2, 1930, 1602-2, box 2, folder 2, RHT Papers, UW. For the north

end clubs, see April 2, 1930, 1602-2, box 2, folder 2, RHT Papers, UW. For the federation, see February 28, 1933, 1602-2, box 2, folder 2, RHT Papers. For the general assembly, see RHT diary, May 22–June 7, 1931, 1602-2, box 2, folder 2, RHT Papers, UW. For the sermons, see RHT diaries, April 11, 1937, 1602-2, box 2, folder 3; and February 6, 1938, 1602-2, box 2, folder 4, RHT Papers. RHT admired Lord Charnwood's *Lincoln*, buying a copy for Rex and one for himself, RHT diary, March 14, 15, and 31; May 23 and 27, 1932, 1602-2, box 2, folder 2, RHT Papers, UW. For the 1932 reminiscence, see "Sketches," 1932 entry, 1602-2, box 2, folder 10, RHT Papers, UW. For political quotations, in order, see RHT diary, November 3, 1936, 1602-2, box 2, folder 3, and 1940, box 2, folder 4, RHT Papers, UW. For earlier elections, see RHT diaries, November 8, 1932, 1602-2, box 2, folder 2; and November 6, 1934, 1602-2, box 2, folder 3, RHT Papers, UW.

37. RHT to Shorrett [*sic*], 26 March 1930, 89/1, box 6, folder 9, RHT Papers, UW. RHT diary, May 17, 1933, 1602-2, box 2, folder 2, RHT Papers, UW. RHT diary, 27 August 1936, 1602-2, box 2, folder 3; and October 28, 1938, 1602-2, box 2, folder 4, RHT Papers, UW. The history involves many entries from June 26, 1939 through November 14, 1940, see RHT diaries, 1602-2, box 2, folder 4, RHT Papers, UW.

38. For first quotation, see the original introduction to *That Man Thomson*, 89/1, box 6, folder 1, RHT Papers, UW. For RHT's relationship with the UW Press, see RHT to W.M. Read, 18 April 1947, 1602-2, box 1, folder 4, RHT Papers, UW. For the press during those years, see Catherine Royer, "The University of Washington Press: Publishing Arm of the University," *PNQ* 50 (October 1959): 157–60. Material on the autobiography is voluminous. For the contract, see RHT diary, October 24, 1945, 1602-2, box 2, folder 5; and Read to RHT, 11 January 1947, along with other correspondence and successive drafts of the manuscript, 89/1, box 6, RHT Papers, UW. For correspondence about the project, see also the Grant Hubbard Redford Papers, Coll Mss 245, box 27, folder 1, Special Collections and Archives, Utah State University, and the University of Washington Press Archives, hereafter UWPA. For the closing quotations, see *That Man Thomson*, 8.

39. RHT, small 1946 diary, March 22; and April 20, 1602-2, box 2, folder 6; *Times*, November 4, 1946; Hepler interview; and Thomson death certificate, January 7, 1949, state file no. 105, Vital Statistics, Department of Public Health, Seattle and King County, WA. For the will, dated August 11, 1947, see file 110051, vol. 86, pp. 715–17, King County Probate Court.

40. Obituaries are in *Times*, January 7, 1949; and *P-I*, January 8, 1949. For the reception, see *University of Washington Daily*, February 1, 1950; and Marion Wing Thomson to Read, 3 February 1950, UWPA. For the school, see Leonard Savitch to Mrs. Frank J. Morrill, 10 January 1964; and Don C. Kessler to Marion Thomson, 10 April 1969, 1602-2, box 3, folder 18, RHT Papers, UW. For the treatment plant, see the news release, September 12, 1963, in 1602-2, box 3, folder 13, RHT Papers, UW. For the scholarship, see the mayor's proclamation, September 8, 1993, 1602-2, box 3, folder 19, RHT Papers, UW.

41. Hepler interview.

42. RHT, *That Man Thomson*, quotations on 129, 130, 131, and see also 132.

A septuagenarian or octogenarian, Thomson strides along Third Avenue in downtown Seattle at a pace belying his age. The photograph is undated, but the clothing of passersby, sidewalk features, and cars at curbside suggest a time following his 1930–31 service as city engineer. His high collar indicates an indifference to contemporary male styles. *University of Washington Libraries, Special Collections, UW 24229.*

14
"R.H."—The Meaning of a Busy Life

THOMSON LIVED DURING the heyday of the civil engineer. Dizzying advances in applied science and technology during the late 19th and early 20th centuries elevated the civil engineer, and especially the city engineer, to elite status in the public eye. In a systematic, interrelated fashion, city engineers focused these advances on solving the problems of rampant urban growth. When undertaking this enormous responsibility, city engineers benefited from the concurrent organizational reform of urban government—reforms enabling the engineer's office to function at least somewhat apart from constant political intervention. The development of a quasi-independent bureaucracy allowed city engineers to oversee urban improvements and apply the best professional judgment, while being relatively unhampered by political favoritism in the selection of products, services, or contractors. [1]

City engineering benefited from the improvements in reinforced concrete, structural steel, asphaltic macadam, and materials testing. Almost incredible advances came in applied electricity, motive power, and sanitation and water purification systems, as well as fresh insights into the etiology of disease. In addition, management techniques borrowed from the corporate world, the growth of inexpensive, rapid communication and transportation systems, the exchange of information through professional meetings and publications, and a vision for an urbanized world without material limits all allowed city engineers to expand their impact on urban development.

City engineers benefited from two additional factors allowing for their remarkable achievements. The first was based on the sensational rise in real estate values caused by the intense demand for urban property and the capitalist tradition of treating land and improvements as commodities, susceptible to sale and resale. However uneven or unfair those urban values (and their assessments) might be from a Marxist or similar perspective, they provided city governments with a deep well of income to draw upon in financing improvements within the purview of city engineering. The second development, the creation of capital surpluses and markets, allowed cities to float bond issues to pay for improvements. Bond purchasers, seeking investment outlets for their surplus capital, put up the funds for the immediate construction of improvements. Cities repaid investors over time, either from property tax revenues dedicated to bond repayment, or from a portion of the monies derived from an improvement's operation, as in the case of Seattle's Cedar River gravity water system. This mechanism—cities tapping capital markets to fund improvements, then repaying bond investors through taxes or revenues—is so commonplace today that it seems unremarkable. But it was not so to George F. Cotterill, Thomson's friend, erstwhile subordinate, and former mayor of Seattle. In a 1928 address, "What Part Has an Engineer in the Development of a Municipality Such as Seattle?" Cotterill pointed to rising property values and bond issues as the engines of public improvement. [2]

Of course there were limitations to the engineering approach. City engineers typically did not develop the comprehensive plans that focused on the separation of urban functions, the protection of residential areas, and the direction and control of new growth. City engineers, too, usually did not have an urban patriot's vision for instilling beauty in the city environment, such as in house lot improvements, tree plantings, parks and boulevards, and civic centers. In general, engineers already were fully involved with ad hoc solutions to pressing problems, such as street extensions and paving, sewer construction, lighting, and grading and regrading. This left little time for other issues. By default, engineers consigned much to the architectural planners and landscape architects who were the principal designers of proliferating city plans in the late 19th and early 20th centuries. Yet, city engineers remained deeply involved in the vision of a city as a whole, even if they rarely produced inclusive plans. Engineering's very attention to streets, paving, sewers, lighting, and grading forced them to consider the city as a unit. [3] Unlike some engineers, Thomson appreciated urban and rural beauty, as well as the sublimity of wilderness. He linked urban beautification to civic patriotism as did other proponents of the City Beautiful.

Thomson, 44 years of age in 1900, could be considered to have been born too soon to enjoy the fullest benefits of the era of the city engineer. His early birth nevertheless was an advantage, for he was well entrenched when his profession's boom years arrived. He lived to see the era of the great dams and the first wave of extensive concrete highway construction, but he died in the decade before the federal interstate highway system began crisscrossing the country. The interstate system—often linked with urban renewal and airport expansion—was America's last unfettered expression of engineering dominance. As the expressway system plowed through urban and rural areas, creating its own disruptions of lives and property, a reaction against purely engineering solutions set in, especially against broad programs designed only to accommodate cars and trucks. One repudiation occurred in Seattle when voters rejected the R.H. Thomson Expressway.

The naming of the R.H. Thomson Expressway was the culmination of efforts within the Seattle chapter of the American Society of Civil Engineers to honor their famous member. Initially, the Seattle group wished to name a portion of Interstate 5 after Thomson, but they learned that the U.S. Bureau of Public Roads had a policy against using the interstate system to memorialize individuals.[4] Meanwhile, Seattle's city government was planning a new north-south expressway designed to run parallel and east of Interstate 5 and Highway 99 (the latter is located west of I-5). This third multilane road would slice through the eastern part of the city near the west shore of Lake Washington and would require the construction of many appurtenances, including ramps, at least one large interchange, and a third bridge across Lake Washington. Initially, this latest paean to automobility was called the Empire Way Expressway. Voters approved it as part of a package of improvements in 1960 (this was before the interstate system's negative aspects such as traffic embolisis and aural, visual, and atmospheric pollution became obvious). In 1962, after some lobbying, the city council renamed it the "R.H. Thomson Expressway."[5]

By 1970, preliminaries for the expressway were underway. But 1970 was not 1960. In 1970, the results of constructing more roads for urban traffic relief, such as Interstate 5, were plain—they bred more traffic. The R.H. Thomson Expressway plans included a large interchange in the Central District, then almost entirely an African-American residential area. Residents denounced it as racist. They were not alone in protesting. Park lovers decried plans to run the expressway through Ravenna Park, a quiet wooded ravine north of the University of

Washington. Other residents in affected neighborhoods attacked the expected increase in noise and automobile exhaust pollution. In 1972, the public voted down the R.H. Thomson Expressway.[6] How Thomson would have reacted cannot be known, but a guess is that he would have approved of the road, if not the name. But by then, too, he might have supported the revival of regional mass transit, which voters rejected earlier in 1969.[7]

One certainty about Thomson's career is that he did not join the so-called "revolt of the engineers," if that meant organizing to establish professional independence from corporations and businesses. He simply was too busy to spend much time with such concerns, or to worry about larger questions regarding an engineer's relationship to society. Besides, this was mainly an East Coast preoccupation. A participant from the "far corner," the Pacific Northwest, would have needed to spend precious time in train travel to participate in the intramural debates of the ACSE and other organizations. He did believe in the superior knowledge of the professional engineer, especially knowledge that was tempered by experience, but again he left the promotion of "professionalism" largely to others. There is no evidence that he bothered to read Thorstein Veblen's sardonic 1921 critique, *The Engineers and the Price System*. Veblin claimed that "the older generation of the craft," meaning people like Thomson, "have been pretty well commercialized," that is, corrupted by the business system of producing scarcity in order to maintain prices. Younger engineers, Veblen argued, were capable of forcing businesses to produce abundantly because they were the only ones who understood how the system worked. If they would strike, everything would stop. Veblen believed captains of industry and finance had long ago lost the ability to understand their technologically advanced businesses. Had Thomson read Veblen, he probably would have disputed Veblen's premise that businessmen consciously limited production. Rather, they were limited only by demand, which was in turn constrained by the inability of nations to unclog the channels of trade. He did not believe that engineers, young or old, normally had interests divergent from those of their employers. Although highly intelligent and an avid reader—when he had the time—Thomson was not an intellectual. A fair conclusion about him is that he considered himself a doer who bent his intellect to the solution of clients' problems, not an abstract thinker or theorizer.[8]

Thomson's engineering was in any case a means to an end. He altered Seattle's urban landscape and undertook consulting jobs in order to improve the material

Soon after this 1939 photograph was taken, Thomson closed his office in the Seaboard Building and continued his consulting work from home. Now 83, he had at last converted to soft-collar shirts. *University of Washington Libraries, Special Collections, UW 24318.*

conditions of living. Implicit in his work was a belief that an improved standard of living released humans from anxiety about their physical survival and encouraged enjoyment in life and spiritual fulfillment. His commitment to professionalism and to his Presbyterian faith—of which more later—produced his 1905 statement, already quoted: "There is so much crying to be done for the relief of the common people, and they are so blind themselves, and there are so few who care, that it seems impossible for me to quit."[9] To a later age suspicious of professional competence and religious hubris, this sentence, lifted from the context of a long letter, could appear arrogant. Yet in later times, a secular arrogance of some internet bloggers, university administrators and faculties, newspaper columnists, television commentators, and other self-appointed molders of opinion have become the norm. It is important to remember, then, why Thomson

undertook engineering in this earlier age. He saw it as a path to personal fulfillment, surely, but at the same time as his essential contribution to improving the quality of life for citizens. It was, in the now largely lapsed meaning of the word, his calling.

Keeping Thomson's vision firmly in mind is important in view of later analyses that argue against his understanding of his own actions. What he really was doing, these critiques say, was creating a second, precarious "human-made environment," producing space for capitalist exploitation, and ridding the city of "new migrants" and other undesirables by wrecking their houses. Such analyses are useful ways of looking at the urban world but they risk the conclusion that Thomson was delusional or ignorant of his own impulses.[10] That was not so. Thomson was a realist who understood how his world worked. If long-term and desirable residents were in the way of necessary improvements, even their houses and businesses went, along with anyone or anything else blocking his vision of progress. He appealed to the profit motive, frankly and openly. He was too much a businessman himself to do otherwise. Money, profit, and specific urban restructurings, however, were never ends in themselves. They were part of the means to a better urban future.

Thomson's career and life demonstrates how impossible it is to compartmentalize an individual. Religion, which informed his views regarding engineering, plus family and Republican politics, all anchored his existence in an uncertain world. His Presbyterianism was Christ-centered and not deeply theological.[11] No surviving correspondence or other documents express a conviction that he was among John Calvin's elect, predestined for heaven. What may be inferred is a firm faith impelling a powerful obligation to work for the "common people," an obligation of the elect. Whatever his possible fate in an afterlife, Thomson behaved as though the Almighty, in shaping the earth, had left plenty for His human agents to perfect while they were on the planet. Family was extremely important to him, as his love for Addie and their children attested. Family was intertwined with his Presbyterian faith. He looked to both for solace and inspiration.

The third anchor, his Republican politics, related more immediately to the secular world. The Civil War confirmed his Republicanism, a political conviction never abandoned. In the early years of the 20th century his outlook was reformist. A few letters criticized the overweening behavior of large corporations but Thomson was too much the businessman to countenance revolutionary socioeconomic change. As late as the 1930s he was investing in mining stock. After World War I he moved with his party away from reform and toward skepticism of the value of social and economic experiments, though he never modified his belief in public works as an agent of positive economic and social improvement.[12]

Finally, Thomson was an intensely urban man, yet his granddaughter remembered him saying how he "enjoyed being out in the woods" when superintendent of Strathcona Park,[13] though he often returned to Seattle, and Victoria and Vancouver, British Columbia. Broomgerrie was a pleasant retreat, but only as a temporary interlude between longer stays in Seattle. The city remained his base, no matter how far afield his travels and consulting took him. Republican though he was, he early abandoned party affiliations at the city level, embracing instead the urban progressive conception of nonpartisanship. In 1898 he was alienated enough from

Seattle's "open town" atmosphere to declare his support for the local Populists if they would "put up a law and order ticket." He worked closely with several Democrats, including his friends William Hickman Moore and George F. Cotterill. He told a close friend in 1907 that "William Hickman Moore is Mayor, and is running the town right." The next year he wrote to another correspondent saying how "my friend, Mayor Moore, was defeated by the Republican Machine." In 1911 a Beta fraternity brother was elected mayor of Butte, Montana, on the Socialist ticket. Thomson congratulated him, writing "that the Socialism which you advance is the fellowship illustrated by the life of our Lord and Savior, Jesus Christ."[14]

It may be true, as Edwin T. Layton Jr. wrote in *The Revolt of the Engineers*, that engineers entertained a "nostalgia for a simpler, individualistic social order such as once prevailed in rural and frontier settings."[15] If so, Thomson was unlike other engineers. He reminisced about boyhood and young manhood in Hanover, Indiana, scarcely more than a village then or later, but reminiscence and nostalgia are different things. Almost as soon as he arrived in California he began searching for the next big, rich city, the next San Francisco. He found it in Seattle. He could have remained in Healdsburg or one of its nearby communities where life was much like it was in Hanover. He did not.

In another respect, Thomson was an urban man of his era, for like many other progressives he embraced municipal public ownership. His 1905 trip to Europe convinced him of the efficiency and effectiveness of municipal owned utilities. He had, of course, already battled for city-owned water and lighting systems. After his European investigations, he added municipal refuse collection to the list. Around the turn of the century, he had been close to the engineering firm of Stone & Webster and its subsidiary, the Seattle Electric streetcar company, but over the years he gradually developed a holistic view of municipal ownership that included public transit. He seems to have arrived at his conclusions in part pragmatically, believing by the time of World War I that Seattle Electric could not operate profitably under any reasonable franchise terms. Furthermore he was offended by what, in his judgment, was the company's arrogance and intransigence.[16] He also looked on approvingly of San Francisco's controversial and ultimately successful Hetch Hetchy water supply program because it would break the grip of a private water company.[17]

&OCR&

In serving Seattle, Thomson made mistakes. When so intent on building a new dam at the throat of a Cedar River canyon, he overlooked the porosity of the Cedar's right bank at that point. The right bank failed, predictably, but thankfully without loss of life. The results were expense for the city and discredit on his department. Regrading Dearborn Street did not reap the short-term economic benefits that Thomson envisioned, while its displacement of African-American householders opened him to charges of race and class prejudice. The charges have no more substance than claiming he was prejudiced against Denny Hill's middle and upper-middle class whites because he masterminded the destruction of their neighborhood. Absolving him of prejudice does not, however, alter the fact that regrading Dearborn Street was less than a good idea. Thomson will always be second-guessed about the leveling of Denny Hill, especially after the limitations of horse-drawn transportation, the electric trolley, and foot traffic over any but short urban distances are now all but forgotten. As Henry Petroski reminds us in his thoughtful, delightful book, "to engineer is human"[19]—engineers learn from their mistakes in their determination to succeed. No doubt Petroski is correct at the microlevel regarding individual buildings, bridges, and vehicles, at least until a new design tool such as the computer comes along to upset the usual way of doing things and present a new set of pitfalls and challenges. Thomson sometimes attempted to justify his mistakes, but he also tried to learn from them.

The macrolevel is a different matter. Thomson's vision of an ever-expanding city, breaking through its transportation barriers to consume still more of its penumbra, is flawed at its core. At some point this expansion cannot be sustained—environmentally or fiscally. Or if it can, the sustainment must come at the expense of any sense of common purpose or identity among the spreading communities making up the megalopolis.

With those caveats entered, there is no question that Thomson improved life in Seattle and elsewhere through his labors. Roy O. Hadley, an admirer of his friend "R.H.," typed a hagiographic retrospective of Thomson's life a few days following his death. "His achievements," Hadley wrote, "are woven into Seattle and the surrounding region so durably that they are taken for granted even as Puget Sound, Lake Washington, and Mount Rainer." He continued: "Every time a resident draws Cedar River water, whenever he walks a level street where once rose a high hill, if he rides over smooth pavement with easy grades on downtown thoroughfares of this city or drives along many scenic highways and bridges throughout the Evergreen State, he enjoys the fruits of the life of R.H. Thomson."[20]

Hadley went on to detail other achievements, "known to but few" younger Seattleites in 1949. That was because most of Thomson's admiring contemporaries were gone. "I have outlived my own generation," Hadley reported Thomson remarking years before he died. With his death, an awareness of his work faded even more. During his lifetime, Thomson labored to alter or overcome nature for the benefit of urban dwellers. As early as the last year of that life, his work was considered as naturally a part of Seattle's landscape as the surrounding waters and mountains. His work may not be as permanent as the waters and mountains, but it was at least as utilitarian. Seattle's voters stopped the R.H. Thomson Expressway in 1972, but nobody on either side of the debate proposed ripping out the Cedar River water conduits or the North Trunk Sewer, or turning off the lights.

Notes

1. Stanley K. Schultz and Clay McShane, "To Engineer the Metropolis: Sewers, Sanitation, and City Planning in Late-Nineteenth Century America," *JAH* 65 (September 1978): 389–411; and Peterson, *Birth of City Planning*, 21–25.
2. See 38, box 14, folder 6, Cotterill Papers, UW.
3. Ibid., and, for a recent study of planning, see Carl Smith, *The Plan of Chicago*.
4. J. Curtis Parker to G. Wellington Rupp, 5 January 1961, copy in 1602-2, box 3, folder 13, RHT Papers, UW.
5. Gordon S. Clinton to William D. Shannon, 3 July 1961, copy in ibid.
6. MacDonald, *Distant Neighbors*, 158–59; Klingle, "Urban by Nature," 435–38; and Phelps, *Public Works in Seattle*, 117–23.
7. Klingle, "Urban by Nature," 437.
8. Edwin T. Layton Jr., *The Revolt of the Engineers: Social Responsibility and the American Engineering Profession* (Cleveland: Case Western Reserve University Press, 1971), 25–33, 54–74, 109–27, 180–95. Thorstein Veblen, *The Engineers and the Price System*, intro. by Daniel Bell (1921; 1963; repr. with Bell intro from 1963, New Brunswick, NJ: Transaction, 1983), 85 for quotation, and 127–30 for Veblen's argument about younger engineers.
9. Quoted in Klingle, "Changing Spaces," 207.
10. For first quotation, see Walter Schoeder, "Environmental Setting of the St. Louis Region," in Andrew Hurley, ed., *Common Fields*, 37. For second quotation, see Klingle, "Changing Spaces," 208. For space for exploitation, see Edward W. Soja, *Postmetropolis: Critical Studies of Cities and Regions* (Malden, MA: Blackwell, 2000), 95–116.
11. For RHT's biblical literalism, see RHT to "Dear Sir" and enclosure, 1 September 1926; 89/1, box 6, folder 9, RHT Papers, UW.
12. For criticism of a large corporation, see RHT to Samuel Hill, 16 August 1913, 89/1, box 5, book 12, RHT Papers, UW. For mining investments, see RHT diaries, May 27, 1932, 1602-2, box 2, folder 2; and July 1, 1937, 1602-2, box 2, folder 3, RHT Papers, UW.
13. Hepler interview.

14. For Populists, see RHT to C.J. Moore, 15 February 1898, 89/1, box 1, folder 1, RHT Papers, UW. For Moore see, first quotation, RHT to William Carnes, 9 July 1907; and for second quotation, RHT to James B. Nelson, 1 March 1908, both in 89/1, box 2, book 5, RHT Papers, UW. For the socialist, see RHT to L.J. Duncan, 5 April 1911, 89/1, box 4, book 10, RHT Papers, UW.

15. Layton, *Revolt of the Engineers*, 64.

16. For RHT's closeness to Stone & Webster, see, among many examples, RHT to Stone & Webster, 28 October 1899, 89/1, box 1, book 2, RHT Papers, UW. For his alienation from the streetcar company, see RHT to Frank P. Mullen, 22 October 1906, 89/1, box 2, book 4; and RHT to A.L. Valentine, 12 October 1910, 89/1, box 3, book 9, RHT Papers, UW.

17. RHT to Wesley L. Jones, 6 January 1914, 89/1, box 5, book 13, RHT Papers, UW.

18. Klingle, "Urban by Nature," 135, notes that Sandy Moss, an African American, and his family lost their house to regrading, which destroyed the "social fabric" of Seattle, and was, by implication, racist. Klingle's indictment of RHT is even more severe in "Changing Spaces," 197, where he notes that Moss's "tragic" situation "did not move" RHT, "who aimed the hoses at Beacon Hill." This is metaphorical excess, and adds nothing to a reasoned critique of RHT.

19. Henry Petroski, *To Engineer Is Human: The Role of Failure in Successful Design* (1985; New York: Barnes and Noble, 1994).

20. Hadley, "Tribute to R.H. Thomson," UWPA.

A Note on Sources

The major archival sources regarding Reginald Heber Thomson's life are in the large collections of letters, diaries, reminiscences, scrapbooks, and other items held by the Special Collections Division of the University of Washington Libraries. In addition to the Thomson papers, the repository includes materials pertaining to Richard A. Ballinger, Thomas Burke, George F. Cotterill, Daniel H. Gilman, the King County Board of Commissioners, John J. McGilvra, the Seattle Lighting Department, and James Edwin Whitworth.

However, for a fuller picture of Thomson's activities, especially during his first term as city engineer, other archives were consulted with the Seattle Municipal Archives being the most prominent. When I researched the Seattle municipal collection, most of the Thomson material was housed in the Puget Sound Regional Archives, a branch of the Washington State Archives. At the time, the City of Seattle materials were being returned in batches to the new, larger home of the Seattle Municipal Archives, where the staff was reviewing and cataloging the newly received items and continuing their program of transferring the documents from paper to microform. Therefore the citation systems for much of the documents under my review were being superseded as I used them. While I have cited the documents from the regional archives and those at the municipal archives in the form that they then existed, the changes at the time and later have rendered these citations rather obsolete. My solution was to limit the annotation for these two archives to the briefest possible documentation in the belief that any single source could be traced to its final form at the Seattle Municipal Archives.

Other essential sources are included in the Manuscript Collection of the Minnesota Historical Society, where the papers of the James J. Hill family and the Great Northern and Northern Pacific railroads are housed. Principally for my purposes, the papers of J.J. Hill, Louis Hill, and the United Securities Corporation were accessed. The Maryhill Museum archives threw light on the relationship between Thomson and the museum's founder, Samuel Hill. The British Columbia Archives and Records Service were essential for detailing Thomson's work in Strathcona Park and elsewhere in British Columbia. Archives at the Marion County Historical Society (Indiana), the Healdsburg Museum

(California), and the Santa Rosa Public Library (California) held newspaper clippings, local histories, and other material important for understanding Thomson's early years. Many of Thomson's scholastic records survive in the Joseph Wood Evans Memorial Special Collections and Archives Center of the Agnes Brown Duggan Library at Hanover College, Indiana.

The Washington State Archives in Olympia, the Thurston County courthouse in Olympia, and the King County courthouse in Seattle hold records of court cases in which Thomson was involved. The National Archives and Records Administration, Pacific Alaska Region branch, retains records of Thomson's activities as a United States deputy mineral surveyor. The archives at the Washington State Museum and Burke Memorial Museum were useful in gaining a better understanding of the Young Naturalists Society even if they contained little about P. Brooks Randolph himself.

The ranch house of Thomson's in-laws at the former Mark West Station south of Healdsburg survives today as the centerpiece of an office park. A visit helped me visualize the setting of Addie Laughlin's life before she married Thomson. Visits and walks in Hanover, Marion, and Healdsburg, not to mention Seattle and its environs, improved my understanding of Thomson's engineering challenges and solutions, as well as the settings of his personal life.

Many books and articles informed this study and are acknowledged in the notes. The best comprehensive Seattle history following contemporary professional standards is Richard C. Berner's *Seattle in the Twentieth Century*, in three volumes. Since I made extensive use of volumes I and II, I should note, with respect, where I differ with Berner's interpretations regarding Thomson and related matters. For example, readers who care about this matter will find my disagreement with Berner's interpretation of the Bogue Plan's failure in note 31 of Chapter 9. In general, Berner's depiction of a pusillanimous and rather disorganized Thomson is based, I believe, on the attitude of Harry A. Chadwick, the weekly *Argus* editor. Berner extensively relied on the *Argus* in his research and accepted at least some of Chadwick's hypercritical views of Thomson. Chadwick, a captivating writer, never let his ignorance of engineering or Thomson's relationships to others stand in the way of authoritarian pronouncements about them.

Moreover, Berner unintentionally libeled Thomson on page 135 of the first volume, *Seattle, 1900–1920,* when having Thomson writing, "I have always opposed contracting debts for municipal luxuries such as Boulevards and Parks and other wild and vicious speculations." Thomson never wrote those words, instead it was John J. McGilvra who wrote them to Thomson; see the *Seattle Times,* November 18, 1895, page 7.

Other important sources, cited in the notes, include the Seattle daily and weekly press, newspaper editions outside of Seattle, as well as items from the professional engineering press. Although not often cited in *Shaper of Seattle,* Paul Dorpat's pictorial volumes are invaluable as guides to the physical alteration of the city over the years. Titled *Seattle: Now & Then,* they were published by Tartu Press in Seattle from 1984 to about 1994. Volumes I and III are in their second editions.

Bibliography

Archival Collections

British Columbia Archives and Records Service—
Strathcona Park and British Columbia documents.

Burke Museum, University of Washington—
R.B. Randolph Collection.
The Young Naturalists Society Records.

Hanover College, Joseph Wood Evans Memorial Special
Collections and Archives Center (Indiana)—
*Fortieth Annual Catalogue and Circular of Hanover College,
Hanover, Indiana, 1871–1872* (Madison, IN: Courier House,
1872).
*Hanover College Board of Trustees Minutes, June 9, 1896–Sept.
25, 1927.*
Recitation Register 1862–1888 Grades.

Healdsburg Museum (California)—
Local histories, newspaper clippings, etc.

Marion County Historical Society (Indiana)—
Local histories, newspaper clippings, etc.

Maryhill Museum—
Samuel Hill archives.

Minnesota Historical Society—
Great Northern Railway Collection.
James J. Hill and Hill family papers.
Northern Pacific Railroad Collection.

Municipal Archives, City of Seattle—
Records of the Corporation Counsel.
Records of the Department of Engineering.
Records of the Office of the City Clerk.

National Archives and Records Administration, Pacific Alaska
Region—
Record Group 49, Bureau of Land Management.

Utah State University archives—
Grant Hubbard Redford Papers.

University of Washington, Special Collections—
Richard A. Ballinger Papers.
Thomas Burke Papers.
George F. Cotterill Papers.
Daniel H. Gilman Papers.
King County Board of Commissioners Collection.
John J. McGilvra Papers.
Seattle Lighting Department Collection.
Reginald H. Thomson Papers.
James Edwin Whitworth Papers.

University of Washington Press Archives—
Papers concerning *That Man Thomson*.

Books and Monographs

Abbott, Carl. *Portland: Planning, Politics, and Growth in a Twentieth Century City.* Lincoln: University of Nebraska Press, 1983.

Aldrich, Mark. *Death Rode the Rails: American Railroad Accidents
and Safety, 1828–1965.* Baltimore: Johns Hopkins University
Press, 2006.

Ambrose, Stephen E. *Nothing Like It in the World: The Men Who
Built the Transcontinental Railroad, 1863–1869.* New York:
Simon and Schuster, 2000.

Armbruster, Kurt E. *Orphan Road: The Railroad Comes to Seattle,
1853–1911.* Pullman: Washington State University Press,
1999.

Bagley, Clarence B. *History of Seattle from the Earliest Settlement to
the Present Time.* 3 vols. Chicago: S.J. Clarke, 1916.

Baker, Charles H. *Life and Character of William Taylor Baker.* New
York: Premier Press, 1908.

Baker, Frank S. *More Glimpses of Hanover's Past, 1827–1986.* Seymour, IN: Graessle-Mercer, 1988.

Baldwin, Neil. *Edison: Inventing the Century.* New York: Hyperion,
1999.

Balmer, Randall, and John R. Fitzmer. *The Presbyterians.* Westport,
CT: Greenwood, 1993.

Barman, Jean. *The West Beyond the West: A History of British Columbia,* rev. ed. Toronto: University of Toronto Press, 1996.

Barnhart, John D., and Dorothy L. Riker. *Indiana to 1816: The
Colonial Period.* Indianapolis: Indiana Historical Bureau and
Indiana Historical Society, 1971.

Beaton, Welford. *The City That Made Itself: A Literary and Pictorial
Record of the Building of Seattle.* Seattle: Terminal, 1914.

Berner, Richard C. *Seattle, 1900–1920: From Boomtown, Urban
Turbulence, to Restoration.* Seattle: Charles Press, 1991.

_____. *Seattle, 1921–1940: From Boom to Bust.* Seattle: Charles
Press, 1992.

Berry, Brian J.L. *The Human Consequences of Urbanization.* New
York: St. Martin's, 1973.

Blackford, Mansel G. *The Lost Dream: Businessmen and City Planning on the Pacific Coast, 1890–1920.* Columbus: Ohio State
University Press, 1993.

Boswell, Sharon A., and Lorraine McConaghy. *Raise Hell and Sell
Newspapers: Alden J. Blethen and The Seattle Times.* Pullman:
Washington State University Press, 1996.

Bromberg, Nicolette *Picturing the Alaska-Yukon-Pacific Exposition:
The Photographs of Frank H. Nowell.* Seattle: University of
Washington Press, 2009.

Buerge, David M. *Seattle in the 1880s,* ed. Stuart R. Grover.
Seattle: Historical Society of Seattle and King County, 1986.

Burke, Padriac. *A History of the Port of Seattle.* Seattle: Port of
Seattle, 1976.

Carmony, Donald F. *Indiana, 1816–1850: The Pioneer Era.*
Indianapolis: Indiana Historical Bureau and Indiana Historical
Society, 1998.

Chittenden, Hiram M. *The Harbor Island Episode.* Seattle: author,
1915; retyping, 1917.

Clark, Norman H. *Deliver Us from Evil: An Interpretation of American Prohibition.* New York: Norton, 1976.

_____. *The Dry Years: Prohibition and Social Change in Wash-
ington,* rev. ed. Seattle: University of Washington Press, 1988.

Colton, Craig E. *An Unnatural Metropolis: Wresting New Orleans
from Nature.* Baton Rouge: Louisiana State University Press,
2005.

Crittenden, Katharine Carson. *Get Mears: Frederick Mears, Builder
of the Alaska Railroad.* Portland: Binfords and Mort, 2002.

Davis, Louise. *History of Sonoma County and Geyserville.* Geyserville, CA: 1985.

Davis, Margaret Leslie. *Rivers in the Desert: William Mulholland
and the Inventing of Los Angeles.* New York: HarperCollins,
1993.

Denny, Emily Inez. *Blazing the Way: True Stories, Songs, and
Sketches of the Puget Sound and other Pioneers.* Seattle: Rainier,
1909.

Dodds, Gordon B. *Hiram Martin Chittenden: His Public Career.*
Lexington: University Press of Kentucky, 1973.

Donahue, Peter. *Madison House: A Novel.* Portland: Hawthorne Books and Literary Arts, 2005.

Dorpat, Paul. *Seattle: Now & Then*, vols. I and III. Seattle: Tartu, 1984–circa 1994.

_____, and Genevieve McCoy. *Building Washington: A History of Washington State Public Works.* Seattle: Tartu, 1998.

Dunbaugh, Edwin L. *The Era of the Joy Line: A Saga of Steamboating on Long Island Sound.* Westport, CN: Greenwood, 1981.

Fairbanks, Evelyn. *The Days of Rondo.* St. Paul: Minnesota Historical Society Press, 1990.

Fein, Albert, ed., *Landscape into Cityscape: Frederick Law Olmsted's Plans for a Greater New York City.* Ithaca: Cornell University Press, 1968.

Ficken, Robert E. *Washington Territory.* Pullman: Washington State University Press, 2002.

Fogelson, Robert M. *The Fragmented Metropolis: Los Angeles, 1850–1930.* 1967; reprinted with a foreword by Robert Fishman. Berkeley: University of California Press, 1993.

Gray, Alfred O. *Not By Might: The Story of Whitworth College, 1890–1965.* Spokane: Whitworth College, 1965.

Hanford, C.H., ed. *Seattle and Environs, 1852–1924.* Chicago: Pioneer, 1924.

Harries, Merion, and Susie Harries. *The Last Days of Innocence: America at War, 1917–1918.* New York: Random House, 1997.

Hines, Thomas S. *Burnham of Chicago: Architect and Planner.* New York: Oxford University Press, 1974.

Hobbs, Richard. *Catastrophe to Triumph: Bridges of the Tacoma Narrows.* Pullman: Washington State University Press, 2006.

Hockaday, Joan. *Greenscapes: Olmsted's Pacific Northwest.* Pullman: Washington State University Press, 2009.

Hynding, Alan. *The Public Life of Eugene Semple.* Seattle: University of Washington Press, 1973.

Illustrated History of Sonoma County, California. Chicago: Lewis, 1889. Salem, MA: Higginson, 1997.

Isenberg, Alison. *Downtown America: A History of the Place and the People Who Made It.* Chicago: University of Chicago Press: 2004.

Issel, William, and Robert W. Cherney. *San Francisco, 1865–1932: Politics, Power, and Urban Development.* Berkeley: University of California Press, 1986.

Johnson, J.B. *The Theory and Practice of Surveying*, 16th ed. New York: Wiley, 1908.

Kelley, Robert L. *Gold v. Grain: The Hydraulic Mining Controversy in California's Sacramento Valley.* Glendale, CA: Arthur H. Clark, 1959.

Kiely, Edmond R. *Surveying Instruments: Their History and Classroom Use.* New York: Bureau of Publications, Teachers College, Columbia University, 1947.

Klingle, Matthew. *Emerald City: An Environmental History of Seattle.* New Haven: Yale University Press, 2007.

Kroll's Atlas of Seattle. Seattle: Kroll Map Company, 1912.

Lamb, John. *The Seattle Municipal Water Supply Plant.* Seattle: Seattle Water Department, 1914.

Layton, Edwin T., Jr. *The Revolt of the Engineers: Social Responsibility and the American Engineering Profession.* Cleveland: Case Western Reserve University Press, 1971.

LeBaron, Gaye, Dee Blackman, and Harry Hanson. *Santa Rosa: A Nineteenth Century Town.* Santa Rosa: Clarity, 1985

Lessoff, Alan. *The Nation and Its City: Politics, "Corruption," and Progress in Washington, D.C., 1861–1902.* Baltimore: Johns Hopkins University Press, 1994.

Lowenthal, David. *George Perkins Marsh: Prophet of Conservation.* Seattle: University of Washington Press, 2000.

MacDonald, Norbert. *Distant Neighbors: A Comparative History of Seattle and Vancouver.* Lincoln: University of Nebraska Press, 1987.

Mann, Charles Riborg. *A Study of Engineering Education: Prepared for the Joint Committee on Engineering Education of the National Engineering Societies.* New York: Carnegie Foundation for the Advancement of Teaching, 1918.

Martin, Albro. *Railroads Triumphant: The Growth, Rejection, and Rebirth of a Vital American Force.* New York: Oxford University Press, 1992.

McCarthy, Michael P. *Typhoid and the Politics of Public Health in Nineteenth Century Philadelphia.* Philadelphia: American Philosophical Society, 1987.

McCullough, David G. *The Johnstown Flood.* London: Hutchinson, 1968.

_____. *The Path between the Seas: The Creation of the Panama Canal, 1870–1914.* New York: Simon and Schuster, 1977.

McShane, Clay, and Joel A. Tarr. *The Horse in the City: Living Machines in the Nineteenth Century.* Baltimore: Johns Hopkins University Press, 2007.

McWilliams, Mary. *Seattle Water Department History, 1854–1954: Operational Data and Memoranda.* Seattle: City of Seattle Water Department and Dogwood Press, 1955.

Meinig, D.W. *Transcontinental America, 1850–1915*, vol. 3 of *The Shaping of America.* New Haven: Yale University Press, 1998.

Melosi, Martin V. *The Sanitary City: Urban Infrastructure in America from Colonial Times to the Present.* Baltimore: Johns Hopkins University Press, 2000.

_____. *Thomas A. Edison and the Modernization of America.* Glenview, IL: Scott, Foresman/Little Brown Higher Education, 1990.

Menefee, C.A. *Historical and Descriptive Sketch Book of Napa, Sonoma, Lake, and Mendocino.* Napa City, CA: Reporter Publishing House, 1873.

Mighetto, Lisa, and Marcia Montgomery. *Hard Drive to the Klondike.* Seattle: University of Washington Press, 2002.

Miller, Char. *Gifford Pinchot and the Making of Modern Environmentalism.* Washington, DC: Island Press, 2001.

Miller, Howard. *The Revolutionary College: American Presbyterian Higher Education, 1707–1837.* New York: New York University Press, 1976.

Millis, William Alfred. *The History of Hanover College from 1827 to 1927.* Hanover, IN: Hanover College, 1927.

Morgan, Murray. *Skid Road: An Informal Portrait of Seattle*, rev. ed. New York: Viking, 1960.

Mulholland, Catherine. *William Mulholland and the Rise of Los Angeles.* Berkeley: University of California Press, 2000.

Munro-Fraser, J.P. *History of Sonoma County, California.* Oakland: Pacific Press, 1879; Petaluma, CA: Charmaine Burdell Veronda, 1978.

NAVSTAR: Global Positioning System Surveying: Technical Engineering and Design Guides as Adapted from the U.S. Army Corps of Engineers, No. 28. Reston, VA: ASCE Press, 2000.

Nesbit, Robert C. *"He Built Seattle": A Biography of Judge Thomas Burke.* Seattle: University of Washington Press, 1961.

Newell, Gordon, ed. *The H.W. McCurdy Marine History of the Pacific Northwest.* Seattle: Superior, 1966.

Newell, Gordon R. *Ships of the Inland Sea: The Story of the Puget Sound Steamboats.* Portland: Binfords and Mort, 1960.

Nye, David E. *Electrifying America: Social Meanings of a New Technology.* Cambridge, MA: MIT Press, 1997.

Oliver, John W. *History of American Technology.* New York: Ronald Press, 1956.

O'Reilly, Shauna and Brennan. *Alaska Yukon Pacific Exposition.* Charleston, SC: Arcadia, 2009.

Penick, James L. *Progressive Politics and Conservation: The Ballinger-Pinchot Affair*. Chicago: University of Chicago Press, 1968.

Peters, Tom F. *Building the Nineteenth Century*. Cambridge, MA: MIT Press, 1966.

Peterson, Jon A. *The Birth of City Planning in the United States, 1840–1917*. Baltimore: Johns Hopkins University Press, 2003.

Petroski, Henry. *Engineers of Dreams: Great Bridge Builders and the Spanning of America*. New York: Knopf, 1995.

_____. *To Engineer Is Human: The Role of Failure in Successful Design*. New York: St. Martin's, 1985; New York: Barnes and Noble, 1999.

Phelps, Myra L. *Public Works in Seattle: A Narrative History of the Engineering Department, 1875–1975*, ed. Leslie Blanchard. Seattle: Seattle Engineering Department and Kingsport Press, 1978.

Pitzer, Paul C. *Building the Skagit: A Century of Upper Skagit Valley History, 1870–1970*. Portland: Galley Press, 1978.

Raymond, William G. *Plane Surveying for Use in the Classroom and Field*, 2nd ed. New York: American, 1914.

Reisner, Marc. *Cadillac Desert: The American West and Its Disappearing Water*, rev. ed. New York: Penguin, 1993.

Revell, Keith D. *Building Gotham: Civic Culture and Public Policy in New York City, 1898–1938*. Baltimore: Johns Hopkins University Press, 2003.

Reynolds, Terry S. *Stronger Than a Hundred Men: A History of the Vertical Water Wheel*. Baltimore: Johns Hopkins University Press, 1983.

Righter, Robert W. *The Battle over Hetch Hetchy: America's Most Controversial Dam and the Birth of Modern Environmentalism*. New York: Oxford University Press, 2005.

Rise, Thurman B., M.D. *The Hoosier Health Office: A Biography of Dr. J.N. Hurty and the History of the Indiana State Board of Health to 1925*. Indianapolis: Indiana State Board of Health, 1946.

Rohrbough, Malcom J. *Days of Gold: The California Gold Rush and the American Nation*. Berkeley: University of California Press, 1997.

Rosenberg, Charles E. *Explaining Epidemics and other Studies in the History of Medicine*. New York: Cambridge University Press, 1992.

Rubey, Harry, George Edward Commel, and Marion Wesley Todd. *Engineering Surveys: Elementary*, 3rd ed. New York: Macmillan, 1950.

Rugh, Susan Sessions. *Our Common Country: Family Farming, Culture, and Community in the Nineteenth-Century Midwest*. Bloomington: Indiana University Press, 2001.

Sale, Roger. *Seattle: Past to Present*. Seattle: University of Washington Press, 1976.

Sayre, J. Willis. *This City of Ours*, Seattle: Seattle School District No. 1, 1936.

Schaffer, Ronald. *America in the Great War: The Rise of the Welfare State*. New York: Oxford University Press, 1991.

Schmid, Calvin F. *Social Trends in Seattle*. Seattle: University of Washington Press, 1944.

Seasholes, Nancy S. *Gaining Ground: A History of Land-making in Boston*. Cambridge, MA: MIT Press, 2003.

Sharpe, Elizabeth M. *In the Shadow of the Dam: The Aftermath of the Mill River Flood of 1874*. New York: Free Press, 2004.

Simpson, John Warfield. *Dam! Water, Power, Politics, and Preservation in Hetch Hetchy and Yosemite National Park*. New York: Pantheon, 2005.

Slayton, Robert A. *Empire Statesman: The Rise and Redemption of Al Smith*. New York: Free Press, 2001.

Slotkin, Richard. *Lost Battalions: The Great War and the Crisis of American Nationality*. New York: Henry Holt, 2005.

Smith, Carl. *The Plan of Chicago: Daniel Burnham and the Remaking of the American City*. Chicago: University of Chicago Press, 2006.

Smith, Norman. *A History of Dams*. London: Peter Davies, 1971.

Soden, Dale E. *The Reverend Mark Matthews: An Activist in the Progressive Era*. Seattle: University of Washington Press, 2001.

_____. *A Venture of Mind and Spirit: An Illustrated History of Whitworth College*. Spokane: Whitworth College, 1990.

Soja, Edward W. *Postmetropolis: Critical Studies of Cities and Regions*. Malden, MA: Blackwell, 2000.

Speidel, William C. *Sons of the Profits*. Seattle: Nettle Creek, 1967.

Stark, Andrew. *Conflict of Interest in American Public Life*. Cambridge, MA: Harvard University Press, 2000.

Stein, Alan J., and Paula Becker. *Alaska-Yukon-Pacific Exposition, Washington's First World's Fair: A Timeline History*. Seattle: HistoryLink, 2009.

Stewart, Lowell O. *Public Land Surveys: History, Instructions, Method*. 1935; Minneapolis: Meyers, 1977.

Tarr, Joel A. *The Search for the Ultimate Sink: Urban Pollution in Historical Perspective*. Akron, OH: University of Akron Press, 1996.

Thomson, Reginald H. *That Man Thomson*, ed. Grant Redford. Seattle: University of Washington Press, 1950.

Thomson, S.H. *Discussion of the Doctrine of Human Depravity, in New Albany Presbytery, September 2, '73; April 2, '74*. Madison, IN: Courier Steam Printing, 1874.

_____. *Our Fall in Adam: Discussion, Exegentical and Doctrinal, of Romans V. 12–21*. Cincinnati: Elm Street Printing, 1878.

Thornbrough, Emma Lou. *Indiana in the Civil War Era, 1850–1880*. Indianapolis: Indiana Historical Bureau and Indiana Historical Society, 1965

Trautwine, John C. *The Civil Engineer's Pocket-Book* 19th ed., rev. by John C. Trautwine Jr. and John C. Trautwine III. Philadelphia: Trautwine, 1916.

_____, and John C. Trautwine Jr., *The Civil Engineer's Reference Book (Formerly "Pocket-Book")*. John C. Trautwine, 21st ed. London: Chapman and Hall, 1937.

U.S. Bureau of the Census, *Historical Statistics of the United States*. Washington, DC: GPO, 1975.

_____. *Seventeenth Census of the United States: Census of Population: 1950*, 2: pt. 47. Washington, DC: GPO, 1952.

Veblen, Thorstein. *The Engineers and the Price System*, intro. by Daniel Bell. 1921; 1963; repr. with Bell intro. from 1963, New Brunswick, N.J.: Transaction, 1983.

Wells, David F., ed. *Reformed Theology in America: A History of Its Modern Development*. Grand Rapids, MI: Erdmans, 1985.

Wilson, William H. *The City Beautiful Movement*. Baltimore: Johns Hopkins University Press, 1990.

Windle, John T., and Robert M. Taylor Jr. *The Early Architecture of Madison, Indiana*. Madison and Indianapolis: Historic Madison, Inc., and Indiana Historical Society, 1986.

Wynne, Robert Edward. *Reaction to the Chinese in the Pacific Northwest and British Columbia, 1850 to 1910*. New York: Arno, 1978.

Seattle Histories*

Bagley, Clarence B. *History of Seattle from the Earliest Settlement to the Present Time*. 3 vols. Chicago: S.J. Clarke: 1916.

Berner, Richard C. *Seattle, 1900–1920: From Boomtown, Urban Turbulence, to Restoration*. Seattle: Chares Press, 1991.

_____. *Seattle, 1921–1940: From Boom to Bust*. Seattle: Charles Press, 1992.

Dorpat, Paul. *Seattle: Now &Then*. 3 vols. Seattle: Tartu, 1984–1994.

Haarsager, Sandra. *Bertha Knight Landes of Seattle, Big-city Mayor.* Norman: University of Oklahoma Press, 1994.

Hines, Neal O. *Denny's Knoll: A History of the Metropolitan Tract of the University of Washington.* Seattle: University of Washington Press, 1980.

Jones, Nard. *Seattle.* Garden City, NY: Doubleday, 1992.

Morgan, Murray. *Skid Road: An Informal Portrait of Seattle,* rev. ed. New York: Viking, 1960.

Nelson, Gerald B. *Seattle: The Life and Times of an American City.* New York: Knopf, 1977.

Nesbit, Robert C. *"He Built Seattle:" A Biography of Thomas Burke.* Seattle: University of Washington Press, 1961.

Ochsner, Jeffrey Karl, and Dennis Alan Anderson. *Distant Corner: Seattle Architects and the Legacy of H.H. Richardson.* Seattle: University of Washington Press, 2003.

Sale, Roger. *Seattle: Past to Present.* Seattle: University of Washington Press, 1976.

Speidel, William C. *Sons of the Profits.* Seattle: Nettle Creek, 1967.

*This list repeats some titles noted under Books and Monographs.

Book Chapters

Corbett, Katharine T. "Draining the Metropolis: The Politics of Sewers in Nineteenth Century St. Louis," in Andrew Hurley, ed., *Common Fields: An Environmental History of St. Louis.* St. Louis: Missouri Historical Society Press, 1997.

Hatch, Melville H. "The Young Naturalists' Society (1879–1905)," in Melville H. Hatch, *Studies Honoring Trevor Kincaid.* Seattle: University of Washington Press, 1950.

Melosi, Martin V. "Technology Diffusion and Refuse Disposal: The Case of the British Destructor," in Joel A. Tarr and Gabriel Dupuy, eds., *Technology and the Rise of the Networked City in Europe and America.* Philadelphia: Temple University Press, 1988.

Peterson, Jon A. "The Impact of Sanitary Reform Upon American Urban Planning: 1840–1890," in Donald A. Krueckeberg, ed., *Introduction to Planning History in the United States.* New Brunswick, NJ: Center for Urban Policy Research, 1983.

Sandweiss, Eric. "Paving St. Louis's Streets: The Environmental Origins of Social Fragmentation," in Andrew Hurley, ed., *Common Fields: An Environmental History of St. Louis.* St. Louis: Missouri Historical Society Press, 1997.

Schoeder, Walter. "Environmental Setting of the St. Louis Region," in Andrew Hurley, ed., *Common Fields: An Environmental History of St. Louis.* St. Louis: Missouri Historical Society Press, 1997.

Tarr, Joel A. "Sewerage and the Development of the Networked City in the United States, 1850–1930," in Joel A. Tarr and Gabriel Dupuy, eds., *Technology and the Rise of the Networked City in Europe and America.* Philadelphia: Temple University Press, 1988.

Journal Articles

Abbott, Carl. "Regional City and Network City: Portland and Seattle in the Twentieth Century," *Western Historical Quarterly* 23 (August 1992).

Baker, Frank S. "Michael C. Garber, Sr., and the Early Years of the Madison, Indiana, *Daily Courier,"* *Indiana Magazine of History* 48 (December 1952).

Benson, Keith R. "The Young Naturalists' Society: From Chess to Natural History Collections," *Pacific Northwest Quarterly* 77 (July 1985).

Campbell, Robert A. "Blacks and the Coal Mines of Western Washington, 1888–1896," *Pacific Northwest Quarterly* 73

(October 1982).

Cole, Terrence M. "Promoting the Pacific Rim: The Alaska-Yukon-Pacific Exposition of 1909," *Alaska History* 6 (Spring 1991).

Cottman, George S. "Internal Improvements in Indiana," *Indiana Magazine of History* 3 (December 1907).

Ficken, Robert E. "Seattle's 'Ditch': The Corps of Engineers and the Lake Washington Ship Canal," *Pacific Northwest Quarterly* 78 (January 1986).

Frykman, George A. "The Alaska-Yukon-Pacific Exposition, 1909," *Pacific Northwest Quarterly* 53 (July 1962).

Gunns, Albert F. "The First Tacoma Narrows Bridge: A Brief History of Galloping Gertie," *Pacific Northwest Quarterly* 72 (October 1981).

Hanson, Howard A. "More Land for Industry: The Story of Flood Control in the Green River Valley," *Pacific Northwest Quarterly* 48 (January 1957).

Harmon, Rick. "The Bull Run Watershed: Portland's Enduring Jewel," *Oregon Historical Quarterly* 96 (Summer-Fall 1995).

Johnston, Norman J. "The Olmsted Brothers and the Alaska-Yukon-Pacific Exposition: 'Eternal Loveliness,'" *Pacific Northwest Quarterly* 75 (April 1984).

Klingle, Matthew. "Changing Spaces: Nature, Property, and Power in Seattle, 1880–1945," *Journal of Urban History* 32 (January 2006).

Leonard, Frank, "'Wise, Swift, and Sure,'? The Great Northern Entry into Seattle, 1889–1894," *Pacific Northwest Quarterly* 92 (Spring 2001).

"Madison, Indiana, October 16, 1851," *Indiana Magazine of History* 43 (June 1947).

Nash, Linda. "The Changing Experience of Nature: Historical Encounters with a Northwest River," *Journal of American History* 86 (March 2000).

Royer, Catherine. "The University of Washington Press: Publishing Arm of the University," *Pacific Northwest Quarterly* 50 (October 1959).

Tarbill, Von V. "Mountain Moving in Seattle," reprint from the *Harvard Business Review,* Vol. 8, July 1930.

Wiley, Harvey W. "The Education of a Backwoods Hoosier," *Indiana Magazine of History* 24 (June 1928).

Wilson, William H. "How Seattle Lost the Bogue Plan: Politics versus Design," *Pacific Northwest Quarterly* 75 (October 1984).

_____. "The Mythic and (Virtually) Unknown Reginald H. Thomson," *Columbia: The Magazine of Northwest History* 15 (Winter 2001–2002).

_____. "'Names Joined Together as Our Hearts Are,' The Friendship of Samuel Hill and Reginald H. Thomson," *Pacific Northwest Quarterly* 94 (Fall 2003).

_____. "Reginald H. Thomson and Planning for Strathcona Park, 1912–1915," *Planning Perspectives* 17 (October 2002).

_____. "The Rising and the Setting of Seattle's Sun," *Pacific Northwest Quarterly* 92 (Spring 2001).

Periodical Articles

Ballinger, Richard A. "Seattle: A Metropolis Built in a Single Generation," *American Review of Reviews* 39 (June 1909).

Callaghan, James J. "A Basis for Better Things All Around," *Town Crier,* September 27, 1913.

Clayborn, Hannah M. "Teenage Rancheros on the Tzabaco: The Piñas of Dry Creek," *Russian River Recorder* 30 (Summer 1985).

Closson, C.C. "Seattle's Regrade Projects: A Letter to the Editors of the *Town Crier,"* *Town Crier,* August 26, 1911.

"Denny Hill Regrade No. 2, Seattle, Washington," *Western Construction News* 5 (July 25, 1930).

Dimock, H. "Street Grades in Seattle," *Proceedings of the Pacific Northwest Society of Engineers* 3 (May 1909).

"Healdsburg Schools, 1853–1880," *Russian River Recorder* 23 (April 1982).

Keller, Philip R. "Washing Away a City's Hills," *World Today* 19 (July 1, 1910).

Matthews, M.A. "Commission Government for Seattle," *Town Crier*, September 6, 1913.

_____. "In Moving Up to Better City Government," *Town Crier,* September 20, 1913.

"Not By Bread Alone: A Social History of the Healdsburg Public Library," *Russian River Recorder* 34 (Fall 1988).

Overstreet, R.M. "Hydraulic Excavation Methods in Seattle," *Engineering Record* 65 (May 4, 1912).

Powell, Archibald O. "The Proposed Lake Washington Canal: A Great Engineering Project," *Engineering News* 63 (January 6, 1910).

"Railways and Water Pollution, with Special Reference to the Water Supply of Seattle," *Engineering News* 56 (December 27, 1906).

"The Regrading of Seattle, Washington–I," *Engineering Record* 57 (May 9, 1908).

"The Regrading of Seattle, Washington–II," *Engineering Record* 57 (May 16, 1908).

"Report on Possible Pollution of the Water Supply of Seattle by a Proposed Railway throughout the Drainage Area," *Engineering News* 56 (August 30, 1906).

"Seattle Completes Denny Hill Regrade No. 2," *Western Construction News* 5 (January 25, 1931).

Thomson, S. Harrison. "The Mosaic Account of Creation," *Methodist Quarterly Review,* 4th ser, 4 (October 1852).

Way, W.F. "Handling Earth by Belts," *Engineering News-Record* 105 (Nov. 27, 1930).

Zimmerman, Louis P. "The Seattle Regrade, with Particular Reference to the Jackson St. Section" *Engineering News* 60 (November 12, 1908).

Theses and Dissertations

Benoit, Paul. "The Man-Induced Topographic Change of Seattle's Elliott Bay Shoreline from 1852 to 1930 as an Early Form of Coastal Resource Use and Management." Master's thesis, University of Washington, 1979.

Dick, Wesley Arden. "The Genesis of City Light." Master's thesis, University of Washington, 1965.

_____. "Visions of Abundance: The Public Power Crusade in the Pacific Northwest in the Era of J.D. Ross and the New Deal." PhD diss., University of Washington, 1973.

Doig, Ivan Clark. "John J. McGilvra: The Life and Times of an Urban Frontiersman, 1827–1903." PhD diss., University of Washington, 1969.

Fitzsimons, Gregory Grey. "The Perils of Public Works Engineering: The Early Development of Utilities in Seattle, Washington, 1890–1912." Master's thesis, University of Washington, 1992.

Flagg, Herbert Judson. "A Study of the Methods of City and Town Surveying." B.S. thesis, University of Washington, 1912.

Klingle, Matthew William. "Urban by Nature: An Environmental History of Seattle, 1880–1970." PhD diss., University of Washington, 2001.

Pittari, John J., Jr. "Practical Idealism: Frederick Law Olmsted, Jr. and the Modern American City Planning Movement." PhD diss., University of Washington, 1997.

Razak, Alan Jay. "Redeveloping the Redevelopment: The Denny Regrade." Master's thesis, University of Washington, 1981.

Reiff, Janice L. "Urbanization and the Social Structure: Seattle, Washington, 1852–1910." PhD diss., University of Washington, 1981.

Roberts, Rex. "A Study of the Growth and Expansion of the Seattle Municipal Government." Master's thesis, University of Washington, 1942.

Rockafeller, Nancy Moore. "Public Health in Progressive Seattle, 1876–1919." Master's thesis, University of Washington, 1986.

Talmadge, Charles Eugene. "The Growth of the Puget Sound Naval Shipyard and Its Influence on the City of Bremerton." Master's thesis, University of Washington, 1983.

Thorndale, William. "Washington's Green River Coal Company: 1880–1930." Master's thesis, University of Washington, 1965.

Newspapers

Healdsburg Enterprise
Portland Oregonian
Russian River Flag
Seattle Argus
Seattle Daily Press
Seattle Post-Intelligencer
Seattle Star
Seattle Sun
Seattle Telegraph
Seattle Times
Seattle Town Crier
Seattle Union Record
University of Washington Daily

Electronic Resources

"Henry Yesler's Native American daughter Julia is born on June 12, 1855," http://www.historylink.org/essays/output.cfm?file-id=3396.

Index